EXPLORATIONS
IN
COGNITION

A Series of Books in Psychology

EDITORS:
Richard C. Atkinson
Jonathan Freedman
Gardner Lindzey
Richard F. Thompson

EXPLORATIONS IN COGNITION

Donald A. Norman   David E. Rumelhart

CENTER FOR HUMAN INFORMATION PROCESSING
UNIVERSITY OF CALIFORNIA, SAN DIEGO

and the LNR Research Group:

Adele A. Abrahamson   Yaakov Kareev   Stephen E. Palmer
Marc Eisenstadt   James A. Levin   David E. Rumelhart
Dedre Gentner   Marigold Linton   Greg W. Scragg
Ronald M. Kaplan   Allen Munro   Albert L. Stevens
                       Donald A. Norman

W. H. FREEMAN AND COMPANY
San Francisco

Library of Congress Cataloging in Publication Data

Norman, Donald A.
  Explorations in cognition.

  Bibliography: p. 408
  Includes index.
  1. Languages—Psychology. 2. Cognition.
3. Linguistic analysis (Linguistics) I. Rumelhart,
David E., joint author. II. Title
BF455.N65   153   74–32244
ISBN 0-7167-0736-5

Printed in the United States of America

2   3   4   5   6   7   8   9

Contents

Preface   ix

   The LNR Research Group   x
   Organization of the Book   xi

Acknowledgments   xiii
Addresses of the LNR Research Group   xv

Part I   INTRODUCTION   1

1   Memory and Knowledge   3
   DONALD A. NORMAN and DAVID E. RUMELHART

   The Analysis of Language   4
   The Representation of Information in Memory   8
   Conceptual Structures for Perception   21
   The Representation of Memories as Plans   29
   Summary   32

Part II   THEORY   33

2   The Active Structural Network   35
   DAVID E. RUMELHART and DONALD A. NORMAN

   Structural Networks   35
   Predicates, Concepts, and Propositions   40
   Primitive Meaning Structures   44
   Representation of Quantified Statements   61
   Summary   63

3   Reference and Comprehension   65
   DONALD A. NORMAN and DAVID E. RUMELHART

   The Problem of Reference   65
   Conversational Postulates   77
   Conversational Postulates and the Problem
     of Reference   83

4 Linguistic Theory and the LNR Structural Representation   88
ALLEN MUNRO

Lexical Decomposition   89
The Predicate Approach   97
Referents   102
Generic Quantification   103
Truth in Semantic Representation   105
Presupposition   107
Summary   112

Part III   LINGUISTIC ANALYSIS   115

5 On Process Models for Sentence Analysis   117
RONALD M. KAPLAN

Components of Comprehension   117
Augmented Transition Networks   121
Predicting Psychological Processes   134

6 Errors in Reading: Analysis Using an Augmented Transition Network Model of Grammar   136
ALBERT L. STEVENS and DAVID E. RUMELHART

The Syntactical Analysis   137
Experimental Method   144
The Prediction Experiment   146
The Reading Experiments   150
Summary   155

Part IV   THE COMPUTER MODEL   157

7 The Computer Implementation   159
DAVID E. RUMELHART and DONALD A. NORMAN

The One-System Hypothesis   159
Basic Units and Operations   161
Interaction between the Parser and the
   Interpreter   171
Summary   177

8 A Language Comprehension System   179
DAVID E. RUMELHART and JAMES A. LEVIN

Verbworld Definitions   180
Verbworld as a Comprehension System   188
Extensions to Verbworld   203
Summary   208

Part V   STUDIES OF LANGUAGE   209

9   Evidence for the Psychological Reality of Semantic
     Components: The Verbs of Possession   211
     DEDRE GENTNER

     Representation of the Possession Verbs   212
     Memory for Chunks   227
     Semantic Structure and the Acquisition of
         Meaning: An Experimental Analysis   233
     Summary   246

10   Experimental Analysis of the Semantics of Movement   248
     ADELE A. ABRAHAMSON

     Semantic Analysis of Recall   248
     Analysis of the Recall   250
     Semantic Elements for Animate Movement   261
     The Representation of the Recalls   269
     Summary   272

Part VI   STUDIES OF VISUAL PERCEPTION
             AND PROBLEM SOLVING   277

11   Visual Perception and World Knowledge: Notes on
     a Model of Sensory-Cognitive Interaction   279
     STEPHEN E. PALMER

     Visual Representation   281
     Visual Processing   294
     Summary   307

12   Aspects of Human Problem Solving: The Use of
     Internal Representations   308
     MARC EISENSTADT and YAAKOV KAREEV

     Section 1   EXPERIMENTAL ANALYSES   309
         The Games   309
         The Apparatus   313
         Studies of the Internal Representation   314
         Search through the Problem Space   324

     Section 2   THEORETICAL ANALYSES   329
         Theoretical Aspects of Internal
             Representation   330
         Top-Down Analysis: Searching for a Pattern   330
         Bottom-Up Analysis: Suggestions from
             the Stimulus   334
         Theoretical Aspects of Search through the
             Problem Space   339
         Implementation   342
         Summary   345

Part VII   EXTENSIONS   347

13   Answering Questions about Processes   349
GREG W. SCRAGG

LUIGI   350
Representational Structures   352
Answering Questions   363
Summary   372

14   Memory for Real-World Events   376
MARIGOLD LINTON

Temporal Judgments of Events   377
Empirical Studies   381
The Take-Two-Items-a-Day-for-Five-Years
    Study   387
Reflections on the Study of Memory   402

Epilogue   405

Higher-Order Conceptual Units: Schemata   406
Processing Structures   408
Cognitive Science   409

Bibliography   410

The Study of Cognitive Processes   410
References   411

Index   423

Preface

This book is a study of mental processes. Our goal is the experimental and theoretical understanding of human cognitive processes. Here, we present one step along the path: the study of the representation and use of knowledge within the human cognitive system.

Historically, workers in cognitive psychology have been interested in the stages of human information processing, starting with sensory analysis, through perception and pattern recognition, attention, and short-term memory. When we started the studies of human long-term memory that led to the work reported in this book, we viewed our work in this tradition, and our initial interests were on those experimental factors and strategies of the subjects that would affect the amount of material that was stored permanently within memory. But the more we studied memory, the more we came to be dissatisfied with this approach. It became clear that subjects organized the material they were asked to learn according to many different strategies, all based upon their past experiences with the world. When new material was learned, it entered a highly complex, tightly interconnected network of prior knowledge. The secrets of memory were linked to the structure of that network of knowledge.

Accordingly, our research branched out to cover a wide range of topics. We have examined language, problem solving, and pattern recognition. We have studied visual processes, and we have looked at the development of memory structures in children. In addition, we have examined memory in a naturalistic setting, where the events to be remembered are those that actually occurred in the life of the subject, and we have considered the implications of our understanding of memory structures for a theory of learning and for educational practices. Most of this material is discussed in this book.

THE LNR RESEARCH GROUP

Originally we were three — Peter Lindsay, Donald Norman, and David Rumelhart — all faculty members in the Department of Psychology at the University of California, San Diego (located in La Jolla, California). The three of us had worked together in studies of perception, attention, and memory. Our first ideas led to the development of a simple semantic network representation, and these ideas were first presented in a paper written for a symposium on organization and memory organized by Endel Tulving and Wayne Donaldson in Pittsburgh during 1971 (Rumelhart, Lindsay, and Norman, 1972). Peter Lindsay left at this point to travel west, eventually returning to Canada.

As we expanded our interests and examined problems in a wider and wider domain, the work went through several significant stages of evolution. The reasonably simple semantic networks with which we had started changed into a more dynamic, functional structure, one that we have come to call a structural network. The ideas were tested by simulation on a large digital computer. The size of the research group grew as more and more of our graduate students entered the research and as we hired professional personnel to help supervise the programming and electronic facilities.

Our graduate students have played a vital role in the continued development of the ideas reported in this book. They have been critical, demanding, inventive, and catalytic. They are an integral and essential part of the research effort. Thus, it is proper that this book be by all of us: by what we have come to call the LNR research group. "LNR" (or sometimes "ELINOR") is an acronym for the research group formed and directed by Lindsay, Norman, and Rumelhart. We have reached a natural plateau in development. Moreover, the members of the group that comprise the "we" of this book are changing. Thus, it is an appropriate time to describe the basic philosophy and nature of the research.

Two of the participants in this venture are not really members of the LNR research group, but we count them as honorary fellows. Marigold Linton spent a sabbatical year from the San Diego State

University with us and added to our interest in and understanding of the storage of real events; this work is reported in Chapter 14. Ronald Kaplan visited several times from Harvard University, and his work on the development and psychological assessment of parsers has been influential. His work is reported in Chapter 5.

Although the book is authored by a large group of people, we like to think of it as authored by a single source: the LNR research group. All the authors have been members of the group or have interacted with it. All share the same framework, all view things with similar philosophies. There are differences, of course, but the single common thread of the active structural network approach to the studies of cognitive processes dominates the work and provides unification of what might otherwise have been diverse investigations. Each of the participants in the research activity has made important and valuable contributions. This book represents the common efforts of the whole group.

ORGANIZATION OF THE BOOK

The book has seven parts. Part I is an introduction to the problems that we have studied and to the philosophy with which we have pursued our investigations. Chapter 1 previews much of the work described in the rest of the book, but very generally. Details and justification of the approach are saved for the later, more specialized chapters.

Part II presents the basic theoretical approach. Here, we first develop the ideas that underlie the notion of the active structural network as a representational format for knowledge. Then, we provide a general discussion of some fundamental issues in the problems of reference and comprehension of information. These ideas are mainly developed from a consideration of the human use of language, although we believe that the work is not restricted to linguistic information (as later chapters demonstrate). The last chapter in Part II (Chapter 4) reviews some aspects of these ideas and contrasts them with developments in linguistic theory.

Starting with Part III, the book becomes less general. We discuss the processes involved in the analysis of language, explain and justify the system we have adopted, and show how it can aid the study of reading. In Part IV, we show how the ideas about language processing and memory representation can be implemented in a computer, both as a demonstration of the completeness and adequacy of the ideas and as a vehicle for future testing and development.

Parts V, VI, and VII present individual research studies of particular aspects of the representational system that were discussed in the earlier chapters. These final chapters extend the theoretical work to other domains of inquiry—experimental studies of language and memory, the development of language in children, visual perception, problem solving, and question answering.

September 1974   *Donald A. Norman*

                                                   David E. Rumelhart
                                                   LA JOLLA, CALIFORNIA

Acknowledgments

We owe large debts to the industry and kindness of many people. We have had lengthy meetings with several score of the leading workers in the fields relevant to this work, in seminars that we convened at the Center for Human Information Processing in La Jolla and at various meetings and symposiums around the country. The LNR research group has twice invaded the Stanford campus. In addition, John Anderson and Gordon Bower (then, both at Stanford) once descended upon us; Bower opened his notebook of questions and relentlessly worked his way through it for approximately six hours while we struggled at the blackboard.

We especially would like to thank Bert Raphael of the Artificial Intelligence Laboratory at the Stanford Research Institute for his valuable interactions with us, and for cheerfully, albeit unexpectedly, paying for dinners for about thirteen of us at a luxurious Chinese banquet. Daniel Bobrow, now at the Xerox Palo Alto Research Center, and Allan Collins, the late Jaime Carbonell, Bill Woods, and Joe Becker, all of Bolt, Beranek and Newman, have also been especially helpful.

Gordon Bower reviewed the entire manuscript with great care, commenting with characteristic understatement. His critique was extremely valuable, and it led to a thorough revision of every chapter. The book is much improved because of his efforts. Danny Bobrow served a valuable role as overseer throughout the entire course of the research. First he gave us guidance on the computer implementation, shaking his head in dismay at our first systems. Then he encouraged us during the writing phase, finally allowing himself to be locked in a house with Norman and Rumelhart for two days while all three worked on the final version of Chapter 7.

An important component of our work was the development of a computer program that incorporated our ideas about language processing and representation (described in Chapter 7 and used in many of the other chapters). This was a major project in itself, and the resulting program became one of the largest and most complex interactive programs operating on the campus computer center computer (a Burroughs 6700). Accordingly, many people helped to write and maintain the program. Robert Olds and Robert Schudy got the system running (and then kept it running). Chris Murano programmed the original English language parser. Several undergraduates worked for us in documenting and programming, most importantly Dennis Bell, Mark Miller, and Robert Neches. The experimental laboratory also contained a good deal of equipment, for it was controlled by two small digital computers. Andy Sturman and Robert Olds have been responsible for the smooth operation of this laboratory. Julie Lustig helped organize the otherwise chaotic daily meanderings of man and machine, and Sheila deMaine kept the paperwork moving and the spirits up.

The research would not have been possible without adequate experimental facilities, and for them we are very much indebted to our sponsoring organizations. The initial research, most especially on the experimental aspects of perceptual, attentional, and short-term memory processes, was supported by a grant from the National Institute of Neurological Disease and Stroke, National Institutes of Health, NS 07454. This support has continued throughout the project. The research on long-term memory, especially the computer simulation of language and memory structures, was supported by a grant from the National Science Foundation, GB 32235X. The Center for Human Information Processing at the University of California, San Diego, helped defray the costs of some of the seminars at La Jolla.

Donald A. Norman spent the 1973–1974 academic year on sabbatical leave at the Center for Advanced Study in the Behavioral Sciences at Stanford, California. The Center provided the facilities and freedom to finish this book. Were it not for that year at the Center, this work probably could not have been completed. Special thanks are due Joan Warmbrunn for her cheerfulness and skill during the repeated typing of the manuscript. Val Falkenberg performed an intelligent and efficient typing of the final manuscript. Throughout all the stages of compiling the book, Julie Lustig has played a major role — encouraging the authors, editing the manuscripts, and finally correcting proof.

Addresses of the LNR Research Group

NAME	ADDRESS
Adele A. Abrahamson	Department of Psychology Rutgers College Rutgers University New Brunswick, New Jersey 08903
Marc Eisenstadt	Department of Artificial Intelligence University of Edinburgh Edinburgh, Scotland
Dedre Gentner	Department of Psychology University of Washington Seattle, Washington 98105
Ronald M. Kaplan	Xerox Palo Alto Research Center 3180 Porter Drive Palo Alto, California 94304
Yaakov Kareev	School of Education Hebrew University of Jerusalem Jerusalem, Israel
James A. Levin	Information Sciences Institute University of Southern California 4676 Admiralty Way Marina Del Rey, California 90291
Marigold Linton	Department of Psychology University of Utah Salt Lake City, Utah 84112

Allen Munro   Department of Psychology
                       University of California, San Diego
                       La Jolla, California 92037

Donald A. Norman   Department of Psychology
                       University of California, San Diego
                       La Jolla, California 92037

Stephen E. Palmer   Department of Psychology
                       University of California, Berkeley
                       Berkeley, California 94720

David E. Rumelhart   Department of Psychology
                       University of California, San Diego
                       La Jolla, California 92037

Greg W. Scragg   Istituto per gli Studi Semantici e Cognitivi
                       6976 Castagnola
                       Villa Heleneum, Switzerland

Albert L. Stevens   Department of Psychology
                       University of California, San Diego
                       La Jolla, California 92037

EXPLORATIONS
IN
COGNITION

PART I

INTRODUCTION

CHAPTER 1

Memory and Knowledge

DONALD A. NORMAN and DAVID E. RUMELHART

As cognitive psychologists, we are interested in a wide domain of inquiry: how people perceive, represent, remember, and use knowledge. In our studies of language, of visual perception, of problem solving, and of education, we find that the theme that links them all together is the single unifying concept of the nature of the representation of information within human memory. In this book we present our ideas on the representation and use of information within memory, and we discuss and demonstrate these ideas in several different areas.

This chapter is a sampler: It introduces a number of the topics that will be discussed in more detail later in the book. Its purpose is to set the scene, to introduce our philosophy of approach, and to describe the nature of the problem areas that we have studied. As is appropriate in a sampler, we have brought together a number of disparate examples. Each example is discussed in sufficient detail to make whatever point is being discussed at the moment, but full specification and further elaboration and justification of those points must await the later chapters. Thus, our goal here is to set forth the issues and the questions.

THE ANALYSIS OF LANGUAGE

People use language to convey information about their ideas or feelings. The speaker or the writer has a reasonably wide choice of the manner of forming his sentences. Moreover, different people, or the same person at different times, may communicate the same ideas or feelings with different expressions. If the listener or reader of language is to understand what is being conveyed to him, he must be able to go beyond the words of the language and determine the underlying message. He should encode and keep a representation of that message that contains the meaning of the communication.

Suppose we were to tell someone that

(1)   Peter put the package on the table.

We would expect the listener to have acquired knowledge of the fact that Peter was the cause of the event that changed the location of the package from wherever it had been to the top of the table. It should not matter how we stated that particular sentence. Indeed, the following conversation conveys exactly the same information, although the words are quite different:

(2A)   That package on the table, how did it get there?

(2B)   It was Peter, he did it.

The ability to paraphrase the same information in different ways is an important property of language. We must ensure that our system for representing information within memory is capable of handling the problems of paraphrase.

It is important to stress this point. We can only handle the problem of paraphrase by encoding the underlying meaning of our experiences. If we encode the words themselves, we will not recognize that sentence 1 is really the same as the conversation of sentences 2A and 2B. We need to be able to dissect language as we receive it into its basic underlying meaning structure: We must represent the propositions of language, not the words that are used. Thus, we require a format that allows us to transform the knowledge about Peter into a statement that says something like

(3)   Peter has performed some operation (as yet unspecified) that has caused the package to change its location from its previous location (as yet unspecified) to its present location, on top of the table.

We have taken the approach that the basic experience that is to be encoded should be represented in terms of its underlying, more primitive, propositions. Thus, we represent the events about Peter and the package in a way that can be considered a formalization of the statements in (3). In fact, we do not stop with the statements shown there, but continue to expand the representations of such things as the package (a physical object that has certain specifications), Peter (a male, human), and the table. The notion of performing this type of expansion of the basic events and concepts into their underlying conceptual ideas is related to the work of Roger Schank (1972b, 1973b), although his methods differ from ours. It is also closely related to the work of the generative semanticists in the field of linguistics (see the discussion in Chapter 4).

The encoding of information in terms of underlying primitives will be discussed in some detail in following chapters. The representation is a powerful one. It does more than simply allow us to address the problem of paraphrase; it also provides a basic information framework for events that govern the way in which all information is interpreted. Suppose a new sentence about Peter comes along:

(4)   Peter said that because the package was heavy, his arms hurt.

It is possible to go back to the framework provided by (3) and add two new items. First, there is an obvious inference that the method used by Peter to get the package to the table was to carry it in his arms, or at the very least, by some means that required exerting effort with his arms. Second, the representation of the package itself can be modified to add the information that it has the quality of being heavy, but not so heavy that it cannot be carried.

Knowledge of the World

One important aspect of language processing is that much more than the knowledge of words is required to understand a sentence: There must be general knowledge about the world as well. To understand a sentence, we appear to combine general knowledge about the world with knowledge of the structure of language and the meaning of the parts of the sentence. Often a good deal of problem-solving behavior is required to determine the exact meaning that is conveyed by language. As an example, consider another aspect of Peter and his package. We use for this example a pair of sentences from a discussion by Minsky (1968, p. 22):

(5A)   Peter put the package on the table.

(5B)   Because it wasn't level, it slid off.

The problem posed by the sentences is to determine the processes that the human language user applied to (5B) to match the pronouns with their appropriate referents: The first "it" in sentence 5B most probably refers to the table; the second "it" must refer to the box. Syntactical knowledge alone cannot identify the referent with which each "it" belongs. To see this, consider the following pair of sentences:

(6A)   Peter put the package on the table.

(6B)   Because it was round, it rolled off.

Sentence 6B has the same syntactic structure as (5B), yet in (6B) the first "it" probably refers to the package, not the table.

To decipher sentences 5B and 6B properly requires some knowledge about objects, about causes of movement, about the things that can roll and slide, and, in general, about the ways things behave. Moreover, logical elaboration can be added freely, because if we wondered

(7)   Where is the package now?

we could easily construct an answer something like, "It's not clear, but probably on the floor."

When concepts are represented within a person's memory, they must fit within the framework provided by general knowledge of the world. This world knowledge is extensive, encompassing all a person's experiences and all information that he has learned. Much of this knowledge is so well integrated and so frequently used that it is applied with little or no conscious effort.

The Structural Framework

One view of the role of world knowledge is to consider it as a structural framework upon which newly acquired information must be fastened. This skeletal or schematic representation then guides both the interpretation of information and the search for new information to fill the gaps left in the structure. This notion is especially clear for the analysis of language and visual perception.

For example, verbs imply a particular structure of concepts and other events. Thus, in the phrase

(8)   . . . put the package . . . ,

the verb "put" carries with it a framework that must be filled if the phrase is to be understood. A verb like "put" can have many different meaning frames. In this example, "put" requires a **physical object** (the package), a **location**, and an **agent** (someone who instigates the action). Moreover, the **object** must be movable (as in "put the package on the chair") or createable (as in "put the answer in the square"). There are further constraints. When a **physical object** such as a package is put somewhere, then it is assumed to have had a prior **location**, even though this assumption was not specifically stated. Moreover, the place where the package has been put must be capable of holding the object, at least temporarily. Finally, the **agent** (say, Peter) must be capable of causing the object to have moved.

Words such as "put" can occur within a number of different frameworks. We can "put an idea into his head," or "put the matter right," or even "put the motion to a vote." Not all meanings require physical objects or imply movement or locations. But, we claim, each will have its own special framework and each has its own special requirements and implications.

The notion that knowledge is packaged into conceptual frameworks that guide in the interpretation of a person's experiences is not new. Under the name of "schema,"[1] the idea has a long history in psychology, where it is most frequently associated with the work of Bartlett and Piaget. We find the idea valuable, for once an appropriate frame or schema has been established, then it can help provide meaningful interpretation for a variety of situations. We repeatedly use this notion in our analyses of language in many of the chapters that follow. In addition, we use frames and schemata as the conceptual basis for the analyses of visual perception (Chapter 11) and game playing (Chapter 12). Just how a person establishes the appropriate frame or schema for a situation from the many that are potentially available, or how a frame is modified when it is no longer appropriate, are difficult problems. Some recent thoughts on these problems, especially in the domain of visual perception and language, are presented by Minsky (in press) and Winograd (in press).

---

[1]The singular form is "schema"; the plural is "schemata."

THE REPRESENTATION OF INFORMATION IN MEMORY

The goal is to represent the conceptual relationships that we believe exist within human memory in a precise and formal manner. The representation must be flexible enough to encompass a wide range of human capabilities. It must not be restricted to a single domain or to a single activity. Thus, it must be able to handle the concepts expressed in natural language, but it should not be restricted to linguistic information. Sensory, experiential, emotional, and cognitive aspects of information must all be present. We would like a homogeneous representational format, so that information can be used in similar manner by all mental processes regardless of its initial source or eventual use. The representation should also be useful in suggesting possible experimental tests.

In this section, we briefly illustrate the type of representational format that we have adopted. This is but a brief introduction, and the intent is only to give a rough overview of the approach. Not all the notation and not all the concepts will be discussed or justified; that is left for later chapters. In particular, Chapter 2 presents a detailed discussion of the representational issues and of the philosophy that we have adopted. Chapter 4 compares our work with some of the current work in linguistics. Chapter 7 gives a demonstration and explanation of how the representational ideas have been programmed into a working computer program. Most of the other chapters can be considered theoretical extensions and/or experimental tests of the ideas.

The Active Structural Network

Our approach can be illustrated by reconsidering the analysis of sentences 5A and 5B:

(5A)   Peter put the package on the table.

(5B)   Because it wasn't level, it slid off.

We want the memory structure to reflect the important underlying propositions. First, there is the existence of the objects that the sentences refer to: Peter, a package, and a table. Next, there are the several events that occurred: Peter was responsible for getting the package on the table; the table was tilted, and as a result, the package slid off it. Figure 1.1 shows how we start the analysis. This figure is a hybrid. It combines a diagrammatic sketch of the information that

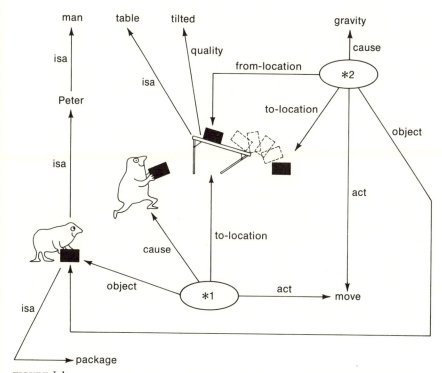

FIGURE 1.1

A diagrammatic representation of the active structural network showing the concepts and events that underlie the sentences "Peter put the package on the table" and "Because it wasn't level, it slid off." The two nodes labeled *1 and *2 are instances of the movements involved. The arrows indicate relations. The label on an arrow specifies the type of relation, and the direction of the arrow indicates the direction in which that relation is to be interpreted.

is to be conveyed with an introduction to the representation of that information.

The basic system that we use for representing information is that of semantic networks. The structure, formally, is a directed graph, with nodes connected to each other by labeled, directed relations. We have expanded upon the procedures normally used in semantic networks, adding the ability to include active procedural information — programs that say how a particular task should be performed. In addition, we have devised a fairly elaborate notational system for incorporating the schemata that we believe underlie human memory into the network representation. For these reasons, we call our structures *active structural networks.* A detailed description of them is given in Chapter 2. For the moment, consider Figure 1.1.

The basic conceptual information shown in Figure 1.1 is that Peter caused the package to move from its earlier location to the top of the table, and that gravity was the causal agent that then acted upon the package, causing it to move from the table top onto the floor. The first movement is represented by a node—the oval numbered *1. The oval is one form of a node, and the labeled arrows that lead from the oval to the concepts (or words) in the figure are called the relations. The relations show how the different nodes and structures in the figure are related to one another. Thus, looking at node *1, we see that it represents an instance of the act of move. This particular instance of move has as its cause, Peter (shown diagrammatically), and the object being moved is a package (again, shown diagrammatically). The location to which the moved object went (the to-location) is the table. The second node, the oval labeled *2, is another instance of move. Here, the cause is gravity, the object is the same package, and the movement takes place from a from-location (the table top) to a to-location (the floor).

The two ovals in Figure 1.1 represent the two major propositions. The other concepts shown in the figure are also represented within the structural network as nodes, although this diagram does not really show how. The picture of the table is shown to be an instance of a node. The relation isa can be read to mean "is an instance of." Thus, the picture of the table is an instance of the concept of table. The drawings of the package and of Peter are instances of the nodes that are named "package" and "Peter."

Clearly, the representation shown in Figure 1.1 is not yet complete. We need a procedure that allows us to represent not only the basic sentences that are under analysis, but the underlying conceptual structure that they must represent. Figure 1.2 shows how we can expand sentence 5A. The top part of the figure represents the basic sentence structure itself: Peter put the package on the table. The bottom part of the figure illustrates the encoding of the underlying conceptual structure.[2]

Expressed in words, Figure 1.2 conveys the idea that when Peter put a package on the table iswhen an event (of which Peter was the agent) caused the result that caused the package to change its location from a place unspecified to a new place, on top of the table.

The action done by Peter to move the package is not known: Hence, it is specified by the dummy action named DO in the figure. The node labeled CAUSE shows that the event indicated by DO had the result

---

[2]In this figure, and in general throughout the book, we simplify the drawings by omitting the relation "act" between a node and the action of which it is an instance. We then label the node with the name of its action or concept. Thus, in Figure 1.2, the propositions that are labeled put, CAUSE, DO, CHANGE, and LOC (location) are actually instances of the actions defined by those labels.

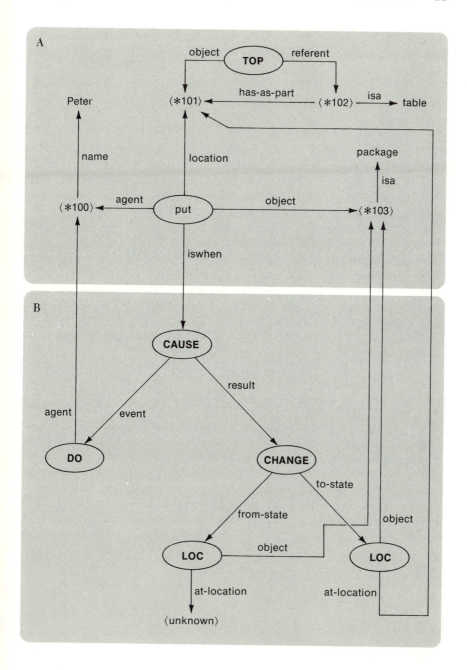

FIGURE 1.2

A shows the basic representation of the sentence "Peter put the package on the table." B shows the result after the sentence has been expanded into the underlying conceptual structure.

of causing a change, the node represented by **CHANGE**. This change was from a state represented by the **LOC** node on the left (which specifies only that the package had some unknown location) to a state represented by the **LOC** node on the right (which specifies that the package is at a location given by node *101).[3] The node *101 represents a physical object that is the top part of the object represented by node *102 and, thus, the top part of the table.

The representation for sentence 5B should show that when the package slid, it changed location from a position on the table to a position at the edge of the table, where the first position was higher than the second. Moreover, the movement was caused by the force of gravity. The package was in contact with the table during the movement, and afterward, it had traveled beyond the edge of the table where, no longer being supported, it fell to a new supporting surface. This is not the place to continue with a detailed analysis. The point is that the representational system must be able to show the underlying conceptualizations of any information that is to be stored. A large set of conceptual frameworks or schemata is required to organize and interpret the information. Moreover, this conceptual knowledge will often need to use widely based, general world knowledge.

The Primitive Structure of Verbs

Throughout this book we represent the underlying meaning structures of events. If our analysis is correct, then this has important implications, not only for the way in which events of the world are understood, but also for the way in which a person acquires knowledge. In Chapter 9, Dedre Gentner reports an experimental investigation of the way children acquire their understanding of language. Gentner examined the hypothesis that verbs are composed of more basic underlying units. This hypothesis implies that a child should not be able to understand a verb until he has first come to understand the propositions that underlie it and the way those underlying structures are combined. Thus, the sentences

(9)   Mary gives a toy to Bert.

or

(10)   Mary takes a toy from Bert.

---

[3]The numbers preceded by asterisks (as in *103, pronounced "star 103") are arbitrary names assigned to the nodes for convenience in referring to them. The numbers have no other significance.

state something about the direction of transfer of possession of the objects and about the person who has initiated the action. If a child is to understand (9) and (10), he must understand the concepts of *possession, change,* and at least some level of *causality.* When we use the verbs "buy" and "sell," as in

(11)   Mary buys a car from Bert.

or

(12)   Bert sells a car to Mary.

we are using, in part, the same primitive notions of *possession, change,* and *cause* that underlie the verbs "give" and "take," as well as the social conventions involved in the purchase of an object, and the fact that there is an exchange of two items, the car and money. At the age of 3 years, children understand the verbs "give" and "take." But up to the age of 5½ years, some children still have difficulty with the verbs "buy" and "sell." In general, Gentner finds that children who have not yet acquired the full meanings tend to equate the word "buy" with the action "take," and the word "sell" with the action "give." The error shows that they have not yet acquired all the fundamental components of the verbs, and the form of the error is useful in letting us deduce just what components do exist and how they are combined. These issues are discussed in considerable detail in Chapter 9, but it is informative at this point to recognize the implications of the representational system for language behavior.

Building Cohesive Structures

The expansion of sentences that has just been illustrated automatically gives the memory representation the power to answer questions that require inference. In a computer implementation of these ideas of sentence comprehension that is discussed in Chapter 8, David Rumelhart and James Levin show how a number of the basic kinds of "wh" questions (questions about *who, where, what, why,* and *when*) can be answered by means of a process that examines the stored information. Thus, suppose someone says:

(13)   Dave was in Pittsburgh from June through July.

Now, our assumption is that the human language-understanding system interprets (13) in a manner such as that shown in Figure 1.3A. If someone then says the sentence

(14)   He went to Pittsburgh by plane from San Diego.

then we assume that the processing system can represent this new information in a way that takes advantage of the structure that was created previously—as shown in Figure 1.3B. Notice that new structures need not be added to memory if relevant old ones already exist. And finally, if someone says,

(15)   Because of the trip, he got a suitcase.

the structure shown in Figure 1.3C is added. The details of this structure are not important at the moment (they will be explained in Chapter 2), but essentially, this structure represents the fact that the event of going to Pittsburgh was the cause of Dave's getting a suitcase. Moreover, Dave got the suitcase by performing some causal act (which is not specified and, therefore, is simply represented by the node labeled **DO** in Figure 1.3C) that had the result of getting a suitcase into his possession (the node labeled **POSSESS**).

We have now shown how a sequence of sentences can result in a single, cohesive structure with memory. These structures can also be used to answer questions. The process of answering questions about the incidents discussed in sentences 13, 14, and 15 is essentially one of determining what information is sought and then examining the structures within the memory network until the appropriate ones are found. Then, by matching the information found with the information sought, an answer can be generated. To do all this is not quite so easy as it might seem. Some cognitive mechanism must exist that can examine the structures within memory and perform the necessary searches and comparisons.

The system that is capable of integrating new information into cohesive structures, making use of old information as much as possible, and then properly interpreting questions and seeking out the information that is sought, is rather complex. It involves a good deal of linguistic and general world knowledge, the ability to examine and interpret the structures of memory, and the necessary processes to construct an appropriate answer from the knowledge that has been found. Several of the chapters in this book discuss the types of issues that are encountered in such systems—primarily Chapter 7 (which discusses the mechanics needed to perform these operations on a computer simulation of the tasks), Chapter 8 (which describes a specific set of cognitive processes for understanding, for creating

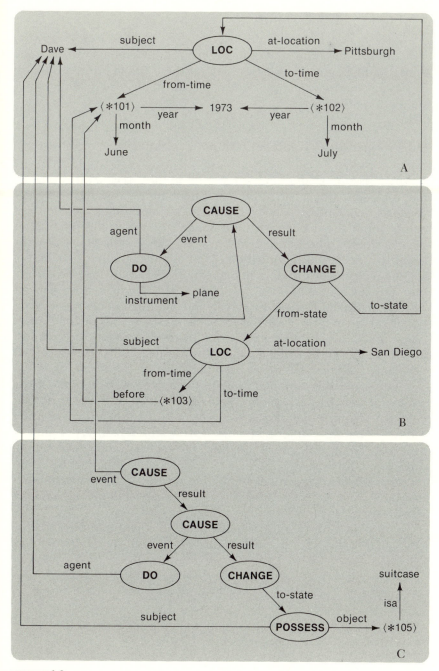

FIGURE 1.3

How information received at different times can be used to form one cohesive structure. A shows the sentence "Dave was in Pittsburgh from June through July." B shows "He went to Pittsburgh by plane from San Diego." C shows "Because of the trip, he got a suitcase."

structures of the type shown in Figure 1.3, and for answering questions), and Chapter 13 (which discusses the types of processes necessary to answer more complex questions, questions that involve mental simulation of events).

On Propositional Representation

A critical issue in the research reported in this book is the format for the representation. The representational format we have adopted suggests that humans retain knowledge in the form of specific statements about the conceptual information present in the information that is stored. The alternative view is that information — most especially perceptual information — is retained as an image that is somehow analogous to the original experience. Many people believe that they have mental images of scenes that they have experienced. This is particularly true in visual and auditory perception: Many people claim to "see" or to "hear" in their mind an accurate, detailed image of past experiences; many can call up from memory the "sounds" of the voices of their acquaintances or "music" that they have experienced. Similar statements are made about all of the senses.

Are these images compatible with the representation of the active structural network? The issues that are involved in this question are complex. There is no easy resolution. Yet, it is our impression that the two apparently differing points of view are, in reality, not quite so different. To separate out all the issues is not easy, and any attempt to do so is bound to raise numerous new issues. It is important to discuss these problems, however, for they are critical to the understanding of much work in contemporary cognitive psychology and artificial intelligence.

To start with the most elementary level at which the problem is often stated, there are two extreme forms of representation:

- A propositional system in which concepts are expressed as statements about the conceptual relationships among the items in the proposition.

- An analogical representation, in which an accurate image of the original scene is maintained.

Thus, if we had piles of blocks on a table, a propositional system might encode the information by such statements as

(16A)   Block A is above block B.

(16B)   Block A is to the right of block C.

and so on. An analogical representation would be like a photograph — an accurate pictorial image of the table and blocks.

This comparison is not really very accurate. It provides a caricature of both alternatives. In considering a representational format, one must ask about the desired properties of that representation. In part, one wishes to have a representation that allows an easy transaction of operations that need to be performed, whereas operations that are not necessary may be hard to do. With the human memory system, there are a number of different operations that will be required. Sometimes a person needs to perform perceptual tasks, to perform pattern recognition, or to manipulate objects mentally (see Shepard and Meltzer, 1971). At times, a person needs to know conceptual relationships.

Humans are flexible in their use of information. They can read upside-down print (although not easily, unless they practice). They can perform mental manipulations of sensory information, and they can recognize sights, sounds, touch, taste, and smells, including visual and tactile texture and auditory timbre. All of this implies the encoding of some sort of direct sensory information. Similarly, they can answer questions about the information that has been stored in ways that imply the storage of conceptual information. We suspect that people are capable of using different forms of representation of the information stored within their memory, and that they are capable of either retrieving an appropriate form or of transforming the information stored into whatever format is most appropriate for answering the questions put to them.[4]

In considering these issues, it is important to note what it means to have a good mental image of something. As soon as a person realizes that mental images — even analog ones — are not the same as photographic reproductions of the original sensory experience, then the door is open for a merger of the two supposedly conflicting ideas about representation. To have a good mental image implies that the mental phenomenon is somehow analogous to the original perception. The mental image is reasonably complete and continuous (to all apparent purposes), and the operations that can be performed upon that image are homomorphic with the operations that can be performed upon perceptions.

The fact that a person "perceives images" when recalling perceptual experiences from memory does not mean that information is stored within memory in that way. It only implies that they are processed as images. Thus, one could very well store information within

---

[4]These issues have been discussed at length in the literature on psychology and artificial intelligence. The critical discussion for us, which has formed the basis for this section, is summarized in Bobrow (in press).

the memory system in one format, and then, when occasion demands, use that information to regenerate the image of which one then becomes aware (see Bower, 1972). The regenerated image could be a reasonably complete analogy to the original perception of the real world, with all the properties that people ascribe to their images. The regenerated image is likely to contain errors, of course, and the errors will be conceptual ones that reflect the underlying propositional base from which they were constructed. It is the existence of gross conceptual errors in what appears to be a highly detailed accurate memory image that lends support to this suggestion. (Several examples will be presented later in this chapter.)

There is an alternative explanation of mental images. All that the introspective arguments tell us is that the form of the information reconstituted from memory as an "image" is similar to that of the form of the original perception. But of what form is the original perception?

We know the perceptual information undergoes considerable transformation as it is processed by the sensory nervous system. Physiological mechanisms pull apart the components of the arriving signals and perform intricate types of frequency, temporal, and spatial transforms on the signals. Feature detectors pull out significant parts of the wave forms. And then context, meaning, and past experience play a large role in the interpretation of the information, evidently in the very initial stages of perception and pattern recognition. Items in focal attention stand out as *figure,* with all else perceived as *ground.* Relationships among the various parts of the perceptual field become a fundamental part of what we call the perception of the sensory world. Suppose, for the sake of argument, that the perceptual system that analyzes the arriving sensory signals produces as the result of its operations a conceptual, propositional representation. If so, then the first stage of conscious awareness of the world is already in the form of propositions. Thus we "see" the objects in front of us as books or as pieces of paper, not as gradations of light energy that arrive at the retina: The natural perception of the world is in terms of meaningful patterns.

If this be so, then when we re-create an image from memory, the propositions that we are able to recall are in a form similar to those that we originally perceived. Hence, the claim that we "see" or "hear" a facsimile of the original perception.

There is more to the argument. The major other points concern the need to get access to information that is stored within memory, and to get that access, one must retrieve the individual components of experiences. A detailed argument about the problem of retrieval is provided by Pylyshyn (1973) in his review article and critique of the concept of mental imagery. In fact, Pylyshyn states this particular point so well that it seems best simply to present the argument from his paper.

We take our quotation from the section where Pylyshyn is discussing the commonly held view that people store accurate images of the world and then, when the occasion arises, recall those images and examine them. Thus, this view of things holds that a person is able to re-experience some aspects of the original and, in that reexamination of the image, discover the information that is being sought. This view, says Pylyshyn, runs into difficulty because

> . . . we can retrieve information about a whole scene or any part of it by addressing aspects of the *perceptually interpreted content* of the scene. Even if we confine ourselves to the retrieval of phenomenal images, we can argue that the content of such images must be already interpreted—in spite of the fact that we seem to be "perceiving" them as we would novel stimuli. This must be so because retrieval of such images is clearly hierarchical to an unlimited degree of detail and in the widest range of aspects. Thus, for example, I might image a certain sequence of events at a party as I recall what happened at a certain time. But I might also image someone's facial expression or the jewel in their ring or the aroma of some particular item of food without first calling up the entire scene. Such perceptual attributes must therefore be available as interpreted integral units in my representation of the whole scene. Not only can such recollections be of fine detail but they can also be of rather abstract qualities, such as whether some people were angry. Furthermore, when there are parts missing from one's recollections, these are never arbitrary pieces of a visual scene. We do not, for example, recall a scene with some arbitrary segment missing like a torn photograph. What is missing is invariably some integral perceptual attribute or relation, for example, colors, patterns, events, or spatial relations (we might, for example, recall who was at the party without recalling exactly where they were standing). When our recollections are vague, it is always in the sense that certain perceptual qualities or attributes are absent or uncertain—not that there are geometrically definable pieces of a picture missing. All of the above suggest that one's representation of a scene must contain already differentiated and interpreted perceptual aspects. In other words, the representation is far from being raw and, so to speak, in need of "perceptual" interpretation. The argument is not simply that retrieval of images would involve a bewildering cross-classification system while retrieval in other forms of representation would not. The point is that because retrieval must be able to address perceptually interpreted content, the network of cross-classified relations must have interpreted objects (i.e., concepts) at its nodes. . . .

We may assume, then, that the representation differs from *any conceivable* picture-like entity at least by virture of containing only as much information as can be described by a finite number of propositions. Furthermore, this reduction is not reasonably accounted for by a simple physical reduction such as that of limited resolution. What type of representation meets such requirements? A number of alternative forms of representations are discussed in a subsequent section. For the present, it suffices to point out that any representation having the properties mentioned above *is much closer to being a description of the scene than a picture of it.* A description is propositional, it contains a finite amount of information, it may contain abstract as well as concrete aspects and, especially relevant to the present discussion, it contains terms (symbols for objects, attributes, and relations) which are the *results* of—not inputs to—perceptual processes."[5]

The real issue, it would seem to us, is that the representational format of information that is stored within the human memory system must be one well suited to the kinds of operations that are performed upon it. Arguments about the mode of representation are often really arguments about the type of relations that get encoded. How good is the mapping between the perceptual units and the memory units, between the perceptual operations and the ones of cognitive deduction? How dense or complete is the information that is encoded? Does it include all the information in which one might conceivably later be interested, or does it include only a selected subset of those relationships that were noted at the time of the initial encoding? In the former case, with a rich, dense body of information, retrieval of a particular item might be difficult. In the latter case, with selective encoding, retrieval of information that was not specifically encoded either may be impossible or may require a long chain of deductions.

We believe that the human cognitive system is capable of flexibility in the way it represents the information that it uses. Propositional representation would appear to be well suited for permanent storage of the meaning and interpretation of the events that a person experiences. At times, analogical representations would appear to be better suited for the operations that one wishes to perform upon mental structures. But because the fundamental differences between the two forms of representation are not clear, and because it appears to be possible to transform one form of representation into the other, we do not feel that this apparently basic issue is, in reality, a fundamental one about mental representation.

---

[5]From Z. W. Pylyshyn, "What the mind's eye tells the mind's brain: A critique of mental imagery," *Psychological Bulletin*, 1973, **80**, 10–11. Copyright 1973 by American Psychological Association. Reprinted with permission of author and publisher.

CONCEPTUAL STRUCTURES FOR PERCEPTION

The active structural network representation of information within memory is a very general scheme. To this point, our examples and discussions have primarily been taken from the use of language. We believe it to be important to be able to represent information from different perceptual systems within a common memory framework. As a result, we have studied some nonlinguistic events, attempting to determine just how these might be represented within the common structural network representation. Chapters 11 and 12 discuss the format for the representation of nonlinguistic information, and to some extent Chapters 13 and 15 do also.

A useful source of information about the nature of the encoding process for nonlinguistic information are the errors that people make as they attempt to remember previously experienced events. In this section, we give examples of these errors in three situations:

- Memory for the floor plan of an apartment.
- Memory for the appearance of the front of a building.
- Memory for the configuration of pieces in a board game.

The Floor Plan Problem

External knowledge about the world imposes constraints on the possible interpretations of information retrieved from memory. Consider how someone draws a floor plan from memory. Buildings have walls and supporting structures. If a staircase occurs on one floor, then it must appear in a corresponding location on the next adjoining floor. Toilets are often located one above the other, especially in public buildings. There must be passageways for people to get from one room to another, and all rooms must have entries. When a floor plan is remembered, all these facts place constraints on the possible result, helping the process of reconstruction. In drawing floor plans, the role of inferred knowledge is made clear because the constraints of building construction are well known. In most memory retrieval tasks, external knowledge is also used, but usually its role is not so easy to discover.

We get clues about the way different types of knowledge interact by examining errors. Consider the following example. In the married students' housing at the University of California, San Diego, all apartments have a balcony that is entered from the living room. Figure 1.4 shows the architect's floor plan of the apartment. Residents of these apartments have some surprising ideas about their own apartments. Figure 1.5 shows a typical floor plan drawn by a resident

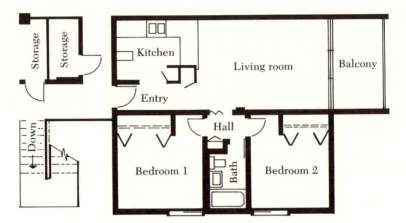

FIGURE 1.4
A floor plan of the second-floor apartments for married students at the University of California, San Diego. Note that the balcony is separated from the living room by a sliding-glass door. There is a brick wall on both sides of the balcony.

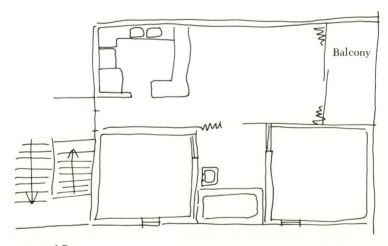

FIGURE 1.5
Drawing of an apartment done by a long-term resident. Note that most of the details are well remembered, but that the balcony is drawn incorrectly: As shown in Figure 1.4, the balcony actually protrudes from the building. Forty-seven percent of the people tested made this error.

of one of the apartments; note the balcony. People who lived in the apartments for long periods (measured in years in some instances) thought the balcony was constructed flush with the exterior of the house, whereas, in fact, it extended beyond (in the normal way). The reason for the confusion is clear from the real floor plan in Figure 1.4. This balcony design is unusual in that there is a solid wall on both sides of the balcony; the wall on the right is confused with the outer wall of the adjoining bedroom. (The fact that the balcony extends out of the building is clear when the building is viewed from the outside.) The error reveals the constructive nature of the retrieval process. Forty-seven percent of the 15 people who were tested made this same error in drawing the balcony, even though some of them sketched the plan while they sat within the living room itself. Another 20 percent of those tested had difficulty in drawing the balcony, correcting themselves several times. The error and the difficulties reveal some of the conceptual factors that are important in reconstructing non-linguistic information from the representational structures contained within memory.[6]

The memory representation is not simply an accurate rendition of real life, but in fact is a combination of information, inference, and reconstruction from knowledge about buildings and the world in general. It is important to note that when the mistake was pointed out, all the students were surprised at what they had drawn. Moreover, people who live in the first-floor apartments (and therefore often enter their home through the balcony) do not make this mistake.

Memory for a University Building

Now consider another related example. Figure 1.6 shows a picture of the Psychology-Linguistics Building at the University of California, San Diego. Stephen Palmer conducted a very simple set of experiments on the graduate students who worked in the building. He asked them to draw pictures of its front. The distortions that resulted were informative.

All of the students who drew these pictures had worked in the building; they performed their experiments there, had their offices there, and had classes and parties there. Moreover, the view shown in the figure is the one that most people use to enter the building at the start of each school day. Each student had seen the building for several years—in some instances from the time the building had been constructed.

---

[6]Yaakov Kareev helped to collect these drawings.

FIGURE 1.6
The north side of the Psychology-Linguistics Building at the University of California, San Diego.

Figure 1.7 shows the drawings of two of the students. In the entire collection of drawings a number of gross conceptual errors are present. First, one drawing shows there to be one too many levels: four floors instead of three. Second, both drawings in Figure 1.7 show the entrance located appreciably to the left of its actual, centered location on the building face. Third, the number of windows is grossly underestimated: Most people drew far too few. The numbers shown by the two students are 9 and 10. The correct number is 42. Fourth, most people drew the building much narrower than it actually is, in relation to its height.

These are all conceptual errors. None of them can be explained by an inability to draw well, or by simple memory lapses or distortions of a pictorial image within the head. All represent wrong concepts of the building. Each has a possible rational explanation, although we do not really know the causes of the errors.

For example, the gross underestimation of the number of windows says something about the numerical precision of the memory representation. From this error, we would wish to conclude that the representational format takes into account the shape and form of the individual windows, plus the fact that the window is repeated a "large" number of times. Then, perceptual problems in counting

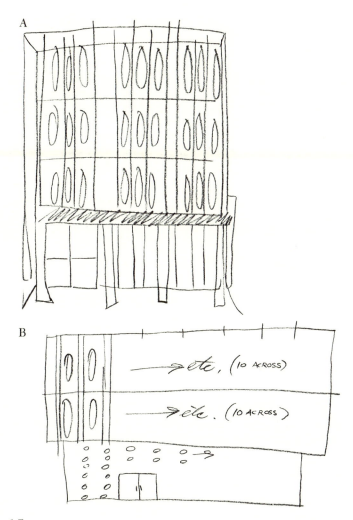

FIGURE 1.7
Two drawings of the north side of the Psychology-Linguistics Building (shown in
Figure 1.6) done by graduate students who worked in the building and always
entered from this direction. (Drawings collected by Stephen Palmer.)

or subitizing numbers as high as 42 would tend to cause the number
to be re-created as much too small a value.

   Some of these ideas have been tested by Palmer. For example,
he also presented the students in his experiment with the drawings
of the building that are shown in Figure 1.8. They tended to select
Figure 1.8A as the most accurate representation, whereas the correct
drawing is shown in 1.8B. Note that the selected version contains

A   C

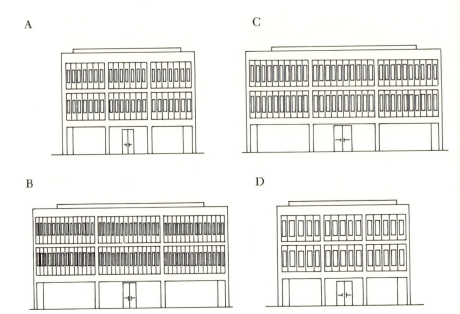

B   D

FIGURE 1.8
Four versions of drawings of the north side of the Psychology-Linguistics Building
used in a recognition memory test conducted by Stephen Palmer. Subjects thought
that *A* was the more accurate drawing, even though it is not. Compare with Figures
1.6 and 1.7.

too few windows and is not sufficiently elongated. Thus, the kinds of
conceptual errors that the students make show up both in their drawings and in visual recognition. Further discussion of the nature of
the representation for visually perceived scenes and objects is presented by Palmer in Chapter 11.

Memory for Board Games

In this example, based upon the research reported by Marc Eisenstadt
and Yaakov Kareev in Chapter 12, a person's memory for the configuration of pieces in a board game was shown to be dependent upon
his conceptualization of the game. The memory for the board appeared
to be more like a reconstruction based upon the conceptual nature
of the game than upon an accurate image of the board.

In this experiment, Eisenstadt and Kareev trained their subjects
to play two board games: Go and Gomoku. Both of these games are
played on the same type of board with the same pieces. Go is an
oriental game in which the two players alternately place black and

white stones, respectively, on the board, each hoping to surround (and therefore control) as much territory as possible. Surrounded pieces are captured. Go is a sophisticated game, and although the rules are simple, the game is considered perhaps even more difficult than chess. Gomoku is played with the same pieces on the same board, but in Gomoku the task is to get 5 adjoining pieces in a row, either vertically, horizontally, or diagonally. Figure 1.9 shows a typical board position for both Go and Gomoku. (In their studies,

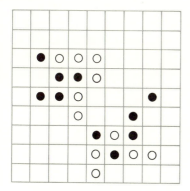

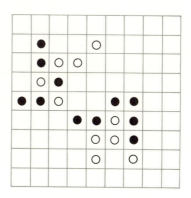

Gomoku game, Black's move   Go game, White's move

FIGURE 1.9
Subjects were shown these board positions briefly and were later asked to recall them. When they were shown the left board, they were told that it was from a game of Gomoku, and that they should determine the best move for black. When they were shown the right board, they were told it was from a Go game, and that they should determine the best move for white. Both board positions are transformations of one another: The right position is the same as the left after being rotated and flipped, and after the white pieces are changed to black and the black changed to white (see Chapter 12 for details).

Eisenstadt and Kareev used a 9-square by 9-square board with the pieces placed within the squares: The games are normally placed on a 19 by 19 board and the pieces are placed on the intersections.) Subjects were trained to play both games. Then they were presented with the configuration shown on the left of Figure 1.9 and told that it came from a game of Gomoku and that their task was to select the best move. After their selection, they were given a blank board and asked to recollect as much as possible of the original board positions. This is the task we want to consider: the memory for the board positions. Later, after many other tasks had intervened, the subjects were shown the board position on the right of Figure 1.9 and told that it had come from the game of Go. As before, their task was to select the best move and then, later, to recall as much of the board as possible. Both board positions are actually the same, except that the right one has been constructed by rotating and turning over the left position and then changing black to white, thereby reversing the colors of the pieces. (Of course, the actual experiment had all the relevant counterbalancing of positions and order of testing.)

What was remembered depended upon which game a subject thought he was seeing. Scoring only those board pieces relevant to the game of Go, the subjects who thought the board was for Go did much better than those who thought it to be Gomoku. Similarly, scoring the recall of only those pieces relevant to a Gomoku game, those subjects who believed the board to be for Gomoku did much better than those who thought it was for Go, as is clearly shown in Figure 1.10. The point is that subjects retained the image of the board

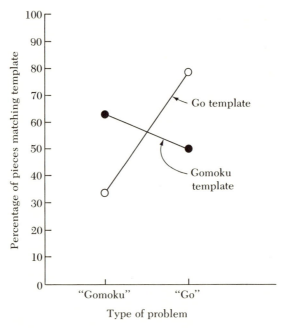

FIGURE 1.10
Results of the experiment illustrated by Figure 1.9. Subjects remembered best those parts of the board positions that were important pieces for the game they thought the position represented (see Chapter 12 for details).

as interpreted by their knowledge of the particular game. A subject's memory did not contain an accurate perception of the board, but rather an image that had already been interpreted.

THE REPRESENTATION OF MEMORIES AS PLANS

In the human cognitive system, all input and output information comes through the sensory and motor systems. Thus, a concept such as a *table* or an action such as *to walk* is probably not specified in terms of detailed refinements on the semantic level, but rather as a sensorimotor image of our experiences. We could think of *walk* as a form of motion in which the *actor* and *object* are the same and in which the *method* is by means of a certain set of motions made by the feet of the actor. We could think of *stroll, saunter,* and *amble* as more specific types of walking. But these definitions seem unwieldy: We know what these types of walking are through our sensorimotor routines for performing them.

One way of cutting the tangled definitional web is to determine the place for sensorimotor images. Fortunately, one method is readily available: We let the primitive definition of actions be the sensorimotor instructions for performing those actions. This by itself is not enough. If the representation of a sentence such as

(17)   Move the object to the table.

involves the sensorimotor commands for movement, then thinking of the sequence also is likely to lead to the movement. This is not what we want. We need several different ways of using the same sensorimotor representation. We should be able to do at least three different things with a given sensorimotor plan:

- The sensorimotor system can be examined, as data.
- The sensorimotor system can be activated, causing the action.
- The sensorimotor system can be simulated, causing an internal representation of the action sequence.

The Representation of a Plan

Consider what the structure of a program for performing an action might look like: some information stored in memory can also be used as instructions to act upon the memory itself. Suppose you are asked to state what two concepts (say, dogs and cats) have in common—how would you do it? Presumably, you would perform some operation equivalent to getting access to the representation for the two concepts and comparing the attributes associated with each. Those that were similar for both would be the things in common; the others would be ignored.

The set of steps that is followed in making the comparison is a *procedure* or a *program*. The program must be translatable into the format for representing events in the data base. It is important that we be able to store our plans and programs in this manner, for then they can be examined, modified, or performed. Because a sequence of instructions is both a program and data, it can be changed in the same way as other information stored in memory can be modified. Just as one can modify his knowledge of concepts and of events, so too can one modify actions.

The ability to represent information within memory as plans has several important implications. As we have seen, it allows a person to learn plans, and then either to manipulate the plans of actions as data or to perform them. It can be argued that the ability to analyze and modify the sequences of instructions that comprise plans is a critical component of the learning process.

In Chapter 13, Greg Scragg examines some of the implications of the ability to use plans in these various ways. Scragg examines how a person might use the knowledge about a kitchen, about foods, and about recipes to answer questions. Some of the questions can be answered by examination of the information stored in memory (questions such as, "Where is meat usually kept?"). Other questions require examination of the procedures for performing actions in order to determine the answer (questions such as, "What are the ingredients in a ham and cheese omelette?"). Other types of questions require that the task be simulated mentally, by performing the activities mentally and then examining them to see what consequences would result (questions such as, "If John were to make an omelette, what utensils would he dirty?"). Scragg's goal was to take the ideas that we had developed for the representation of information within active structural networks and to construct a computer program that could answer questions about processes; that is, he wanted to be able to hold a conversation between himself and the computer.[7] In this conversation, the statements of the human are shown in this type font. The responses of the program are shown in *this type font*.

---

[7] The computer simulation system is described in Chapter 7; Scragg's work is discussed in Chapter 13.

> Where are the cookies?

I think they are on the shelf.

> I ate the cookies.

OK.

> Where are the cookies?

There are none.

> Make a baked Virginia ham and very sharp Cheddar cheese sandwich.

OK.

> What did you use to make the sandwich?

Baked Virginia ham, very sharp Cheddar cheese, San Francisco sourdough bread, lettuce, mustard, a knife, a plate.

To this point the conversation has concerned actions that have actually been performed. Here are examples of statements that require examination of the routines for doing actions in order to state what would probably happen if they were to be performed:

> If I make a cake, what utensils would I need?

*You would need a pan, a measuring spoon, a stirring spoon,
a bowl, an icing knife, a measuring cup, a sifter.*

> How do you make spaghetti?

*First you make the sauce.
Add onions and mushrooms to a pan.
Brown them.
Then ——— (etc.)*

> Before putting onions in the pan, put butter and oil in the pan.

OK.

This conversation illustrates some of the requirements that a representational system must have. The knowledge should be in a form that is useful for many purposes. It should be possible to describe the information stored in memory, to modify it, to perform according to it, to imagine the results of using it, and to compare things by analogy to it.

SUMMARY

This chapter has presented a preview of much of the material in the book. The basic intent was to provide an introduction to the major issues that have guided our research. Thus, this chapter has focused primarily on discussions about the representation of information within memory, with sufficient examples to illustrate the points and to provide a guide and introduction to some of the chapters of the book.

The main point of these examples is that complex cognitive acts accompany the processes of language understanding and of recognizing perceptual events. Information in memory consists of all of our knowledge of the world. The process of understanding involves a large variety of cognitive processes, all working together to integrate new information into the structures that already exist in a person's mind.

PART II

THEORY

CHAPTER 2

The Active Structural Network

DAVID E. RUMELHART and DONALD A. NORMAN

STRUCTURAL NETWORKS

The fundamental premise that underlies all of the work reported in this book is that information within human memory can be represented by means of what we call an *active structural network*. The word "active" means that the structures are both data and process. The knowledge structures are represented by a labeled, connected network or graph that consists of a set of *nodes* interconnected by a set of *relations*. Each relation is an association between two nodes and has two important properties: It is labeled and it is directed. The interpretation of a relation that interconnects two nodes depends both on the label and on the direction in which the relation is traversed. Using a relation in the direction opposite to its label is equivalent to using the *inverse* relation. Relations, then, are bidirectional but not symmetrical. These relations are used by the memory system to encode logical or semantic associations among nodes.

Figure 2.1A illustrates the most elementary unit of our representational system. Here two nodes, a and b, are shown associated by relationship R. The arrowhead defines the direction in which the

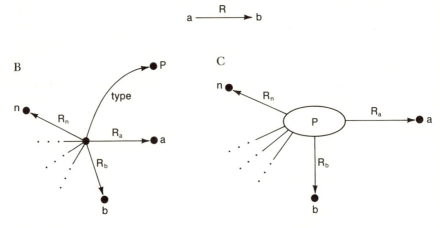

FIGURE 2.1
The basic network structures. *A* shows the relation R between two nodes a and b.
In general, an n-ary function P (a,b, . . . ,n) is represented by a node whose structure is
shown in *B*. The notation shown in *C* is usually used to denote n-ary functions.
When this notation is used, the connection between the node and the name of the
predicate is not always drawn.

label on the arrow should be interpreted. The link between the
nodes can be traversed in either direction, yielding the following
pair of descriptions of Figure 2.1A:

(1)   a R b
         b R-inverse a

For example, if R has the label **superset**, the **R-inverse** could have
the label **subset**:

         a subset b = b superset a

There are no restrictions on the number of associations any particular
node may have with others. Although associations between nodes
are always represented by binary relations, nonetheless, any *n*-ary
function (or predicate) can be represented by a concatenation of relations. Thus, the *n*-ary function

(2)   P(a, b, . . . , n)

can be represented by the structure shown in Figure 2.1B, in which
the *n* relations (R_a through R_n) indicate the *n* terms of the predicate.

The central node in Figure 2.1B represents an instance of the predicate P, and the name of the predicate is determined by following the relation labeled type from the central node. We often use the structure shown in Figure 2.1C in place of that of 2.1B to simplify the representation and to emphasize the central role of the name of the predicate.

Every definable piece of information in the memory system is encoded in the format of a node plus its relations. The node is the only addressable unit in the memory system; there are nodes for all of the ideas that make up the knowledge of the system.

Primary and Secondary Nodes

Although all nodes are named in the system (that is, addressable), the names do not necessarily have natural language equivalents. When a node does correspond to a concept named in natural language, then we still must distinguish its usage in different contexts by distinguishing between *primary* and *secondary* nodes. A *primary* node is the only node in the memory system that refers directly to a natural language concept. Such nodes may contain abstracted definitions of that concept expressed in the relational format. *Secondary* nodes represent the concepts as they are used in specific contexts — a *token* use of a primary type node.

A secondary node is generally an instance of some specific primary one. The relation type, or one of the relations that are forms of the type relation,[1] is used to point from a secondary node to its primary or type node.

The importance of this distinction can be appreciated by consideration of the problems that occur when a single concept must be referred to many times, but in different circumstances. Suppose that the concept of "hitting" is used in two sentences:

(3)   John hits the ball.
(4)   Mary hits the house.

The difficulty is shown in Figure 2.2A. Here, the two uses of the act "hit" are confused with one another. To resolve the difficulty, we distinguish between the definitional node for "hit," the *primary* (or type) node, and the particular use of that node, the *secondary* (or

---

[1]The two most common forms of type relation that will be used throughout the book are isa and act. In general, isa is the type relation used for concepts and act the type relation used for propositions. In this chapter, only the relation type is used.

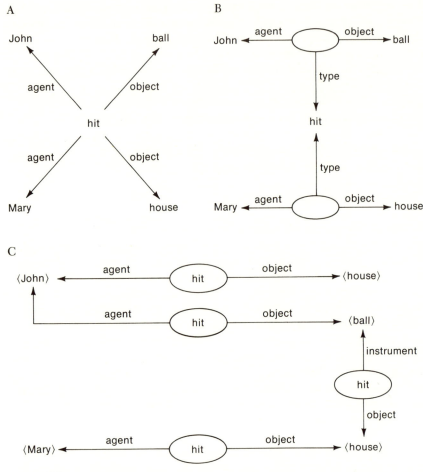

FIGURE 2.2
An example of the need to distinguish between primary and secondary nodes. A
shows how the absence of secondary nodes (or token nodes) makes it impossible to
separate the components of two different events. B and C show appropriate
representations. Secondary or token predicate nodes are represented by ovals;
secondary or token concept nodes are represented by angular brackets.

token) node. Figure 2.2B illustrates how the use of secondary nodes
keeps information about these two events separate.

The solution shown in Figure 2.2B is an illustration for events,
but similar problems also arise with the use of concepts. Suppose
that John also hit a house, but one different from the one hit by Mary.
We need two secondary nodes to represent the two houses. In fact,

we need secondary nodes for all of the concepts in Figure 2.2B in order to handle all possible contingencies. This is shown in Figure 2.2C, where we have added the following information:

(5)   John hit a house (different from the one hit by Mary).

(6)   The ball hit by John hit the same house that Mary hit.

The solutions shown in Figure 2.2B and C also indicate our notation. Secondary nodes that correspond to particular events (or *n*-ary predicates) are represented by ovals, and the name associated with its primary node is either written within the oval or pointed to by means of the relation **type**. Secondary nodes that correspond to particular concepts are represented by angular brackets, and again the name associated with the primary node is either written within the brackets or pointed to with the relation **type**. The relation **type** connecting a secondary node to its primary is always present conceptually (although it is sometimes deleted in a drawing to simplify the resulting diagram). Figure 2.2C shows the simplified notation.

Addressing the Network

Although Figure 2.2 shows names printed beside the nodes, this is not accurate. Nodes are abstract entities; they are where the set of relations that comprise a concept come together. The natural language name for a node is itself a form of information, and it too must be given some representation. This information is contained in a *vocabulary*. When the concept represented by a node has a name in natural language, then that fact is represented by a relation that points from the node to the location in the vocabulary that contains the appropriate words. The vocabulary contains the orthographic and pronunciation information for the name.

Figure 2.2C is incomplete. The notation should actually be represented as is shown in Figure 2.3. In general, we use the notation shown in Figure 2.2C in order to simplify the diagrams, but the reader should be aware that all natural language names are not a part of the node space; rather, they are a part of the vocabulary.

It is tempting at this point to describe the elements that comprise the vocabulary in terms of the same type of network structures that we use for the structural network. The vocabulary contains the information about the spelling patterns and sound patterns for the words contained within it, and these patterns must themselves be comprised of underlying elements that are related to one another, probably by

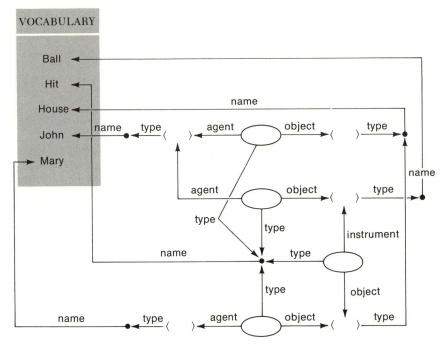

FIGURE 2.3
The structure shown in Figure 2.2C is incomplete. The complete structure includes
a *Vocabulary*, which specifies the names of all nodes and which provides
orthographic and pronunciation information.

some form of structural network. This representational issue, however, lies outside the domain of this book. Let it be noted that the
translation of visual images or acoustical sounds into appropriate
lexical entries (as well as the reverse transformation from the lexical
entries to sounds or written words) is accomplished by a complex
perceptual process: The simplification implied by Figure 2.3 does
not reflect the complexity of the actual representation.

PREDICATES, CONCEPTS, AND PROPOSITIONS

At this point we need to define some terms. Our goal in the next few
sections is to demonstrate just how we encode the meanings of words,
especially how we decompose a single word into a more primitive,
underlying structural representation. Before we do that, however,
we need to define the terms "predicate," "concept," and "proposition" in a formal manner.

Predicates

A predicate is a general function that specifies the relations that might exist among some set of concepts. The term *predicate* refers to the function itself. The term *argument* refers to the type of concept that can be used within the predicates.

The general representation for a predicate, P, is

(7) $P[\text{range}_1, \text{range}_2, \ldots, \text{range}_n]$.

P is the name of the predicate. The term *range$_i$* is a name that specifies the range or set of legal values for the ith argument of the predicate. As an example of this, let us consider the representation for one of the possible meaning senses of the verb "give." "Give" has a variety of meanings, so before we begin, it is important to understand in what sense we mean to represent this word. Most words can be used in a variety of contexts, often with quite different meanings. We allow a single vocabulary item to stand for any arbitrary number of type nodes in the structural network, each type node corresponding to a different sense of the word. In any given situation, of course, only one specific sense is relevant. It is the task of the processes of language comprehension to determine which of the possible senses is meant, being guided in the selection by syntactic, semantic, and pragmatic information. As we give examples of word definitions in this chapter, it is important to remember that we do not claim that any single definition can convey all the possible interpretations and uses of a word; rather, any single definition is intended to apply only to one single interpretive sense.

For the current example, we wish to demonstrate the general representation for one of the possible meaning senses of the verb "give": in particular, the sense that denotes one person placing an object in the possession of another person. The general predicate for this sense of "give" can be expressed formally like this:

(8)   give[agent, object, recipient, time]

In this definitional structure, all the arguments have names that denote their ranges, or, more specifically, that give the set of restrictions that apply to the concepts that can be used to fill those arguments. Thus, the first argument of the predicate "give" has the name "agent." This is a selectional restriction, for it means that the only concept that can be used to fulfill that part of the predicate is one that denotes an animate being capable of instigating the action. In general, whenever an argument position in a predicate is filled, the concept that is inserted at that position must satisfy the selectional restrictions imposed by the range specified by the name of the argument.

This notation for predicates has a direct relationship to the diagrammatic notation that we have been using for the structural network. Thus, consider a particular instantiation of the predicate "give" — say, the sentence

(9)   Mary gives John a dollar.

This sentence allows us to fill in most of the arguments of the predicate, with the exception of the argument for the **time** of the event (unless we wished to designate the event as being in the present). Each of the concepts used to satisfy the predicate is, of course, a *secondary* concept, which we illustrate by using angular brackets. Thus, sentence 9 is represented in equivalent fashion by the structural diagram shown in Figure 2.4 or by the predicate of the form

(10)   give[⟨Mary⟩, ⟨dollar⟩, ⟨John⟩, time].

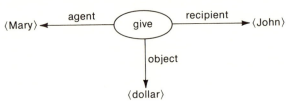

FIGURE 2.4
Mary gives John a dollar.

The concepts that satisfy the arguments of a predicate are always represented by nodes. Note that the ranges of the arguments are represented in the structural diagram by the names of the relations between the predicate node and the node that represents the concept that is filling the argument. Because **time** was not specified in sentence 9, it simply is omitted from the representation shown in Figure 2.4. In general, predicates have some obligatory arguments that must be fulfilled whenever they are used. (**Agent, object,** and **recipient** are all obligatory for the predicate in sentence 9 and are also optional arguments that need not be filled. **Time** is optional for the predicate in sentence 9.)

In the example illustrated by (9) and (10), the predicate is given a name. It is not necessarily true, however, that predicates need correspond to any particular English term, just as a node in the structural network need not have an exact correspondence to a word in a natural language.

Although we have illustrated the use of a predicate for a verb, predicates can also correspond closely to other grammatical classes of the language, including adjectives, adverbs, conjunctions, and nouns. These will be discussed later.

Concepts and Propositions

Predicates refer to relationships, concepts refer to the things related. Concepts act as the constants that replace the variables of predicates, thereby generating descriptions of particular events or states. We call a predicate with all of its obligatory variables filled a *proposition*. Example 10, therefore, is actually a proposition.

Although whenever an argument of a predicate is filled, it must be by a concept, a proposition can also serve as a concept. Thus, in

(11)   Mary told Helen that she gave John a dollar.

the predicate for "tell"

(12)   Tell[agent, recipient, time, object]

has its argument position for **object** satisfied by proposition 10. Thus:

(13)   Tell[⟨Mary⟩, ⟨Helen⟩, time, Give[⟨Mary⟩, ⟨dollar⟩, ⟨John⟩, time]].

The structural network diagram for proposition 13 is shown in Figure 2.5.

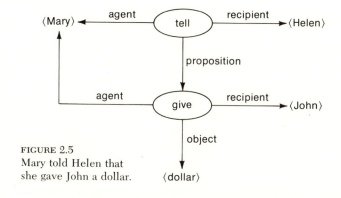

FIGURE 2.5
Mary told Helen that
she gave John a dollar.

Concepts sometimes refer to some idea that has a particular name in natural language. This is often true of concrete items that can be uniquely specified, such as Abraham Lincoln, or England. Most concepts do not have simple names, however. Consider the concept of the event that occurred the other day when a stray dog walked into class and licked the hand of the instructor. This event need not have any unique name by which it can be called, but it will have a unique node within the structural network that corresponds to it. That node can be referred to uniquely by means of a *description* (for example, the phrase used in the earlier sentence).

Propositions comprise an important class of concepts. All the concepts we have considered thus far are simple, in that they denote some particular object or class of objects. Propositions express facts about concepts, objects, activities, and the relationships of these three. Propositions differ from other concepts in that they can take on a truth value. Other concepts can only be said to correspond to existent or nonexistent objects. As we have illustrated, propositions can serve as arguments to higher predicates. The embedding of propositions within propositions provides one of the more important tools for our structural representations.

PRIMITIVE MEANING STRUCTURES

Representational Constraints

The simple propositional structures shown in the preceding section do not take us to our goal; we need to expand the representation. We do so by analyzing the predicates into a set of semantic primitives that seem to underlie the meanings of predicates. Consider these sentences:

(14A)   Mary gave a dollar to John.

(14B)   John took a dollar from Mary.

(14C)   John got a dollar from Mary.

All these sentences are related in meaning, but they differ enough that they have different implications and thus cannot be considered to be paraphrases of one another. Therefore, their underlying semantic structures differ, yet they must be related.

The meaning of sentence 14C seems to be shared by both (14A) and (14B). Sentence 14C tells us that Mary once had possession of a dollar, but that it is now in John's possession: The dollar was transferred from Mary to John. Sentence 14B implies that John instigated the transfer, and we do not know whether or not Mary approved. Sentence 14A implies that Mary instigated the transfer. From considerations like these, we see that many words must have some underlying primitive representations, and that, moreover, words like "give" and "take" are not primitive. A word like "get" is closer to a primitive structure, but examples are easily devised that show that "get" cannot qualify as a semantic primitive, either. Concepts like "transfer," "possess," and "instigate the transfer" seem to be much more likely candidates for the role of semantic primitive.

In attempting to arrive at a set of primitive structures, we start off with a list of different psychological criteria that guide the analysis and, thereby, the development of the underlying primitive structures. The psychological criteria that we find important are:

- completeness
- invariance under paraphrase
- the preservation of overlap in meaning
- continuity
- extendibility
- psychological validity

The Completeness Criterion. A minimal requirement for any semantic system is that it be *complete.* It must be capable of representing any information that we might want to store. In this chapter, we emphasize linguistic information, and so we interpret the statement primarily to mean that the representation be capable of representing any idea that can be expressed linguistically. Despite the emphasis on linguistics, we also keep in mind the need to account for nonlinguistic concepts as well. Basically, we believe the primitives that underlie language are general cognitive building blocks, not just linguistic ones (see, for example, how these structures are used to represent nonlinguistic concepts in Chapters 11 and 12).

Invariance under Paraphrase. The semantic representations should be invariant under paraphrases of the same information. No matter how information is received or expressed, expressions that have the same meaning should have the same semantic representation.[2]

---

[2]The mapping from the formal structure to the primitive structure is many-to-one. Many formal propositions may have a single common primitive structure. This means that the reverse process, that of generating sentences from the underlying primitive propositions, is not uniquely determined. Thus, different utterances can result from the same structures. In fact, this provides us with an experimental tool that can be used to study the underlying representations. (This is the technique used by Adele Abrahamson in Chapter 10.)

The Preservation of Overlap in Meaning.   Many lexical items have overlapping meanings. Sometimes the meaning of one item seems to be wholly contained within the meaning of another; sometimes the meanings seem only to share elements; at other times the meanings appear to be entirely unrelated. Our representation should reflect these situations.

If people judged that the meaning of sentence 15A

(15A)   Henry went to a store.

were wholly contained within that for (15B),

(15B)   Henry drove to a store.

then this judgment would constrain our representations for these senses of the words "go" and "drive": The representation for this sense of the word "drive" would have to contain the representation for this sense of the word "go" as one of its subparts.

In a similar fashion, if people judged that the meaning of sentences 16A and B

(16A)   Henry strolled to a store.

(16B)   Henry sauntered to a store.

were closely related, but that neither was wholly contained within the other, then the representation for these senses of the meanings of the words "stroll" and "saunter" should share elements in common, but neither should contain the other as a subpart.

The Continuity Criterion.   The semantic representations should exhibit certain continuity characteristics. Small changes in meaning should cause only small changes in representation. Sentences with similar (but different) meanings should have similar (but different) representations.

The Extendibility Criterion.   A semantic structure must never be closed. It should always be possible to link new information onto previously constructed semantic structures. We communicate by passing back and forth information about internal data structures, and these structures do not respect the bounds that grammar places on sentences. New information about a concept may arrive at any time. The representational system must be capable of expansion whenever information is received.

Psychological Validity.   The representations should be consistent with what is otherwise known about the human information-processing system. The strengths and weaknesses of human performance should be reflected by the strengths and weaknesses of the representational system. Ideally, the representation should be relevant to a number of different cognitive activities: It should tell something of how knowledge in general is represented, acquired, and used.

The various criteria that have just been discussed constrain the possible representational formats. Thus, the structures described in this book might at times appear to be arbitrary, but they are not. They have been derived from a lengthy evolutionary process of selective modification and elimination. Moreover, as we consider new experimental and logical issues, we will probably be forced to modify the structures further. The constraints that we have already attempted to satisfy have caused us to make many revisions of our conceptions. It is hoped that this will minimize the impact of future changes.

In the next sections we emphasize linguistic considerations, especially for the basic representational structures for verbs and nouns. The structures are generalizable to nonlinguistic contexts, as later chapters in this book will illustrate. The very nature of language — its capability of communicating the underlying structure of human experience — helps guarantee the generality. Thus, in the sections that follow, much of the analysis of verbs can be applied directly to the *structure of events*; much of the analysis of nouns can be applied directly to the *structure of concepts*.

Verbs

In our examination of the verbs of English we have identified at least four different classes of primitive predicates that underlie verb meanings: *stative, change, causative,* and *actional.* Each of these four kinds of predicates is associated with a different aspect of verb meaning. The *stative* component of a verb conveys the fixed relationship that holds among its arguments for a specified period. The *change* component tells simply that a change of state has occurred. The *causative* component communicates the source of, or reason for, the change. The *actional* component describes the behavior involved in the performance of the action specified by the verb. All verbs seem to contain at least one of these primitive components and a single verb may contain all of them.

This classification of verbs is intended as a possible framework for a complete analysis of all verbs in English. We do not claim that these

four categories are exhaustive, but we do believe that they are necessary. The classification is our own, although it is closely related to
ongoing work in other laboratories. The work of Roger Schank
(1972b, 1973b) is perhaps most similar to ours.

Considerable work has been described in the linguistic literature
that is related to these classifications. In Chapter 4 of this book, Allen
Munro provides a review of the linguistic work, including a comparison of those theories with the ideas introduced in this chapter. In
Chapter 10, Adele Abrahamson introduces a slightly different, although related, analysis for verbs of motion. Dedre Gentner tests
some of these concepts in her studies, which are reported in Chapter
9. In his article on psycholinguistics in the *Annual Review of Psychology*, Johnson-Laird (1974) suggests that yet another component
of verbs is *intention*, a concept that is related to our *cause* (see Johnson-Laird, 1974, pp. 143–144). Miller (1972) has performed a thorough
analysis of verbs of motion that differs from but is consistent with the
present analysis.

Statives. The simplest component of verbs communicates the
information that a particular state of the world holds for some specified
period. We call this the *stative* component. Two important statives
are those of *location* and of *possession*. We refer to these primitives
by the names **LOC** and **POSS**, respectively. (The stative primitive for
location is discussed later in this chapter and again in Chapters 8 and
10. The stative primitive for possession is discussed in Chapter 9.)

Consider the following sentence:

(17)   A stadium was located in the park from 1956 to 1963.

This sentence is a good example of the use of the stative for location:
It simply expresses the state of location of the stadium. To represent
sentence 17, we use the primitive predicate for stative location, the
predicate that we call **LOC**. **LOC** is a predicate that takes four arguments in this form:

(18)   **LOC** [object, at-loc, from-time, to-time].

Each of the four arguments in (18) specifies the range of the concepts
that may be used to fill them. Thus, for the predicate **LOC**, the first
argument must be filled by an **object**; the second must be filled by
any concept that can serve as a **location** at which the concept that
plays the role of the **object** can be located. The last two arguments
specify the initial time (**from-time**) and the final time (**to-time**) for

which the predicate is true. (The argument range specified by **at-loc** is one of a general class of location ranges, including the general case of simply **loc**, for any concept that can serve as a location, and such specialized aspects as **to-loc**, **on-loc**, **in-loc**, and so on.)

Sentence 17 is represented in terms of predicate 18 in the form illustrated by Figure 2.6.

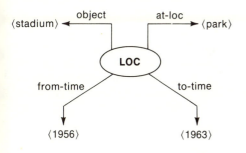

FIGURE 2.6
Statives. Here, the primitive stative of location, **LOC**, is used to convey that "A stadium was located in the park from 1956 to 1963."

Specific verbs are defined in terms of the underlying primitives. This will be explained and illustrated in detail in Chapter 8, but as a simple example, consider the rather basic stative verb of location, "locate." This verb can be used in several different ways; one of the possible meanings of the verb is that used in sentence 17. We represent the definition of the predicate "locate" in terms of the underlying **LOC** in the following manner. (The arrow in the definition may be read as "is defined to be" or, more simply, as "is when.")

(19)   locate [object, location, time$_i$, time$_f$] $\rightarrow$ **LOC**[object, at-loc, to-time, from-time].   .

In the structural network, the relation **iswhen** connects the predicate with its primitive structure, as shown in Figure 2.7. Figure 2.7 illustrates the first step of defining a procedure within the structural network. The letters **O**, **L**, **T**$_i$, and **T**$_f$ are free variables, constrained by the range specified by the relation names. When any particular sentence that uses the verb "locate" is analyzed, then we find the particular arguments used in the sentence and assign the variables to them. (In more technical language, we bind the arguments to the variables.) This example does not show much of the power of the representation, because the stative predicate **LOC** is very similar to the verb "locate." The power of this analysis will become more apparent in the succeeding sections and chapters.

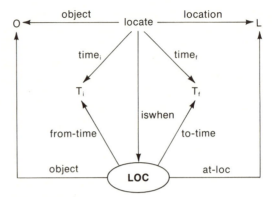

FIGURE 2.7
One sense of the verb "locate" is captured by the
stative **LOC**, with the formal definition as shown
in this figure.

Change of State. The next verb component denotes a change
from one state to another, but where the cause of the change remains
unspecified. Consider sentence 20:

(20)   The train moved out of the station at 3 o'clock.

This sentence represents a change between two statives of location.
Before 3 o'clock, the train was located at the station; after 3 o'clock,
the location is not specified, except that it is not that of the station. The
important new component that is added here is that of *change of
state*. We represent this change in the manner shown in Figure 2.8,
where the predicate primitive **CHANGE** describes the relationships
between the two stative location components that are involved in the
change.

The primitive predicate **CHANGE** is defined in such a way that the
language-understanding system can use it to construct the form of
structural network shown in Figure 2.8. (The system that creates
these structures is described in Chapter 8.) The structure that results
from a change of state component should:

- indicate that the former state (**from-state**) terminates at the time
  of the change;

- indicate that the final state (**to-state**) was initiated at the time of
  the change;

- construct a new token node for **CHANGE** with each of the
  arguments filled with appropriate concepts.

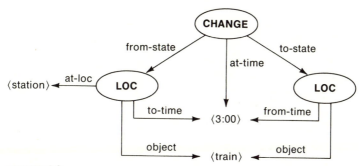

FIGURE 2.8

Change of state. The primitive **CHANGE** conveys a change of state between two statives. This figure shows a change in location: "The train moved out of the station at 3 o'clock."

The structure shown in Figure 2.8 illustrates that use of the verb "move" with the meaning sense shown in sentence 20 (in which there is a change in location of a physical object) requires the use of two instances of **LOC** that are related to each other through one instance of the predicate **CHANGE**.

Causatives.   When a change of state takes place in such a manner that the causal action can be identified, then we must include the causal component in the structural representation of the event. Consider these three sentences:

(21A)   Ambrose woke up.

(21B)   A cowboy woke up Ambrose.

(21C)   A cowboy woke up Ambrose by putting water on him.

Sentence 21A is a simple change of state, of the sort described in the previous section. Sentence 21B, however, adds to the statement of (21A) the causal agent for the change of state, namely, the cowboy. Finally, sentence 21C provides some more elaboration on the causal act of (21B).

Sentence 21A is represented by the structural network shown in Figure 2.9A. To represent the event described by sentence 21B, we must specify that some event took place to cause the change of state in Ambrose. That event is not specified by the sentence, however, except that we know that a cowboy was the agent. Such lack of specification is common in causal components of events, and so we represent such an action by means of the primitive activity **DO**. The action

A

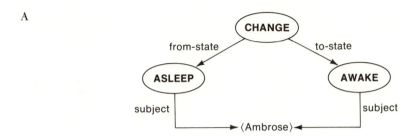

B

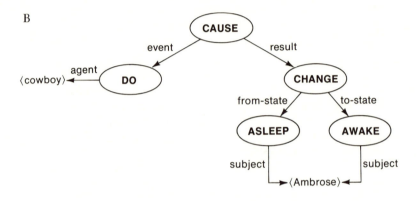

C

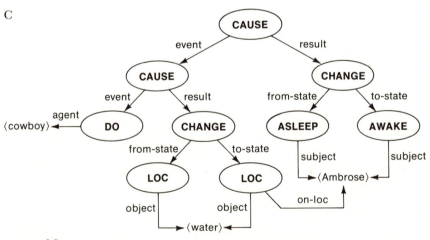

FIGURE 2.9
Causative. *A* shows a simple change of state: "Ambrose woke up." *B* shows that
a cowboy did something to cause Ambrose to awaken: "A cowboy woke up
Ambrose." *C* shows some elaboration on the event that **CAUSE**d Ambrose to awaken:
"A cowboy woke up Ambrose by putting water on him."

DO is simply an abstract activity, specified as much as possible by the sentence, but primarily serving as a marker that something has taken place. Figure 2.9B shows the representation within the structural network for sentence 21B.

In Figure 2.9B we see the basic components that we have used for all causal structures. The predicate **CAUSE** combines the causal event with the result of that event. In the structure shown in Figure 2.9B, the causal event is only minimally specified as some abstract event **DO**, for which a cowboy was the agent. Each component of the structure, however, may be further elaborated upon. Thus, sentence 21C further elaborates upon the nature of the causal event by specifying that the cowboy put water on Ambrose. This action of the cowboy is, in fact, a change of state, and it is illustrated in Figure 2.9C. Note that this figure shows how the elaboration of the causal event can contain within it even further causal events. Thus, examination of Figure 2.9C shows that:

- Ambrose changed from being asleep to being awake.

- Ambrose's awakening was caused by a change of state of some water from some unspecified location to a location on Ambrose.

- The cause of the change of location of the water was some unspecified action, of which a cowboy was the agent.

Such elaboration could continue indefinitely.

Actionals. Actional components are important aspects of verbs, but they are the least well-developed part of our verb representations.[3] For example, the verb "stroll" differs from the verb "saunter," and "talk" differs from "preach" only with respect to how the actions are actually performed. These differences are reflected in what we call the *actional* components of the verbs. (Actional components are closely related to the linguistic "manner.") It may well be that semantic primitives are associated with sensorimotor schemata for carrying out actional components, or perhaps with the perceptual procedures that recognize them. Actional components, which are discussed in Chapter 4, are important for verbs that describe actions performed in the world. Abrahamson's component of *implementation* in Chapter 10 is one aspect of *actionals*.

---

[3]"Actional": of or pertaining to action or actions (*Oxford English Dictionary*). We will occasionally use the word as a noun, despite its formal classification as an adjective.

Configurations of Semantic Primitives in Verb Definitions

The preceding sections illustrate how we construct the representational structures for predicates. These ideas are used throughout the book, and in particular, Chapter 8 presents a number of specific definitions of words, using the components defined in this chapter as the basic building blocks. Chapters 9 and 10 provide some experimental tests of the psychological reality of these semantic components.

In this section we summarize and formalize the concepts developed in the preceding sections and present formal definitions for the concepts of **STATE**, **EVENT**, and **ACTIONAL**. These definitions, presented in the form of a rewrite rule, can be considered a formal specification of the structural schemata for verb definitions that are used in this book. (In the specification of the rules, it is important not to confuse the words **STATE**, **EVENT**, and **ACTIONAL** with their English language equivalents. To aid in distinguishing these formal terms from the English words, they have been printed in **THIS TYPE FACE**.)

STATES. **STATES** are relatively enduring relationships among objects, and they are represented by *stative* components. There are probably a large number of semantic primitives for statives, but in this chapter we have mentioned only a few (**LOC**, **POSS**, **AWAKE**, and **ASLEEP**) and described only one in detail (**LOC**). Three rules summarize the characteristics of **STATES**.

> Rule 1:   A primitive stative, **STATE**, may apply on any arbitrary number of objects.

STATE $\rightarrow$ **STATE** [object$_1$, object$_2$, . . . , object$_n$, from-time, to-time]

> Rule 2:   Any repetitive or continuing action (for example, walking) is a state.

STATE $\rightarrow$ **ACTIVITY** [agent, from-time, to-time]

> Rule 3:   Any conjunction of **STATE**s is also a **STATE**.

STATE $\rightarrow$ **STATE**$_1$ and **STATE**$_2$ . . . and **STATE**$_n$

EVENTS.   An **EVENT** is a category that represents those things that can be caused or that can cause other **EVENT**s. Basically, **EVENT**s are processes that happen in time, where the internal structure of the process is considered important. This class consists of all *change-of-*

state, causative, and *actional* verbs. The definition for **EVENT** can be formalized by four rewrite rules.

Rule 4:   A change of state is an **EVENT**.

$$\text{EVENT} \rightarrow \text{CHANGE } [\text{STATE}_i, \text{STATE}_f]$$

Rule 5:   A causal relation between any two **EVENT**s is itself an **EVENT**.

$$\text{EVENT} \rightarrow \text{CAUSE } [\text{EVENT}_i, \text{EVENT}_f]$$

Rule 6:   Any **ACTIONAL** is an **EVENT**.

$$\text{EVENT} \rightarrow \text{ACTIONAL } [\text{actor, from-time, to-time}]$$

Rule 7:   Any conjunction of **EVENT**s is also an **EVENT**.

$$\text{EVENT} \rightarrow \text{EVENT}_1 \text{ and } \text{EVENT}_2 \ldots \text{ and } \text{EVENT}_n$$

ACTIONS. **ACTIONAL** components can be viewed as either **STATE**s or **EVENT**s, depending on the role they play in the verb. In many abstract verbs, the **ACTIONAL** components are only poorly indicated, or are not indicated at all. Then the dummy **ACTIONAL** component **DO** is substituted for the exact **ACTIONAL**. Rules 8, 9, and 10 summarize the roles that primitive **ACTIONAL**s can play.

Rule 8:   The dummy component **DO** can play the part of an **ACTIONAL** component.

$$\text{ACTIONAL} \rightarrow \text{DO } [\text{actor, from-time, to-time}]$$

Rule 9:   Any primitive **ACTIONAL** may operate on any arbitrary number of objects.

$$\text{ACTIONAL} \rightarrow \text{DO } [\text{actor, object}_1, \text{object}_2, \ldots, \text{object}_n, \\ \text{from-time, to-time}]$$

Rule 10:   Any conjunction of **ACTIONAL**s is also an **ACTIONAL**.

$$\text{ACTIONAL} \rightarrow \text{ACTIONAL}_1 \text{ and } \text{ACTIONAL}_2 \ldots \text{ and } \text{ACTIONAL}_n$$

Although these ten rewrite rules are most likely neither necessary nor sufficient to characterize the possible configurations of semantic primitives, they do seem to be appropriate for all of the verbs that we have analyzed thus far.

These ten rewrite rules provide some formalization of the descriptions of the verb components provided in the preceding sections.

They form the basis for the family of verb definitions that are presented in Chapter 8. These definitions, coupled with the active processes of language understanding, help provide the mechanisms for building the active structural representation for the information that is conveyed by a sentence. In a real sense, a sentence does not exist in memory after it has been interpreted; rather, the sentence is used to provide instructions as to how to modify the structures of memory to convey the deep, underlying components that comprise meaning.

Adjectives and Nouns as Predicates

Thus far, our discussion of predicates has mostly been concerned with verbs. It is our view, however, that nearly all substantive terms should be represented by a configuration of underlying predicates. This section illustrates how we represent nouns and adjectives as predicates. Consider these sentences:

(22A)   This is red.

(22B)   This is a ball.

In our analysis of these sentences, both "red" and "ball" are represented as predicates that take a concept as an argument. Thus, in the analysis of (22A) and (22B), the node that serves as the referent of "this" is found in memory. Then the predicate term (either "ball" or "red") is asserted about that node. The copula, "is," presumably serves to convey information about time and tense. (Neither adjectives nor nouns can do this in English.) The structural representation for these sentences is shown in Figures 2.10A and B. Adjectives and nouns can take more than one argument. In the sentence

(23)   This is the **father** of John.

FIGURE 2.10
Adjectives and nouns as predicates.
Node *500 represents a concept
that is red; node *501 represents a
concept that is a ball.

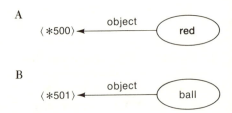

the referents for both "this" and "John" serve as arguments for the noun "father." In the sentence

(24)   John is **eager** to please his father.

the adjective "eager" has two arguments; one is the concept "John," the other is the entire proposition that John pleases his father.

Just as the semantic structure of verbs is expressed as a configuration of primitive predicates, so too, we believe, is the semantic structure of nouns and adjectives. Nouns and adjectives often seem to be kinds of stative predicates, so that the structures underlying nouns and adjectives frequently are those defined by rules 1–3 in the preceding section. We have not yet carried out as detailed an analysis of nouns and adjectives as we have of verbs, but since most nouns and adjectives are neither the names of primitive predicates nor the names of activities, they are properly represented as a structure of the type generated by rule 3: a conjunction of stative predications. Thus, for example, we might expect the noun "person" to look something like

(25)   person[X] $\rightarrow$ mortal[X] **AND** biped[X] **AND**
        [able[X, talk[X]], . . .

Definition 25 says that if an object "X" is a "person," then it is mortal, it is a biped, and it is able to talk (and has other properties not shown in sentence 25). In similar fashion, adjectives such as "mortal" can be defined:

(26)   mortal[X] $\rightarrow$ alive[X] **AND** future[die[X]].

This definition means that if an object "X" is said to be "mortal," then that object is "alive" until some time in the future, when it will die. (This definition, like all the others outlined here, is designed solely to illustrate our representation and should not be taken to be a complete definition of the word "mortal.") The network structures associated with these definitions are illustrated in Figure 2.11.

The role of time in noun and adjective representations is not as clear as it is with verbs. Still, with many nouns and adjectives the time relationships are important, for they specify the appropriate duration when the predication holds true. Nouns that signify roles, such as "student" or "teacher," clearly require some sort of temporal specification, for a person playing a particular role does not do so for all time.

A

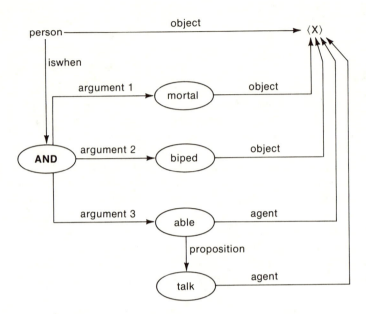

B

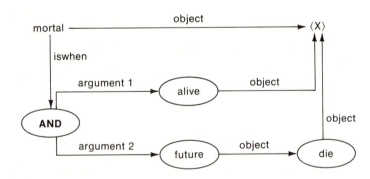

FIGURE 2.11
A person is an object that is mortal, biped, and able to talk (among other things). When an object X is mortal, it has the property of being alive, but also of dying at some time in the future.

Like verbs, both nouns and adjectives also can be expanded into primitive representation. The same criteria that were examined for the representational constraints of verbs apply. Just as the meanings of the verbs "give," "take," and "get" overlap, implying an underlying primitive structure, so too do the meanings of such nouns as "chair," "throne," "seat," and "support" overlap and again imply a shared underlying primitive structure.

It has typically been supposed that there are a number of distinctions between noun and verb definitions. For example, it might be supposed that a noun definition simply consists of the specification of the set of physical characteristics that are common to all objects named by that noun. However, it is clear that all nouns could not be specified by such a set. For example, abstract nouns name entities with no physical realization. Furthermore, even concrete nouns must be defined in terms of abstract relational characteristics.

Functional Definitions. What is a chair? According to the dictionary, it is a seat, usually movable, for one person. Often, we are told, it has four legs and a back, and it may have arms. A seat is defined as a surface on which another surface can rest. To determine whether a particular object is a chair, we need to determine whether it has a surface that can serve as an adequate support that is the appropriate size for holding a person. If the surface is too small, it is not a chair; if it is too large, it still might be a seat—perhaps it is a bench or a couch—but it is not a chair. Then again, it might not be a seat at all if it is, say, the flat roof of a ten-story building. But what is not a chair now might serve as one later. The definitions are relative; they depend upon the functional uses of the object. Although a flat-topped building is not usually a chair, it could serve as one if we were to postulate an appropriately sized giant (although it still would not be readily movable). The game we are describing here has overtones of Wittgenstein's problems with definitions: It is not possible to create a fixed set of defining characteristics that will not sometimes be violated.

Prototypes and the Representation of Noun Concepts. In the early days of research on semantic networks, it was felt that most concepts could be described by their place in the hierarchy of things, with descriptive and definitional features assigned either at the node representing the concept or at the higher-level nodes that represented superset, superpart, or other similar relationships. This is the way that we did it (Rumelhart, Lindsay, and Norman, 1972; Lindsay and Norman, 1972). This is how Collins and Quillian did it (Collins and Quillian, 1969; Quillian, 1968, 1969), and so, too, did Anderson and Bower (1973), Simmons (1973), and Kintsch (1972b). Even Schank (1972b), who strongly emphasized procedural definitions, does so only for verb structures, calling concepts PP's (for picture producers) and stating that they are usually thought of by themselves, and do not need to be related to other concepts. Only Winograd (1972, 1973) seemed to treat nouns as active procedures.

As psychological studies began to bear on these issues, it became clear that simple hierarchical structures could not describe a person's understanding of concepts. (Collins and Quillian, 1972, have discussed some of these issues.) Perhaps the most interesting studies, however, were those performed by Rosch (1973, 1974) and by Rips, Shoben, and Smith (1973). They showed that some items were better exemplars of semantic categories than others. Their results can be interpreted to mean that there is a psychological distance measure on the semantic space. Thus, a dog is a good exemplar of the category of animals, but a spider or a fish is not. Similarly, in the minds of most adult subjects, whales seem more similar to fish than to mammals.

These studies appear to show that simple set membership relations cannot suffice for the definitional properties of concepts. In the simple view of semantic network, if both a stork and a robin are classified as birds, there should be no difference in the amount of time it takes a subject to state the truth of either fact. Actually, subjects take longer to decide that an animal like a stork is a bird than to decide that an animal like a robin is a bird. Items that seem "close" to the most typical member or prototype of the category are quickly judged to be members. Items "further" from the prototype take longer to be classified. It would appear that the "appropriateness" of an object to a semantic category is considered in making semantic judgments (see Smith, Shoben, and Rips, 1974).

The notion of a prototype has a particularly simple representation within our view of nouns as predicates. Consider, for example, the following definition of "human":

(27)   human[X] $\rightarrow$ mortal[X] **AND** biped[X] **AND** exist[head[X]] **AND** mammal[X].

The structural representation of (27) is illustrated in Figure 2.12. Within the network there is a node for the variable, X. Notice in the figure that the variable X in this definition has exactly the properties of a *prototype* for that concept. Whenever a noun such as "human" is predicated of some node, all of the properties of the prototype X are thereby applied to it. In the literature on semantic networks, this property is usually called passing the properties of a node to its descendants.

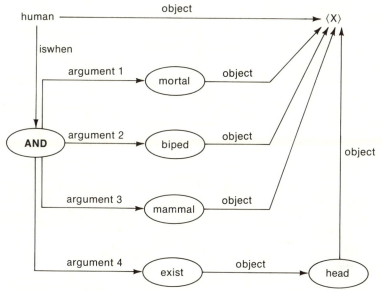

FIGURE 2.12
Node X is the protypical human: All instances of humans have all the
properties of node X applied to them.

REPRESENTATION OF QUANTIFIED STATEMENTS

Quantification has traditionally been a central issue in the development of semantic representations. Quantifiers have been especially
difficult to deal with within the domain of semantic networks. Rather
than developing a uniform way of dealing with all quantified statements, we have developed two different methods. The appropriate
method of representation depends on the nature of the quantified
statements and the nature of the set over which the quantification is
applied. These two methods are:

- *Individual quantification:* to represent the quantified
  statement as a sequence of individual propositions about each
  member of the set;

- *Generic quantification:* to modify the definition of the quantified
  term.

We now discuss the conditions under which each of these representations is used and the details of how they are employed.

Individual Quantification

The first case is the simpler. In the sentence

(28)   A dog barked.

the quantifier "a" specifies the creation of a new node for a particular dog to which the predicate "bark" is applied. Similarly, in

(29)   Every person in this room wears glasses.

we represent the sentence by adding the information "wears glasses" to each of the nodes that represents a person in the room. Obviously such a technique is viable only when the set over which the quantification applies has only a small number of members, all of whom can be exactly specified. This procedure works well for many cases of quantification, but, of course, it cannot be applied when the sets are either large or not well individuated.

Generic Quantification

The second method of representing quantified statements occurs in *generic quantification*. By generic quantification we mean any statement that applies in general over a large, open-ended class of elements in a set. For example, the following three propositions represent three different senses of generic quantification:

(30A)   All men are mortal.

(30B)   Most birds can fly.

(30C)   All animals have a head.

These statements all are intended to tell us something about the class of "men," "birds," and "animals."

Generic quantification is performed with the aid of active procedural representations. A procedure is constructed that performs the assertions stated by the quantifier, and that procedure is stored, unevaluated, as a part of the definition of the set. This means that the procedure is still represented with variables. Thus, example 30A would cause the definition for "men" to be augmented by the addition of the procedure that asserts mortal [X] as:

(31)   man[X] → [former definition of "man"] **AND** mortal[X].

Now, whenever definition 30A for "man" is asserted about a concept, the predicate "mortal" will also be asserted.

Example 30B poses a slightly different problem than did example 30A. In the latter example, the quantifier is not asserting a universal relation but only a probabilistic one. The definition of "bird" is augmented in the following way to represent this predication:

(32)   bird[X] $\rightarrow$ [former definition of "bird"]
         AND probable[able[X,fly[X]]].

The third example is certainly the most interesting and difficult of the three. On one reading, (30C) can be paraphrased in this way:

(33)   If something is an animal, then there is an object that is its head.

In general, there will be a different head for each animal. Thus, whenever we predicate "animal" of any concept, we must find the other concept that represents the head of the animal. We accomplish this by introducing a function called head that finds or creates the concept for the thing that is the "head" of its argument. The definition of "animal" is thus augmented in the following way:

(34)   animal[X] $\rightarrow$ [former definition of "animal"]
         AND exist[head[X]].

where "exist" is a predicate that asserts that its argument must be a concept in memory.

This section does not cover all the issues raised by quantification, but it does illustrate some of the more fundamental problems and some of the approaches that we have taken. Some further discussions of related issues occur in the next chapter when we consider problems of specific and intensional reference. Additional discussions of some of these issues can be found in the works of Anderson and Bower (1973, Chapter 13), Simmons and Bruce (1971), and Winograd (in press).

SUMMARY

We view our predicate terms as active procedures capable of carrying out a variety of tasks. This point should be remembered when our work is compared with other propositionally based representational systems in mathematical logic and generative semantics. Although logicians and generative semanticists have proposed semantic representations that bear a good deal of structural similarity to our own, we have an additional commitment to the view that predicates (especially semantically primitive predicates) should be treated as procedures as well as structural entities. Thus, rather than treat our predicates as static objects on which computations are done, we treat our predicates as names of procedures that contain the strategies relevant to computations of facts about those predicates. Our view of treating nouns (as well as verbs, adjectives, and quantifiers) as predicates implies that these terms should also correspond to the names of procedures that comprehend these concepts. Thus far, we have only alluded to three goals that the procedures associated with our predicate should accomplish:

- We have shown how definitions of terms can themselves be executable and that the decomposition of predicate terms can be naturally carried out by the processes that constitute the definitions of these predicates.

- We have indicated that the primitive semantic predicates are processes that can appropriately construct data structures in the network representing particular instantiations of the primitive predicates.

- We have suggested that predicates can be procedures that compute the goodness of fit of any given term for any given concept.

In Chapter 8 we describe in more detail the nature of the processes associated with semantically primitive predicates. Defining them to be procedures allows us to build simple retrieval and question-answering systems with the same definitions used for the normal evaluation of our predicate terms.

This chapter has covered the fundamental properties of the active structural network representation, including the basic framework for the representation of verbs. These aspects of the representation are only part of the story, however. In the next several chapters we fill in the picture. We start with a discussion of the problems of reference. Then we explore the processes by which sentences are interpreted into their structural representation. Finally, we consider the processes that operate within the network to construct and interpret the structures.

CHAPTER 3

Reference and Comprehension

DONALD A. NORMAN and DAVID E. RUMELHART

THE PROBLEM OF REFERENCE

A central issue in communication is ensuring that each participant is talking about the same concepts. In a conversation the speaker often wishes to communicate some structure within his memory to the listener. To do this, the speaker must specify those concepts, so that the listener can either discover them within his own memory structures or create them. How the speaker specifies those structures depends upon what he believes the listener to know. Language provides numerous conventions to specify the referent for conversation: sometimes by a unique name, sometimes by use of very explicit description, sometimes by inference, sometimes only in the most casual manner.

Consider the following task, reported by Olson (1970). A gold star was placed under a small wooden block on a table. A person who saw the act was asked to tell someone who did not see it just where the gold star was. The listener could see the table. The block was a white wooden cylinder, about one inch across. How the speaker described the block depended upon what else was present on the table. If a cylindrical black block (the same size as the white one) was also on the table, the location of the star was described as

(1)   It's under the white one.

If only the white cylindrical block and a square block were on the table, then the location was described as

(2)   It's under the round one.

If three blocks were on the table in addition to the one over the star (a cylindrical black one, a square black one, and a square white one), then the description of the star's location was:

(3)   It's under the round, white one.

The point is that the same object is being described in three different ways. These results should not be surprising, but they indicate something of the problem of reference. The task is to determine which concept is being talked about. Just how a concept or an object needs to be described depends upon the set of alternatives from which it must be distinguished. Normally, in language, only enough information is provided for the listener to determine for himself just which of the several possibilities is being referred to. Difficulty in communication arises when the speaker misperceives the state of the listener, so that a concept is either ambiguous to the listener or, worse, interpreted with a reference different from the one intended.[1]

Consider a sentence like

(4)   They are frightening monkeys.

Until we know the proper referent for the word "they," we cannot decipher the meaning of sentence 4 without ambiguity. If we know that the speaker is using the word "they" to refer to the monkeys themselves, then (4) can be interpreted as a statement of the apparent ferocity of the monkeys. If the word "they" refers to something that is known to be frightening the animals, then (4) has a different interpretation.

Usually, the topic of reference is not defined within the same sentence as the one that is being analyzed. In conversations, lectures, and written language, the referents are established either within the surrounding sentences, or within the context in which the entire communication is embedded, or even by a set of various socially accepted postulates. Full knowledge of the meaning of most real utterances usually requires full knowledge of the situation in which they were produced.

In our analysis of language, we assume that every noun phrase—in

[1]The reader should consult the paper by Olson (1970) or the related one by Osgood (1971) for further examples and discussion.

fact, every sentence—is an expression of reference. By using the term "reference," we do not restrict ourselves to physical objects in the world, but rather to concepts within a person's memory, whether actually existing at the time or of potential existence. Whenever we use this definition, we immediately discover one of the critical aspects of human communication: The concepts within one person's mind are almost certainly different from the concepts in everyone else's. The problem of reference, then, is the problem of specifying for the other person just which concept is meant, either with sufficient precision that the concept can be found, or with sufficient specification that it can be created. Indeed, a major difference between a sentence that a listener finds intelligible and one that is not, is often the degree to which the roles of the various concepts of the sentence have been made explicit. In grammatical sentences, syntax helps to define the appropriate role for each part of the sentence. In ungrammatical sentences, substantial context, supplied either by the situation or by other sentences, is required to determine the appropriate mapping of the concepts of the utterance onto the appropriate memory structures. Spoken language is often much less grammatical than written language, probably because within the normal context of spoken language there is a rich ensemble of contextual information from which to draw in assigning appropriate interpretations.

The approach that we take in this chapter differs from that normally found in the literature created by linguists, philosophers, and workers in the field of artificial intelligence. The concerns of these workers differ from those of the psychologist. As psychologists, we study the mechanisms and the processing involved in the identification of concepts. We are concerned with the problem of reference as a problem of communication. We want to know how information is transferred from the speaker to the listener, and our emphasis is on the psychological representation of the information and on the cognitive processes that are involved.

The philosopher and the linguist are interested in different aspects of language and communication. A person in the field of computer science or artificial intelligence often seems to be interested in the same problems as the psychologist, but does not share the desire to be restricted to those mechanisms that satisfy the known facts about human memory and human decision making. For the reader who wishes to examine the problems of reference from the linguistic and philosophical points of view, the collections of papers in the book *Semantics*, edited by Steinberg and Jakobovits (1971), and in the book *Semantics and Natural Languages*, edited by Davidson and Harman (1972), provide excellent (albeit advanced) dissertations on numerous aspects of the problem.

In this chapter we first examine some of the more formal aspects of reference. Then we treat socially determined properties of reference, most especially those properties that have been labeled *conversational postulates*. Finally, we examine some of the discussions of reference that appeared in the earlier sections of this chapter, using some of the tools developed in the treatment of conversational postulates.

The Speaker's Point of View

We begin the study of reference from the point of view of the speaker. First, the speaker must decide whether the listener has knowledge somewhere within his memory structures of the concept under discussion. If so, the speaker must find an effective way of indicating which of the many possible memory structures represents the one relevant concept. If not, the speaker must define the concept sufficiently that the listener can create a new memory structure that will serve as a satisfactory reference for the ensuing discussion. Second, social and pragmatic constraints affect the manner of communication. The specification of the definition of the concept must be as efficient as possible. Social conventions must be followed, taboos must be avoided.

Specific Reference. When the speaker has a particular concept in mind, we call this situation one of *specific reference*. First, consider the situation where the speaker knows that the listener has no advance knowledge of the concept. This is the simplest case for the speaker, for then he has control over the amount of information that is introduced. He only needs to describe the concept with the degree of specificity required by the conversation. For example, to introduce the new concepts of a specific picture, book, and man to a listener, sentences of this form may be used:

(5A)   John bought a **book** and a **picture** yesterday.

(5B)   John saw **an old man** with a **long beard** carrying a scythe.

In these sentences, the determiner "a" or "an" suffices to introduce the fact that a new concept is being defined.

Now consider the situation where the speaker assumes that the listener does know about the concepts that he wishes to discuss. Here, the speaker has a more difficult problem than before: He cannot be sure exactly how much the listener knows about the topic, nor can he know exactly how many other concepts exist within the memory of the listener that are potentially confusable with the desired one. The tools of language that the speaker may use in this situation are powerful, and they mostly allow abbreviated reference to the desired concepts. This power can often lead to problems.

Two of the most common methods of reference used when the speaker believes the listener to know of the relevant concepts are *pronominalization* and *definite description*.

(6)   He gave her the book.

In sentence 6, the definite determiner "the" signals the listener that a definite, particular book is meant. The pronouns "he" and "her" are similar signs. Definite descriptions can be expanded as much as is necessary to eliminate ambiguity, as the experiment by Olson reported in the opening pages of this chapter showed. Thus, in sentence 6, the phrase "the book" is a possible means to distinguish the book from, say, a painting. Similarly, all of the following definite descriptions can be used to refer to the old man of sentence 5B:

(7A)   he

(7B)   the man

(7C)   the old man

(7D)   the old man with a beard and a scythe

(7E)   the old bearded man with a scythe whom John saw

Whether the speaker should use a phrase as simple as (7A) or as complex as (7E) depends upon his judgment of the listener. This, in turn, depends upon how long it has been since the topic was last introduced and the number and type of alternative concepts from which it must be discriminated.

This problem of specification is not restricted to language, but arises any time that one wishes to refer to a concept stored within the structural network of memory. Exactly this problem of specification of a concept (or of an event) within memory is the central issue in the study of memory for real events by Linton, Chapter 14 of this book.

Often, a concept is specified by means of nonlinguistic information. In normal conversations, context is usually established by the physical surroundings or by other nonlinguistic considerations. When a person leaves your home, it is meaningful to ask,

(8)   Would you please close **the door** as you leave?

and, moreover, have full confidence that the listener will know which door is intended. Similarly, it is entirely appropriate to ask,

(9)   How's Mary?

of someone whose wife is named Mary, no matter how many other persons named Mary either the speaker or the listener might know. Similarly, once a speaker has uttered sentence 10A,

(10A)   John moved into a new house last year.

he can then use definite reference for all parts of that house:

(10B)   **The kitchen** is beautiful.

Once a concept is introduced into a conversation, further reference can be made to its parts under the assumption that the listener now knows of them.

Intensional Reference.   Up to this point we have discussed the case in which the speaker has a particular concept in mind. A philosophically and psychologically more troublesome case arises when the speaker has in mind only a definition of a class of concepts—not simply a particular instance. In the least troublesome of these cases, the speaker is deliberately vague, but he does not expect any lack of precision in his listener. The simplest examples of this case occur in questions and commands. Consider, for example,

(11A)   Think of a **number from 1 to 10.**

and

(11B)   Give me a **sheet of paper.**

In each of these examples, the speaker had no particular instance in mind, only the general concept. The listener, however, was asked to find a particular instance of that concept.

The major difference between *specific* and *intensional* reference has to do with the specificity of the referent. Specific reference always conveys existential import: A specific item is being referred to, for which a unique concept exists in the mind of the speaker. Intensional reference need not refer to any particular concept or item. For example, in negative statements and in conditionals one often refers to concepts for which there cannot be any particular instance, as in the "car" and "whale" of these examples:

(12A)   Susan doesn't own a car.

(12B)   If you see a whale, tell me where to look.

The most difficult case of *intensional reference* occurs when the speaker is not attempting to refer to any particular concept in the mind of the listener, but is making a *generic statement* about the class itself. This case is troublesome because it allows for many ambiguities. Consider these examples:

(13A)   John wants to buy **a car that will get 30 miles to the gallon.**

(13B)   John wants to buy a car that will get 30 miles to the gallon, but he can't find one.

(13C)   John wants to buy a car that will get 30 miles to the gallon, but the owners won't sell it.

Sentence 13A is ambiguous. The phrase in **bold-faced type** can either refer to a particular car, one that is known to the speaker, or define a (possibly empty) class of cars. Sentences 13B and 13C provide sufficient extra information to determine the specific meaning that is intended.

The following examples are somewhat different:

(14A)   **The first man on the moon** could easily have been Russian.

(14B)   The first man on the moon could easily have been Russian, but an American got there first.

(14C)   The first man on the moon could easily have been Russian, but his parents moved to the United States before he was born.

This situation differs from that illustrated by the sentences in (13). The critical phrase in (13) (a car that . . .) is introduced by the indefinite determiner "a," whereas the critical phrase in (14) (the first man on the moon . . .) is introduced by the definite determiner "the." The difference results from the fact that the phrase of (13) could refer either to a single unique car (as in 13C) or to a class of cars in which all share the characteristic of good gas mileage (example 13B). The phrase of (14), however, must refer to a unique person.

Definite and indefinite articles can be used in intensional reference as true generic statements. Such statements apply to classes of individuals:

(15A)   **A snake** can be dangerous.

(15B)   **The collie** is a good dog with children.

These sentences differ from other intensional uses of referring expressions, but generics seem to allow quantifiers; "any," "all," "some," or "each" can usually be substituted for the determiner (any snake . . . , any collie . . .).

The Listener's Point of View

From the listener's point of view, there are two kinds of referring expressions: *definite* and *indefinite*. A definite referring expression uses either a definite article, a proper name, or a pronoun. An indefinite referring expression uses an indefinite article (such as "a" or "some"). The strategies employed by the listener differ in the two cases.

Indefinite Referring Expression. There are three basic cases to consider. In the first, the indefinite expression is simply interpreted as an instruction to the listener to create a new instance of the concept within his memory structures. In the second case, the speaker is either unsure about the knowledge of the listener, or he is, in essence, demonstrating his own lack of knowledge, even though the listener may be able to supply a specific reference. Finally, the speaker may be wishing to communicate an intensional reference.

The first case is illustrated by the first phrase in (16):

(16)   an old man with a beard, carrying a scythe

The use of the indefinite article "an" signals the fact that the listener is not expected to know of the man being mentioned (or of the scythe, either). The listener is expected to create a new node within his memory structures that corresponds to an old man, with a beard, who is carrying a scythe.

The second case is one in which the speaker is being vague about the referent, but the listener in fact knows the specific concept that is being referred to and tells the speaker so.

(17A)   Speaker: John wants to buy a car that gets 30 miles to the gallon.

(17B)   Listener: I know. He showed it to me.

Similarly, when the speaker uses an intensional reference to ask the listener something, the listener is being specifically requested to supply the particular instance.

(18A)   Speaker: Who was that bald man with a long beard?

(18B)   Listener: Peter Lindsay.

It appears that in the case of indefinite referring expressions, the listener first looks for the specific referent in memory. If he finds it, he may tell the speaker, as illustrated in (17B) and (18B). If the listener fails to find a referent in his memory, he must determine whether the speaker was using specific or intensional reference. If specific reference was intended, the listener should create a new concept as in (16). If intensional reference is intended, the listener must store the information in an appropriate generic form.

Now consider the last case: The speaker wishes to communicate an intensional concept.

(19A)   John wants to buy a car.

(19B)   John wants to buy a car, and he is test driving it right now.

(19C)   John wants to buy a car, but he can't find one he likes.

Sentences 19B and 19C represent the specific and intensional interpretations of (19A), respectively. Figure 3.1A illustrates the structural network representation of the specific interpretation of (19A). Figure 3.1B illustrates the representation for the intensional interpretation. Note that our representation of the intension is accomplished by the introduction of an unbounded variable (X) and by putting the intensional phrase directly under the *want* predicate. Thus, the network representations for the intensional form of (19A) would read something like:

(20)   John wants to buy some object X, and he wants X to be a car.

A

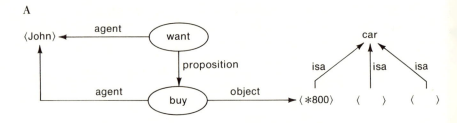

B

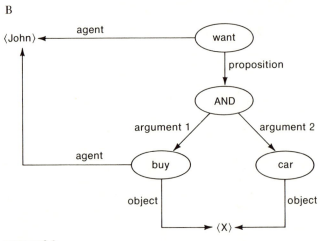

FIGURE 3.1
Two interpretations of "John wants to buy a car." In *A*, we assume that John has a specific car in mind, the one represented by node *800. In *B*, we assume intensional reference: John wants to buy some object X, and he wants X to be a car.

Definite Referring Expressions.   When the listener hears a definite referring expression, the usual problem arises of determining whether it is meant in an intensional manner or whether it is an actual, explicit reference to a concept. When the listener decides that he is expected to be able to identify the concept within his own knowledge structures, he must use whatever information is available to him to make the search through memory for the appropriate node structure. If no unique structure can be found, either because none exists or because there are several, the listener then has a choice of options: He could exert more effort, hoping thereby to find the appropriate referent; he could interrupt the speaker and ask for clarification; or he could ignore the difficulty and treat the reference as if it were an indefinite one. Often, the strategy that is followed is determined by the various social conventions governing the conversation: Does the listener wish to display his ignorance to the speaker? Is there any convenient way to ask for clarification without disrupting the conversation? Does the point seem important enough at this point to justify the effort that would be required to clarify it? The search process itself is guided by a number of different cues that are available to the listener, perhaps the most important of which is the underlying assumption that the speaker would not have used that particular expression had he not thought the listener capable of disambiguating it.

In choosing a strategy, the listener must take into account the knowledge structures of both parties in the conversation. This has three aspects:

- The knowledge structure of the listener.

- The listener's understanding of the knowledge structure of the speaker.

- What the listener believes the speaker believes to be true about the knowledge structure of the listener.

Actually, the listener's use of information about what he believes the speaker to believe about the listener's own belief can be expanded to a ludicrous extent. For example, the listener might decide that the speaker has deliberately referred to a definite concept to discover whether the listener will accept it without question, thereby acknowledging that he does know about it, despite the fact that the listener professes ignorance. Such convoluted reasoning chains arise continually with the invocation of conversational postulates.

A common occurrence of this form of reasoning is easy to illustrate. Consider the situation where the speaker (Hubert) is an old friend of the listener (Mary), but they have not seen each other for five years. Hubert knew both Mary and her husband (Peter) at the time of their marriage, ten years ago. Mary now has a two-year-old son, Peter, who is named after his father. Hubert asks:

(21)   How's Peter?

If this question were asked by Mary's mother, it would be ambiguous. When asked by Hubert, however, Mary reasons that he must mean her husband, for Hubert is not likely to know about the son. This type of reasoning occurs frequently in conversations.

More typically, however, definite expressions are handled by a standard set of heuristics, of which three[2] are useful to mention at this point: the determination of definite reference by

- unique instance;
- recency;
- foregrounding.

The strategy of unique instances can be applied whenever the concept being referred to is unique in the mind of the listener. Thus, if a child knows of only one ocean and one sun, to tell the child that "the sun sets over the ocean" is completely unambiguous and the appropriate concepts are readily found.

The next two strategies are related. If the concept has been mentioned recently (so that the referent is still active within short-term memory), then it is a good heuristic that the instance that is still active is the appropriate one. In a pair of sentences such as

(22A)   I saw John driving a cute little car yesterday.

and

(22B)   The car was about the same size as my bicycle.

the referent for the phrase "the car" in (22B) is clearly established by the phrase "a cute little car" in (22A).

Even if the actual concept itself was not recently mentioned, the disambiguation might be handled by what Chafe (1972) has described as "foregrounding." Chafe has argued that whenever a new concept is introduced into a conversation, that concept introduces a number of auxiliary aspects into the local context or foreground. The task of the listener is to keep track of this foregrounded material, and when pronouns or other definite referring expressions occur, to use it to help determine which referent is intended. A simple example of the use of a foregrounded concept can be constructed by modifying the story of (22) slightly:

(23A)   I saw John driving a cute little car yesterday.

(23B)   The wheels were about the size of dinner plates.

---

[2]Our computer model of language understanding uses these heuristics (plus a few others) in its computation of definite reference, and the actual operation of the program is discussed in Chapter 8. At this point, we discuss only the general philosophy of the procedures. Interesting discussions of some of the problems can be found in the Ph.D. theses by Charniak (1972) and by Winograd (1972) of the MIT Artificial Intelligence Laboratory.

The phrase "the wheels" is unambiguous because mention of "a car" in the preceding sentence has brought to the foreground all attributes of that car, even though they were not mentioned specifically.

These strategies require that the concepts be mentioned within the recent past. Had five or six other sentences been inserted between the two sentences of (22) or (23), none of which referred to the car or anything dealing with it, then the search through recent short-term memory would not have worked so well. To see this, consider this version of the story:

(24)   I saw John driving a cute little car yesterday. He was going south while I was going home after diving. The visibility wasn't good, but I did manage to get some abalone. I even saw a huge sea bass hiding in the kelp. Anyway, as I was saying, the wheels of John's car were about the size of dinner plates.

With example 24 there is probably difficulty in recovering the reference for "the wheels." In fact, most speakers would realize the difficulty faced by the listener and would insert cues to help, as we have illustrated in the example: The return to the topic matter is signaled by the phrase "as I was saying"; the search for disambiguation of the wheels is helped by inclusion of the modifier "of John's car."

CONVERSATIONAL POSTULATES[3]

As we have seen, both speaker and listener must make a number of common assumptions in order to use language effectively. The communication process requires that they take each other's knowledge into account as they converse. Little would be accomplished were the speaker to speak of concepts and things of which the listener had no knowledge whatsoever, for to do so would be to speak unintelligibly. Similarly, were the speaker to say only that which was already known by the listener, the result would be boredom.

Both participants in a conversation (and, equally, the writer and his expected set of readers) must follow the same set of rules if the communication between them is to be effective. These rules are numerous and not well known at the present time. The study of them has just

---

[3]The ideas in this section have come from numerous sources. We have been aided considerably by conversations with Ken Jennings and Aaron Cicourel of the Department of Sociology at the University of California, San Diego. Allen Munro has helped create some of the analytical techniques and examples used in this section. The major papers that we have used are those by Gordon and Lakoff (1971) and Grice (1967), the book by Searle (1969), and the collection edited by Sudnow (1972).

begun, but some linguists, philosophers, sociologists, and even a few psychologists have started to examine exactly which nonlinguistic rules help govern the linguistic utterances that take place within a conversation. The set of rules is called *conversational postulates* (often abbreviated CP). The principal philosophy that underlies the postulates and, therefore, that governs the interaction between individuals, seems to be summarized by the two statements:

(25)   Be sincere.

(26)   Be relevant.

Rule 25 simply says that both participants play fairly: One is not trying to con the other (although these postulates also work well in describing how and what one person does when he is trying unduly to influence or confuse the other).

Rule 26 is the critical one. From a liberal interpretation of its use of "relevant," we derive several critical principles:

(27A)   Do not say to others that which they already know.

(27B)   Do not be superfluous.

Combining the rule of sincerity, we get:

(27C)   Do not mislead.
         Do not tell more than you know.
         Do not tell less than you know.

These rules turn out to be useful in examining the flow of information within conversations. Let us examine some possibilities that illustrate the principles.

(28)   Some of Dave's children are boys.

When a listener hears this sentence, he assumes one of the principles of (27C): "Do not tell less than you know." The speaker in (28) has used the word "some," which implies either that some of the children are girls or that the speaker himself does not know about the rest. If the listener believes that the speaker knows Dave's children, then he infers that some of the children are girls. He will be upset later on to learn that all are boys. Notice that statement 28 is technically true; if *all* of the children are boys, then clearly *some* of them are also. A skilled lawyer or debater might cleverly make use of conversational postulates and statements like (28) to mislead deliberately, but, technically, without stating a falsehood.

An interesting demonstration of the power of subtle cues within a referential statement to bias a witness's response to a question has been given by Loftus and Zanni (1973). The subjects in the experiment saw a short movie of an automobile accident. Afterward they were asked to answer questions about the accident, both about possible causes and about the outcomes. Imbedded in the series of questions was one of the form of either (29A) or (29B) (half of the subjects saw form A, the other half saw B):

(29A)   Did you see a broken headlight?

(29B)   Did you see the broken headlight?

As Loftus and Zanni pointed out, a skillful lawyer would be sure to use question 29B. By conversational postulates, a statement like (29B) implies that there really was a broken headlight, and the only issue is whether or not the observer saw it. Question 29A makes no implication about its existence. As might be expected, a different pattern of responses was received for each of the two questions. (In fact, in the film, there was no broken headlight.)

If someone makes a statement that is believed to be self-evident, the polite listener who wishes to tell the speaker that he is stating the obvious has a choice of several ways of responding. One is to respond with another statement that is even more obviously true. If someone says,

(30)   I am beginning to suspect that I misbehaved last night.

one possible response is

(31)   I am beginning to suspect that the sky is blue.

The speaker of (31) obviously knows that his listener knows that he knows the sky is blue, so if that sentence is really designed to be relevant to the conversation, then the apparent violation of the conversational principle is the clue that (31) was spoken in sarcasm. Considerations of consistency and relevance help guide the interpretation of sarcastic remarks, such as

(32A)   The sky is blue. (*The preceding statement was rather obvious.*)

(32B)   The earth is flat. (*The preceding statement was rather wrong.*)

(32C)   Pigs may fly. (*The preceding statement was not really wrong, but it was highly unlikely.*)

In related ways, it is possible to analyze how polite requests or commands often are made through use of these conversational postulates, rather than by direct statement of the request. (The direct request would often be considered to be impolite.) Thus, the questions

(33A)   Can you take out the garbage?

or

(33B)   Could you tell me the time?

asked of someone who obviously can do these things are actually requests. (For a fuller discussion of the use of statements like these to convey requests, see Gordon and Lakoff, 1971.)

Violations of CP's: Grice's Analysis

Deliberate violations of the conversational rules are often useful ways to signal the actually desired meaning of a statement. A good treatment of the rule of violations is provided by Grice in his paper on logic and conversation (Grice, 1967). It is useful to examine briefly his ideas, as the unpublished manuscript is not readily available to everyone. To do so, however, it is first necessary to go over Grice's versions of the basic conversational postulates. As you will see, these are very closely related to the ones already discussed.

Rules for the Speaker. Grice is concerned with implicatures, which he defines as the things implied by a statement. Conversational implicatures often derive as much from the conversational postulates as from the formal content of the utterance. Grice says there are four main headings for the conversational postulates: *quantity*, *quality*, *relation*, and *manner*. There are rules for each.

Quantity:

- Make your contribution as informative as possible.
- Do not be more informative than required.

Quality:

- Do not say what you believe to be false.
- Do not say that for which you lack adequate evidence.

Relation:

- Be relevant.

Manner:

- Be perspicuous.
- Avoid obscurity (prolixness is not virtuousness).
- Avoid ambiguity.
- Be brief.
- Be orderly.
- Be polite.

All these rules do not carry equal weight. Thus, someone who rambles, taking minutes to say what could be said in seconds, perhaps wandering unnecessarily from the topic, is not considered as serious a violator of these rules as someone who utters falsehoods.

Rules for the Listener.   The listener (or reader) must make use of the conversational postulates in reverse, seeking to interpret just what hidden meaning might be contained within the communication that has been received. Thus, the recipient assumes that language flows smoothly back and forth among the participants, with each statement relevant to the topic, and neither saying too much nor too little. Anytime that a violation of the conversational postulates is perceived by the listener or reader, it is taken to be a signal that some nonobvious meaning is intended. Consider these examples:

If something is overspecified, then the overspecification is assumed to be an important signal about the content of the communication. Thus,

(34)   I went to work yesterday.

demands no particular response (unless it is known that yesterday was a holiday, and then specification of the day becomes meaningful). The statement

(35)   I ran to work yesterday.

draws attention to the mode of going.

The following discussion and examples are from Grice. Consider the following letter of recommendation from a professor about his student:

(36)   Gentlemen:

> I am very pleased to be able to recommend Henry Jones to you. Mr. Jones is a model student. He dresses well and is extremely reliable. I have known Mr. Jones for three years now, and in every way I have found him to be most cooperative. His wife is charming.

> Sincerely,

The letter contains nothing but positive, factual statements, yet it guarantees that Jones will not get whatever he was seeking. The letter violates the maxim of informativeness: It says nothing relevant to the person who is trying to evaluate Henry Jones, and that, of course, is the message. The true meaning cannot be evaluated properly, however, unless the recipient also understands the social conventions.

Volunteering too much information in response to a question can also be subject to interpretation. Perhaps it is best summed up by the remark of Gertrude in the play scene of *Hamlet*, "The lady doth protest too much."[4]

Violations of relevance are sometimes used as signals to drop the subject.

(37)   At a genteel tea party A says, "Mrs. X is an old bag." There is a moment of appalled silence, then B says, "The weather has been quite delightful this summer hasn't it?" B has blatantly refused to make what *he* says relevant to A's preceding remark (from Grice).

A failure to be brief, a failure to use one word instead of many, is also a signal. Thus, to say, "Ms. X sang 'Home Sweet Home,'" means something quite different than to say, "Ms. X produced a series of sounds which correspond closely with the score for 'Home Sweet Home'" (from Grice).

---

[4]For us to specify the quotation in this way is a violation of the rule, "Do not say more than you know." By our violation of the rule, you, the reader, are supposed to be impressed by the quality of our literary knowledge. In fact, we got the quote wrong the first time, and the exact quotation and the context in the play that led to the statement had to be provided for us by Norman Anderson, who is indeed a Shakespearean scholar.

CONVERSATIONAL POSTULATES AND THE PROBLEM OF REFERENCE

Reference by Definite Description and Conversational Postulates[5]

Consider the problem of reference by definite description. In one sense, a description such as "the sum of 4 and 3" can be replaced by the number "7." But as we have already indicated, this is not always desirable. If we really meant the number "7," why was it not used directly? We normally follow the conversational postulates that prohibit us from saying something without a purpose. Thus, suppose someone says,

(38)   The Mayor of La Jolla took my children camping.

Let the name of the Mayor be Alison Thompson. Then, in some sense, 38 is equivalent to

(39)   Alison Thompson took my children camping.

To interpret (38) as (39) is to miss the point of using sentence (38) in the first place. When a person says that the Mayor has done something (as in sentence 38), there is a strong implication that the fact that she is Mayor is relevant. This follows directly from the conversational postulates.

In sentence 38, by specifying the "Mayor," the speaker has automatically foregrounded all the properties of mayorhood: city hall, politics, prestige, importance, and so on. Now that foregrounded information can be used in a further sentence. It is to be hoped that the listener will have recognized the relevance of these topics to his judgment about the pretentiousness of the speaker, or perhaps the friendliness of the Mayor, and so on.

When a particular phrase is used, it is often the side effects of the phrase that are useful. These side effects introduce seemingly irrelevant concepts that then become foregrounded and that then have implications for the listener. It would be wrong, therefore, for our analyses to bypass the implications of the method of reference and instead simply to substitute the referent for the reference term. This is true even when the specific concept is being referred to.

---

[5]The basic idea for this section, and in particular, the problems that we brought about by substituting the computed value of an operator for the operator itself during the analysis of a sentence, were pointed out to us by Andrew Ortony, first in conversation at the Psychonomic Society meeting in 1973 and then in correspondence. (Some of these points are raised in Ortony, 1974, and Anderson and Ortony, in press.)

The Given-New Distinction

Haviland and H. Clark have proposed an interpretation of the process of sentence comprehension that combines a number of the features of reference, conversational postulates, and the search for an appropriate memory representation that have been discussed in this chapter (Haviland and H. Clark, 1974; H. Clark and Haviland, 1974; H. Clark, 1973a). The given-new distinction is described in this way:

> The Given-new Strategy is based on the premise that the listener typically knows a good deal about the topic of conversation, the physical setting of the speech act, the beliefs of the speaker, etc., even before he attempts to understand a particular sentence. For lack of a more precise representation at this time, we presume that this previous knowledge is coded in memory in the form of a complex interrelated set of primitive propositions of the type typically used by linguists in semantic representations. Thus, what the listener sees, what he thinks the speaker's beliefs are, what he has learned in the past, and what he knows from the immediately preceding sentences are all coded in such an interrelated form. Each sentence the listener then encounters contains some given information and some new. He must treat the given information as if it were an address, a pointer, or an instruction specifying where the new information is to be integrated into the previous knowledge. In brief, the Given-new Strategy is to treat the sentence as a two-part message: the given information is an address in memory, and the new information is content to be placed in the address. The strategy, therefore, consists of at least three conceptually separate stages: (1) discovering the structure of the sentence, determining what is given information and what is new; (2) finding the address in memory as determined by the given information; and (3) placing the new information at that address.
>
> Imprecise as the Given-new Strategy is at the present time, it has several rather interesting consequences. First, it claims that the listener must attempt to match the information found in the presuppositions of a sentence with some aspect of his previous knowledge. If the presuppositions of the sentence do not match something the listener already knows, the Given-new Strategy will fail and he will have to try an alternative procedure. One alternative is to treat the presuppositions as new information as well as set up a new structure in memory essentially unrelated to facts he already knows. Thus, if the presuppositions match previous knowledge, the sentence should be easy to comprehend; if the presuppositions do not match, or match only in some rather oblique way, the sentence should take longer to comprehend.

Second, the Given-new Strategy leads the listener to believe that the presuppositions of a sentence contain given information and the assertion new information. If, in fact, the assertion contains given information, this strategy should fail badly. The listener will be forced to alter his strategy and take more time in comprehending the sentence. In addition, he will find sentences with such inversions relatively unacceptable.[6]

Here, then, is an explicit statement of a strategy that combines our conceptions of reference with a statement about the relative processing difficulty that a listener will face in interpreting sentences. Moreover, by making the relatively straightforward assumption that both listener and speaker understand the principles of the given-new contract, the principles of conversational postulates themselves fall out of the general processing structures. Thus,

> The speaker agrees to provide information he thinks the listener already knows as Given information, and information he thinks the listener does not already know as New information. The listener, for his part, agrees to assume that the speaker is trying to provide, as best he can, known and unknown information as Given and New information in the sentence. (H. Clark, 1973a).

World Knowledge and Reference

In normal speech, the classes of information that a speaker will assume can be used to decode the referent seem to have no limits. Thus, consider this children's story, taken from the Ph.D. thesis of Charniak of the MIT Artificial Intelligence Laboratory:

(40)   Janet wanted a nickel. Her piggy bank was in her room, so she went there and got it. "I will get that nickel," she said. She shook the piggy bank very hard. Finally it came out (Charniak, 1972).

Several different questions are raised by this story. For example, what do the two "its" refer to? To determine the answers we need considerable knowledge about the world. We are not told that the piggy bank actually contains a nickel—this fact is deduced from the story itself. We must know that a nickel is a coin, a small cylindrical metal object that can be used as money. Coins can be stored in piggy

---

[6]From H. H. Clark and S. E. Haviland, "Psychological processes as linguistic explanation." In D. Cohen (Ed.), *Explaining linguistic phenomena.* Washington, D.C.: Hemisphere Publishing Corp., 1974, pp. 105–106. Copyright 1974 by Hemisphere Publishing Corp. Reprinted with permission of authors and publisher.

banks, especially by children. Piggy banks are small, pottery (nowadays plastic) replicas of pigs that are hollow and completely sealed except for a slot on the top through which coins can pass only if they are oriented properly. Normally, it is an easy task to insert a coin into a piggy bank, but to excise one from the bank requires a good deal of effort, skill, and luck.

Knowing all of this, plus a good deal more, then we can deduce that the first "it" of story 40 (. . . she went there and got *it*. . .) refers to the piggy bank, whereas the second "it" (finally *it* came out) refers to the nickel.

Sometimes, even knowledge of the physical world is not sufficient. Consider this story, also taken from Charniak:

(41)   Mother made some cookies and left one out on a plate. She put the plate on the kitchen table, and went into the living room. "I am sure Janet will like it," thought Mother (Charniak, 1972).

Several problems appear in this story, starting with the word "one" in the first sentence. This task is relatively easy: The only possible set of objects so far talked about from which a single one could be extracted is comprised of the cookies. The task would be more difficult if the first sentence had been replaced with this:

(42)   Mother made some cookies. When she was finished, the kitchen was dirty. There were dirty bowls and cups, cookie sheets, and utensils. She put one on a plate on the kitchen table.

Story 42 is clumsier, but the "one" clearly refers to a cookie here, just as "it" did in (40). The last "it" in (41) also poses a problem ("Janet will like it"). Clearly, recency does not work, for we would then think that "it" referred to the living room. To understand what is referred to requires that we know about the likes and dislikes of children.

Finally, to understand some references we need conversational postulates. Consider these two pairs of sentences:

(43A)   Do you see that blue block on the piece of paper?

(43B)   What color is it?

(44A)   Do you see that block on the piece of yellow paper?

(44B)   What color is it?

The item referred to by the word "it" in sentence 43B is different from the one referred to by sentence 44B. In the former sentence, it is the paper that is meant; in the latter sentence, it is the block. Here, the underlying principle seems to be that a person rarely asks a question that also contains its own answer. The principle is derived from the conversational postulate, "Do not be superfluous." (This example comes from the thesis of Winograd, 1972.)

The discussion of Charniak's study of children's stories gives us the excuse to terminate the chapter with one last example, a common children's joke. It is a good example because it combines a violation of a conversational postulate with an irrelevant search for the referent of a pronoun. The joke works only because the normal process of deciding that a referent is intended and then solving for the appropriate concept takes place rapidly, smoothly, and with so little conscious effort that we usually are not even aware that we have done any processing at all. Hence the repeated success with the same joke—time, after time, after time.

(45)   Child: Do you know the word "hippopotamus?"
         Adult: Yes.
         Child: Spell it.
         Adult: H-I-P-P-O-P-O-T-A-M-U-S.
         Child: Ha, ha. No. I-T.

CHAPTER 4

Linguistic Theory and the LNR Structural Representation[1]

ALLEN MUNRO

The earlier chapters in this book have discussed our studies of two aspects of language understanding: the nature of the representational structure and the nature of the processes that search for, interpret, and create structural representations. In this chapter I compare the approach to the study of language presented in this book with that of some contemporary linguists. I have been selective in my analysis of the linguistic literature, treating only those issues and the works of those writers that are directly relevant to issues that have concerned the LNR research group.

Most of the comparisons made here are between the structural representations of the LNR research group and similar semantic representations developed by generative semanticists. These linguists regard their semantic representations as closely related to, if not indistinguishable from, underlying syntactic representations. The nature of the argumentation that has led these linguists to their representations has usually been quite different from the way we have justified our representations. However, since the LNR group and these generative semanticists both claim to have developed representations for the semantic structure of utterances, a comparison of these representations is warranted.

---

[1] Pamela Munro has made many helpful recommendations on several drafts of this chapter.

LEXICAL DECOMPOSITION

Generative Semantics

One important aspect of the LNR structural representation is the expansion of lexical items into their underlying structures. The generative semantic theory of lexical decomposition has influenced this development.

In 1965, Lakoff introduced the use of "primitive" predicates in syntactic deep structures (see Lakoff, 1970c). These primitive predicates are the components of more complex lexical items. Two such semantic primitives are **BECOME** and **CAUSE**.[2] Lakoff suggested that a sentence like (1), for example,

(1)   The stagehand darkened the auditorium.

could be derived from a deep syntactic structure similar to that shown in Figure 4.1.

To justify the use of the abstract semantic primitives **BECOME** and **CAUSE** in structures like Figure 4.1, Lakoff suggested that the logical structure

(2)   **BECOME** [dark [room]]

has as an English surface realization

(3)   The room darkened.

He points out that many English verbs ending in -en (for example, "harden," "redden," "brighten") are derived from adjectives that can be represented as arguments of **BECOME**. Lakoff calls the verbs whose deep structural representations include **BECOME** "inchoative verbs." (He sometimes uses the term **INCHO** as a semantic primitive in place of the more English-like **BECOME**.) As we shall see, the inchoative verbs correspond to "verbs of change" in the memory model — verbs that have the structural component **CHANGE** as part of their representations.

CAUSE in Lakoff's system is an abstract verb that, when combined with inchoative verbs, results in verbs of causation. For example, the logical form of the transitive verb "darken" in (1) is

(4)   **CAUSE** [the stagehand, **BECOME** [dark[the auditorium]]].

---

[2]Lakoff and other generative semanticists use the convention of capitalizing primitive verbs to distinguish them from ordinary lexical items. I follow the convention used throughout this book of also setting them in **THIS TYPE FONT**.

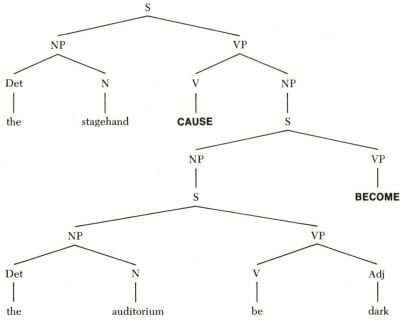

FIGURE 4.1
A representation for the deep syntactic structure of "The stagehand darkened the
auditorium," following Lakoff (1970c). The abbreviations used in this figure (and
subsequent figures) are:

Adj,	adjective	NP,	noun phrase	V,	verb
Det,	determiner	S,	sentence	VP,	verb phrase

These proposals of Lakoff were adopted and extended by
McCawley (1967, 1968a, 1968b, 1972). He argued that sentences can
be correctly correlated with their meanings only if the grammar includes transformations that apply to trees that terminate in semantic
primitives rather than in lexical items. He proposed that a tree like
that shown in Figure 4.2[3] represents sentences like

(5)   Jean killed Pat.

The structure of Figure 4.2 is sufficient to account for the ambiguities that arise with simple modifications of sentence 5. (McCawley

---

[3]McCawley proposed in 1970 that in underlying syntactic representations, English
word order should be represented as *verb-subject-object* (VSO). Hence, V is the leftmost component of each sentence in Figure 4.2. One effect of underlying VSO word
order is that the propositions of Figure 4.2 (represented by the various subscripted S's)
have the form of propositions in symbolic logic (for example, **ALIVE** [Pat], and so on).
The x of Figure 4.2 represents the unknown actions of Jean that caused Pat's death.

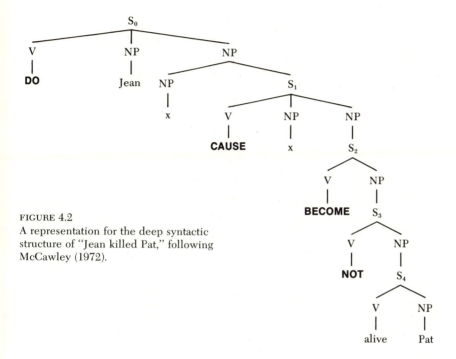

FIGURE 4.2
A representation for the deep syntactic
structure of "Jean killed Pat," following
McCawley (1972).

credits Morgan with this observation.) Thus, sentence 6 has several
interpretations.

(6)   Jean almost killed Pat.

Three interpretations of (6) can be described this way:

(7A)   Jean almost did something that would have killed Pat.

(7B)   Jean did something that almost caused Pat to die (but it actually
         didn't affect Pat).

(7C)   Jean did something that caused Pat to be seriously injured, but
         Pat recovered.

These three ambiguities are easily accounted for by the fact that the
modifier "almost" may be added to the structure of Figure 4.2 at any
one of three places: to modify **DO**, **CAUSE**, or **NOT**.

Dowty (1972) continued the linguistic developments of Lakoff
and McCawley. His analysis of the nature of the primitives **DO** and
CAUSE is very similar to that of the LNR group. He hypothesizes that
CAUSE is a relation between two *propositions* in semantic structure
(rather than a relation between an individual and a proposition, as in
McCawley's analysis). Dowty means that a person cannot *cause* an

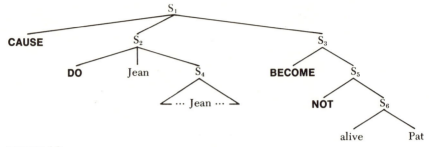

FIGURE 4.3
A representation for the deep syntactic and semantic structure of "Jean killed Pat," according to Dowty (1972).

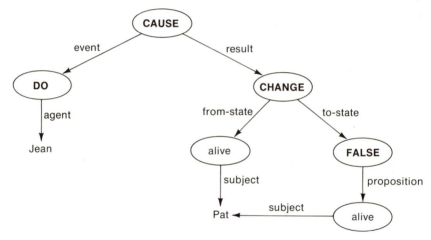

FIGURE 4.4
The LNR memory model representation for "Jean killed Pat."

event; only his *doing* something can cause the event. He extends McCawley's representation of "kill," proposing Figure 4.3[4] as the representation for (5).

Notice the similarity in structure between Figure 4.3 and the memory model representation of (5) in Figure 4.4. Both of these representations express the concept that Jean did something, and that it was this action which was the cause of Pat's becoming not alive (or changing to the state of not being alive). The major structural difference is that Dowty's representation does not make explicit the former state, in which Pat was alive.

---

[4]The symbol ⟨··· Jean ···⟩ in this figure corresponds to McCawley's x in Figure 4.2. It stands for the proposition that describes the actions of Jean's that had the effect of causing Pat's death.

Dowty suggests Figure 4.3 as one of two possible structures for sentences like (5). This structure does not specify whether Jean intended her actions to cause Pat's death. The presence of **DO** in S_2 of Figure 4.3 makes explicit the intentionality of the subject (Jean) only with respect to the proposition S_4 (which represents some action of Jean's), not with respect to the whole proposition S_1. The structure for

(8)   Jean (intentionally) killed Pat.

is discussed in the next section on **DO**. The memory model structure shown in Figure 4.4, like Dowty's Figure 4.3, preserves the vagueness of sentence 5 regarding Jean's intentionality.

The Primitive **DO**

In the memory model, predicates of activity are represented as having an underlying **DO** semantic element, sometimes left unspecified, sometimes elaborated by various adverbial modifiers. Here I trace the development of related linguistic theory and compare it with our representations.

Statives and Actives.   Lakoff (1966) discovered a number of different linguistic tests that can be applied to a verb or adjective to distinguish between those that are stative and those that are active (or nonstative). Active verbs and adjectives can be used in imperative commands:

(9A)   **Do** that again.

(9B)   **Eat** that food.

(9C)   Be **careful**.

Stative verbs and adjectives cannot be used in imperative commands.[5]

(10A) ? Be **tall**.[6]

(10B) ? **Know** the answer.

---

[5]Unfortunately, examples of stative commands are hard to develop, in part because the human understanding system seems obliging in its attempts to make sense out of any construction. Thus, "Be tall" does have several possible interpretations, most of them based on metaphorical extensions of "tall." Similarly, "Know the answer" can become interpreted by transforming the stative sense of "know" into an active form meaning "do something that will cause you to be in a state of knowing." Even our prototypical example of a stative, the verb "locate," takes a "change of state" meaning when used in a command: "Be located in Venezuela." Thus, it would seem that Lakoff's tests must be regarded more as diagnostic tests for stativity than absolute indicators.

[6]Here I follow the standard generative linguistics usage of ? to mark sentences of questionable grammaticality and * to mark ungrammatical sentences.

In a similar vein, Lakoff observed that only active verbs can be used in the progressive.

(11A)   I am learning this proof.

(11B)   *I am knowing this proof.

Only actives can be replaced by the verb "do" (a sort of "pro-verb" in certain constructions, just as nouns are replaced by pronouns) in the following sorts of constructions.

(12A)   What I **did** was to kiss him again.

(12B)   *What I **did** was to know the answer.

(12C)   What she **did** to please me was to be careful.

(12D)   *What she **did** to please me was to be tall.

(12E)   I learned the answer, although John told me not to **do so**.

(12F)   *I knew the answer, although John told me not to **do so**.

These latter observations, together with ten syntactic arguments that are too complex to recapitulate here, led Ross (1972a) to postulate that active verbs involve the verb **DO** in deep structure, whereas stative verbs do not. Ross claimed that ". . . every verb of action is embedded in the object complement of a two-place predicate whose subject is identical to the subject of the action verb, and whose phonological realization in English is *do*" (Ross, 1972a, p. 70). He suggested that a sentence such as

(13)   Frogs produce croaks.

has the underlying structure shown in Figure 4.5[7]

The Memory Model: Structures with **DO**.   The **DO** of such structures as shown in Figure 4.5 is obviously related to the **DO** in memory model structures like that represented by Figure 4.4. In both Ross's analysis and that of the memory model, **DO** is understood as a marker of possible intentionality. The precise relationship between **DO** and intentionality, however, remains to be worked out. The **DO** of the structure for the act of "kill" in Figure 4.4 indicates that Jean inten-

---

[7]Some languages provide surface evidence for the deep structure proposed by Ross, shown in Figure 4.5. In the American Indian language Mojave, for example, **DO** may appear in the surface structure of any active sentence that takes a transitive verb (see P. Munro, in press).

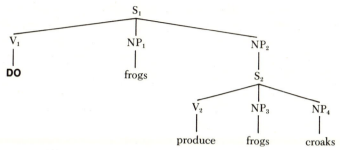

FIGURE 4.5
Ross's (1972a) representation for "Frogs produce croaks."

tionally did those actions that led to Pat's death, but the structure does not specify that Pat's death was part of Jean's intention. Dowty (1972) suggests the addition of a higher **DO** dominating the causal structure, as in Figure 4.6, to represent a sentence like

(8)   Jean (intentionally) killed Pat.

Stative verbs in the memory model do not have a higher **DO** structure. Therefore, the subjects of stative verbs and adjectives are *not* interpreted by the model as intentional agents.

A second function of **DO** in the memory model is that it provides a proposition that represents the vagueness of the hearer's knowledge about a causal event. The **DO** represents a lack of knowledge about which of the many possible actions that Jean may have been guilty

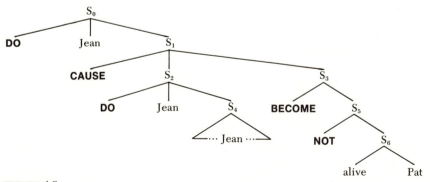

FIGURE 4.6
A representation for the deep syntactic structure of "Jean (intentionally) killed Pat," following Dowty (1972).

of was actually responsible for the death of Pat. Notice that the **DO** can often be expanded by using an additional phrase. The *manner* of the action can often be expressed in a prepositional phrase introduced with "by." Similarly, the instrument can be expressed in a prepositional phrase introduced by "with." Thus:

(14A)   Jean killed Pat by making the coffee too strong.

(14B)   Jean killed Pat with a flower pot.

Conceptual Dependency Analysis

The work of Schank (1972b, 1973a, 1973c) has been quite influential in the development of the lexical decomposition approach in the memory model. His work suggests that a large proportion of semantic representation can be accounted for with a remarkably small set of semantic primitives.

Some of Schank's proposed structures may account for semantic distinctions that are either lost or difficult to find in the representations suggested in this book. His notion that there are several distinctly different primitive **CHANGE**s has led us to question whether the memory model **CHANGE** is sufficiently detailed. (Schank calls his **CHANGE** a **TRANS**.) For example, to give someone an object is a *physical* transfer (**P-TRANS**); to remember something is a *mental* transfer (**M-TRANS**); and to tell someone something is a *conceptual* transfer (**C-TRANS**). Our single, unified **CHANGE** has the virtue of capturing the semantic unity of Schank's various **TRANS**es, but may fail to capture some important distinctions that his system elucidates.

Similarly, Schank discriminates among several different kinds of primitive *causes*. His *Result, Reason, Initiation,* and *Enable* are all ordinarily represented in our system by a unified primitive causal component, **CAUSE**. Some recent developments in our attempts to model text understanding have led us to suspect that the representation of the semantic distinctions among these various types of causes may have desirable consequences for a text-understanding system (see Rumelhart, in press). Nonetheless, it is our belief that all these *causes* have some primitive underlying **CAUSE** component in common. The best solution may prove to be one that makes use of a set of near-primitive causal predicates such as those suggested by Schank, all of which have in common some more basic component such as our **CAUSE**.

THE PREDICATE APPROACH

The development of our commitment to a propositionally based system has paralleled a similar development in linguistic theory. We discovered that the expansion of predicates into underlying primitives yields useful dividends in question-answering, paraphrase, and in the representation of meaning in general. As a result, we have been led to extend the predicate analysis to parts of speech other than verbs. Thus we join a long tradition in logic and a more recent trend in linguistics.

Adjectives

Linguists have long been aware that in many languages, quite possibly in the majority of languages, adjectives are members of the same syntactic class as verbs. In other words, what we call adjectives in English are often verbs that take a single argument in other languages. If this were the case in English, most adjectives would behave like ordinary intransitive verbs. Thus, instead of saying

(15A)   The car is red.

we would say

(15B)   The car reds.

George Lakoff (1970c) observed that adjectives in English are, for the most part, indistinguishable from verbs with respect to syntactic rules. He claims there are only three differences, the primary one being the fact that adjectives take the auxiliary verb "be" when used as predicates.

In the memory model, most adjectives are represented as stative predicates with three arguments, as in Figure 4.7, which represents a concept of a *red house*.

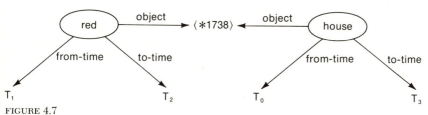

FIGURE 4.7
A memory model representation for the concept of *a red house*.

Not all adjectives are necessarily stative. Some adjectives (such as "surprising," "careful," "polite," "obnoxious," "tactful," "officious") are ambiguous in that a particular use of the adjective could be represented either by a simple stative or by a predicate of action, which would require a **DO** in the structural representation. Context determines whether a given instance of such an adjective should be represented as a simple stative or as a stative dominated by the activity predicate, **DO**.

Nouns

Logicians since Frege (1879–1882/1972) have treated common nouns as predicates that take a single argument. This approach is very similar to that of the memory model. Most nouns are represented as stative predicates with one substantive argument, which is the node that represents the hearer's concept of the referent under discussion. For example, in Figure 4.7, node *1738 is the hearer's concept for a particular house. Whether stative noun-predicates require other arguments, such as *time*, is an unsettled issue. Ordinarily, the time arguments of nouns are simply the dates marking the "creation" and "destruction" of the individual in question.

Bach (1968) has shown that time arguments for some instantiated noun-predicates are not markers of the span of an individual's existence but rather of the time span for which that predicate holds true for the individual. This is evidenced by the occasional use of temporal modifiers with noun-predicates, as in

(16)   The then chairperson of the board had a different philosophy.

Bach points out that not all nouns are simple stative predicates. Some, such as "fool," "idiot," "prince," and "comedian," can also be activity predicates — they may be used in the diagnostic environments for activity verbs.

(17A)   Don't be a fool.

(17B)   Stop being a comedian.

This suggests that the underlying representations of some uses of these nouns must include the **DO** activity predicate.

Adverbs

We have not yet developed a comprehensive approach to adverbs in our system, but the development that has occurred is related to linguistic studies (Lakoff, 1968, 1970a, 1970b) in which adverbs are analyzed as higher predicates — that is, predicates that take propositions as arguments. Our current approach centers on classifying the various types of adverbial predicates, and then determining the scope of those adverbs in the semantic representation. The development described here has been influenced by Schank's (1972a) treatment of adverbs, which can also be formulated in predicate terms.

One type of adverb that takes a proposition as an argument is a sentence adverb. For example, a simple sentence like

(18A)   John went to school.

may be modified by a sentence adverb such as "certainly," "probably," or "fortunately." Figure 4.8 shows that when sentence 18A is modified by the sentence adverb "fortunately," the node that represents the whole of the sentence is the one modified. In the underlying representational structure, sentence adverbs are analyzed as verbs that take sentential subjects, as is shown by the possibility of paraphrasing Figure 4.8 as

(18B)   That John went to school is fortunate.

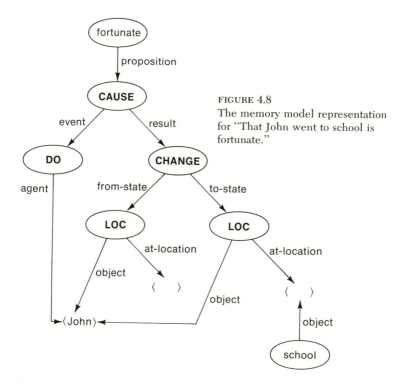

FIGURE 4.8
The memory model representation for "That John went to school is fortunate."

In the LNR representation for several other types of adverbs, the propositional arguments of the adverbs are subcomponents of the sentences in which they occur. For example, "manner" adverbs have a smaller scope than sentence adverbs. By our analysis, there are two sorts of manner adverbs. Those of the first type can modify the **DO** predicate of a semantic structure. For example, "happily," "sadly," "cleverly," "resourcefully," and "reluctantly" can be represented as predicates that take two substantive arguments—the *agent* and the *action*, both represented in the **DO**.

The second type of manner adverbs includes "quickly" and "slowly." Some of the sentences in which these adverbs are used, such as

(19)   The ball rolled slowly down the incline.

would seem not to have a **DO** as part of underlying structure. These adverbs should be represented as predications on the **CHANGE** portion of the underlying proposition. Actually, the decomposed structure of an adverb like "quickly" should probably be some predication about the relative duration of the **CHANGE** predicate. Such a predication would have as arguments some of the arguments of the **CHANGE** structure.

Certain prepositional phrases, such as "with a knife" and "by car" in

(20)   Seymour sliced the salami with a knife.

and

(21)   John went to school by car.

have traditionally been analyzed as instrumental adverbs. Lakoff (1968) pointed out that only active predicates may be modified by instrumental adverbs. This observation suggests that instrumental adverbs ought to be associated with the **DO** in representations of sentences like (20) and (21). In LNR representations, prepositional phrases like "with a knife" in (20) are represented by treating "knife" as an "instrumental" argument of **DO**.

A number of basic adverb types remain to be investigated within the context of the memory model. For example, adverbs with variable scope in semantic representation, such as "almost," "hardly," "basically," and "barely," have not yet been studied. We expect that the extension of the predicate approach to more adverb types, as well as to other parts of speech, will be one important object of future semantic research in our group.

Modal Verbs

Thus far our analysis of surface sentences has assumed, in effect, that the main verb of a sentence is the highest predicate of the sentence; that is, the other constituents of the sentence appear in the representation as arguments of the main verb. We have neglected the effect of tense markers, such as -ed; the auxiliary verbs, such as "have" and "be"; and the modal verbs, such as "can," "must," "should," and "will." Chomsky (1957) analyzed all of these as constituents of the "auxiliary component" of sentences.

In the current computer implementations of the theory, all input sentences are presumed to be in the past tense, and auxiliary verbs are essentially ignored. The analysis of auxiliaries (including tense) into higher verbs, as has been proposed by Ross (1969) and McCawley (1971b), offers a way to improve the system. The details of this proposal have been worked out only for the representation of modal verbs. For example, the expansion of

(22)   John can go to school.

into the structure shown in Figure 4.9 makes use of a higher predicate **ABLE**. **ABLE** has as an argument the proposition "John go to school" in this representation.

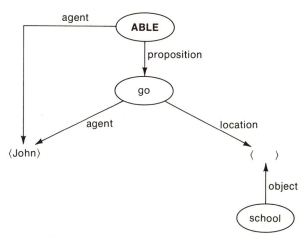

FIGURE 4.9
A memory model representation for "John can go to school." (Note that the predicates "go" and "school" have not been fully comprehended in this structure—see the section on partial comprehension in Chapter 8.)

This sort of higher-predicate analysis finds independent justification in the analysis of sentences such as

(23A)   John is likely to succeed.

Linguists have proposed that (23A) should be derived (through a transformation called subject raising) from the same deep structure source as

(23B)   It is likely that John will succeed.

In these sentences, the adjective "likely" may be thought of as a predicate that takes the propositional argument "John will succeed." A similar relationship seems to hold between the sentences

(24A)   John may succeed.

and

(24B)   It may be that John will succeed.

This leads us to conclude that "may" and "likely" have similar forms in underlying representation, each taking the propositional argument "John will succeed."

Further work on modal verbs is certainly needed in the LNR model, since the approach mentioned here addresses only one type of modal interpretation, namely, the epistemic uses of the modal verbs. Nonetheless, higher-verb analysis seems a fruitful approach to the auxiliary system in English.

REFERENTS

In the structural representation of the memory model, mental concepts are represented by nodes. Nodes are of two kinds: concepts for objects or events in the world, and representations of abstract, genericlike concepts. The latter class, which is essentially that of type nodes, is discussed in some detail in Chapters 3 and 8 (see the type-token distinction discussion in Chapter 2). These nodes are the representations of statements that are true for the members of some *class* of objects or events.

The function of reference programs, such as the procedure the discussed in Chapters 3 and 8, is to "return with a node"—to provide nodes as the arguments of predicates in input sentences. For a predicate to be instantiated as a proposition—as an instance of an event in the memory structure—it must have each of its "substantive" or required arguments filled. It is the function of the reference procedures to find the intended nodes or to create new nodes of appropriate form.

Early workers in transformational linguistics did not find it necessary to make use of the concept of "referent" in theories of grammar. Lees and Klima (1963), for example, developed a theory in which pronominalization rules functioned without considerations of reference. However, Chomsky (1965) claimed that lexical items must be designated as "referential" in order that certain transformations could apply correctly. He introduced the notion of *indices*, which are markers on the deep structural representations of nouns that distinguish whether two or more instances of the same noun are coreferential. Chomsky made it quite clear, however, that these indices are simply convenient tags within deep structure, and they do not represent a speaker's concepts.

McCawley (1968b, 1971a) has proposed a theory of reference in which Chomsky's concept of an index is put to much the same use as are token nodes in the memory model. He suggests that, in semantic representation, the arguments of a proposition are best thought of as indices rather than as nouns or noun phrases. Unlike Chomsky, McCawley specifically believes that the indices represent the speaker's mental concepts, and thus should be thought of as existing "in the mind of the speaker rather than in the real world; they are conceptual entities which the individual creates in interpreting his experience" (McCawley, 1971a, pp. 223–224).

In addition to capturing many of the phenomena that motivate McCawley's essentially "psychological" theory of reference, the approach described in Chapter 3 is in accord with much of the linguistic evidence discussed by other linguists interested in reference (see, for example, Postal, 1970; Perlmutter, 1971; and Karttunen, 1971a).

GENERIC QUANTIFICATION

Sentences such as

(25)   Man is mortal.

are interpreted by the memory model to imply a modification of the definition of "man." After (25) has been received, the definitional structure for "man" is modified so that all present and future instances of "man" known by the model have the property of being mortal. Sentences like (25) are interpreted in the universal, generic sense.

Not all generic statements imply universal quantification, however (see, for example, Lawler, 1972, 1973). Although a sentence such as (25) seems to be paraphrasable as

(26)   All men have the property of being mortal.

other generic sentences cannot be paraphrased in a similar manner. For example, a sentence such as

(27)   Dogs chase cats.

does not mean the same as

(28)   All dogs chase all cats.

For most readers, (27) means that many dogs will occasionally chase some cats.

In Chapter 2 it was suggested that the difference in interpretation between the quantifications implied by (25) and (27) can be expressed through the use of modals:

(29)   A man must be mortal.

(30)   A dog may chase a cat.

Here (29) should be read as

(31)   A man is certainly mortal.

The effect of this input (31) is to add to the definition of "man":

(32)   man[x] $\rightarrow$ [certain[mortal[x]]]**AND**[previous definition of "man"]

Similarly, (30) should here be read as

(33)   A dog possibly chases cats.

Sentence 33 adds (34) to the definition of "dog":

(34)   dog[x] $\rightarrow$ [possibly[chase[x, cat[y]]]]**AND**[previous definition of "dog"].

Here the problem for the memory model is how to determine when a generic use requires "must" and when it requires "may." The solution probably involves the nature of the predicate. Generic sentences involving stative verbs like "hate" are more likely to have universal interpretations than are generics involving active verbs. Thus, if

(35)   Pedro hates vegetables.

then it is correct to say that

(36)   Pedro hates beans.

But a different conclusion follows when we use an active predicate, such as "chase," as in sentence 27, or "eat," as in

(37)   Maria eats vegetables.

If we know that (37) is true, then we do not conclude that

(38)   Maria eats beans.

The situation is, unfortunately, more complicated than a simple active-stative distinction would suggest. First, the understood quantification of various verbs seems to be dependent on the pragmatics associated with the verbs. "Hating," being a mental operation, can be performed universally, on an entire class, such as "all vegetables." "Eating," however, is a physical operation that has its physical limits: Only *some* elements of a very large class can be eaten by an individual. Hence the quantification of (37) is *some*. Other important determiners of the universality of quantification for various generics (discussed by Lawler, 1973, and Kanouse, 1972) include embedded negation (generic sentences with *hate* have more universal interpretation than those with *love*) and "mental" or "emotion" verbs (generic sentences with *love* are more universal than those with *eat*).

Current memory model implementations do not take into account these factors. Although a great many facts about generics do seem to be accounted for by the treatment of generics discussed in Chapter 3, the semantic phenomena associated with generics remain a source of future research problems.

TRUTH IN SEMANTIC REPRESENTATION

In order to deal with the problems of conflicts of information within memory, we need a system for representing a hearer's confidence in the truth or falsity of stored information. The memory model is reasonably efficient in this regard, applying a three-valued truth system to its propositions: true, false, and unknown. In his paper "Hedges," in which he discusses some syntactic constructions that speakers use to qualify their statements, Lakoff (1972) hinted that there should be a range of possible truth values, ranging on a continuous scale from **TRUE** through **POSSIBLE** to **FALSE**. I believe this idea has a number of deficiencies. Note that of all these truth values, only two have special linguistic status. In sentences, **TRUE** seems to be an understood value unless there is some specific overt marker for one of the other values; and **FALSE** (**NEG** in the linguistic literature) has special grammatical functions that the other proposed truth predicates do not have. Many predicates seem to contain **FALSE** as an atomic predicate; for example, "dead" is defined as **FALSE** (alive) (see Figure 4.4). No verb that I can think of might contain the atomic predicate **VERY-IMPROBABLE** or anything like it. This is not to say that concepts like **VERY-IMPROBABLE** do not have linguistic and psychological validity, but rather that they are more complicated— they have more underlying structure—than simple truth values.

I suggest that there are only two *truth* values, **TRUE** and **FALSE**. Of these, only **TRUE** is really primitive. A number of psychologists (see, for example, Wason and Johnson-Laird, 1972; H. Clark, 1971) have shown that negative concepts are more difficult to comprehend than non-negative ones. Many different types of reaction-time experiments have shown that sentences with either surface or hidden negatives (such as the semantic negative in the word "absent") require significantly more processing time.

However, there is a possibly continuous range of certainty values from absolutely certain (+1) to completely unknown (0). Table 4.1 shows what could be called English modal predicates or truth-certainty predicates, each factored into one of the two truth values and one of the various certainty values. The certainty values are repre-

TABLE 4.1
Modals predicated on x factored into certainty and truth values.

| | | | Truth value predicated on x | |
			TRUE(x)	**FALSE**(x)
			x is	x is
Certainty value predicated on truth of x		**CERTAIN**	certain	impossible
		ALMOST-CERTAIN	almost certain	almost impossible
		FAIRLY CERTAIN	very probable	very improbable
		⋮	⋮	⋮
		UNKNOWN	unknown	unknown

sented in the table as predicates that take truth values as arguments. Modal predicates are terms in English that can often be used to express a speaker's judgment of the truth and the certainty of the truth of a proposition. Thus,

(39)   **CERTAIN[FALSE**[x]] → it's **impossible** that x

(40)   **FAIRLY CERTAIN[FALSE**[x]] → it's very **improbable** that x

Thus far, this schema has not accounted for the meaning of predicates like "possible." Karttunen (1972) points out that, by Grice's principles of cooperation (see the discussion in Chapter 3), one should not tell a listener that "x is possible" if one knows for a fact that x is certain (or, perhaps, even if one only knows that x is probable), because to do so would not be maximally informative. In most conversational situations, therefore, when a speaker predicates "possible" of something, he is only stating that he has no knowledge that makes that thing certainly false. "Possible" is thus only the negation of a point value, namely, **CERTAIN[FALSE**[x]]. It thus allows a range of values. The claim that "possible" has the underlying structure **FALSE[CERTAIN[FALSE**[x]]] may be open to experimental test, perhaps using reaction times. This claim can be contrasted with proposals for a three-valued (or n-valued) logic system, such as those made by Lakoff. (Compare this proposed structure for "possible" with one that can be derived for "uncertain" by a similar line of reasoning. Here again only a point is denied, this one at the other end of the scale, if "uncertain" is defined as **FALSE[CERTAIN**[x]].)

The implementation of these nested-component representations for truth and certainty is one aspect of current efforts of the LNR group to model semantic structures in the memory model.

PRESUPPOSITION

The nature of the phenomenon of presupposition is still in considerable dispute among linguists and philosophers. As we shall see, there is as yet no agreement as to its proper representation in the semantic representations of sentences, or even as to whether the phenomenon has reality independent of ordinary sentence implications. For a review of some recent linguistic work on presupposition, see Karttunen (1973a, 1973b); Katz (1973); and Keenan (1971).

The presupposition of a sentence is usually defined as those conditions that must hold in order for a sentence to be either true or false (Strawson, 1950; Keenan, 1971). For example, sentence 41A is said to presuppose its complement clause, (41B):

(41A)   John regrets that Sam walked to school.

(41B)   Sam walked to school.

If (41B) is not true, then an utterance of (41A) is said to be neither true nor false, but some other truth value, perhaps "nonsense."

Many linguists have defined linguistic presupposition as that portion of the meaning of an utterance that holds for both a sentence and its negation. Thus, the presupposition of

(41C)   John didn't regret that Sam walked to school.

is the same as that of (41A), namely,

(41B)   Sam walked to school.

In this section I examine several types of presupposition and show how they are treated in the memory model.

Factives

The first type of presupposition I consider is that of the factive verbs. Kiparsky and Kiparsky (1971) point out that verbs such as "forget," "regret," "comprehend," "ignore," and "know" all have the property that their complement clauses are presupposed, as examples (41A)–(41C) have shown. Yamanashi (1972) suggested that the common effect of factive verbs is the result of one primitive semantic component that they have in common. He identified this component as **KNOW**, a primitive that dominates the dependent clauses of these sentences in deep structure. This explanation accounts for the effect of many of the factive verbs, although the factive lexical item "fact" (as in "It's a fact that x") may not so clearly have **KNOW** as part of its deep structure.

The memory model treatment of factive verbs is very similar to that of Yamanashi. In the system of verb definitions discussed in Chapter 8, the verb "know" has the predicate **INFORMATION** as a more primitive lexical component. Thus, one sense of "know" is defined in this way:

(42)   X knows proposition P means the **INFORMATION** about P is located in X's memory.

The predicate **INFORMATION** has the special property that it automatically assigns a truth value of true to its propositional argument. Therefore, the proposition P in a sentence of the form "X knows that P" is automatically called true. Similarly, the lexical item "fact" has **INFORMATION** as part of its definition. Most factive verbs include an instantiation of **INFORMATION** as part of their representation because they have "know" as a component. For example, one sense of a word like "regret" might possibly be defined in this way:

(43)   X regrets proposition P means that X knows P makes X sad.

Implicatives

Karttunen (1971b) observed that certain verbs, such as "manage," "remember," and "bother," have special presuppositional properties. These verbs, which he called *implicatives*, have the property that their complement clauses are asserted or implied, while some additional semantic element—different for the different verbs—is presupposed. The propositional objects of implicative verbs (unlike those of factive verbs) are negated when their embedding verbs are negated. Thus, although

(44A)   Pam managed to solve the problem.

implies that

(44B)   Pam solved the problem.

the sentence

(44C)   Pam didn't manage to solve the problem.

does not imply (44B). Rather, (44C) implies the negation of (44B). In addition, each of the various implicative verbs carries a unique presupposition that seems to be invariant under negation. The presupposition of "manage" is one of *trying*; thus both (44A) and (44C) have (45) as a presupposition:

(45)   Pam tried to solve the problem.

Similarly, "remember to do" is said to presuppose an obligation to do, and "bother" presupposes ease of accomplishment.

A

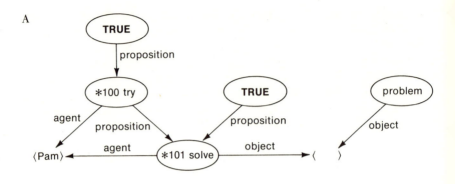

B

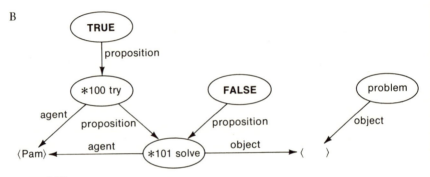

FIGURE 4.10
A: The memory model representation for "Pam managed to solve the problem."
B: The memory model representation for "Pam didn't manage to solve the problem."

In the memory model, the predicate expansions of the various implicative verbs handle these phenomena. For example, the LNR representation of (44A) is shown in Figure 4.10A. The node that stands for sentence 44A is not node ∗100, but node ∗101. This means that when (44A) is negated, as in sentence 44C, node ∗101 is negated, leaving node ∗100, the presupposition of trying, unaffected (as in Figure 4.10B).

Definite Descriptions

The notion of presupposition, as developed by Frege (1960) and Strawson (1950), was concerned with the truth of sentences like

(46)   The present King of France is bald.

These theorists proposed that the truth of (46) is neither true nor false, since its presupposition, that the King of France exists, does not hold.

In our model, there is no special "presupposition" procedure that invokes a special interpretation during the comprehension of a sentence such as (46). As the section on definiteness in Chapter 3 explained, a referent for "the present King of France" is searched for in memory and if none is found, then one is created. Intuitively, this seems like a good model of what might happen if (46) were heard by an individual who had no preconceptions about the existence of a present King of France (say, a person who was ignorant that France is a republic).

Suppose now that a sentence such as (46) is heard by one who is aware that France is a republic. The search in memory for the referent for the noun phrase, "the present King of France," retrieves the information that no such individual can exist. The philosophy used by the LNR group is that such contradictory pieces of information are treated as messages about possible interpretations. The discovery of such an error during comprehension then invokes the mental procedures that have the effect of conversational postulates. This may result in a number of interpretations by the hearer, such as that the speaker of (46) is ignorant; that the information currently within the hearer's memory is incorrect; that the speaker knows what he is saying and, therefore, is deliberately uttering a falsehood (perhaps to be ironic, perhaps to deceive); and so on. The point is that conflicts in presuppositional aspects of sentences are treated no differently than are conflicts in the directly asserted parts of the sentences.

Presupposition and the Memory Model: A Summary

In the work of the LNR research group, the notion of presupposition does not have special status. We have no special "presupposition" structures in our representation. The semantic representations of the presuppositions of input sentences are searched for in the memory data base to see if they represent old or new information in precisely the same manner that the nonpresuppositional components of sentences are searched for. If no "old" copy of the information is found, then the new information is added to the pre-existing memory structure. (Some of these presuppositions are, of course, not invoked when the hearer is only partially comprehending the input; see the discussion of these issues in Chapter 8.) The intuitional phenomena about the meanings and pragmatic uses of sentences that are accounted for by "presupposition" in other theories are handled by various processing strategies: Presupposition is simply a natural result of ordinary predicate expansion, definite reference routines, and conversational postulates.

The three types of presuppositional constructions discussed in this section (factives, implicatives, and definite descriptions) are not the only types of presupposition handled by the memory model. In particular, the "presuppositional" phenomena associated with questions and with various lexical items follow naturally from processing strategies and definitions. For example, a word like "stop" implies a cessation of some activity that is presupposed to be taking place. Part of the definition of "stop" in the memory model includes that there be a "previous state of activity," which is changed; a word like "again" has the presupposition that there was a previous event that is repeated. These words and most others are handled without formal acknowledgment of their presuppositional implications, by the normal structure-searching and structure-building routines of the memory model. As a further example, see Gentner's explanation (Chapter 9) of how the failure of negation to apply to the "presuppositions" of verbs of change is explained by the interaction of conversational postulates with the structure of the change verbs.

Our approach, in which the phenomena of presupposition fall out from the interaction of input and what might be called the hearer's world knowledge, resembles some recent proposals in linguistics. Karttunen (1973b) suggests that linguists ought not to concentrate on representing the presuppositions of sentences, but rather on understanding the relationship between sentences and their contexts. A context, he says, may satisfy the presuppositions of a sentence. Practically, a context must entail a number of propositions in the speaker's mental representational structure in order to satisfy the presuppositions of an input sentence. In our work, if some of these propositions are not part of "context" (the previous knowledge in memory), then those propositions are assumed to be indirectly asserted by the input utterance. If some of the propositions are actually contradicted in the data base, then conversational postulates are called in to find an appropriate nonliteral interpretation of the utterance.

SUMMARY

In this chapter I have compared the theories of the LNR research group with some analyses in linguistic theory. I have confined myself to a review of certain descendants of standard theory in transformational linguistics. Much of the work in this tradition is still highly constrained by the formal nature of the concept of a transformational grammar. A grammar is not traditionally conceived of as a device in the speaker-hearer's cognitive arsenal, but rather as a formal tool for the description of languages. Our work has different goals, in that we have tried to treat a wide variety of cognitive functions within a common framework. We view language as but one aspect of cognitive skills. As I have tried to show, our work and that of certain linguists has led to some converging results, particularly as to the nature of semantic representation. We have profited in particular from the work of the generative semanticists, especially Lakoff, McCawley, and Ross. Two "nonmainstream" linguists who have had particular impact on our thinking are Schank, who has developed some insightful representational devices, and Chafe (1970, 1972), whose concern with input-processing heuristics and with the nature of semantic representation closely parallels ours.

It must be acknowledged, however, that there has been little concrete interaction between linguists and psychologists. We have not been prepared to adopt the terminology and theoretical constructs of transformational linguistics, and linguists have not been convinced that our approach can provide them with modeling tools that they cannot create within the framework of their own tradition. I believe that we may expect more interaction as cognitive psychologists and linguists approach certain new topics. For example, some members of our research group have begun an effort at modeling the understanding of texts within the theoretical framework described in this book (see Rumelhart, in press). We have profited from learning of the work on text analysis done by certain European linguists, as exemplified by van Dijk (1972, 1973, 1974). We believe that our system, with its emphasis on the connectedness of semantic structures—which may be contrasted with the traditional single sentence unit of analysis in linguistics—may offer a powerful tool for this sort of study.

Other similar lines of research are being carried out in parallel by linguists and cognitive psychologists. For example, the approach to conversational postulates exemplified in Gordon and Lakoff (1971) has stimulated our attempts to simulate conversational postulates. Recent linguistic interest in pragmatics suggests that a model with the capacity for representing the speaker-hearer's world knowledge is required. Correspondingly, one of our most lasting concerns has been to model the intimate interaction between world knowledge and language understanding. Other points of possible future contact between the two fields include the areas of "functionalism" in linguistics (Bever and Langendoen, 1971; Langacker, 1974) and studies of variation in natural language (Ross, 1972b, 1973). We may thus hope for a richer and more fruitful interaction with the linguistic community as its theories and those of cognitive psychologists interested in language continue to evolve.

PART III

LINGUISTIC ANALYSIS

CHAPTER 5

On Process Models for Sentence Analysis

RONALD M. KAPLAN[1]

How does the human listener comprehend sentences? This is a question of major concern to psychologists interested in language, and it has been intensively investigated. Language comprehension, one of our most intricate cognitive capabilities, happens so automatically and with so little conscious effort that it is not easily susceptible to scientific observation or introspective analysis. Thus it is not surprising that there is still no satisfactory explanation of how the listener deciphers and assimilates the conceptual relationships that are conveyed by spoken and written language.

COMPONENTS OF COMPREHENSION

A common way to approach a phenomenon or system as complicated as language comprehension is to find some way of decomposing it into less complicated, more manageable subdomains, to study these in isolation from one another, and then, when the separate components are well understood, to study their interactions. The success of this kind of enterprise depends, of course, on discovering the "right" decomposition: one whose components are individually simpler than the total system and combine in relatively simple ways. There is

[1]This chapter is derived from Ronald Kaplan's doctoral dissertation, submitted to the Department of Psychology and Social Relations, Harvard University. The work was partially supported by grant GS-39836 from the National Science Foundation.

little to be gained from a decomposition in which the internal operations of one component are substantially influenced by the internal operations of other components. In such a case, simple accounts of the components in isolation leave unsolved the major problem of explaining their interactions.

In utilizing a decomposition approach, there are two important points to bear in mind. First, a decomposition can be an effective aid to understanding and explanation even though its components do interact in many different ways. The stipulation is only that the interactions be "relatively" simple, not that they be completely absent. Thus, Simon (1969) has used the term "nearly decomposable" to describe systems for which a "right" decomposition can be found. Second, it is not clear that an effective decomposition exists for every complicated system we might choose to investigate, and the effort spent in searching for one might in fact be wasted. On the other hand, if the right decomposition for a system cannot be found, then it is doubtful that the system is amenable to explanation in any real sense. Decomposition is perhaps the only way to approach a complicated phenomenon.

Syntax and Semantics

The phenomenon of human language comprehension is often viewed as being nearly decomposable into such traditional linguistic domains as syntax and semantics. Roughly speaking, the syntactic component takes the words of a sentence, combines them into phrases, and determines the logical relationships that hold among them. It pays attention to comparatively local and superficial aspects of sentences such as inflections, word order, and the stable properties of words that a simple dictionary might contain. The semantic component has deeper, more global concerns. It must provide a meaningful interpretation of the phrases constructed in syntactic processing. Thus, under this decomposition, semantics has to do not only with the meanings of individual input elements and the significance of various syntactic relationships, but also with knowledge of previous inputs, memory for previous events, and general knowledge of the world. The semantic component must relate all these different sources of information to create a single interpretation that fits into the context of previous experience, both linguistic and nonlinguistic.

Of course, syntax and semantics are not completely independent. Countless examples can be adduced to demonstrate the widespread and intricate ways in which these two components interact. Semantic interpretations depend upon syntactic relationships, which themselves may depend upon the results of semantic processing. Such interactions do not necessarily undermine the fruitfulness of this decomposition. However, they do impose strong criteria for evaluating theories of the individual components. A complete explanation of comprehension must eventually account for syntax-semantics interdependencies as well as for their operations in isolation. A theory of an individual component must be assessed according to how easily it accommodates explanations of interaction.

The discussions in this chapter emphasize the syntactic component of language comprehension. I present a framework for modeling the psychological processes by which the words of a sentence are organized into their underlying syntactic relationships. This framework does provide channels for semantic interaction, but these are not of central interest here. The semantic component is discussed in several other chapters of this book. (Chapters 7 and 8 in particular offer more elaborate hypotheses about the nature of syntactic-semantic interactions.)

Knowledge and Process

The framework outlined here suggests another near decomposition of human comprehension, one that cuts across the syntax-semantics distinction. Within this framework, a model of comprehension includes a theory of the native speaker's linguistic *knowledge* and a theory of the cognitive *processes* that apply this knowledge to the task of comprehending specific sentences.

The syntactic knowledge component is an explicit, formal account of the meaningful sentences of the language. It represents the principles by which words combine to convey basic syntactic relationships. It must provide each possible sentence with a structural description that not only serves as a basis for semantic interpretation, but also accurately reflects the native speaker's intuitions about such sentential properties as grammaticality, ambiguity, and systematic paraphrase. Indeed, the native speaker's judgments about these matters constitute a major source of evidence for the design of the knowledge component.

These requirements on the knowledge component are very similar to the conditions of adequacy for a transformational grammar (Chomsky, 1965), and indeed, the model of competence proposed by the linguist might in fact be a realization of a knowledge component. But there is one crucial difference: A competence grammar need not have anything to do with performance, with psychological processes. The knowledge component, however, is assessed as to how well it can be combined with a process component. The process component is a model of the psychological operations involved in sentence comprehension. It is realized as an imaginary computing device, a *processor*, which interprets the abstract linguistic information provided in the knowledge component and applies it in the analysis of particular inputs. The processor furnishes a basis for *testing* the theory against actual human performance by specifying various processing resources that will be expended at different points in the analysis of a sentence. These could include such items as memory load and processing effort, and the theory must indicate how these are to correspond to measurable aspects of human performance. (For more details and a fuller discussion of some psychological tests of these issues, see Kaplan, 1974.) It might be the case that a linguistic competence grammar could serve as the knowledge component of a comprehension model. It might allow for interactions with a process component in a revealing way. This was an early approach to building comprehension models, most clearly expressed in the Derivational Theory of Complexity.

The Derivational Theory of Complexity (for example, Fodor and Garrett, 1966) incorporates a linguistically motivated transformational grammar as the formal model of syntactic knowledge. The associated processor has not been specified in full detail, but the application of a single transformation in a sentence's grammatical derivation is taken as the basic unit of processing effort. In the early 1960's, the bulk of the experimental results seemed to support this model of comprehension. For example, Miller and McKean (1964) found that the passive and negative transformations had an additive effect on cognitive complexity. However, a series of later studies went against the transformational complexity metric. For example, Slobin (1968) observed a *reduction* in psychological difficulty when the agent-deletion rule is applied in passive sentences. Thus, it appears that a count of transformations applied is not a good predictor of human processing effort, and most attempts to construct transformationally based accounts of comprehension have been abandoned.

Perceptual Strategies. The basic notion underlying a theory of perceptual strategies is that the language comprehender is sensitive to the superficial properties of sentences. He follows a set of relatively simple strategies to discover the grammatical relationships present in sentences. The most elaborate discussion of this approach has been provided by Bever (1970).

Consider the following sentence:

(1)   Tarzan ate bananas until Jane came home.

This sentence has two clauses in it, each essentially a self-contained sentence. The person who hears or reads sentence 1 has two problems to solve: He must determine first the grammatical relationship that holds between the two clauses and then the internal structure of each. Bever suggests that people use at least two strategies to do this. First, the first noun-verb-noun sequence in the sentence is initially taken to be the main clause. Second, within each clause the first noun is taken to be the subject, the verb is the action, and the second noun the object. Bever argues that strategies of this nature provide a useful guide for the language comprehender, leading rapidly to the correct interpretation of the sentence in the majority of cases. In sentences for which the perceptual strategies fail, there is usually difficulty in comprehending the sentence, as in:

(2)   The boat floated down the river sank.

In sentence 2, the perceptual strategy assigns the status of subject and object incorrectly, so that when the reader of the sentence has completed the analysis with the word "river," the presence of the word "sank" causes momentary confusion. This is resolved only when he realizes that the perceptual strategy led to an erroneous first impression, and that the sentence is actually equivalent to

(3)   The boat that floated down the river sank.

A collection of strategies by themselves constitute neither a complete nor a coherent model of comprehension. There are several difficulties. Each strategy in the collection is a *heuristic*, often helpful, but not guaranteed to work in all cases. Sentences for which the strategies fail are indeed often more complex to comprehend than those for which the strategies work, but nonetheless, they are still comprehensible. The simple statement of the perceptual strategies is insufficient in that it does not cover all possible situations and it does not specify what should take place when the strategies fail.

AUGMENTED TRANSITION NETWORKS

In this section I present a formal notation for representing information about syntactic possibilities. Like the formalism of transformational grammar, this notation permits intuitions about linguistic structure to be expressed in a precise and revealing way. Along with the notation, I provide the general outline of a processor that interprets the notation, applying the grammatical descriptions to determine the logical relationships conveyed by particular input sentences. I also point out a variety of resources needed by the processor to carry out its computations. The operations of the processor and the resources it requires appear to be plausible predictors of human processing. This impression is substantiated by experimental evidence mentioned in later sections.

The notation presented here is closely related to the *augmented transition network* (ATN) formalism for natural language grammars. It has evolved from previous work by Woods (1970), Bobrow and Fraser (1969), and Thorne, Bratley, and Dewar (1968). I explored its psychological relevance (Kaplan, 1972), and demonstrated its capacity for formalizing a number of Bever's (1970) perceptual strategies. The Woods and Kaplan papers are both recommended because they include examples more detailed than those presented in this chapter. The processor is an extension and generalization of syntactic analysis programs devised by Kay (1973) and Woods (1973); Kaplan (1973a, 1973b) provides a technical discussion of the principles underlying its design.

Basic Mechanisms

I start with the linguistic observation that the words of simple noun-verb-noun sentences in English fulfill the syntactic functions of subject, action, and object, respectively. A notation for formalizing this fact is presented in Figure 5.1: The notation describes how *functional names* are to be assigned to *sequences* of linguistic elements. The arrows in Figure 5.1 are called *arcs* and they represent the temporal sequence of elements—N (for noun), V (for verb), and N. The

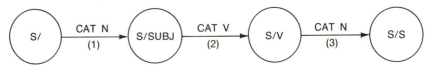

FIGURE 5.1
A simple transition network grammar. CAT N means that the word must fulfill the CATegory of noun. V stands for verb, S for sentence. The numbers in parentheses identify the arcs in the discussion.

Arc	Action
(1)	Assign the name SUBJECT to the current word.
(2)	Assign the name ACTION to the current word.
(3)	Assign the name OBJECT to the current word.

circles that join the arcs are called *states*. A *naming action* is associated with each of the arcs; these are listed in the table that accompanies the figure. In general terms, the processor works its way through both the words of an input sentence and the states and arcs of the diagram, formulating hypotheses about the logical relationships in which each word participates on the basis of its superficial context. Let us follow in detail the analysis of the simple sentence 4:

(4)   Tarzan likes Jane.

By convention, the starting point for the processor is the first word of the sentence and the state labeled S/.[2] The arc leaving this state has the label **CAT N**, so the processor consults the dictionary entry for "Tarzan" to see if it belongs to the grammatical **CAT**egory of nouns. Since the word "Tarzan" is marked as a noun, it satisfies the label on the arc. Hence, the associated action is executed, naming "Tarzan" as the **SUBJECT**. Then the processor performs a *transition*: It shifts its focus of attention to the state to which the arrow of the arc points (state **S/SUBJ**), and it examines the next word of the sentence.

At state **S/SUBJ**, the processor goes through a similar set of operations. It compares the current word ("likes") with the category specified by arc 2. Because the current word can be a verb, the condition is satisfied, so the word is named as the **ACTION**. Now the processor makes a transition to state **S/V**, and the next word in the sentence becomes the center of attention. In the same manner, "Jane" is named as the **OBJECT**, and when state **S/S** is reached, the syntactic analysis of the sentence is finished. The proper logical relationships have been determined and are represented by the list of functional names that have been assigned:

> [SUBJECT= "Tarzan"
>   ACTION= "likes"
>   OBJECT= "Jane"]

This summary of the sentence's syntactic structure is available for other comprehension components to use.

---

[2]States are given names that uniquely identify them to the processor. Other than being unique, there are no formal restrictions on how names are constructed. However, in working with more complex networks, it is helpful to adopt a convention of using mnemonic labels for states. Thus, the label S/ in Figure 5.1 identifies the first state of the network that describes a simple sentence (S); S/S is the last state of the sentence network; and other S/−labels give a rough indication of how far the analysis of the sentence is likely to have progressed by the time the state is reached. For example, the label S/SUBJ signifies that the state is entered after the SUBJECT has been found.

Alternatives and Scheduling. I now enrich the notation to allow the grammar to accept sentences in which noun phrases have determiners:

(5)   The ape likes Jane.

The expanded grammar is shown in Figure 5.2.

The first state in this new network has two arcs leaving it, arcs 1 and 4. This indicates that there are two ways in which a sentence may begin: either with a noun or with a determiner (DET). Notice that Figure 5.2 does not indicate the order in which the arcs should be considered. Although we could imagine processors capable of simultaneously exploring both possibilities, we shall assume a device that can examine only one arc at a time. Thus our processor must make a choice whenever it is faced with alternative possibilities, and our model of language comprehension must include a separate statement of just how the processor should *schedule* the examination of arcs at each state. For state **S/** the processor might be given this scheduling rule:

Try arc 1 before arc 4.

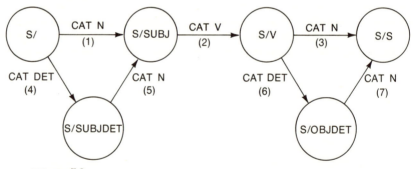

FIGURE 5.2
A simple transition network grammar that accepts Determiners (DET).

Arc	Action
(1)	Assign the name SUBJECT-HEAD to the current word.
(2)	Assign the name ACTION to the current word.
(3)	Assign the name OBJECT-HEAD to the current word.
(4)	Assign the name SUBJECT-DETERMINER to the current word.
(5)	Assign the name SUBJECT-HEAD to the current word.
(6)	Assign the name OBJECT-DETERMINER to the current word.
(7)	Assign the name OBJECT-HEAD to the current word.

To simplify the present discussion, rules of this sort are represented directly in the grammar diagrams instead of in separate lists. The order of arcs leaving a particular state corresponds to the appropriate scheduling rule. In effect, the processor examines the arcs in clockwise order, starting with the arc closest to the top of the circle.

The processor begins the analysis of sentence 5 by considering arc 1 and the word "the." Since "the" cannot be a noun, the transition specified by arc 1 cannot be performed. The processor therefore tries the next arc, arc 4. This time the transition is acceptable. The word "the" is named the **SUBJECT-DETERMINER** (as specified in the table of actions accompanying Figure 5.2). Now the processor's attention shifts to state **S/SUBJDET** with the current word being "ape." The analysis continues successfully to state **S/SUBJ**, and then, with the word "likes," to state **S/V**, where another ordering choice must be made. Following the scheduling rule, arc 3 is considered first. "Jane" is a noun, so arc 3 is successful, thereby completing the analysis of the sentence. Arcs 6 and 7 were not attempted in this sentence, but other sentences might require their use.

Seeking and Sending. The grammar illustrated in Figure 5.2 fails to express an important linguistic intuition, namely, that the constituents before and after a transitive verb in English permit the same syntactic patterns — they are both noun phrases. The redundant arc configurations at states **S/** and **S/V** are symptomatic of this failure. Figure 5.3 introduces a modification of the notation that allows intuitions about phrase structure to be captured. The grammar shown in Figure 5.3 describes the same sentence patterns as Figure 5.2.

Figure 5.3 shows two separate networks. The upper network corresponds to the main-clause grammar of Figures 5.1 and 5.2, while the lower one represents a subnetwork for the internal structure of noun phrases (abbreviated **NP**). In general, an ATN grammar can have any number of separate subnetworks, and the processor can be instructed to move back and forth between them. The instructions appear in the arc labels, which have been expanded so that they are now specified as one of three types:

CAT
SEEK
SEND

To see how this new description is interpreted, let us again analyze sentence 5:

(5)   The ape likes Jane.

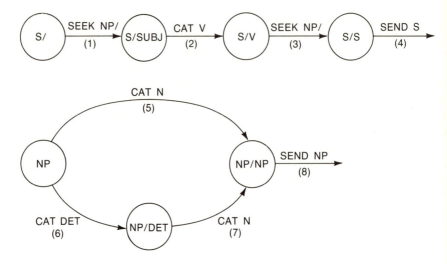

FIGURE 5.3
An augmented transition network that is equivalent to the grammar shown in Figure 5.2. The label **SEEK x** transfers control to the subnetwork at state **x**. The **SEND** arc resumes from where the **SEEK** was initiated (see text).

Arc	Action
(1)	Assign the name **SUBJECT** to the current phrase.
(2)	Assign the name **ACTION** to the current word.
(3)	Assign the name **OBJECT** to the current phrase.
(4)	None
(5)	Assign the name **HEAD** to the current word.
(6)	Assign the name **DETERMINER** to the current word.
(7)	Assign the name **HEAD** to the current word.
(8)	None

As before, the processor begins at state **S/**, comparing the arc leaving the state with the first word of the sentence. At this point in the analysis, a noun phrase is required: The processor must "seek out" a noun phrase. This operation is invoked by the label **SEEK NP/** on arc 1. In general, a label on an arc of the form **SEEK x** instructs the processor to shift its attention to the state labeled **x**. The current word does not change when a **SEEK** operation is performed.

Now the processor enters the separate subnetwork for **NP**. It starts by examining the arcs leaving state **NP/**, first considering arc 5, the one labeled **CAT N**. Since the current word, "The," cannot be interpreted as a noun, arc 5 is rejected, and arc 6 is attempted instead. This method succeeds, bringing the focus of attention to state **NP/DET** and making "ape" the current word. From state NP/DET, the processor makes the transition of arc 7 to state NP/NP, where the analysis of the noun phrase is complete. Arc 8 marks the end of the noun phrase subgrammar: The SEND NP label instructs the processor to shift its attention back to the arc that had originally requested the NP/ network. Thus, at the end of the phrase "The ape," the processor executes the naming action associated with arc 1 and continues at state S/SUBJ.

The word "likes" permits a successful transition of arc 2 to state S/V, where another SEEK NP/ arc is encountered. A sequence of events similar to the earlier sequence now takes place and, finally, when the second noun phrase is completed (the single word "Jane"), the processor again returns to the point from which it came. Thus, after this second traversal of the NP/ network, the arc 3 transition is resumed. At state S/S the sentence analysis is complete, as indicated by the instruction to the processor on arc 4: SEND S.

Notice that a simple list of functional names is no longer sufficient to represent the syntactic structure of this sentence. The NP/ grammar was invoked twice, and each time an assignment was made for the name HEAD. The SUBJECT and OBJECT HEADs are distinguished in the following way: The processor maintains a separate record of name assignments for each subnetwork that it enters. When a SEND arc is executed, the list of names for the current subnetwork is sent as a unit to the appropriate SEEK arc. The naming action on the SEEK applies to the whole list, not just a single word. The result is a hierarchical structure of names:

```
[TYPE = S
 SUBJECT = [TYPE = NP
            DETERMINER = "The"
            HEAD = "ape"]
 ACTION   = "likes"
 OBJECT   = [TYPE = NP
             HEAD = "Jane"] ]
```

Each level in this structure has an instance of the name TYPE to denote the kind of phrase being represented. The processor assigns a symbol x to this special name when it executes a SEND x arc.

The SEEK and SEND arcs provide a significant addition to the capabilities of the transition network notation. There are no restrictions on the states that a SEEK arc may refer to. Any part of the network can thus be used and reused by other parts. In particular, a SEEK arc located at one place in a grammar may refer to the subnetwork to which it itself belongs. For example, in order to handle sentences that contain embedded clauses, the network that describes main clauses must be able to use itself as one of its components. A simple description of this syntactic pattern would be impossible without the SEEK-SEND combination.

It is not enough to say *what* the processor should achieve for SEEK and SEND arcs; we must also specify *how* it is to do it. On encountering a SEND arc, the processor must be able to resume the particular SEEK arc that led to the SEND, and avoid returning to any others. In Figure 5.3, the processor must return to arc 1 after analyzing the subject noun phrase, not arc 3. Thus, the processor must have some way of remembering the sequence of SEEK arcs that led to the current subnetwork. Push-down stores are a simple mechanism for recording the necessary information, although there are other methods that permit greater scheduling flexibility (see Kaplan, 1973b, for a detailed discussion of this point). Whichever technique is used for scheduling and place keeping is also a prime candidate as a predictor of psychological complexity.

Expanding the Transition Network: Passive Sentences

The strategy of assigning the SUBJECT and ACTION roles to the first noun and verb is appropriate for active sentences, but it leads to the wrong interpretation for passives such as:

(6)   The apes were liked by Jane.

One way of handling passives is to add an alternative path all the way from state S/ to state S/S that describes the arrangement of phrases in passive sentences and assigns the correct names to them. However, instead of doing this, I shall use a less redundant and more intuitive grammatical description. Until the past participle verb is encountered, passives have the same form as actives:

(7)   The apes were thieves.

This fact can be expressed by using a single set of arcs to describe the common initial segment. In the analysis of sentence 6, the arcs instruct the processor to name "The apes" as the SUBJECT and "were" as the ACTION of the sentence. These tentative assignments are *revised* when the past participle and prepositional ("by") phrase are discovered. "The apes" is relabeled as the OBJECT, "Jane" is relabeled as the **SUBJECT**, and "were" is interpreted as an auxiliary to the main **ACTION** "liked." Figure 5.4 shows a transition network that handles active and passive sentences in this way. Arc 12 permits intransitive verbs, as in:

(8)   The ape slept.

Names.   The grammar shown in Figure 5.4 includes a variety of naming actions and a separate specification of additional conditions on the arcs. The naming operations specified in previous figures have only made assignments to the current word or phrase, and the assignments have only been used to create the final structural description of the sentence. However, the strategy for passives requires that names assigned at one point in a path through the grammar be open to revision later on along the path. Thus, Figure 5.4 illustrates several new ways of operating on names: An additional name can be assigned to a previously named element; a name can be removed from an element to which it was previously assigned; and a previously assigned name can be shifted to another element. An example of each of these actions is found on arc 9, the key arc for passive sentences.

Additional Conditions.   Up to now, the decision whether a transition is admissible has depended only on the current word in the sentence and the label on the current arc (**CAT V, SEEK NP/**, and so on). A **CAT** arc only accepts words belonging to a particular grammatical category, whereas a **SEEK** arc stipulates that a segment of the sentence beginning with the current word meet the requirements of another subnetwork. But the human listener is sensitive to certain constraints that hold between the current word and *preceding* elements of the sentence, and the notation outlined so far gives us no way to express them. Subject-verb agreement in English is a good example of such a constraint; it accounts for the fact that the ambiguity in sentence 9A is not perceived in (9B–C):

(9A)   Flying planes can be dangerous.

(9B)   Flying planes is dangerous.

(9C)   Flying planes are dangerous.

To permit constraints of this sort to be expressed, a new column has been added to the table that accompanies Figure 5.4. This column lists a set of additional conditions that must be met before the corresponding arc can be taken. These conditions usually involve lexical features of previously named constituents, although they can also be used to express more complicated constraints on the current element than the arc label permits. The table also introduces a notational abbreviation: The special name ✱ (called star) is used for the frequent references to the element that is currently the processor's focus of attention.

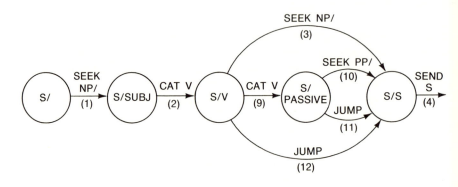

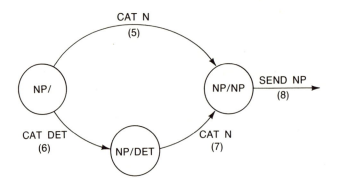

FIGURE 5.4

An augmented transition network grammar for passive and active sentences (having both transitive and intransitive verbs). This grammar has three subnetworks: one for sentences (S), one for noun phrases (NP), and one for prepositional phrases (PP).

Let us consider the analysis of sentence 6 to see how the grammar in Figure 5.4 operates.

(6)   The apes were liked by Jane.

As usual, the processor starts with the first word of the sentence at state S/. Thus, * names the word "The." The processor executes the SEEK NP/ found on arc 1, which brings it to the subnetwork for noun phrases. The phrase "The apes" is properly recognized as a noun and the processor returns to arc 1. Since the actions on a SEEK arc are executed with * referring to the structural description of the phrase just analyzed, "The apes" becomes the SUBJECT. Now the processor goes to state S/SUBJ, with * being the word "were."

At this point the processor is considering arc 2. The arc's label requires that the current word be a member of the category of verbs, while the table further stipulates that * be in tensed form, agreeing in

Table for Figure 5.4.

Arc	Additional conditions	Actions
(1)	None	Assign the name SUBJECT to *.
(2)	* must be a tensed form and must agree with SUBJECT in person and number.	Assign the name ACTION to *.
(3)	The ACTION must allow a noun phrase to follow it.	Assign the name OBJECT to *.
(4)	None	None
(5)	None	Assign the name HEAD to *.
(6)	None	Assign the name DETERMINER to *.
(7)	None	Assign the name HEAD to *.
(8)	None	None
(9)	* must be the past participle of a verb that can take the passive and the ACTION must be a form of "be."	Assign the name ACTION to *; assign the name OBJECT to SUBJECT; remove the name SUBJECT.
(10)	The prepositional phrase must start with the preposition "by."	Assign the name SUBJECT to the object of the preposition.
(11)	None	None
(12)	The ACTION does not require a noun phrase to follow it.	None
(13)	None	Assign PREP to *.
(14)	None	Assign PREPOBJ to *.
(15)	None	None

person and number with whatever constituent has been named as the
SUBJECT. Thus arc 2 would be disallowed if * were the word "was."
In the case of sentence 6, all the conditions are satisfied, so the word
"were" becomes the ACTION. Note that both the names SUBJECT and
ACTION have now been assigned incorrectly, given our intuitions
about the sentence's meaning. Arc 3 is scheduled first at state S/V, so
the subnetwork for noun phrases is entered with the word "liked" as
*. This time the result is unsatisfactory: * is neither a determiner nor
a noun, so the processor is blocked at state NP/.

This situation is a consequence of the scheduling rule for state
S/V. Arc 9 represents the possibility of a passive structure, and no
problem would have arisen if it had been scheduled first. Unfortunately, reversal of the scheduling rule does not offer a general
solution—it conceals the difficulty in this instance, but the problem
crops up again in active sentences such as (10):

(10)   The apes were frustrated thieves.

In sentence 10, attempting arc 9 first will lead to a block at state
S/PASSIVE, when the processor encounters the word "thieves"
instead of a by-phrase. The correct analysis of (10) is provided by arc
3, assuming an adjustment to the NP/ grammar to handle prenominal
participles. Thus, for either arc, ordering a perfectly comprehensible
sentence can cause the processor to block. Moreover, even if the
scheduling rules could be altered from one sentence to another,
there is no way of knowing before the arcs are actually attempted
which ordering is most promising for a given input sentence.

The Agenda.   To ensure that a successful analysis is arrived at for
every comprehensible sentence, the alternative arcs leaving a state
must be treated as truly independent possibilities. The fact that one
of them is successful does not mean that the processor can forget
about the others. Thus the notion of scheduling introduced earlier
must be greatly extended. The processor maintains a list of things to
do, called the *agenda*. When the processor makes a transition to a
new state, it does not simply attempt arcs in scheduled order until it
finds an acceptable one. Instead, it immediately places on the agenda
an entry for each arc at the state. An agenda entry consists of the following pieces of information:

> An arc to be attempted
> The position in the sentence at which to apply the arc
> A list of the names currently assigned
> A record of the SEEK arcs that led to the current subnetwork

An entry is thus a complete description of a computation to be performed, and the agenda itself is a record of all untried possibilities for every state in the network that the processor has reached.

The processor updates the agenda whenever it arrives at a new state. It then removes the top-most entry and executes it. If the arc is successful, this updating procedure is repeated at the following state; if the arc fails, no change is made to the agenda. In any event, the entry that ends up at the top of the agenda determines the next move the processor will make.

The rules for scheduling the arcs at each state, which have been represented by the order of arcs in the network diagrams, must now be interpreted with respect to the agenda. They define the relative order in which entries for arcs at a given state will be added. Thus, the fact that arc 3 appears before arc 9 means that the entry for arc 3 will therefore be executed first. But if arc 3 results in a block, as it does for sentence 6, the processor will eventually retrieve and execute the arc 9 entry, which leads to the correct analysis. Given the concept of an agenda, our model of language comprehension must include scheduling rules of a different sort. The processor must be told not only the relative order of arcs at each state, but also the order of arcs at a new state with respect to entries already on the agenda. There are two particularly simple rules of this type: All new entries can be placed either below or above all other items on the agenda. Placing them at the bottom of the agenda results in what is usually called a *breadth-first* application of a grammar to a sentence. If they are placed at the top, the result is a *depth-first* search strategy.

Back to the Passive.   The processing examples just discussed have implicitly assumed a depth-first scheduling rule, and I shall maintain this discipline to continue the analysis of sentence 6. In accordance with these extended rules, the processor will still move forward to state S/V, and agenda entries will be constructed for arcs 3, 9, and 12 at the current word "liked." The arc 3 entry will be removed and executed first, resulting in new entries for the arcs at state NP/. The agenda now has entries for arcs 5, 6, 9, and 12. Arcs 5 and 6 are unsuccessfully attempted, and the arc 9 entry reaches the top of the agenda. With "liked" as the current word, this transition is acceptable, and the actions instruct the processor to revise the set of names it has accumulated. It now recognizes that "were" is not the main verb, but rather is a marker for the passive construction. The present word, "liked," is actually the main ACTION, and what was earlier thought to be the SUBJECT ("The apes") is in reality the OBJECT. The arc 9 transition thus corrects the erroneous initial hypothesis about the structure of this sentence.

Arc 9 leads to state **S/PASSIVE** with "by" as the current word and with the logical **SUBJECT** of the sentence not yet known. Arc 10 **SEEK**s the subnetwork for prepositional phrases (state **PP/**) and serves to identify "Jane" as the **SUBJECT** of the sentence. Once this has been done, the analysis of the sentence is finished. Notice that the final name assignments for sentence 6 are identical to the assignments for the corresponding active:

(11)   Jane liked the apes.

Like the passive rule of a transformational grammar, this network thus expresses the intuition that corresponding passives and actives are paraphrases.

Jumping. The transition network of Figure 5.4 is capable of handling other types of sentences. Two arcs in the figure have not yet been explained: the two labeled **JUMP** (arcs 11 and 12). An arc of type **JUMP** allows the processor to bypass some stages of analysis by "jumping" to a new state without making the normal change in ∗. For example, the subject may be omitted from passive sentences in English by leaving out the prepositional phrase headed by the word "by." In this case, the **JUMP** on arc 11 allows the sentence analysis to terminate successfully without discovering the subject noun phrase. Similarly, arc 12 provides for the possibility that the verb is not followed by an object.

PREDICTING PSYCHOLOGICAL PROCESSES

The grammar shown in Figure 5.4 is still but a miniscule fraction of the syntactic knowledge that would be required for an adequate characterization of the sentences of English. Nevertheless, the notation illustrated in these examples is sufficient for much more extensive syntactic descriptions. Chapter 6 presents an ATN grammar for a reasonably large subset of English, and another large grammar has been designed by Woods and Kaplan (1971). But syntactic knowledge is only one component of an explanatory theory of comprehension. The preceding sections have defined a processor to go along with the notation and to serve as a psychological process component. I conclude this chapter with a brief discussion of the possible correspondence between the operations of the processor and human cognitive operations.

As it applies a particular grammar to an input sentence, the processor must remember several kinds of information and perform a variety of computations. To interpret the grammar correctly, the processor utilizes memory resources for keeping track of:

Functional names assigned
SEEK arcs to be returned to
Entries on the agenda

Computational effort is expended in the following ways:

Attempting arcs
Taking arcs of different types (CAT, SEEK, SEND, JUMP)
Updating the agenda
Assigning names
Revising name assignments
Checking additional conditions

The strongest claim about this framework for explaining comprehension is that these properties of the processor are direct analogs of human sentence-processing mechanisms. Given an intuitively satisfying grammar and a relatively simple set of scheduling rules, the operations performed by the processor in analyzing an input sentence correspond to the mental processes of the native speaker who comprehends the same sentence.

This claim, of course, requires empirical validation, and this is not an easy task. The native speaker's mental processes are not available for direct inspection. Their nature must be inferred from fairly crude observations of comprehension performances, which, for the most part, have to do with the difficulty experienced in processing different sentences under various experimental conditions. Thus, acceptance of the strong correspondence claim depends on the validation of a somewhat weaker hypothesis: The observable cognitive complexity of a sentence is a simple function of the memory and computational effort needed by the processor to analyze it. In terms of the types of memory and operations previously listed, a simple weighted sum of the number of operations of each type should be a good predictor of cognitive complexity.

At present very little experimental evidence exists that can be brought to bear on the validation of this approach to explaining comprehension. The experiments that have been performed appear promising, however. My experiments on processing load (Kaplan, 1974) and the experiments of my colleagues (Wanner, Kaplan, and Shiner, 1974; Wanner and Maratsos, 1974) on the psychological issues involved in the processing of relative clauses show that the augmented transition network grammar can be a powerful tool for our understanding of psychological mechanisms.

CHAPTER 6

Errors in Reading: An Analysis Using an Augmented Transition Network Model of Grammar

ALBERT L. STEVENS and DAVID E. RUMELHART

The process of reading requires the integration of all levels of representation of the text. An active reader does more than simply decode the visual information before him, letter by letter, word by word. Information flow goes in all directions. While the visual and perceptual system is passing up the results of their analyses to higher-level processes, semantic and syntactic systems are passing their information down to bias the perceptual systems. The eventual process of textual reading requires the integration of the bottom-up analysis (working up from the physical features) and the top-down analysis (working dowm from semantic and syntactic considerations).[1]

---

[1] The phrases "bottom-up" and "top-down" are derived from the computer science literature. Consider the tree structure diagram that represents the structure of a sentence. The completely analyzed sentence appears at the top of the diagram; the semantic and syntactical analysis comprises the middle portion of the tree, and the words, or phonetic and visual symbols of the language string, appear at the bottom. Top-down analysis starts at the top of the diagram and works its way down. Bottom-up analysis starts with an analysis of the physical inputs and tries to piece them together in order to work its way up the diagram. We believe that both processes go on at the same time. The tree structure is, of course, highly oversimplified, and the actual processing is not so easily classified into higher- or lower-order components. Nonetheless, the analogy still provides a useful overview.

Empirical evidence on reading comes from several sources. For example, Tulving and Gold (1963) demonstrated that words presented tachistoscopically are recognized correctly more often when they are presented in the context of a sentence than when they are presented in isolation. Goodman (1965) demonstrated that children are far better at reading words in the context of a meaningful passage than in a nonstructured list. These studies show that information derived from the linguistic structure of discourse can be used to aid the recognition of words. Furthermore, most errors in oral reading can be explained by assuming that readers are depending so heavily on linguistic types of information that they actually ignore a certain amount of the visual information (Kolers, 1969; Goodman, 1965). These errors are often visually similar to the correct word, but equally important, they obey linguistic rules that govern their relationship to the rest of the discourse. The errors typically remain uncorrected unless they do not fit with subsequent words.

These studies all suggest that a major component of the reading process must be the interaction of syntax and semantics with sensory analysis. All current models that attempt to characterize the way extravisual contextual information aids word recognition have either taken the effect of each different context as a parameter (Morton, 1970) or proposed a simple equation to characterize context (Rumelhart and Siple, 1974; see Smith and Spoehr, 1974, for a review). In reading, the context is continuously changing. The model that accounts for the reading process must contain a dynamic component that reflects the changing effect of context.

THE SYNTACTICAL ANALYSIS

Consider what a skilled reader must do. He wishes to read the material that is before him, but at a rapid rate. If he is to read textual material at rates in excess of 300 words per minute, he does not have time to go through the identification process for each word as if it were presented in isolation. Fortunately, there is no need to do this. By using his knowledge of the textual material—the conceptual contents, the semantic interpretation, and the syntactic constraints—the skilled reader effectively limits the number of possible alternatives that need be considered at each point in the text. The act of reading becomes, in part, the act of confirmation—confirming that a word from the set of those predicted is in fact present.

A good model of the syntactical analysis of language helps us analyze the process of reading, for it tells us at each point within the sentence just what class of words can be expected to follow. The parser that was described by Kaplan in Chapter 5, the *augmented transition network* (ATN) parser, has several advantages as a component of a model of the reading process. It has a great deal of psychological plausibility. For the purposes of the study reported in this chapter, the most important aspect of the ATN system is its predictive nature. This means that following each word in the sentence there is an explicitly ordered set of expectations with respect to the syntactic class and other characteristics of the next word.

Clearly, syntactic information alone is not sufficient to characterize the structures involved in the reading process. Semantic, pragmatic, and other knowledge must also interact with the visual analysis. Nonetheless, syntactic analyses must play a large role in determining the reading process, and it is instructive to see just how far the analysis of reading can be carried on the basis of syntactic considerations alone.

Accordingly, the plan of the present studies was as follows. First, we selected two prose passages for our study that would be well characterized by a particular implementation of an ATN parser. Then, we examined a reader's performance under two basic conditions: *prediction* and *reading aloud*. In the prediction studies the subject was shown a section of text and was required to predict the word that would follow next. If he was wrong, he was asked to make a second prediction, and if wrong again, a third. In the reading studies, the subject was asked to read the textual material aloud. His verbal output was tape recorded and analyzed to determine the pattern of reading errors. In one of the reading-aloud conditions, the subjects read normal type (all capital letters). In the second reading-aloud condition, the type was visually degraded. We did this in order to increase errors by reducing the quality of the visual input.

At each state of the parsing model the set of possible arcs serves as our model of a subject's expectations with respect to syntactic structures. If, during the parse of a sentence, the subject should make an incorrect transition, problems encountered later in the text may force him to back up and try a different arc.

We compared the performance of the ATN parser both in matching the predictions of the subjects and in accounting for the types of errors that they make while reading aloud. We found that the ATN grammar that was optimal for parsing the sentences in the two texts also turned out to match the subject's predictions quite well. The same grammar also accounted for substitution and insertion errors that were made when subjects read aloud.

The Parser

Following the principles of an ATN parser (see Ronald Kaplan's chapter), we constructed a grammar that was capable of handling the sentences in the experimental texts that we presented to the subjects.

We selected two different texts from a study guide for the preparation for the Graduate Record Examination (Turner, 1972). One text, on Keynesian economics, was about 500 words long, divided into four paragraphs. The other, on the vocabulary of trades, was 310 words long divided into three paragraphs. Each text was edited slightly so that the second and third paragraphs of each could be handled by the grammar that we were studying. An excerpt from each text is shown in Figures 6.1 and 6.2.

DIFFERENT OCCUPATIONS DIFFER IN THE CHARACTER OF THEIR SPECIAL VOCABULARIES. THE TECHNICAL VOCABULARY OF TRADES THAT HAVE OCCUPIED GREAT NUMBERS OF MEN SINCE REMOTE TIMES IS VERY OLD. IT CONSISTS OF WORDS THAT HAVE WORKED THEMSELVES INTO THE FIBRE OF OUR LANGUAGE. THUS THE TECHNICAL VOCABULARIES OF BOTH FARMING AND FISHING ARE GENERALLY UNDERSTOOD. THE SPECIAL DIALECTS OF SUCH PROFESSIONS AS LAW, MEDICINE, DIVINITY AND PHILOSOPHY HAVE BECOME FAMILIAR TO CULTIVATED PERSONS AND THEREBY THESE DIALECTS HAVE CONTRIBUTED MANY WORDS TO THE POPULAR VOCABULARY. NEVERTHELESS, EVERY VOCATION POSSESSES A LARGE BODY OF TECHNICAL TERMS THAT REMAIN FOREIGN.

FURTHERMORE, THE PROPORTION OF THESE TERMS RAPIDLY INCREASED IN THE LAST FIFTY YEARS. FOR EXAMPLE, NEW TERMS ARE RAPIDLY COINED IN THE NATURAL SCIENCES, AND THEN THEY ARE ABANDONED WHEN THEY HAVE SERVED THEIR TURN. MOST OF THE NEW COINAGES ARE CONFINED TO SPECIAL DISCUSSIONS AND THEY SELDOM GET INTO GENERAL CONVERSATION. YET, NO PROFESSION IS A CLOSED GUILD. FURTHERMORE, POPULAR SCIENCE ACQUAINTS EVERYONE BOTH WITH MODERN VIEWS AND WITH RECENT DISCOVERIES. AN IMPORTANT EXPERIMENT IS IMMEDIATELY REPORTED IN THE NEWSPAPERS AND EVERYONE IS SOON TALKING ABOUT IT. THUS, OUR COMMON SPEECH IS ALWAYS MAKING NEW TECHNICAL TERMS COMMONPLACE.

FIGURE 6.1
Keynesian economics.
SOURCE: Adapted from *How to Pass High on the Graduate Record Examination Aptitude Test*. New York: Arco, 1972, p. 166.

We constructed a simple ATN grammar that was consistent with the sets of sentences that would be analyzed. (Only the second and third paragraphs of each text were analyzed.) The ATN grammar is shown in Figure 6.3.[2] There are six subnetworks. Parsing begins with the network for declarative sentences (called *statements*). The statement network can require use of the other ones. Thus, in the statement network, state ST/1 can perform a SEEK to either the NP (noun phrase) network or the PP (prepositional phrase) network. Similarly, state ST/2 of the statement network requires a SEEK to the VP (verb phrase). The RCL network is sought only from state NP/3 of the noun phrase network. The last network, that for *sentential complements* (SC), is only invoked during the transition from NP/1 to NP/5 of the noun phrase network. The sentential complement network then requires a SEEK to the statement network. (A sentential complement occurs when a sentence contains another sentence within it; for example, "John knew **that Mary went to the store.**"

The statement network allows a sentence to have an initial noun phrase, followed by a verb phrase, in turn followed by an unspecified number of optional prepositional phrases. (By verb phrase, here we mean verb, optional auxiliary verbs, and optional adverbs: "was slowly running" is a verb phrase). All arguments of the verb (such things as object, instrument, location, and time) are parsed by the prepositional phrase subnetwork (PP), which allows for a deleted or nonexistent preposition when the phrase is the objective argument of the verb. The statement network also allows the verb to take adjectives or adverb-adjective pairs as arguments when there are predicate adjectives.

The noun phrase network is the most complicated of those presented. Its core is the three states NP/1, NP/2, and NP/3, which accept an optional determiner or possessive pronoun, a series of optional adjectives, and a noun. Certain relational nouns may take arguments (hence the SEEK PP/1 arc) and also may be modified by relative clauses. The noun phrase network also parses certain other constituents that can serve as arguments to the main verb. These include

---

[2]The notation shown here differs slightly from that used by Kaplan in Chapter 5 in two ways. First, whereas Kaplan named the states in the ATN system mnemonically, we have chosen to select the initial part of the name of a state to reflect the part of speech being analyzed, and simply to provide a number for the second part of the name. Thus, the first two states of our statement network are named ST/1 and ST/2. Kaplan would have named them, perhaps, ST/ and ST/SUBJ. Second, we permit a SEEK to enter a network at any state, not just the first state. Thus the relative clause (RCL) subnetwork has in it a SEEK ST/2 arc, which indicates that the parser goes to the statement network, starting at the state labeled ST/2 (where it is looking for a verb phrase). This condition is in fact allowed and was used by Kaplan in his parser, but the networks that were described in Chapter 5 never reached the level of complexity that would have required this notation to be explained.

pronouns, a verb suffixed with -ing followed by its arguments, infinitive phrases, and sentential complements. We did not consider conjunctions and adverbial transition elements in applying the ATN grammar to the passages. This required us to skip some words in the analysis. For example, the words not used in the paragraphs shown in Figures 6.1 and 6.2 are underlined. A total of 217 words for the Keynes passage and 152 for the trades passage were included in the analysis.

MOVEMENTS IN RATES OF INTEREST PLAYED A COMPLEMENTARY ROLE BY INSURING THAT ALL INCOME WOULD ULTIMATELY BE SPENT. THUS, IF PEOPLE DECIDED TO INCREASE THEIR SAVINGS, THE RATES OF INTEREST ON THE MORE ABUNDANT SUPPLY OF LOANABLE FUNDS WOULD FALL. THIS WOULD LEAD TO INCREASED INVESTMENT. THE ADDED OUTLAYS FOR INVESTMENT GOODS WOULD OFFSET THE DIMINISHED OUTLAYS BY THE MORE FRUGAL CONSUMERS. IN THIS FASHION, CHANGES IN BOTH CONSUMER SPENDING AND INVESTMENT DECISIONS WERE KEPT FROM CAUSING ANY CHANGE IN TOTAL SPENDING THAT WOULD LEAD TO UNEMPLOYMENT.

KEYNES ARGUED THAT NEITHER WAGE MOVEMENTS NOR CHANGES IN THE RATE OF INTEREST NECESSARILY HAD THIS AGREEABLE EFFECT. HE FOCUSED ATTENTION ON THE TOTAL OF PURCHASING POWER IN THE ECONOMY. THIS TOTAL IS CALLED AGGREGATE DEMAND. REDUCTIONS OF WAGES MIGHT NOT INCREASE EMPLOYMENT; THEY MIGHT MERELY REDUCE AGGREGATE DEMAND. FURTHERMORE, HE HELD THAT INTEREST WAS NOT THE PRICE THAT WAS PAID TO PEOPLE TO SAVE BUT THAT IT WAS THE PRICE THAT THEY GOT FOR EXCHANGING HOLDINGS OF CASH FOR LESS LIQUID FORMS OF INVESTMENT. AND IT WAS DIFFICULT TO REDUCE INTEREST BEYOND A CERTAIN LEVEL. ACCORDINGLY, IF PEOPLE SOUGHT TO SAVE MORE MONEY, THIS WOULDN'T NECESSARILY MEAN EITHER LOWER RATES OF INTEREST OR A RESULTING INCREASE IN INVESTMENT. INSTEAD, THE TOTAL DEMAND FOR GOODS MIGHT FALL UNTIL SAVINGS WERE BROUGHT BACK IN LINE WITH INVESTMENT BY THE PRESSURE OF HARDSHIP WHICH HAD REDUCED SAVINGS IN FAVOR OF CONSUMPTION. THE ECONOMY WOULD NOT FIND ITS EQUILIBRIUM AT FULL EMPLOYMENT, BUT IT WOULD FIND EQUILIBRIUM WITH SOME UNSPECIFIED AMOUNT OF UNEMPLOYMENT.

FIGURE 6.2
The vocabulary of trades.
SOURCE: Adapted from *How to Pass High on the Graduate Record Examination Aptitude Test.* New York: Arco, 1972, p. 276.

FIGURE 6.3

The augmented transition network (ATN) grammar
used for the analyses in this chapter.

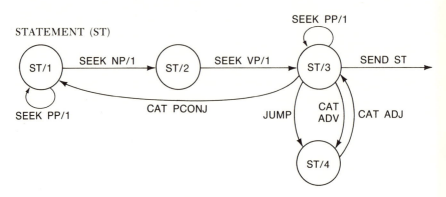

STATEMENT (ST)

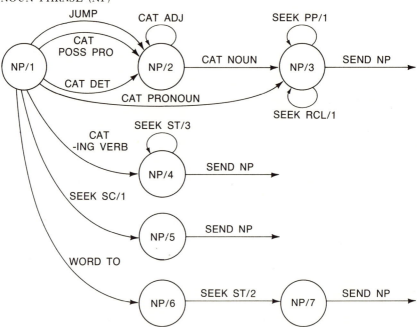

NOUN PHRASE (NP)

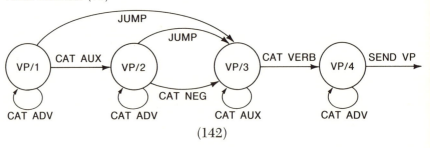

VERB PHRASE (VP)

(142)

PREPOSITIONAL PHRASE (PP)

RELATIVE CLAUSE (RCL)

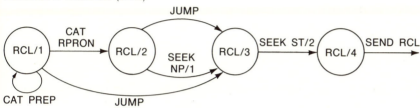

SENTENTIAL COMPLEMENT (SC)

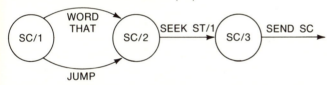

Terms used in the ATN Diagram

ADJ	Adjective	POSS PRO	Possessive pronoun
ADV	Adverb	PP	Prepositional phrase
AUX	Auxiliary verb	PREP	Preposition
CAT	Category; arcs so labeled require a single word of a particular syntactic class, the name of which also appears on the arc.	SC	Sentential complement; an embedded sentence, usually preceded by the word "that."
DET	Determiner	SEEK	Indicates that the state named after the word SEEK should be entered.
-ING VERB	A verb nominalized with an -ing suffix.		
JUMP	Jump; a transfer to another state in the grammar made without using a word in the input string.	SEND	Indicates a return to the state from which the subnetwork was entered.
		ST	Statement; a declarative sentence.
NEG	Negation	VP	Verb phrase
NP	Noun phrase	WORD	Word; arcs so labeled require a particular word whose name also appears on the arc.
PCONJ	Propositional conjunction; used to join two complete propositions, usually "because," "while," and so on.		

EXPERIMENTAL METHOD

There were three separate experiments. In the *prediction* experiment, subjects were asked to anticipate words in a text. In the *normal reading* experiment, we tape recorded our subjects while they read aloud from a text displayed on a television screen. In the *degraded reading* experiment, the conditions were the same as in the *normal reading* experiment, but the contrast of the display was reduced so that the text was difficult to read.

Materials

The materials used were the same for all three experiments: Excerpts from the passages are shown in Figures 6.1 and 6.2 and have already been discussed.

General Procedure

The subjects were tested individually in acoustically isolated booths. The facilities are illustrated in Figure 6.4

Each booth contained a 19-inch black and white television monitor, a small display oscilloscope, a typewriter keyboard, and microphones. The keyboard was slightly to the left of the subject, and the display oscilloscope was above it. The television monitor was slightly to the right of the subject.

The experiment was controlled by the laboratory's PDP-15 computer (Digital Equipment Corporation). The textual display was generated and maintained by a VST-2000 computer terminal, which transmitted the text as a video signal to the room monitor. The display consisted of all capital letters (as illustrated in Figures 6.1 and 6.2). Only one paragraph was displayed at a time. Whenever the subject responded on the typewriter keyboard, his typed words appeared on the display oscilloscope above the keyboard. The computer presented the text, started and stopped the audio tape recorder, and monitored the keyboard.

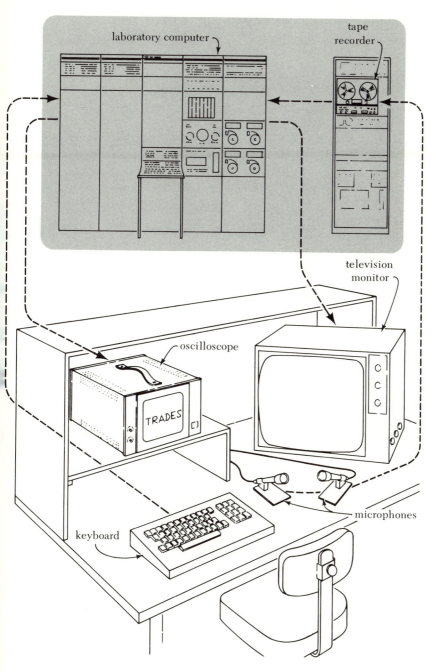

FIGURE 6.4

THE PREDICTION EXPERIMENT

Procedure

Twenty-four undergraduate subjects at the University of California, San Diego, participated in the experiment as part of a course requirement. Each also participated in the normal reading experiment. Subjects were divided into two groups, twelve making predictions about the Keynes passage and twelve making predictions about the trades passage.

The procedure was as follows. The first paragraph of the passage selected for the subject was displayed on the television screen. The subject read that paragraph to himself. This paragraph familiarized the subject with the style and content of the text. When he finished, he pressed a key on the keyboard, starting the prediction phase of the experiment. At this point, the first paragraph was removed from the screen and several words from the next, as yet unseen, paragraph were displayed in its place. The subject was required to predict the word that would follow the last word being displayed by typing his response on the typewriter keyboard. The word that he typed was displayed for him on the display oscilloscope. He signaled completion of the response by depressing the carriage return key. If he was correct, the computer displayed the word "CORRECT" on the oscilloscope; otherwise, it allowed him a second and a third guess. Then, the next three words from the paragraph were added to the television screen and the procedure was repeated. (The first of these words, of course, was the one that the subject had been trying to predict.) When the entire paragraph was on the screen, the display was erased and the procedure was repeated for the third paragraph of the text. At the beginning of the paragraph, the number of words that were displayed initially varied from one to three so that each word in each paragraph was predicted by four of the twelve subjects.

The subjects were instructed that the experimenter was interested only in what they thought the next word would be. They were instructed not to attempt to engage in problem solving, but simply to respond with the first words that came to mind. If they could think of no words (or no second or third alternative), they simply depressed a sufficient number of carriage returns to cause the computer to increment the display. All the predictions were stored and analyzed after the session was over.

Results

We analyzed the predictions in the following manner. For each prediction point we computed just where the subject should be in the ATN. We then tabulated, for each state, the number of times the subject's predictions were generated as a result of traversing each of the possible arcs. It was not always possible to determine precisely which arc was being taken, so a number of conventions were employed in making the tabulation:

- Because it is nearly always true that a noun can be used attributively, in which case it is grammatically an adjective, it often was not possible to determine which arc in NP/2 the subject was using. For these predictions, words that are unambiguously adjectives were classified as adjectives, and all the rest were assumed to be nouns.

- In the case of quantifiers such as "most" and "each," a determination of syntactic category is not possible, so a separate category labeled adjective or noun was constructed and is included in Table 6.1.

- In NP/1, determiners or pronouns such as "this" and "these" are ambiguous and therefore were given a separate category.

- For the same reasons, auxiliaries or verbs such as "be" and "have" were also given a special category.

- Prepositions at the end of a noun phrase can be either in NP/3 or in ST/3. In such cases, we assumed that if the preposition could apply to the noun, then it did (see Hill, 1968). Otherwise, it was assumed to modify the verb and hence was in state ST/3.

The proportion of times each arc was taken for each state is shown in the first column of Table 6.1. It is interesting that the syntactic class of the predictions seems to depend primarily on the state of the grammar from which the subject is predicting. This follows from the degree of consistency with which subjects "choose" the same arc when in a particular state. In fact, the most frequent arc was selected 75 percent of the time. This seems to suggest that there is a reasonably fixed ordering of expectations, conditional only on the state of the network as assessed by the ATN model.

As a point of comparison, we thought it useful to perform a similar analysis on the passages themselves to see if, in fact, the subjects' expectations are realistic and do follow English usage. Thus, each sentence in the passages was analyzed and a tabulation of the proportion of times each arc was traversed from each state was constructed.

The results of this tabulation are shown in column 2 of Table 6.1. It is obvious that the subjects' predictions agree well with the structure of the passages and the ordering of the ATN arcs.

The subjects made a total of 2738 predictions. Of these, 96.7 percent are accepted by the grammar, 1.5 percent are grammatical but

TABLE 6.1
Proportions of transitions from each state in the grammar for subjects' predictions, the actual passages, and reading errors. (Numbers in parentheses are the number of times that state was entered.)

		Statement			
		Subjects' predictions from the prediction experiment	Actual passages	Reading experiments	
				Normal text: substitution errors	Degraded text: substitution errors
State	Arc				
ST/1		(36)	(5)	(1)	(1)
	NP/1	0.972	1.000	1.000	1.000
	PP/1	0.028	0.000	0.000	0.000
ST/2		(423)	(47)	(10)	(32)
	VP/1	1.000	1.000	1.000	1.000
ST/3		(495)	(66)	(10)	(13)
	PP/1	0.873	0.894	0.800	0.692
	JUMP	0.071	0.061	0.200	0.231
	PCONJ	0.030	0.030	0.000	0.077
	ADV	0.026	0.025	0.000	0.000
ST/4		(50)	(5)	(2)	(3)
	ADJ	1.000	1.000	1.000	1.000

		Verb Phrase			
VP/1		(598)	(55)	(10)	(38)
	JUMP	0.448	0.418	0.400	0.921
	AUX	0.198	0.527	0.200	0.026
	ADV	0.033	0.055	0.000	0.026
	AUX or VERB	0.319	—	0.400	0.026
VP/2		(268)	(35)	(8)	(9)
	JUMP	0.858	0.714	1.000	0.556
	ADV	0.104	0.229	0.000	0.333
	NEG	0.037	0.057	0.000	0.111
VP/3		(558)	(52)	(12)	(38)
	VERB	0.934	0.981	0.917	0.974
	AUX	0.005	0.019	0.000	0.000
	AUX or VERB	0.061	—	0.083	0.026
VP/4		(440)	(49)	(8)	(9)
	SEND	0.955	0.980	1.000	1.000
	ADV	0.045	0.020	0.000	0.000

TABLE 6.1 *(continued)*

		Subjects' predictions from the prediction experiment	Actual passages	Reading experiments	
				Normal text: substitution errors	Degraded text: substitution errors
State	Arc				
Prepositional Phrase, Relative Clause and Sentential Complement					
PP/1		(649)	(92)	(13)	(16)
	PREP	0.607	0.620	0.615	0.563
	JUMP	0.393	0.380	0.385	0.437
PP/2		(700)	(92)	(18)	(23)
	NP/2	1.000	1.000	1.000	1.000
RCL/1		(49)	(7)	(1)	(2)
	RPRO	0.735	1.000	1.000	0.500
	JUMP	0.265	0.000	0.000	0.500
RCL/2		(85)	(7)	(3)	(3)
	JUMP	0.800	0.857	1.000	1.000
	NP/1	0.200	0.153	0.000	0.000
RCL/3		(67)	(7)	(3)	(4)
	ST/2	1.000	1.000	1.000	1.000
SC/1		(46)	(3)	(1)	(0)
	"THAT"	1.000	1.000	0.000	—
	JUMP	0.000	0.000	1.000	—
SC/2		(36)	(3)	(1)	(1)
	ST/2	1.000	1.000	1.000	1.000
Noun Phrase					
NP/1		(1057)	(95)	(18)	(21)
	JUMP	0.525	0.568	0.444	0.381
	DET	0.245	0.221	0.111	0.524
	PPRO	0.053	0.076	0.056	0.048
	-ING	0.044	0.032	0.056	0.000
	SC/1	0.044	0.032	0.056	0.000
	PRO	0.039	0.076	0.000	0.048
	"TO"	0.014	0.042	0.000	0.000
	DET or PRO	0.036	—	0.056	0.000
NP/2		(1691)	(155)	(21)	(70)
	NOUN	0.789	0.671	0.857	0.686
	ADJ	0.192	0.329	0.143	0.314
	NOUN or ADJ	0.020	—	0.000	0.000
NP/3		(775)	(93)	(15)	(35)
	SEND	0.658	0.581	0.600	0.743
	PP/1	0.279	0.344	0.333	0.200
	RCL/1	0.063	0.075	0.067	0.057
NP/4 and NP/6		(79)	(7)	(0)	(4)
	ST/3 and ST/2	1.000	1.000	—	1.000

do not fit the model for one reason or another, 1.3 percent are conjunctions, and the remaining 0.5 percent apparently are not grammatical at all. A few of the ungrammatical substitutions can be explained by assuming that a previous word was not quite read properly, as when a plural was read as a possessive. The overwhelming conclusion, however, is that the predictions are grammatical, and that in fact, their syntax adheres for the most part to those constraints dictated by the network we have presented.

To summarize, the model provides a reasonable framework within which most of the predictions can be represented. A majority of the time, the prediction can be narrowed to a single syntactic class. More complex constructions that appear as nominals (such as infinitives, sentential complements, and gerunds) are seldom predicted. Generally, the predictions appear to tend toward what might be termed major constituents, such as nouns and verbs, and less toward modifiers like adjectives and adverbs.

THE READING EXPERIMENTS

Procedure

The "Normal Reading" Experiments. Twenty-four undergraduates, most of whom had participated in the prediction experiment, served as subjects. The subject sat before the television monitor and had the microphone in front of him. When ready to begin, he pressed a key on the keyboard, and the first paragraph was displayed. He read that paragraph aloud and when he finished, pressed the key again, and the next paragraph was immediately displayed. After all paragraphs were displayed, the subject answered five multiple-choice questions about the paragraph and then summarized it orally. The reading of the second and third paragraphs, as well as the summary, was recorded with a tape recorder.

Subjects were instructed not to "perform," but simply to read rapidly. They were asked to attempt to understand the material as best they could, and this part of the instructions was stressed several times. Of course, a subject did not read the same passage about which he had been tested for predictions. Thirteen subjects were recorded while reading the Keynes passage, and eleven subjects were recorded while reading the trades passage.

The "Degraded Reading" Experiment. Eight subjects (different from the ones used in the other conditions) served in this experiment.

All were undergraduates at the University of California, San Diego. The procedure was the same as that for normal reading, with two exceptions: (1) Each subject read both passages, and (2) the image on the television was degraded by turning down the contrast. This caused considerable reduction in the visibility of most vertical lines in the characters.

The Analyses

Each recorded passage was transcribed and then analyzed by digitizing the recorded wave forms and storing them on the computer's disc memory. The analysis program allowed the experimenter to call up any portion of the stored wave form and to display it on an oscilloscope while listening to the displayed wave form. The experimenter was able to move two pointers on the display and to play back the speech signal represented between them. This procedure served as a check on the original transcriptions; any errors found were corrected.

Analysis of Reading Errors. Four types of reading errors were tabulated: substitutions, partial word substitutions, omissions, and insertions. Partial word errors occurred when the reader began the proper word and then started over, or occasionally if the reader began an incorrect word, and then corrected it before finishing the word. The tabulation of errors for both normal and degraded passages is shown in Table 6.2. The proportions are based on the total number of words read. Several aspects of the data are obvious. First, the overall probability of an error is quite low. There were 124 errors out of 5464 in the normal reading and 227 errors out of 3600 words in degraded reading. Second, substitution was the most frequent type of

TABLE 6.2
Types of reading errors occurring in both the normal and degraded experiments. The proportion is based on the total number of words read.

Error type	Normal reading		Degraded reading	
	Total	Proportion	Total	Proportion
Substitution	71	.013	188	.052
Partial word	33	.006	25	.007
Omission	12	.002	12	.003
Insertion	8	.001	2	.001

error for both readings. Third, the degradation produced approximately a fourfold increase in substitution errors, but evidently had little effect on the other types of errors.

Samples of the substitutions that occurred are listed in Tables 6.3 and 6.4 and are printed in capital letters in a type face that is very similar to the text displays used in the experiments. It is clear from the tables that substitutions typically look very similar to the correct word, and that the two often share many letters in common. Moreover, several substitutions, most notably the plural-singular substitutions, share all but one letter with the proper word.

The substitution errors appear to follow both visual and syntactical constraints. To show this, the same analysis used for the predictions and the passages was carried out for the substitutions and insertions. Of the 164 errors in the degraded text, 147 or 91 percent were accepted by the model. Of the 17 not accepted, 8 were nonwords. In the normal readings, 60 of the 72 errors or 83 percent were accepted by the model; 5 of the 12 that were unaccounted for were nonwords and 2 were conjunctions. These errors are tabulated in the third and fourth columns of Table 6.1. Figure 6.5 shows the distribution of predictions and the distribution of errors from a representative state in the grammar, state ST/3. In all states, the distributions of predictions and errors were in close agreement. Both also agreed closely with the state transitions that occur in the passages themselves. Sixty-nine percent of the substituted words were of the same syntactic class as the correct word.

One might expect that reading errors would tend to be the result of taking a higher probability arc when the correct word was actually one of a lower probability. A detailed analysis of the errors indicates that this is not true. There are at least two possible explanations. First, the words within a syntactic class may be more similar to one another than to words in other classes. (This was especially obvious for prepositions, and for adverbs, which often end in -ly.) Second, additional constraints are associated with the text besides syntactic ones. As already noted, visual cues provide an important source of information.

The subjects had a tendency to take the more probable arc in the prediction experiment. Twenty-two percent of the predictions made by the subjects could be interpreted as the result of taking one of the earlier, more probable arcs leading from a state rather than the later arc, which actually was correct. Fifteen percent of the predictions seemed either to result from the selection of an arc that was less probable than the correct one, or to be caused by reasons we could

TABLE 6.3
Sample substitution errors from the "normal" reading condition.

Word in the text	Substituted word	Word in the text	Substituted word
A	AS	HAD	MIGHT
ACQUAINTS	ACQUAINTANCE	HAVE	ARE
ARE	HAVE	IN	OF
	IN	INTEREST	ENTRANCE
BOTH WITH	WITH BOTH	PRESSURE	PEOPLE
BY	FOR		PRESENCE
CONSUMERS	CONSUME	SAVINGS	SAYINGS
	CONSUMER	UNEMPLOYMENT	EMPLOYMENT
	CUSTOMER		LABOR

TABLE 6.4
Sample substitution errors from the "degraded reading" condition.

Word in the text	Substituted word	Word in the text	Substituted word
A	AN	PROPORTION	PERFORATION
	OUR		VOCATION
ABANDONED	HARDENED	SOUGHT	BOUGHT
ABUNDANT	REDUNDANT		SAVED
AT	IF		THOUGHT
	IN	SPENDING	ASCENDING
	OF	SUCH	EACH
BROUGHT	ENOUGH	SUPPLY	SUPPLIES
DIMINISHED	DOMINATED	TERMS	THEME
FULL	ALL	THIS	THE
GENERAL	REAL		THEY
GENERALLY	IN	UNSPECIFIED	EFFECTIVE
	BENEFICIALLY		EXPRESSIVE
IMPORTANT	INFORMANT		INCREASED
LARGE	CERTAIN		UNEFFECTIVE
PRESSURE	PRESENCE		UNEMPLOYMENT
	PROCEDURE		UNSPECIFIC
	RESULT		
	RESULTS		

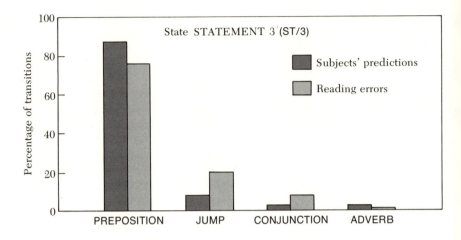

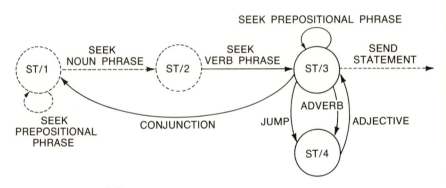

FIGURE 6.5
A comparison of the subjects' predictions with reading errors for
a representative state in the ATN.

not determine. In the prediction experiment, no visual cues were
present to guide the subjects' responses. Approximately 5 percent of
the substitutions were not recognizable as words. It is interesting that
73 percent of these substitutions either were immediately corrected
by the subjects or were preceded and/or followed by excessive pauses.
This would seem to indicate that the readers were often aware that
these nonwords did not make sense. Most of the substitutions happened on a single-word for single-word basis. If the subjects had
been reading in larger chunks, it is likely that there would have been
more errors that crossed word boundaries.

SUMMARY

This chapter has demonstrated the role of syntactic analysis in the processes of reading English text. It has long been known that a person's expectancies play a major role in his perceptual processes. In this chapter, we describe our pioneering efforts to model the dynamic nature of the change in expectancies that occurs as the reader progresses through the words of a text.

The work reported here has several different aspects. We demonstrated that the ATN parser and its associated grammar can account rather well for the expectancies of the subject, including the errors of substitutions and insertions. Part of this result, of course, simply reflects the fact that subjects are sensitive to the intricacies of the grammatical style of the passages that they read. The ATN grammar provided a powerful notational tool for studying the varied intricacies of the grammar, allowing us to record the differences in expectancies throughout the many stages of analysis of the various clauses and phrases that comprise the sentences of the English language.

Our studies of the errors made while reading degraded text point out the interactions between the visual analysis and the grammatical analysis. The reader must use all forms of information, decoding the words presented to him according to the visual cues and the grammatical and semantic constraints.

PART IV

THE COMPUTER MODEL

CHAPTER 7

The Computer Implementation[1]

DAVID E. RUMELHART and DONALD A. NORMAN

THE ONE-SYSTEM HYPOTHESIS

A basic tenet of our approach to the study of cognitive processes is that only a single system is involved. In psychological investigations, the usual procedure is to separate different areas of study: memory, perception, problem solving, language syntax, semantics. We believe that a common cognitive system underlies these areas, and that although they are partially decomposable (in the sense discussed by Ronald Kaplan in Chapter 5), the interactions among the different components are of critical importance. Thus, an important aim of our research efforts has been to study a wide variety of problem areas to determine the nature of the system that allows all components to work together in an integrated manner.

A critical step of our investigations has been the construction and use of a computer implementation of our ideas. The computer model forces us to confront the issues of interaction directly. We want a system that directly and accurately characterizes our ideas about language, about thought, about the representation of information — the ideas described in the preceding chapters of this book. One system has to be capable of handling the representation and processing

[1]We thank Danny Bobrow of the Xerox Palo Alto Research Center for his assistance in writing this chapter.

issues in syntactic and semantic analysis of language, in memory, perception, problem solving, reasoning, question answering, and in the acquisition of knowledge. This chapter describes that system. Later chapters in this book—especially Chapters 8, 12, and 13—show how the computer implementation has been used in the study of language comprehension and question answering, perception and problem solving, and reasoning and question answering.

The computer implementation is called MEMOD (memory model). MEMOD consists of three major components: a *node space*, a *parser*, and an *interpreter*. The memory structure, in the format described in Chapter 2, resides within the node space. The parser takes words as input, and then, by means of an augmented transition network (ATN, as described in Chapter 5), produces the network structures of the active structural network within the node space. The interpreter examines the nodes of the structural network, and by using a portion of the network as a guide to its processing, performs operations on the network, changing the structure where required. The interpreter can also communicate with the user of the system. In general, MEMOD is driven by means of sentences that the user types into the parser.

Four basic ideas have been combined in the construction of MEMOD. First, we use the idea that a semantic network can serve as a representation for the knowledge about many different tasks and areas. Second, we use the idea that procedural information forms an important component of our knowledge structure. These first two ideas, of course, result in the notion of an *active structural network* that is the basis of all our work (see Chapter 2). Third, we use the idea of an ATN parsing model (as described in Chapter 5) to model the process of human language analysis. Fourth, we use the idea of a grammatical *case frame* (somewhat based upon Fillmore, 1968) as a generalized procedure for structuring the representation of declarative and procedural knowledge.

The process of putting these four ideas together has been informative. It was not a straightforward process of simply taking the four different ideas and combining them into a system. When we tried this, we discovered gaps and inconsistencies. The process of constructing MEMOD, therefore, became a case study in scientific method. We postulated a procedure; then we put the components together, modifying the parts to make this possible; then we used the system for a while, discovering its strengths, weaknesses, and conceptual errors. We then repeated the entire process, each time coming up with a better, more powerful computer implementation, each time learning more about our underlying theoretical conceptualizations, and each time learning how to do it better the next time. Thus neither our theoretical conceptualizations (discussed in the earlier chapters of this book) nor our computer implementation (discussed in this chapter) are complete; they are still being modified as we explore new areas and learn new things.

BASIC UNITS AND OPERATIONS

The Structure of the Computer Representation

The first problem is to encode the structural networks into a format appropriate for the computer. Figure 7.1 illustrates how we do this. There are two parts to the figure. The *word index* contains the literal string of letters that represent the names of the nodes. The *node space* encodes the interrelations among the nodes.

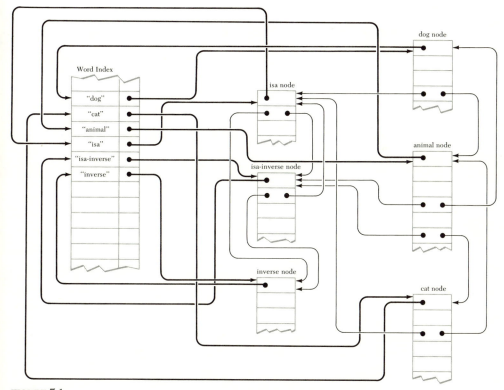

FIGURE 7.1
A schematic representation of the computer structure for dog isa animal, cat isa animal, isa inverse isa-inverse, and the appropriate corresponding inverse relationships.

The word index serves as our entry to the node space.[2] When the system encounters a word, it uses the word index to find the node that corresponds to that word. Similarly, when the system wishes to produce the name of the node as an output, it goes to the appropriate location in the word index to find the string of letters that comprise the name of the node.

A node consists of two parts. First, there is a *header*, which contains technical information about the computer representation of the node (such as its length), and a pointer back to the word index. Second, there is a sequence of *items* on each node. The items are used to implement the labeled relations of the network. To encode the relationship drawn as an arrow labeled R from a node a to a node b, we place an item on node a with a pointer to the node for relation R and a pointer to the node for b. In addition, we place on node b an item consisting of a pointer to the node for relation R-inverse and a pointer to the node for a.

Operations on the Node Space

In order to build and manipulate the structures shown in Figure 7.1, we need to develop a set of basic operations. Typical operations allow the system to:

- create a new node
- connect some node a to some node b with relation R
- forget particular relations between two nodes
- find the first or last item on a node
- find the next or the previous item on a node
- test whether part of the structure on one node is the same as the structure on another node

The portion of the node space shown in Figure 7.1 only illustrates structural information. We need to be able to represent information about processes as well. In particular, we need to represent the kinds of operations just described. We do this by associating some of the nodes in the node space with these operations. Thus, the node for **connect** is associated with the operation of linking nodes together.

---

[2]The structure shown in Figure 7.1 is actually a simplification of the actual implementation. For efficiency of operation, a *node-name index* (not shown in the figure) acts as the interface between the *word index* and the *node space*. Each node is preceded by a *header*, which contains special information about the node. The nodes in the node space are actually arranged in a linear array; the nodes do not actually point to one another, but rather only communicate through the node-name index. None of these changes is important for understanding how these structures are represented.

The operation itself is built into the underlying system language of MEMOD (Algol in our implementation). When we wish to perform some action, we do so by referencing one of these special nodes.

Suppose we wish to **connect** the node for **dog** to the node for **animal** with the relation **isa**:

(1)   Connect dog to animal with isa.

We express this desire by constructing a node of the form shown in Figure 7.2. In the figure, **node ∗3000** is a token of the special node **connect**, which represents the actual performance of the connection of a relation between the two nodes. The relations **object, to,** and **with** point to the arguments required by the action. **Connect** is an example of what we call *basic, built-in* operations. The relation **prim** points to the system language (Algol) description of the operation (indicated by the shaded area in the figure). To perform the action, MEMOD must be able to carry out the instructions pointed to by the relation **prim**. The portion of the system that causes the desired operations to be carried out is called the *interpreter*. The interpreter is a program written in the system language, and it takes as an argument a node that expresses the desired action. In the case illustrated in Figure 7.2, the interpreter is given **node ∗3000** as its argument.

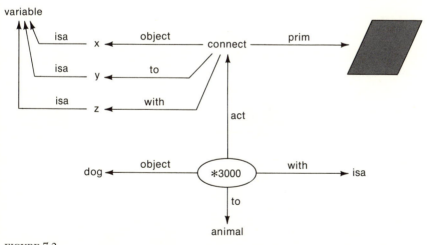

FIGURE 7.2

A node for a basic, built-in operation, and one of its tokens. (Node ∗3000 is the token.) The shaded area pointed to by the relation **prim** represents the computer code, which carries out the operations. In this diagram (and all of the following similar diagrams) token nodes are given arbitrary names for easy reference and discussion. The name ∗3000 is an example; the numbers used for node names have no special significance.

The interpreter operates in this manner. First, it examines the node given to it as its argument (node *3000) and follows the act relation to the node for connect. There, the relation prim indicates that this is a basic, built-in operation. The interpreter then associates the arguments on the *token* node (*3000) with the corresponding variables on the *type* node for connect. The forming of the association between the arguments of a *token* node and the corresponding variables on the *type* node is called *binding the variables to their values*. Once the variables have been bound, the underlying system language code for connect is performed. The process of binding variables and then running the code is called *evaluating the node*. The result of evaluating node *3000 will be the construction of a connection labeled isa from the node for dog to the node for animal (and the inverse connection from the node for animal to the node for dog).

Some basic, built-in operations produce values as a result of their execution. For example, consider the operations in

(2)   Print the firstnode from animal via isa-inverse.

Firstnode is a built-in operation that, in this case, examines the node for animal until it finds the first instance of the relation isa-inverse. Firstnode then returns as its value the node pointed to by that relation. Figure 7.3 illustrates the nodes that would have to be constructed in

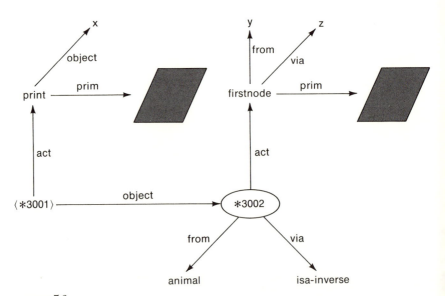

FIGURE 7.3
The node structure for the sentence Print the first node from animal via isa-inverse.

the node space in order for (2) to be carried out. The interpreter starts with node *3001, notes that it must evaluate the argument for the relation object, node *3002. When node *3002 is evaluated, it returns with the value dog, allowing node *3001 to be executed. This results in the printing of the word "dog" on the computer terminal.

To get structures such as those shown in Figure 7.3 into the node space we use the parser. The parser takes a sentence such as (1) and (2) and, with the aid of the interpreter, produced a structure like that shown in Figure 7.3 and causes it to be evaluated.

Defining New Actions

We add appreciable power to the system if we can construct new actions from combinations of old ones. Suppose we wish to have an action that retrieved the first instance of the concept represented by a node. For example, we wish to define the action instance so that the sentence

(3)   Print instance of animal.

will print the word "dog." We define the general concept instance of x with the sentence

(4)   Return with the first node from x via isa-inverse.

In sentence 4, x is a variable that will be bound to the appropriate argument of instance whenever it is used. The operation of return establishes the value for the token of instance.

Because of the fact that instance takes an argument, the word is not simply a noun. We use a new syntactic class for words of this type — the syntactic class of operator. MEMOD accepts definitions of new actions by invoking a special built-in operation of the system — the built-in operation called define. Thus, when the system encounters a sentence of the form

(5)   Define instance as operator.

it responds by first requesting what we call the *definition frame* for the new action, which specifies the argument names and ranges. The system responds to (5) with the request:

(6)   *The definition frame for instance is:*

In this example, the user would respond with

(7)   instance of x.

Now the system asks for the sequence of sentences that constitutes the definition of instance by the request:

(8)   *The definition is:*

The user responds:

(9)   Return with the first node from x via isa-inverse.
        ##

(The symbol ## is used to signify the end of the definition.) At the conclusion of the definition, the interpreter constructs the configuration of nodes shown in Figure 7.4, which constitutes this definition of instance. As we showed in Chapter 2, the definitional structure for the new action is pointed to by the relation iswhen.

Definitions of terms can consist of sequences of sentences. We illustrate this with a definition for one sense of the word "son."

(10)   Define son as predicate.
        The definition frame for son is: x son of y.
        The definition is:
            Connect x to male with sex.
            If age of x is less than 18, then connect x to child with isa.
            Connect y to x with parent-of.
            ##

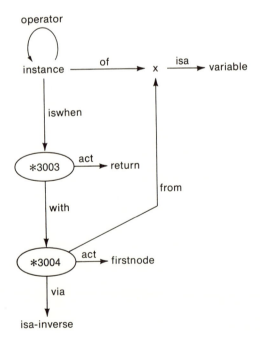

FIGURE 7.4
The node structure for the
definition of instance.

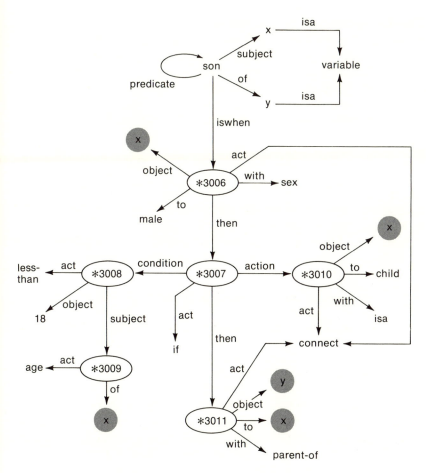

FIGURE 7.5
The node structure for the definition of son.

The structure created by the define procedure is shown in Figure 7.5.[3] We return to this definition later.

---

[3]In Figure 7.5, we introduce a new convention. When a node at the bottom of the figure points to a node at the top, to reduce the visual clutter of the diagram, we simply repeat the name of the top node at the bottom location. Despite the fact that the name appears in different places, there is but a single node in the system, one to which all the relations are connected. To emphasize this fact, we label these repeated drawings of the same node with lighter ("screened") lettering; screened letters indicate that the node is actually a repetition of a node in the diagram, but there is only one such node in the node space.

The Operation of the Interpreter

To this point, we have illustrated how the interpreter handles basic actions. In this section we extend that notion to show how the interpreter operates upon defined structures.

The function of the interpreter is to evaluate a node. The following five statements characterize its operation in evaluating a node x.

1. Evaluate any argument of x that is capable of being evaluated. Then replace each evaluated argument with the value that resulted.

2. Follow any instance of an **act** relation to the type node for x.

3. Bind each variable of the type node to its corresponding argument value on the node for x.

4. If the type node has a **prim** relation, carry out the appropriate basic built-in, operation. If not, evaluate the node pointed to by the relation **iswhen**.

5. If x points to any node with the relation **then**, evaluate that node.

To illustrate the operation of the interpreter, consider a specific sentence:

(11)　Oedipus is the son of Jocasta.

The resulting structure is shown in Figure 7.6. Node *3012 is given as an argument to the interpreter. The interpreter first follows the relation **act** to the node for **son** and then binds the variables x and y to their corresponding arguments (**Oedipus** and **Jocasta**). It then evaluates **node *3006**, the first node for the definition of **son**. The evaluation proceeds in the manner that we described earlier and results in the formation of a new connection in the network, a link labeled **sex** that connects the node for **Oedipus** to the node for **male**. The relation labeled **then**, which connects **node *3006** to **node *3007**, is a message to the interpreter that after completion of the evaluation of **node *3006**, it should then proceed to evaluate **node *3007** (see statement 5 in the characterization of the interpreter). **Node *3007** is an instance of a type of basic built-in operation that we have not yet discussed, the conditional operation **if**. The built-in operations associated with **if** require that the node associated with the condition relation be evaluated (in this case, **node *3008**). If the value of that evaluation is **FALSE**, then the operations specified by the instance of **if** are complete. If the evaluation leads to a value of **TRUE**, then the built-in operations for **if** require the node associated with the

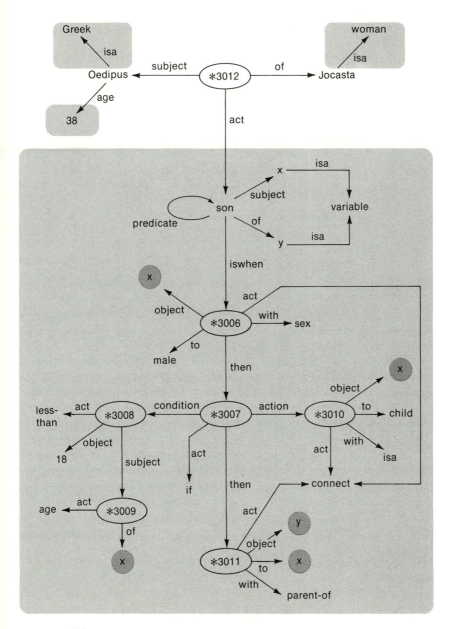

FIGURE 7.6
The node structure for the sentence **Oedipus is the son of Jocasta.** The shaded
area shows the definitional structure for **son** (the same structure as in Figure 7.5).

relation action be evaluated. In our example, the node *3010 is the node associated with the relation action. However, the system believes that the age of Oedipus is 38 (that is, not less than 18), so in fact, the node *3010 is not evaluated. This completes the evaluation of the node that represents the if statement (node *3008), and the interpreter then follows the relation then to perform the evaluation of node *3011. This last node in the sequence is again a simple instance of connect. When the interpreter finishes the operations associated with this node, it has performed all the operations associated with the evaluation of Oedipus as the son of Jocasta; it will have added a statement to the node for Oedipus that his sex is male, and it will have added the relation parent-of from the node for Jocasta to the node for Oedipus.

SOL: A Semantic Operating Language

To produce a viable system capable of representing and acting on procedural as well as structural information, we need a set of basic built-in operations, an interpreter for carrying out those operations, and an input language for expressing declarative, imperative, and interrogative information. In addition, we need a facility for expressing the definitions of new operations in terms of old, previously defined ones. The properties of MEMOD that we have already described—the parser, the interpreter, and the ability to encode both structural and procedural knowledge within the node space—provide us with the power of a programming language. We already have the capability to initiate elementary operations upon the node structure. It is possible to instruct the system how to carry out its information processing. We can store within the node space such information as the strategies for finding the referents to noun phrases, determiners, and pronouns. We can encode strategies for question answering, deductive reasoning, and problem solving. The basic, built-in operations that act upon the node structures provide the basic nucleus for the system: The ability to define new operations built up from previously defined ones provides the power to expand the system indefinitely.

The result of these components is a programming language within MEMOD using the parser, the node space, and the interpreter. The syntax of the language is given by the grammar of the parser, and is, therefore, the syntax of English. The language is called SOL (pronounced "soul"): *semantic operating language*. The natural syntax of English provides for the guidance of the desired operations. Because all statements in SOL enter MEMOD through the parser, SOL can take advantage of the power of natural language. Thus, we can leave out arguments (and let the parser fill them in), we can paraphrase, and we need not use a fixed word order.

Reference is made both easier and more complex by the use of English. The parser allows **SOL** to use pronouns, so that once **MEMOD** has established specific nodes within the network, it is then possible to refer to those nodes by phrases such as **the node** or **that node**, or even as **it**. Local reference is made easier. Global reference, however, is more difficult. To specify a new node, a node that has not been talked about recently, one must provide a unique description of it. In doing this, one encounters all the problems of reference discussed in the early sections of Chapter 3. Once the node structure is found, then again, it is possible to use abbreviated reference.

Perhaps the most important aspect of the use of an English syntax for programming is that it aids our development processes. When we have difficulties with the **SOL** programming language, or when there is some fault in the control processes that causes the **MEMOD** system to malfunction, the process of analyzing the problem often yields new insights into the general issues of language and human control structures. (The syntactic classes recognized by the parser are shown in Box 7.1. Some of the basic, built-in operations are illustrated in Box 7.2.)

INTERACTION BETWEEN THE PARSER AND THE INTERPRETER

In the analysis of an English sentence, the parser and the interpreter work together. To ensure proper communication between these two systems, the node space contains both syntactic and semantic information. Most important, we use ideas derived from the "case grammar" of Fillmore (1968) to allow the parser to know when it has gathered up the necessary subpieces for a unit that is evaluable by the interpreter—that is, when it has filled a "case frame" with arguments that satisfy the appropriate argument constraints. We now illustrate how the parser uses the argument frames for words and how it invokes the interpreter. Consider the sentence

(12)   A happy boy gave Fido to the girl who lives across the street.

In the analysis of sentence 12, the parser uses the syntactic class and case frame information associated with the words "a," "happy," and "boy," to put together the individual pieces of the noun phrase "a happy boy." Once the parser recognizes this noun phrase, it must

BOX 7.1
The syntactic classes recognized by the SOL *parser.*

Actions: Verbs that introduce an imperative sentence.

Adjectives: The adjectives of English are used in their prenominal position.

Adverbs: The adverbs of English, which appear immediately before a verb.

Auxiliaries: The auxiliary verbs of English.

Determiners.

Infix operators: Operators (for example, "plus," "minus," "times") that appear as terms with arguments both preceding and following.

Negatives: Certain adverbs of negation in English (for example, "not," "never," and "n't").

Nouns: The nouns of English that do not require arguments.

Operators: The nouns of English that accept or require arguments (for example, "father" in "father of John," "destruction" in "destruction of the city by the enemy").

Predicates: The verbs and predicate adjectives of English used in declarative statements.

Propositions.

Pronouns.

Propositional conjunctions: Terms serving as sentential connectives (for example, "if," "because," "and," "or").

Qwords.   *Wh-words* initiating questions that stand for a deleted noun phrase (for example, "who," "where," and "what," in sentences like "Who is at home?", "What is that?", "Where is John?").

Qdet.   *Wh-words* that introduce questions, but that must be followed immediately by a noun phrase (for example, "which" in "Which man went to school?", and "what" in "What color is that box?").

Relative pronouns.

Selectors: Quantifiers of English (for example, "each," "any," "most").

BOX 7.2
Some of the basic built-in operations available in MEMOD.

Connect x to y with z: An action that creates a labeled relation z from node x to node y.

Define x as y: An action that initiates the definition of x as a member of syntactic class y.

Evaluate x: An action that causes the node x to be evaluated by the interpreter.

x exists: A predicate that determines whether the node named or described by x exists.

Forget x y z: An action that removes the relation labeled y from between x and z.

x identical to y: A predicate that tests whether node x is the same as node y. It returns a value of **TRUE** or **FALSE**.

If x, then y; otherwise z: A propositional conjunction that tests statement x. Depending on the truth value of statement x, it carries out either the action y or the action z.

Newnode: An operator that creates a new node and returns with that node as its value.

Nextnode from x via y: An operator that finds the next node accessible from x by following relations labeled y from the current position on the node.

Nextrelation from x to y: An operator that finds the next label on the relation from node x to node y from the current position on the node.

Return x with y: An action that causes a truth value of x and node y to be returned as a value of the procedure in which it appears.

find the node in the node space that represents it. Because this phrase is an example of unspecific, intensional reference, a new node will be created to represent the concept of "a happy boy." Now let us examine how this is done.

The determination of the proper structure is made by starting with the concept for "boy," then backing up to the adjective "happy." An adjective is represented in the system as a procedure. Therefore, the parser invokes the interpreter, asking it to evaluate the adjective definition. This has the result of constructing **node *3013** (shown in Figure 7.7), "a happy boy." (A set of possible rules for constructing structures modified by adjectives and nouns is described in Chapter 13.)

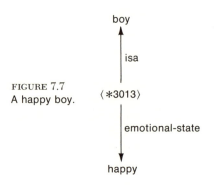

FIGURE 7.7
A happy boy.

Now the parser continues with the sentence, this time beginning with the verb "give," which it identifies as the probable main predicate of the sentence. Construction of the representation for the sentence is guided by the case structure associated with the main verb. Any given English term may be used in a number of different senses, some of which may be different syntactic classes, some of which may be of the same syntactic class but have different case frames, and some of which may both be of the same class and use the same case frames, but have different interpretations. All these possibilities can be expressed within the node structure. Here, let us examine briefly how the different senses are represented, and then examine in more detail the use of one particular case frame.

Consider one possible meaning sense of the word "give." First, we define "give" to be a predicate; then we provide a case frame.

(13A)   Define give as predicate.

(13B)   *The definition frame for give is:* x gives o to y (at-time t).

In the frame described by (13B), the phrase enclosed in parentheses (the time information) is optional and need not be used in any particular sentence. The rest of the arguments are necessary: They must be used. The letters x, y, o, and t are simply the names of the variables of the definition, and the words **to** and **at-time** denote the ranges or the cases associated with the verb. In this simple case, the word **to** indicates the use of the preposition "to" in the sentence; the word **at-time** indicates any preposition that can be used to indicate time information. The variables x and y do not have range specifiers with them in this instance. A variable without a range specification before the verb is taken to be the **subject**. A variable without a range specification after the verb is taken to be the **object**. Thus, in the sentence

(14)   Bert gave a boat to Ernie on his birthday.

the following bindings of the arguments would occur:

x	Bert	(the subject)
y	Ernie	(the recipient)
o	a boat	(the object)
t	his birthday	(the time — which would have to be evaluated further)

When the frame information of (13B) is placed in the node space, the structure for the node for "**give**" would look something like that shown in Figure 7.8.

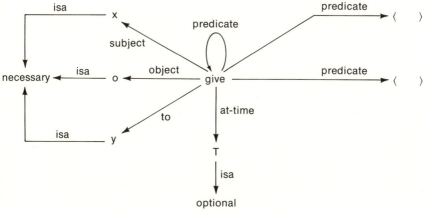

FIGURE 7.8
The frame structure for one sense of the predicate **give**.

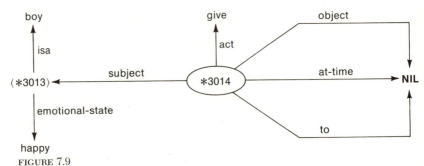

FIGURE 7.9
An intermediate stage of the structure produced during the parse of the sentence
A happy boy gave. . . .

Figure 7.8 indicates that **give** has three alternative word senses, this one and the two others pointed to by the relation **predicate**. The parser uses the frame information contained with this meaning sense for **give** to create a new secondary node that serves as a token of the main predicate, **node ∗3014** in Figure 7.9. When the analysis of the sentence is completed, **node ∗3014** will represent the proposition that stands for sentence 12. Note that the node for **a happy boy**, **node ∗3013**, has been assigned the role of **subject** in this new structure. For the parse to be completed, all the nodes of ∗3014 now filled by **NIL** that correspond to **necessary** arguments in the verb frame must be filled in by appropriate nodes.

Now let us return to the analysis of sentence 12:

(12)   A happy boy gave Fido to the girl who lives across the street.

The unique node associated with the proper name "Fido" is taken as the **object** of **node ∗3014**. At this point the parser and interpreter analyze the phrase, "to the girl who lives across the street." It does this by transforming the relative clause to the question

(15)   What girl lives across the street?

and passing the question as the argument to the procedure for the word **the**. When the interpreter evaluates the definition for **the**, the strategies that comprise that definition will determine the appropriate referent for the phrase. The end result is shown in Figure 7.10. Here, **node ∗3014**, as before, represents the main predicate of sentence 12. Three instances of "girl" are shown, but only one, **node ∗1482**, represents a girl living across the street. (In fact, this girl turns out to be Oedipus' sister.)

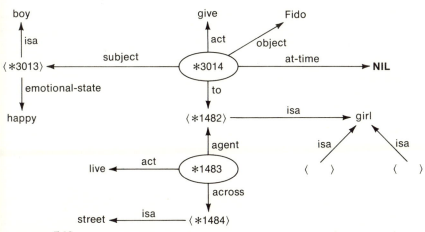

FIGURE 7.10

The complete structure produced by the parse of the sentence A happy boy gave Fido to the girl who lives across the street.

On the completion of the parse, the token of the highest verb of the sentence, in this case node ✳3014, is inserted as one argument to an implicit performative verb that we call the **comprehender**. (The other argument passed to the **comprehender** is a token that indicates the kind of sentence just encountered—declarative, interrogative, or imperative.) The **comprehender** is itself defined in **SOL** statements within **MEMOD** and it can carry out any action definable in the system. In particular, it is normally defined so that it evaluates the token passed to it, thereby invoking the definition of the main verb of the sentence. However, the **comprehender** can be defined to play a much more active role in the interpretation of the input sentence. When the **comprehender** has finished the various jobs required of it, control is returned to the parser, which awaits the input of another sentence. (The role of the **comprehender** is illustrated further in Chapters 8 and 13.)

SUMMARY

We have constructed a computer implementation that allows us to test our ideas over a reasonably wide domain of areas while being consistent and precise about the structure of our theories. Because our programming language **SOL** is expressed in the structural network representation, and because it also operates through the parser, it has become a vehicle for expressing our ideas, even when these ideas are not actually entered into the system. Thus, SOL and MEMOD have become important adjuncts to our thinking and to the development and evaluation of our theories, even when the computer implementation is not actually used.

The use of MEMOD to test theoretical systems is described in three different chapters of this book:

- In Chapter 8, David Rumelhart and James Levin show how the model of comprehension and verb expansion (described in Chapter 2) can be used to develop a system that understands and can answer questions.

- In Chapter 12, Marc Eisenstadt and Yaakov Kareev model the human problem-solving processes, emphasizing the perceptual and cognitive aspects involved in the playing of board games.

- In Chapter 13, Greg Scragg explores the power of MEMOD to examine and simulate its own structures and to observe the operation of its own processes.

The use of the conceptualizations developed within the construction and evaluation of MEMOD have been important for all of the work discussed in this book, even when MEMOD or SOL have not been used explicitly. In four chapters, the tools of the computer implementation have been of special importance for the development of the ideas:

- In Chapter 6, Albert Stevens and David Rumelhart show how the parser can be used as a theoretical tool in the study of the reading process.

- In Chapters 9 and 10, Dedre Gentner and Adele Abrahamson, respectively, examine the experimental implications of the representational format (especially the expansion of verbs into their underlying structures) on memory, understanding, and the child's acquisition of language.

- In Chapter 11, Stephen Palmer shows how the ideas about representation and processing can be applied to the study of visual perception.

CHAPTER 8

A Language Comprehension System

DAVID E. RUMELHART and JAMES A. LEVIN

In this chapter we describe a computer system designed for language comprehension. The system applies the general approach to representation and processing outlined in Chapter 2 within the framework of the MEMOD computer system described in Chapter 7 to produce a procedurally based system for both comprehension and question answering. Our system is called Verbworld. In it, we follow a systematic model for writing definitions of predicates. All of the inferential power of the system is embedded in the procedural definitions. Comprehension of a sentence or answering of a question proceeds in a uniform manner, without the need for any "intelligent" executive program: The intelligence of the system is distributed throughout the semantic network data base.

Comprehending a sentence involves evaluating the procedural definition of the predicate terms in the sentence. Thus, the system comprehends a sentence like "John gave Fido to Mary" by treating it as a call to the procedure give, with the concepts for "John," "Mary," and "Fido" as arguments of the procedure. Then the comprehension of the sentence occurs through the evaluation of this procedure. This evaluation is carried out by the SOL interpreter in the manner discussed in Chapter 7.

We restrict the procedural definitions of surface verbs to dictionary definitions that express the essential relationships. Thus, we might define "give" as "X gives Y to Z means that X causes Z to get Y." Recall from Chapter 7 that the evaluation of a SOL definition consists simply of the evaluation of the definitions of all of the predicate terms used in the definition. Thus, when the sentence "John gave Fido to Mary" is presented to the system, the sentence is, in effect, analyzed as "John caused Mary to get Fido." Furthermore, if **CAUSE** were defined as "X causes Y means that X's **DO**ing **CAUSE**s Y," the system would then, in effect, evaluate the sentence to the form "John's **DO**ing **CAUSE**d Mary to get Fido." Similarly, if "get" were defined as "X gets Y means that X comes to have Y," the evaluation of the sentence would yield "John's **DO**ing **CAUSE**d Mary to come to have Fido." This process of replacing the definition of one term by the definition of another continues in Verbworld until there is a sentence composed entirely of "semantically primitive" terms. In our present example, that would be something like "John's **DO**ing **CAUSE**d a **CHANGE** to Mary **POSS** Fido." At this point the system evaluates the definitions of these primitive terms. The SOL definitions of these primitive terms are relatively unconstrained. They must be defined to build underlying semantic structure, search the data base for relevant information, and return a pointer to any information found or new structure created.

In the following sections, we provide details of how the system works. Do not be misled by the simplicity of the definitions given there. These definitions provide much of the machinery for the language-understanding and question-answering capabilities of Verbworld. In fact, one of the advantages of this approach is the ease with which one can write simple definitions that extend the knowledge of the system to new problem areas.

All of the processes described in this chapter (except those in the last section, headed "Extensions to Verbworld") are implemented within the MEMOD computer system. The examples illustrate the actual operation of that system.

VERBWORLD DEFINITIONS

We distinguished in Chapter 2 between several different aspects of verb meanings: *statives, changes of states, causes* of these changes, and *actionals*. The *stative* component of a verb represents some fixed relationship that holds among the arguments of the verb over some specified period. The *change* component of a verb indicates that some change of state has taken place. The *causative* component communicates the source of, or reason for, the change. The *actional* component communicates the particular activity. Not all of these different verb components are present in all verbs, but all components may appear in a single lexical item.

Statives

The simplest semantic component of verbs is the stative component. This component seems to be present in nearly all verbs. The stative component expresses the information that a particular state of the world holds over some period. The simple locative is an example of a predicate that has only stative components. We call the semantically primitive predicate that underlies locative verbs **LOC** (see Chapter 2). We define our semantic primitives as procedures that build the appropriate underlying structure. Thus, **LOC** is defined in SOL as follows:

(1)   Define as predicate **LOC**.
        The definition frame for **LOC** is:
        X **LOC** at-loc L from-time T1 to-time T2.
        The definition is:
        Return with newtoken for **LOC** subject X at-loc L
        from-time T1 to-time T2.
        ##

Definition 1 is shown exactly as it would be entered into the SOL system. The term **newtoken** is the name of an operator within the definition of a semantic primitive that creates a token of the primitive, with the appropriate constants filled in for the variables. To illustrate its use, suppose the following sentence were entered into the SOL system:

(2)   John **LOC** at UCSD from 1967 to 1969.

When the parser encounters sentence 2, it first determines that **LOC** is the major predicate term. This predicate is evaluated, causing the procedure **newtoken** to build the structure illustrated in Figure 8.1. This structure is returned to the surface level to make it available for further processing.

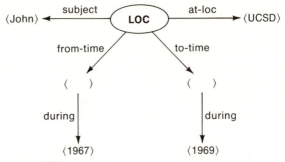

FIGURE 8.1
Underlying semantic structure representing the meaning
of the simple locative stative proposition "John was
located at UCSD from 1967 to 1969."

We are now in a position to define the stative sense of the verb "locate."

(3)   Define as predicate locate.
        The definition frame for locate is:
        X located at-loc L from-time T1 to-time T2.
        The definition is:
        Means that X **LOC** at L from T1 to T2.
        ##

Whenever a clause containing this particular sense of "locate" is encountered (for example, "John was located at UCSD from 1967 to 1969"), the input constants are associated with the variables of definition 3 and the definition is evaluated by invoking **locate**. The invocation of the procedure **locate** causes the proposition with **LOC** as its main predicate to be evaluated,[1] thereby causing the lower-level invocation of **LOC** to be interpreted. All of this has the result of creating a structure similar to that represented by Figure 8.1. The new structure is returned by **LOC** to the definition of "locate." The term **means** in definition 3 is an action that carries out the details of returning this structure. The interpretation of **means** associates the new structure with the surface proposition involving "locate."

---

[1]When we refer to the "evaluation" of a proposition, we mean the interpreting of the definition of the main predicate of the proposition. This is done by invoking the SOL interpreter (see Chapter 7) on the node representing the proposition being evaluated. The structure generated by this process becomes associated with this node and can be referred to as the "evaluation of" the node.

Change of State

Figure 8.2 illustrates the network structure that we assume underlies a simple change of location. Here, our primitive, **CHANGE**, relates two primitive state propositions involving location.

We define **CHANGE** so that it automatically constructs structures like those in Figure 8.2. A SOL definition for **CHANGE** that constructs such structures is given in (4):

(4)   Define **CHANGE** as operator.
           The definition frame for **CHANGE** is:
           CHANGE from-state S1 to-state S2 at-time T.
           The definition is:
           S1 ended at T.
           S2 started at T.
           Return with newtoken for **CHANGE** from state S1 to state S2.
           ##

When interpreted, this definition modifies the ending time of the prior state, S1, and the beginning time of the resulting state, S2, to the time T. Then **newtoken** builds a token of **CHANGE** linking the two states, S1 and S2. This structure is then returned to the calling procedure.

Having now defined **CHANGE** and **LOC**, we are in a position to define an intransitive sense of the verb "move." This noncausative

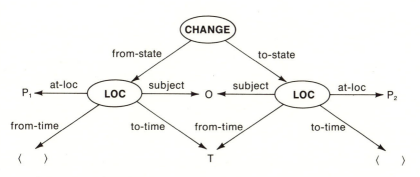

FIGURE 8.2
Semantic structure representing the meaning of
a change-of-locative-state proposition.

sense simply indicates that something changes from one location to another. The **SOL** definition is:

(5)   Define as predicate move.
       The definition frame for move is:
       X moves from-loc L1 to-loc L2 at-time T.
       The definition is:
       Means that a **CHANGE** from the state that X is located
       at L1 to the state that X is located at L2 occurs at T.
       ##

Note that when this definition is interpreted, it evaluates **LOC** twice (through the two uses of **locate**) and returns the structures built by **LOC** to **CHANGE**, where they are integrated into the structure as shown in Figure 8.2. **CHANGE** can now be used to define a variety of simple change-of-state verbs. (One example, "get," is defined later in definition 13.)

Actionals

Within **Verbworld**, very little has been done with actionals. We have looked at rather abstract verbs with very little actional component. In the case of abstract verbs, we have been able to represent the general actional component by the unspecified, abstract action called **DO**. Figure 8.3 illustrates the general form this representation takes.

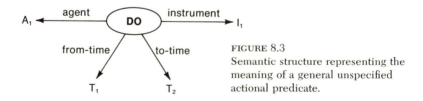

FIGURE 8.3
Semantic structure representing the meaning of a general unspecified actional predicate.

Causatives

The causal component of verb meanings is complex in that there are at least three different sorts of things that we can say "cause" events to occur. The first kind of causal element we called the *agentitive cause*. The animate being who initiated the action leading to the resultant event is specified as the *cause*. For example, in (6), "John" is the *agentitive cause*.

(6)   John opened the door with the key.

The second sort of causal element is the *instrumental cause*. In this case, the instrument used in the action which initiated the resultant event is specified as the *cause*. Thus, in (7), "The key" is the *instrumental cause* of the door's opening.

(7)   The key opened the door.

Finally, a *method* may be specified as the *cause*: the actual event that caused the result. In sentences 8A and 8B, "John's turning the key" is the *method* that caused the door to open.

(8A)   John's turning of the key opened the door.

(8B)   John opened the door by turning the key.

In (6) and (7) we appear to have simple noun phrases as the cause of the event. However, we suggested in Chapter 2 that our primitive causal predicate **CAUSE** should hold only between two events. Thus, even when no causal event is mentioned, we assume that there was an event that served as the causal event. In such cases, we use the abstract actional **DO** (with its agent and instrument arguments as specified from the surface sentence) as a kind of "pro-verb" standing for the unspecified activity. If, however, the actual causal event is specified (as in 8A and 8B), we simply use this event as the first argument of the **CAUSE** predicate.

Figure 8.4A illustrates the structure generated by sentence 6, and Figure 8.4B illustrates the structure generated by sentences 8A and 8B.

Thus, our definition for **CAUSE** must first determine what the causal event is before it can create the appropriate semantic structure.

(7)   Define as predicate **CAUSE**.
         The definition frame for **CAUSE** is:
         X **CAUSE** Y (method M instrument I at-time T).[2]
         The definition is:
         If X is event, call X C, otherwise if M is specified, call the
         evaluation of M C, otherwise call newtoken for **DO** agent X
         Instrument I C.
         Return with newtoken for **CAUSE** event C result evaluation of Y.
         ##

---

[2]In this definition, the parts of the frame that are enclosed within parentheses are marked as optional. Unlike the other arguments, they need not be present in any given sentence. The parentheses act as signals to the parser to mark the arguments "optional" when constructing the frame.

A

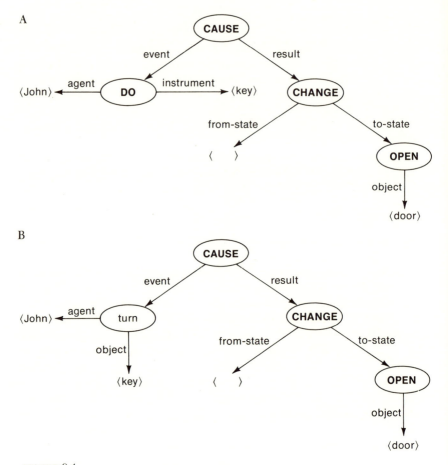

B

FIGURE 8.4
Semantic structure for propositions containing causal elements. *A* represents a sentence with both agentive and instrumental causes: "John opened the door with the key." *B* represents the proposition with an embedded causal event: "John opened the door by turning the key." For simplicity, the expanded structure for the predicate "turn" is not shown.

The first sentence of the definition is devoted to the discovery of the appropriate causal event. First, the subject, X, of **CAUSE** is examined to see if it is an event. If so (as in 8A), it becomes the causal event. Otherwise, if the method, M, was mentioned in the sentence (as in 8B), the structure generated from evaluating proposition M becomes the causal event. If neither subject nor method are events (as in 6 and 7), then a new token of the actional **DO** is created to serve as the cause. After the causal event is discovered, then the structure for the result is generated by the evaluation of the proposition. Finally, the causal event and the result are properly linked by **CAUSE** and the resulting structure is returned.

Now that we have defined several basic components of verb meanings, we can use these as building blocks to define ever broader classes of verbs with increasingly more natural definitions. For example, we can define one sense of the surface form of the verb "cause" very simply in terms of the primitive **CAUSE**.

(8)   Define as predicate cause.
        The definition frame for cause is:
        X causes proposition Y (method M instrument I at-time T).
        The definition is:
        Means that X **CAUSES** Y with I by M at T.
        ##

Similarly, we can now define a transitive sense of the verb "move."[3]

(9)   Define as predicate move.
        move is already defined as **PREDICATE**.
        Redefine? No
        Add a sense? Yes
        The definition frame for move is:
        X move Y (from-loc L1 to-loc L2 at-time T method M
        instrument I).
        The definition is:
        Means that X **CAUSED** Y to move at T from L1 to L2 by M with
        I at T.
        ##

Note that we have defined the transitive sense of "move" in terms of the intransitive sense. Similarly, we can define one sense of the verb "put" in terms of the transitive "move."

(10)   Define as predicate put.
        The definition frame for put is:
        X puts Y at-loc L (instrument I at-time T).
        The definition is:
        Means that X moves Y to L with I at T.
        ##

---

[3]In example 9, **move** already had a prior definition, so before the user was allowed to enter this new definition, **MEMOD** queried him to determine whether he really meant to enter a new definition and, if so, was it intended to replace the old one (a redefinition) or was it a new meaning sense for the word.

This set of definitions can, of course, be extended to include other verbs in other verb families. As we show in the following section, the only additional primitive required to account for a wide range of possession verbs is a primitive stative of possession that we call **POSS**. In general, our system can be extended to other families of verbs with only the addition of new primitive statives and actionals. In fact, the definitions given for **CAUSE** and **CHANGE** will generate all of the primitive structures outlined in Chapter 2. Furthermore, if methods of **CAUSE** are required to be events and the arguments of **CHANGE** to be primitive statives, actionals, or conjunctions of either, then our definitions automatically build those structures allowed by rules 1 through 10 of Chapter 2.

VERBWORLD AS A COMPREHENSION SYSTEM

In the preceding section we concentrated our attention on the use of our semantically primitive predicates as a means of building the appropriate network structure. In this section we show how these same semantic primitives can play an integral role in sentence-verification and question-answering processes.

Sentence comprehension consists of at least four distinct processes within the **Verbworld** system. The first process is the parsing of the input sentences into a canonical form consisting of a predicate name followed by its arguments. We call this the surface proposition. Second, this output is converted into its underlying semantic structure by evaluating the surface propositions generated by the parser. This process was discussed in the preceding section. The third process is the comparison of this structure with previously stored information in search of contradiction, confirmation or partially redundant information with which the new information from the input propositions can be integrated. The fourth and final process is the retrieval of the appropriate contextual information for answering the question. In this section we focus on the processes of verification and information retrieval. Perhaps the most interesting aspect of the **Verbworld** system is the ease with which we can use the primitive predicates themselves to carry out these two tasks.

The essence of the **Verbworld** verification process is to extend the capabilities of the primitive predicates so that they carry out a search for matching information in memory before they build new structures. The new function of the primitives is to try to find a structure already stored in memory that matches the structure the primitive would build. If the primitive finds a match, no new structure is built.

If the primitive does not find that structure, it builds it in memory. Thus, there are three possible results of evaluating an input sentence:

1. If the sentence contains only old information (that is, if all the primitives find matching information in memory), no new structure is built, but the old structure is returned for later use.

2. If the sentence contains only new information (that is, if none of the primitives evaluated find matching information), an entirely new structure is built and returned as described earlier.

3. If some of the information is new and other information is old (that is, some primitives find matching information while others do not), the new structure is built and linked to the old structure. This hybrid structure is then returned.

Question answering is a simple extension of this process. Consider the answering of a yes-no question. If the primitives find an entirely old structure, then the answer is "yes" or "I know that to be true." If the primitives would have built a new structure, then the answer is "no" or "I don't know." Answering wh-questions is only slightly more complex. The process proceeds for these questions as before, except that the argument slots being queried are specially marked. Then, if an old structure is found, the nodes filling the marked arguments are returned. The names of these nodes are given as answers. If an old structure is not found, then the appropriate answer is "I don't know."

The implementation of this processing capability requires only an augmentation of the definitions of the primitives. The definitions of all of the surface terms remain exactly as outlined in the previous section. All of the question-answering and sentence-verification capability is concentrated in the primitive predicates.

Verification

Suppose there is a primitive predicate called **POSS** that represents the possession relationship. In this case, we could define one sense of the verb "have" as follows:

(11)   Define as predicate have.
        The definition frame for have is:
        X have Y (from-time T1 to-time T2).
        The definition is:
        Means that X **POSS** Y from T1 to T2.
        ##

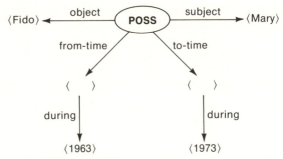

FIGURE 8.5
Semantic structure representing the possession stative
proposition "Mary had Fido from 1963 to 1973." Note
the similarity to Figure 8.1.

If we were now to input the sentence

(12)   Mary had Fido from 1963 until 1973.

the structure shown in Figure 8.5 would be constructed. Now suppose
that one sense of the verb "get" has the following definition:

(13)   Define as predicate get.
        The definition frame for get is:
        X gets Y (from Z at-time T).
        The definition is:
        Means that a **CHANGE** from the state that Z has Y until T to the
        state that X has Y from T occurs at T.
        ##

If at this point we entered the sentence

(14)   Mary got Fido from John.

then the old structure, Figure 8.5, would be augmented by the structure for the new information in (14). The result would be the more
complex structure illustrated in Figure 8.6. By defining a few more
terms, we can illustrate the principles by which the system can be
readily expanded to encompass a reasonable set of English words.
For example, we can define one sense of the word "give" (as in "John
gave the ball to Mary") to be:

(15)   Define as predicate give.
        The definition frame for give is:
        X gives Y to Z (method M at-time T).
        The definition is:
        Means that X **CAUSES** Z to get Y from X by M at T.
        ##

Similarly, we can define one sense of the verb "remember" (as in "John remembered that he gave the ball to Mary") to be:

(16)   Define as predicate remember.
        The definition frame for remember is:
        X remembers proposition Y (at-time T).
        The definition is:
        Means that the **INFORMATION** about Y is moved from X's memory
        to X's consciousness at T.
        ##

In the preceding definition the term **INFORMATION** is an operation whose argument is believed by X to be a fact. Finally, we define one sense of the verb "make" (as in "John made his brother stay home") to be:

(17)   Define as predicate make.
        The definition frame for make is:
        X makes proposition Y (at-time T method M).
        The definition is:
        Means that X **CAUSES** proposition Y by M at T.
        ##

Now, if the sentence

(18)   John remembered that he gave Fido to Mary.

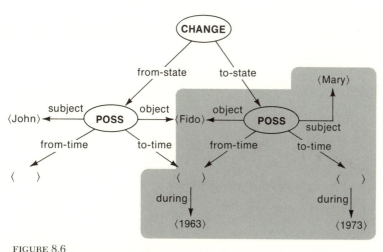

FIGURE 8.6
Semantic structure representing the change-of-possession-state proposition "Mary got Fido from John." The shaded area is the structure that was stored by previous inputs (see Figure 8.5); the unshaded area represents the information added by the new sentence.

is entered into the system, it will further augment the data base, resulting in the structure shown in Figure 8.7. Suppose further that the term "happy" is essentially a surface version of a primitive stative that we will call **HAPPY**. Then, if we input the sentence

(19)   John made Mary happy by giving Fido to her.

the data structure illustrated in Figure 8.8 is returned.

The examples given thus far indicate the ways that incoming information can be decomposed into semantic primitives and integrated into previously existing data structures. We now turn to a discussion of the ways that we can use these same capabilities to retrieve the answers to certain simple questions.

Answering Questions

The kinds of questions a system ought to be able to answer, given that it has stored the information shown in Figure 8.8, are as follows. First, here are some types of *yes-no questions*:

(20A)   Did John have a dog before 1963?

(20B)   Did a woman take Fido from John?

(20C)   Did John know that he gave Fido to Mary?

(20D)   Did John cause Mary to get a dog?

(20E)   Was Mary happy because a man gave Fido to her?

And here are some *wh-questions*:

(21A)   What did Mary get from John?

(21B)   Whom did John give Fido to?

(21C)   Why was Mary happy?

(21D)   From whom did Mary take Fido?

(21E)   How did Mary get Fido?

The answers to these and many other questions are, of course, implicit in the input sentences. Given appropriate definitions for the primitive procedures, the system can retrieve the information necessary to answer these and similar questions.

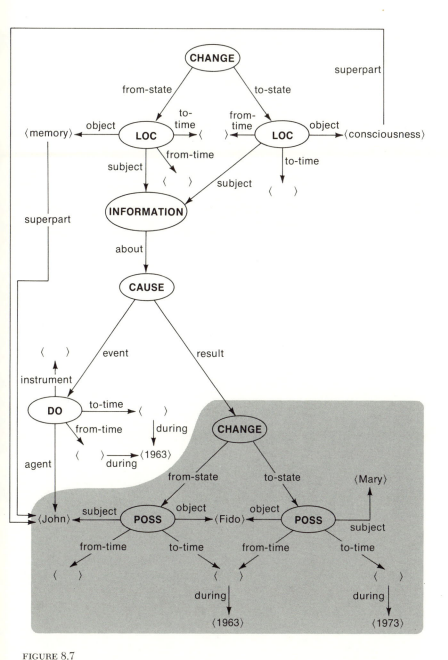

FIGURE 8.7
Semantic structure for the proposition with an embedded propositional argument "John remembered that he gave Fido to Mary." The shaded area is the structure stored by previous inputs (see Figure 8.6).

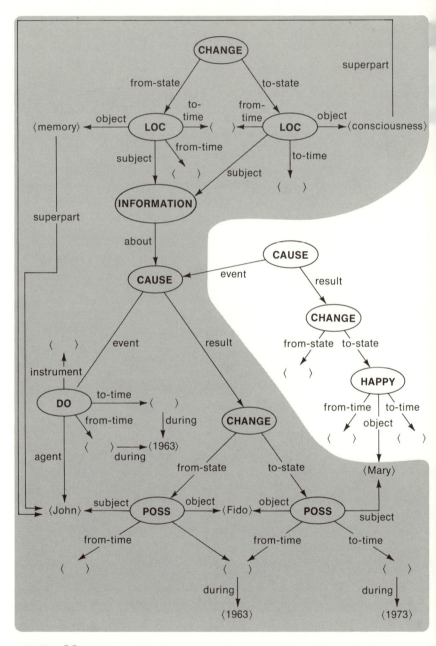

FIGURE 8.8
Semantic structure resulting from the sentence "John made Mary happy by giving Fido to her" and previous knowledge (the area that is shaded—see Figure 8.7).

Yes-No Questions.   When the parser encounters a *yes-no question*, it builds a token of a procedure called **TFques**. The only argument of this procedure is the node structure for the content of the question. This structure is equivalent to the structure created by the corresponding declarative sentence. For example, suppose the sentence

(22)   John had Fido before March 1964.

had been given to the system. The parser would have produced the output shown in Figure 8.9A. Had the sentence

(23)   Did John have Fido before March 1964?

been given, the structure illustrated in Figure 8.9B would have been constructed. Then, the question is answered by evaluating that structure (shown in Figure 8.9B), starting with the **TFques** token. **TFques**

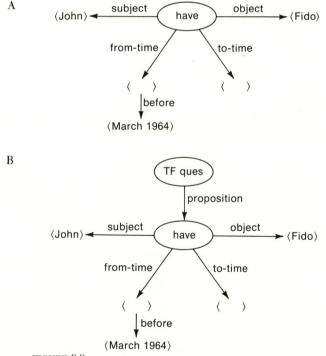

FIGURE 8.9
A shows the parsed structure for the sentence "John had Fido before 1964." B shows the parsed structure for the question "Did John have Fido before 1964?"

evaluates its propositional argument. If the structure corresponding to the propositional argument is found in memory by the primitives, that structure is returned to TFques, which then outputs the answer "Yes." If the structure corresponding to the proposition is not found (or if only part of it is found), the procedure TFques outputs the answer "No, I don't think so."

In the case of sentence 23, the system would find a match in memory (see Figure 8.8) and would answer "Yes." It should be noted that a "yes" answer here involves an inference and is not just a matter of parroting back information that was previously entered. The inference was made by the system when it learned that John had given Fido to Mary. According to our definition of "give," one can give only what one already possesses; hence, since John gave Fido away in 1963, he must have had the dog sometime before March 1964. (The procedures that infer that 1963 is before March 1964 are presented in a later section.)

Other, more subtle inferences can be made in this same way. For example, suppose that one sense of the verb "know" has the following definition:

(24)   Define as predicate know.
        The definition frame for know is:
        X knows proposition Y (from-time T1 to-time T2).
        The definition is:
        Means that the **INFORMATION** about Y is located in X's memory from T1 to T2.
        ##

Now, it should be clear that the Verbworld system could correctly answer the question

(20C)   Did John know that he gave Fido to Mary?

This is inferred from the fact that John remembered the giving (sentence 18), and according to our definition of "remember," one can only remember what one already knows.

This strategy is only slightly complicated by questions like 20A, B, D, and E, in which one or more of the arguments is referred to intensionally by specification of a general class ("dog" instead of "Fido," "woman" instead of "Mary"). In this case, the question can be answered if any member of the class in question was involved in the events or states suggested. To answer these types of questions, it is only necessary to extend the definitions of the pattern-matching procedures used in the search so that successful retrieval occurs whenever any member of the class is found to match the structure in question. In all other respects the question-answering process proceeds as explained previously.

Wh-questions. The process of answering *wh-questions* is nearly identical to that of answering *yes-no questions.* The only difference is that, rather than answering "Yes" when a match is found in the data base, the system answers with those concepts that fill the queried argument slot of the retrieved structure (or structures).

Perhaps the easiest way to explain the answering of *wh-questions* is to give some examples. Suppose the following question were asked of the system:

(25)   Who had Fido before 1964?

In this case the parser builds the structure illustrated in Figure 8.10. Note that this structure differs in only two respects from the one shown in Figure 8.9B for the question "Did John have Fido before 1964?" First, the highest procedure is a token of **who** rather than **TFques.** Second, the queries argument in Figure 8.10 is itself a token of **who. Who** fills the queried argument with the class name **person** (in effect, converting the question "Did a person have Fido before 1964?"), and then specially marks the argument so that a list is constructed containing those elements in the data base that satisfy the constraint. The final answer to the question consists of this list. In the current data base (Figure 8.8), both "John" and "Mary" would satisfy the constraints, and the answer "John and Mary" would be given.

Questions involving "what," "where," "whom," and so on, are all answered by a similar procedure. The only differences are the constraints on the answer set and on the particular argument slot queried.

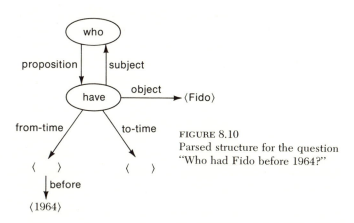

FIGURE 8.10
Parsed structure for the question
"Who had Fido before 1964?"

Other questions cause slightly different problems. A certain set of question words, those we call **Qdets**, appear in constructions like the following:

(26)   Which man had Fido before 1964?

In this case the structure shown in Figure 8.11 is constructed. **Qdets** such as "which" or "what" take two arguments: the constraint on the queried element and on the embedded proposition. A question containing a **Qdet** is answered in the same way as a *wh-question*, except that the **Qdet** question constrains the answer set with its explicit argument. Thus, question 26 constrains its answer set to members of the category "man," returning with an answer set containing only "John."

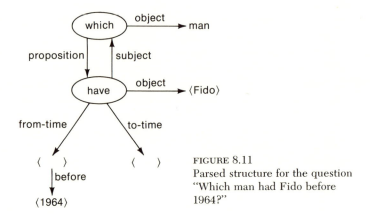

FIGURE 8.11
Parsed structure for the question "Which man had Fido before 1964?"

One other interesting aspect of **Qdets** is that the same procedures can be used to compute restrictive relative clauses. For example, "The man who had Fido before 1964 . . ." requires the same calculations as sentence 26, and in fact the same procedures are used within **Verbworld**.

The Representation of Time in **Verbworld**[4]

One problem not addressed in the previous section is that of locating events in time. All surface verbs in the **Verbworld** system accept temporal arguments. A fairly large portion of the system is devoted to

[4]The model for the structure and processing of time presented here is derived from a representation developed by David Navon.

processing these arguments. Upon input of information about some event or state, the system attempts to match it with information already stored in memory. It is important that the temporal arguments of new information be consistent with those of potentially matching structures in memory. Unfortunately, time specifications are often incomplete. They are often vague (for example, when they include a past-tense verb), but they can be very precise. The temporal-matching procedure must be capable of utilizing all temporal information, whatever the degree of vagueness.

Recall that we have defined each of our primitive *stative* and *actional* components to have starting and ending times. These times are viewed as instantaneous moments. The precise instant at which a moment occurs is, of course, never known. Instead, it is only specified as being either *before*, *after*, or *during* the occurrence of some other event in memory. The most important of these other events are those that belong to a "reference sequence" of events. A sequence of events can serve as a reference sequence if, for any two elements of the sequence, we can always determine which of the two elements occurred first. Thus, the sequence of calendar events is a prime example because, given any two dates at the same level of specification, there are simple rules for determining which came first. Other examples of such sequences are: years in school, sequence of houses lived in, sequence of schools attended. In **Verbworld**, the sequence of calendar dates is the reference sequence most often used. The representation of a segment of that sequence is illustrated in Figure 8.12.

The representation shown in Figure 8.12 allows us to illustrate events with various degrees of temporal specificity. For example, June 9, 1969 is a more precise level of specificity than June 1969 or the year 1969 because it is a subpart of those events. Furthermore,

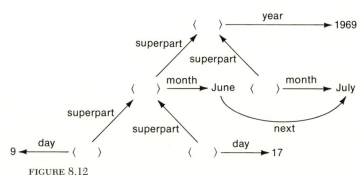

FIGURE 8.12
Representation of one part of the temporal reference sequence.

June 9, 1969 occurred before June 17, 1969 because the two dates are part of the same month and because the number 9 is less than the number 17; June 9, 1969 occurred before July 1969 because June 9 is a subpart of June 1969, which, in turn, occurred before July 1969 (since we know that June comes before July). Finally, June 9, 1969 occurred before any time in 1974 because it occurred in 1969, and the number 1969 is smaller than the number 1974.

The time of some new event cannot always be related to the occurrence of any element of a reference sequence. In such a case, we may know how it relates in time with some other event stored in memory. Such temporal relationships are represented as relations between the starting and stopping moments of the events. For example, if event A occurred before event B, that fact would be represented by connecting the ending time of event A to the beginning of event B with the relation *before*.

When trying to match a new input to a previously stored structure, the system must determine that both the start times and the end times of the two predicates are consistent. Two moments are consistent if neither moment is known to have occurred before the other. If the start time of a stored event was during 1969 and the start time of the newly input event was during June 17, 1969, these start times are consistent, since 1969 is neither before nor after June 17, 1969. Thus, the question of whether one moment is known to be before or after another moment is continually posed while the system is trying to match structures. This question is resolved in one of two ways:

- If there is a string of **before** relations from one of the moments to the other.
- If one moment is **during** or **after** an element of some reference sequence and the other moment is **during** or **before** an earlier element of the same sequence.

Otherwise, the times are assumed to be consistent and a match is made.

Suppose the fact that "Mary got Fido in 1963" is stored (see Figure 8.8). When the input "John gave Fido to Mary on May 17, 1963" is encountered, this new input will be matched to the old, because May 17, 1963 is consistent with the previously stored information. If the input "Mary gave Fido to Peter in May 1972" were encountered, no match would occur. In the old structure, Mary still possessed Fido until a time that is during 1973 (see Figure 8.8), and in the new structure Mary ceased to possess Fido during 1972. Since 1973 is greater than 1972 the times are not consistent.

Reference in Verbworld

Here we simply outline the procedures used in **Verbworld** to discover the appropriate referents.

Indefinite Reference.   We need to consider two cases of indefinite reference — *specific* and *intensional*. In **Verbworld**, all indefinite references are assumed to be specific, except in the case of questions, which are always assumed to be intensional. The job of finding the referent is carried out by procedures invoked by the indefinite articles ("a," "an," "some"). These terms are the names of procedures in **Verbworld** that decide whether the reference is *specific* or *generic*: If it is *specific*, they create new concepts; if it is *generic*, they define the class to which the referent belongs.

Definite Reference.   **Verbworld** always assumes that definite noun phrases are *specific references*. There is no provision for the intensional usage of definite noun phrases illustrated in Chapter 3. (Thus, "the first man on the moon . . ." always refers to a particular person.) The task of finding the intended referent is accomplished by the procedures associated with the definite article or pronoun in question, depending on how the definite noun phrase is expressed.

The Definite Determiner "The."   Suppose the task is to determine the appropriate memory structure for some concept X that has been referred to by the phrase ". . . the X . . . ." (X may be a single word or a complete phrase.) The word "the" automatically invokes a set of strategies that examine the phrase X. The strategies are:

- execution of operators
- relative clauses
- unique instances
- recency within short-term memory
- use in the indefinite sense

In brief, the strategies work as follows. First, if the phrase under discussion, X, contains an operator (for example, "the sum of 3 and 4"), then the phrase itself contains the procedures for disambiguation. These procedures are executed before anything else is done. If the phrase is a relative clause (for example, "the man who discovered America"), it is evaluated to see if this results in a concept unique within the current context. If the phrase is not an operator or relative clause, or if these procedures fail to find the referent, the next strategy is to determine whether the time being referred to is unique in the mind of the listener. If the item is unique (for example, "the Pacific Ocean"), the problem is solved.

If these strategies fail, the immediate context is checked for a recently mentioned exemplar. ("Immediate context" is the set of recently used concepts, indexed by their lexical names.) For example, consider the following pair of sentences:

(27A) A boy dropped a ball.

(27B) Then the boy picked it up.

The reference procedures within the will find in immediate context the node representing the boy who dropped the ball.

If all else fails, the last strategy is to assume that no particular item corresponds to X. In this case, the determiner "the" is being used like the indefinite determiner "a." These strategies constitute possible psychological operations performed by a listener to help disambiguate concepts introduced by the word "the."

Pronouns[5]

Verbworld contains a set of heuristic strategies that are invoked whenever a pronoun is encountered. Pronouns, unlike the definite article, are always assumed to be disambiguated within immediate context. A pronoun is defined by procedures that search through immediate context for the referent. These procedures check candidates for agreement with the pronoun in number and gender.

Different strategies are used depending on whether the pronoun is reflexive. If the pronoun is reflexive, the referent should occur within the proposition in which the pronoun occurs. For other pronouns, the referent procedures look only at previous propositions. First, the topic under discussion is considered as a possible referent. We take the "topic" to be the term that either was previously pronominalized, or was the subject of the previous sentence. If neither of these concepts meets the number and gender constraints of the pronoun, the procedures then look at the object and the remaining noun phrases of the proposition. If none meets the constraints, the preceding proposition is searched. This process continues until either the procedures find an

---

[5]The pronoun procedures used in Verbworld were developed and implemented by Arthur Graesser II.

appropriate referent, or they run out of elements in the context set. At this point they construct a new node for an unknown individual to serve as referent.

Although this essentially syntactic approach is probably a poor simulation of the underlying psychological processes involved in finding pronominal referents, it is surprisingly successful. Our pronoun strategies accounted for about 90 percent of the uses of pronouns in a set of sample sentences drawn randomly from the *World Book Encyclopedia*.

EXTENSIONS TO VERBWORLD

Partial versus Complete Comprehension

The comprehension process that has been described so far might be called *complete comprehension*. Every predicate term is reduced to its most primitive representation and stored in that form. Virtually all inferences are made during the comprehension process. Furthermore, all propositions are treated equally; propositions that play a peripheral role in the sentence are as deeply analyzed as those playing a central role. This hardly seems a realistic characterization of human sentence comprehension. People seem to be able to decide which aspects of the sentences to interpret fully and which aspects to interpret more superficially.

Considerations such as these led us to develop a variable depth strategy. This variable depth strategy allows information to be stored at different levels in the decomposition process. With this strategy, certain questions will be answered more readily than others. In particular, verification of a sentence is easier if it is identical to a previous sentence than if it is a paraphrase of that previous sentence.

An Example. Consider the sentence "John gave Fido to Mary." According to our definition of "give," this sentence is first decomposed into a structure that might be paraphrased, "John caused Mary to get Fido from himself." If the system were to stop the decomposition at this point, it would produce the structure illustrated in Figure 8.13A. Similarly, it could cease processing at the next level of decomposition (Figure 8.13B), or the next (Figure 8.13C), or the next (Figure 8.13D), or totally convert the input into its most primitive elements.

Although this variable depth of processing notion has a number of intuitively pleasing characteristics, it poses a number of implementation problems. First, the data structure, which was pleasantly uniform

A

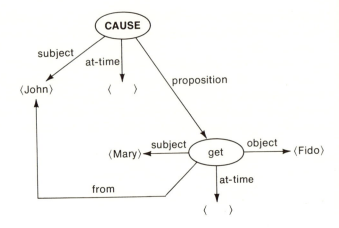

B

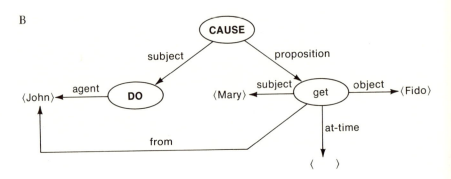

C

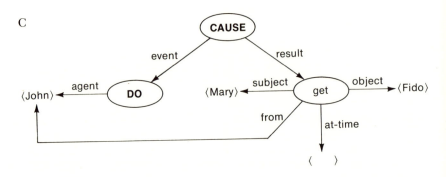

FIGURE 8.13
Representation of the levels of partial comprehension of the sentence "John gave Fido to Mary." A shows the structure resulting from one level of decomposition; B shows two levels; C shows three levels; and D (*facing page*) shows four levels.

up until now, suddenly becomes extremely heterogeneous. In addition, we now have to implement a capability for making inferences at retrieval time as well as at storage time. Nevertheless, these problems pose surprisingly little difficulty within the **Verbworld** system.

The verification of sentences causes no problem. The sentence is comprehended as before, but at each level a check is made to see whether the information is stored at that level. If it is, the comprehension process can be terminated, since the input information is "old." If the information is not found at a given level, the system can accept the input as new information and stop the analysis to build the structure appropriate for that level. Alternatively, the system could probe its memory further by decomposing the information to another level of representation.

Suppose that the information contained in the sentence "John gave Fido to Mary" is stored at the level shown in Figure 8.13B. Suppose further that someone asserts again that "John gave Fido to Mary." In this case, **Verbworld** would find the stored information by decomposing the input sentence one level. Now suppose that someone asserts "Mary got Fido from John." In this case, the appropriate information could be found without decomposing at all. The surface proposition itself would be found in the data structure.

More difficulties arise, however, when information originally was not decomposed enough. Suppose, for example, that the information was stored at the level of Figure 8.13B, and the system was asked the question "Does Mary now have Fido?" In this case, no amount of decomposition of the input question will ever match the stored information.

D

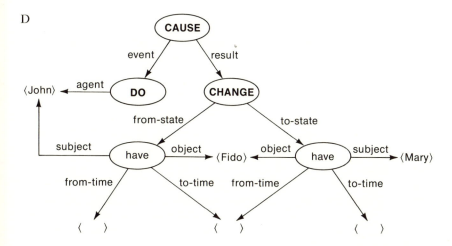

Partial Comprehension and Ambiguity. One of the virtues of partial comprehension is that not much time or effort is spent on understanding and storing unimportant inputs. Another important virtue is that ambiguity can be preserved. Often one hears a sentence that is by itself ambiguous, but that will be disambiguated by later information. If comprehension were always complete, one would be forced to choose a particular interpretation. Partial comprehension allows the option of storing a structure at the lowest level at which it can be unambiguously understood, thus preserving any ambiguity for resolution later, if the need arises. Here is an example:

(28)   The librarian gave the book to Peter.

There are at least two interpretations of this statement. According to one interpretation, there was a transfer of ownership. According to the other, the library retains ownership of the book, but has physically given the book to Peter. These two readings are illustrated in Figures 8.14A and 8.14B.

If there is no clue as to the intended interpretation of the sentence, the ambiguity of the input is preserved by storing the partially comprehended structure illustrated in Figure 8.15. Here the word "have" has deliberately not been decomposed into any of its possible interpretations.

Now, suppose that sentence 28 had actually been:

(29)   The librarian gave the book to Peter. The library had several copies of the volume and no longer needed it.

The second sentence resolves the ambiguity present in the first. If the first sentence in (29) led to the structure shown in Figure 8.15, the second sentence would allow it to be changed to the unambiguous structure shown in Figure 8.14A.

Sophisticated Answering

As currently formulated, the **Verbworld** system should perhaps be called an information-retrieval system rather than a question-answering system. The distinction we have in mind here is between a system that gives answers in a format most amenable to itself versus one that takes into account certain needs and requirements of the person asking the questions. There are a number of ways in which any system can be more or less a question-answering system as opposed to an information-retrieval system.

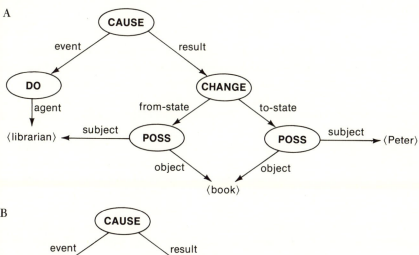

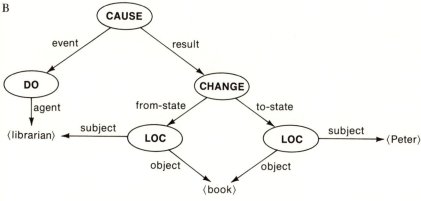

FIGURE 8.14
Two possible representations for the ambiguous sentence
"The librarian gave the book to Peter."

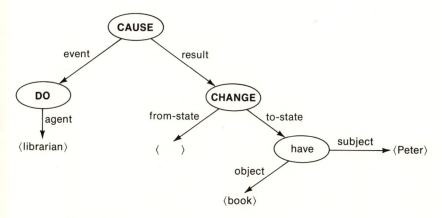

FIGURE 8.15
Partially decomposed representation that preserves the ambiguity
of the sentence "The librarian gave the book to Peter."

At the simplest level, it would be useless for any system to retrieve the relevant information and communicate it to the questioner in some language (or format) that the questioner did not understand. An answer of "Yes," "No," "I don't think so," or any of the answers given by the **Verbworld** system is somewhat better, but such an answer to the question "Do you know the time?" would hardly be satisfactory. Moreover, when a person is asked "Where are you from?" an answer like "Milltown" is only rarely appropriate. It must come as a shock to the lost child to discover that although he knows full well who he is, where he lives, who his father is, and where his mother works, the answers "Johnnie," "on the corner," "Daddy," and "at her office" are not very helpful to the friendly policeman. It also comes as a shock to someone building a question-answering system that figuring out the right answer to the question, tough as that might be, is only part of the problem. Explaining the answer to the questioner is at least as difficult (see the discussion in Norman, 1973).

Although few sophisticated answering procedures have been developed within the **Verbworld** system, in theory it is well suited for the implementation of such procedures. Such developments lie in the future.

SUMMARY

Verbworld is designed to perform language-comprehension and question-answering processes. Of course, such procedures are only a suggestion of ways to establish a psychologically accurate model of language comprehension. Many aspects are left out and many things are probably exaggerated. But **Verbworld** does include many of the principles of human language comprehension.

Verbworld is by no means a finished product. Rather, it is a useful tool for the study of understanding. It has provided a symbiotic relationship between theory development and computer implementation. For the most part, our theoretical ideas have suggested the method of implementation, but in crucial areas such as theory systematization, partial comprehension, and augmentation of answers, the implementation has suggested answers to theoretical issues. The development of **Verbworld** will continue, for it serves both as a useful criterion of the precision of our understanding and as a fertile source of new ideas and problems.

PART V

STUDIES OF LANGUAGE

Evidence for the Psychological Reality of Semantic Components: The Verbs of Possession

DEDRE GENTNER

This chapter is concerned with the way verbs are stored and processed. I use a set of possession verbs as illustrative examples. The first section of the chapter deals with the structural representation of these verbs. The remainder of the chapter is concerned with issues of processing and with experimental tests of the theory.

In this chapter I use the terms "components" and "chunks" to refer to the underlying semantic units of verbs, rather than the term "primitive elements," which is used in the other chapters of this book. I make this change to emphasize that the components analyzed in this chapter need not necessarily represent the members of some universal set of innate semantic features. If such a set exists, most of the components that are described in this chapter are probably combinations of the innate features.

The two main linguistic treatments of the possession verbs are those by Bendix (1966) and Fillmore (1966). Bendix proposed a general analysis of verbs of possession, and in a critique of this work, Fillmore suggested some alternative representations. Schank and his collaborators have also studied verbs of possession (Schank, Goldman, Rieger, and Riesbeck, 1972). My treatment differs from all three of these approaches, although it has some points in common with each.

REPRESENTATION OF THE POSSESSION VERBS

Possession: **POSS**

The first element needed to represent the family of possession verbs is some expression of the state of possession. This stative, which I call **POSS**, indicates possession of an object by a person from some initial time to some final time. For example, the sentence

(1)   Mrs. Vandel owned the Kluge diamond from 1932 to 1939.

FIGURE 9.1

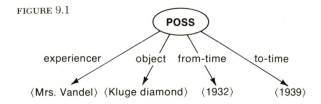

is represented by the structural network shown in Figure 9.1. In this chapter **POSS** represents the intuitive notion of ownership. This does not imply that **POSS** is an unanalyzable whole. It seems clear that **POSS** shares elements of meaning with other statives. One such stative is location (see E. Clark, 1970). Another is "inalienable possession," which is inherently nontransferable "possession," as in sentence 2 (see Kimball, 1973):

(2)   Mrs. Vandel had an imposing appearance.

Knowledge of the components that make up **POSS, LOC**, and the other statives enables us to represent the semantic similarities among these statives and also offers us an analytical approach to the problem of multiple senses of verbs.

Multiple Senses: Metaphorical Extension of **POSS**

A major difficulty in the representation of verbs is the fact that most verbs have many meanings. For example, consider the verb "have" in the following sentences:

(3A)   Sam has a large kettle.

(3B)   Sam has a nice apartment.

(3C)   The kettle has an enamel coating.

(3D)   Sam has good times.

One way of dealing with verb senses is to formulate a definition that serves equally well for all uses of the verb. Bendix's approach is essentially this one (Bendix, 1966). The disadvantage of such an approach is that the resulting definitions are so general that they lose their usefulness for specific instances. For example, a paraphrase of "have" for sentences 3B and 3C would need to omit the notion of ownership; yet ownership is important in the meaning of "have" in sentence 3A.

A second way of handling multiple word senses is to choose one sense as the meaning of the word. Fillmore's claim is that "have" is a real verb when it means "possess" but serves a merely syntactic function in its other senses (Fillmore, 1966). This approach avoids the difficulties presented by an all-inclusive definition. However, it also tends to obscure the semantic relations among the different senses of the verb.

In this chapter the verbs are defined in their basic possessive senses. In my view the other senses of these verbs are not a separate class but are metaphorical extensions of the meaning of the basic sense. In each of these extensions some, but not all, of the elements that characterize **POSS** are preserved.

For example, in sentences 3A and 3B,

(3A)   Sam has a large kettle.

(3B)   Sam has a nice apartment.

the verb "has" conveys the idea that Sam has the right to use the object as it is normally used: to live in the apartment, to cook with the kettle. However, the right to transfer possession of the object is present in sentence 3A but not in sentence 3B. Sam can sell the kettle if he wants to, but not the apartment. In sentence 3D,

(3D)   Sam has good times.

very few of the elements of **POSS** remain.

Moreover, notice that although we can speak of transfer of good times, as in

(4)   Sam gave Chlorette a good time.

the transfer differs from the normal transfer of **POSS** in that Sam can continue to have a good time himself after the transfer. Had he given Chlorette a zircon the situation would be different. **POSS** conveys exclusive possession; if Chlorette owns something, Sam does not. It is understood, though, that the relation between Sam and good times in sentence 3D is not the full **POSS**, but something more like "experiences." The properties of the transfer (giving a good time) are inferred from the properties of the state of having a good time.

The analysis of **POSS** into more primitive components should allow us to describe the elements that take part in a given metaphorical extension. However, in the remainder of the chapter I will be concerned only with the basic possessive senses of the verbs. In this context **POSS** can be treated as simple ownership of concrete objects.

Transfer of Possession: **TRANSF**

TRANSF is a higher-level component that stands for change of possession of an object from one person to another. The argument structure of **TRANSF** is shown in Figure 9.2.[1] The **TRANSF** chunk is similar to the *transfer-of-possession* that Schank and his co-workers call **ATRANS** (Schank, 1973b). The chief difference is that **ATRANS**, like the other primitive verbs in Schank's system, is defined as a unitary action, whereas the **TRANSF** component used here consists of a **CHANGE** component acting on a stative of possession (see Figure 9.2). I prefer the **TRANSF** analysis; first, because it makes apparent the relation between stative verbs like "have" and verbs of change like "give"; and second, because explicit representation of the stative components of verbs helps clarify metaphorical extension.

TRANSF *and Causality: The Abstract Act* **DO**. The **TRANSF** chunk does not specify any causal agency for the change of possession. However, many verbs include a statement about the causal agent as part of their meanings.

---

[1]In this (and later) figures in this chapter, shaded nodes indicate a repetition of a node shown elsewhere in the figure, but duplicated for clarity.

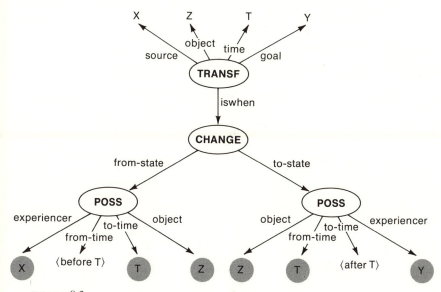

FIGURE 9.2

Transfer of possession: Object Z passes from the possession of person X to the possession of person Y at time T.

Consider the transfer of object Z from X to Y:

> If X instigated the action, we can say X **gave** Z to Y.
> If Y instigated the action, we can say Y **took** Z from X.

A few verbs of possession, such as "grab," "seize," and "hand," specify not only the agent of the transfer but also the action that was performed to cause the transfer to occur. However, in general, the possession verbs tend not to specify actional components. What is specified is which transfers take place and who instigates them, and sometimes why; rarely is it important to know exactly how the transfers are accomplished. Thus, the abstract causal act **DO** is normally used in this chapter to represent the event by which the agent caused the change in possession to occur. This is in keeping with the analyses presented in the other chapters of this book.

Using the components discussed to this point, it is possible to define such verbs as "give" and "take." The structural representations for "give" and "take" are shown in Figure 9.3.

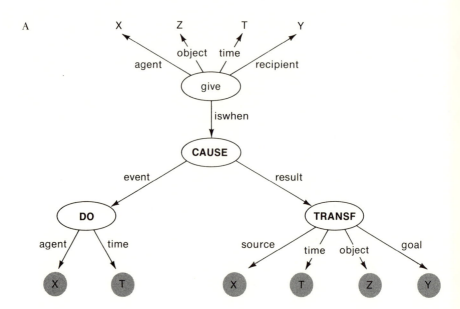

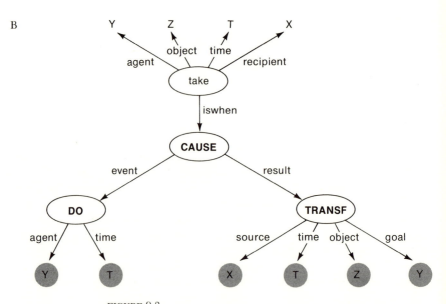

FIGURE 9.3
Structural representations for "give" and "take":
A "X gives Y a Z at time T."
B "Y takes Z from X at time T."

TRANSF, Negation, and Presupposition

The meaning of **TRANSF** includes both the initial state and the final state of possession, as well as the change from one to the other. The sentence

(5)   I took some candy from the children (at time T).

communicates a number of different aspects of the event: the initial state, the final state, the change to the final state, and the cause of the change. Thus, the following ideas are all contained within (5):

(6A)   The children had some candy (before time T). [*The initial state*]

(6B)   I had some candy (for some time after T). [*The final state*]

(6C)   I got some candy (at time T). [*The change to the final state*]

(6D)   I caused myself to get some candy (at time T). [*The causal element*]

All of these submeanings are normally communicated by "take."
    A problem arises with negative sentences. As Fillmore points out, the negation of sentence 5

(5)   I took some candy from the children.

affects only the change to the final state part of the transfer, not the initial state; that is,

(7)   I didn't take any candy from the children.

normally conveys that the speaker did not get any candy but *not* that the children did not have candy. Fillmore builds this difference into his representation of "take." In his system, only sentence 6D, which contains the causal element and the change to the final state, makes up the asserted meaning of the verb. The initial state that the children had some candy is not directly communicated, but is a presupposition. In other words, it is part of the necessary background information (along with the fact that the children exist, and so on) that must be true in order for the sentence to make sense. (A more complete discussion of presupposition is given in Chapter 4.)
    Although Fillmore's representation captures the behavior of "take" under negation, the omission of the initial state from the "asserted meaning" seems clearly wrong for positive sentences. The **TRANSF**

chunk has the advantage that it represents the full positive meaning, including both the initial and final states. To this **TRANSF** representation we can add a conversational postulate that states that negating a change-of-state verb such as "take" does not normally affect the initial state, but affects only the change to the final state.

There is an independent motivation for this postulate. There are indefinitely many negative sentences that could truthfully be uttered. One could edify one's companions with remarks like

(8A)   I didn't take any diamonds from the children.

(8B)   Robespierre didn't take any animal crackers from Sophie Tucker.

and so on. People normally talk about what did not happen only when it might well have happened. It is only plausible to utter a negative sentence when some, but not all, of the chunks that would have been conveyed by the positive sentence are in fact valid. Sometimes the speaker uses special stress to indicate which part of the meaning should be negated, as in

(9A)   I didn't take any **candy** from the children.

(9B)   I didn't take any candy from the **children**.

In the absence of special information, one normally assumes only that the change of state did not occur. With this postulate we can capture the effect of negation on change-of-state verbs while still representing the full positive meaning of the verb.

Obligation: **OBLIG**

The verbs "give" and "take" can be represented simply as actions on the part of a person that result in transfer of possession, but many possession verbs are more complex. Some notion of obligation is included in the meanings of many of these verbs. Sometimes only one person is obligated, as in the verb "owe." More often there is mutual obligation, as in verbs of exchange such as "buy" and "trade." A common pattern is that two actions must be completed to fulfill the meaning of the verb. For example, consider this story:

(10)   Ida and Sam decided to trade speakers since hers were too big for her apartment. She delivered hers to him on Wednesday but by Saturday he still hadn't brought his over.

Here we can see several features of these verbs. First, there is an initial agreement, either explicit or, as in a store where the rules are well known, implicit. Each party agrees to be obligated to perform some action in return for the other party's performing his action. I call the stative component of the verb that denotes this obligation **OBLIG**.

Sometimes a final time by which both actions must be completed is specified. But even if such a time is not made explicit, there is some implicit feeling about the duration, such that the tardy person becomes increasingly in the wrong after some vaguely defined interval following the completion of the other half of the bargain. In informal situations, the completion of one person's action tends to ratify the agreement, and thus confirms the other person's state of **OBLIG**. Words such as "buy" and "sell" normally imply that the transfers of both the object being purchased and the money being paid take place at the same time.[2] Words such as "borrow" and "loan" imply that there is a reasonably long interval between the initial transfer of the object being loaned and the final transfer of the object back to the loaner.

Notice that the notion of **OBLIG** is concerned with the acceptance of a social or moral requirement. One would not use **OBLIG** in the case of a man who was being robbed. The actions that are agreed upon are most often transfer of possession, as in "trade," "buy," or "return." But other sorts of actions are also possible, as in the verbs "hire," "work for," and "contract." Thus **OBLIG** is a stative denoting the social or moral necessity for performing a certain action. The structural format for **OBLIG** is shown in Figure 9.4.

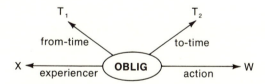

FIGURE 9.4
The argument structure of **OBLIG**: X has been in
a state of obligation since time T1 to perform the
action W by time T2.

---

[2]In this and later analysis, I use the term "money" to include all formal acts that have become equivalent to the actual physical use of money, such as presentation of a check or a credit card to the seller.

Mutual Obligation or Contract: **CONTR**

Some verbs are concerned with a state of obligation that applies to one person only. For example, "owe" and "pay" communicate a state of **OBLIG** on the part of the owner or payer, but do not convey that the other person is in a state of **OBLIG**. However, there are many verbs that involve two co-agents who both agree to be obligated to perform actions. I use the term **CONTR** to refer to the state of mutual obligation to perform stated actions. The structure of **CONTR** is shown in Figure 9.5.

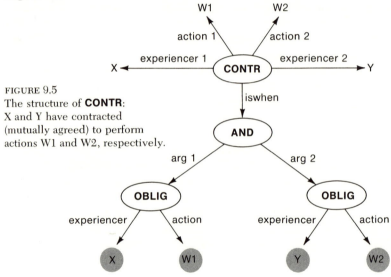

FIGURE 9.5
The structure of **CONTR**:
X and Y have contracted
(mutually agreed) to perform
actions W1 and W2, respectively.

BOX 9.1 *(continued)*

I. COMPONENTS USED IN THESE DIAGRAMS.

CAUSE   The causal connection between an event and its result.

DO   An unspecified action performed by some agent: the abstract actional component of the verb.

CHANGE   A change from one state to another state.

POSS   The state of ownership by the experiencer of the specified object.

TRANSF   The change of possession (transfer) of an object from one person to another.

OBLIG   The state of societal obligation to perform some act or series of acts.

CONTR   The state of mutual societal obligation in which each of two persons is obliged to perform an (in general, different) agreed-upon act.

AND   A general conjunction, all of whose arguments must be fulfilled.

II. RELATION NAMES USED IN THESE DIAGRAMS.

Name of the relation	Symbol normally used for the argument of the relation	Description of the relation
Agent	X	human performer of an action
Experiencer	–	human who undergoes an indicated state
Recipient	Y	human who is the nonagentive participant in an action (the indirect object)
Object	Z	physical object
Source	–	initial possessor of an object
Goal	–	final possessor of an object
Argument (arg)	–	one of the argument relations of the conjunction **AND**
Action	W	action to be performed

(continued)

BOX 9.1 (*continued*)

III. STRUCTURAL REPRESENTATIONS OF A SET OF POSSESSION VERBS.

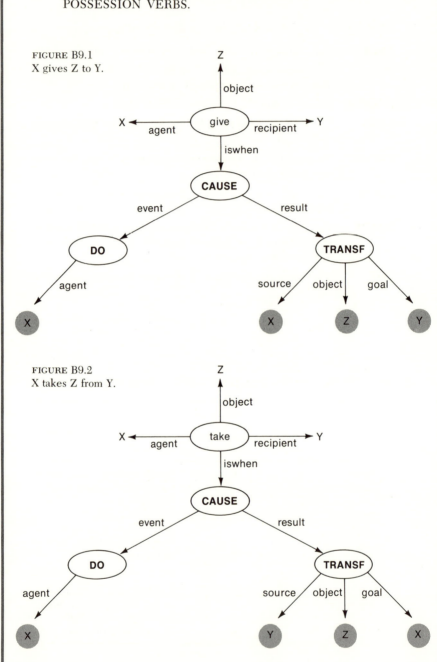

FIGURE B9.1
X gives Z to Y.

FIGURE B9.2
X takes Z from Y.

(*continued*)

BOX 9.1 *(continued)*

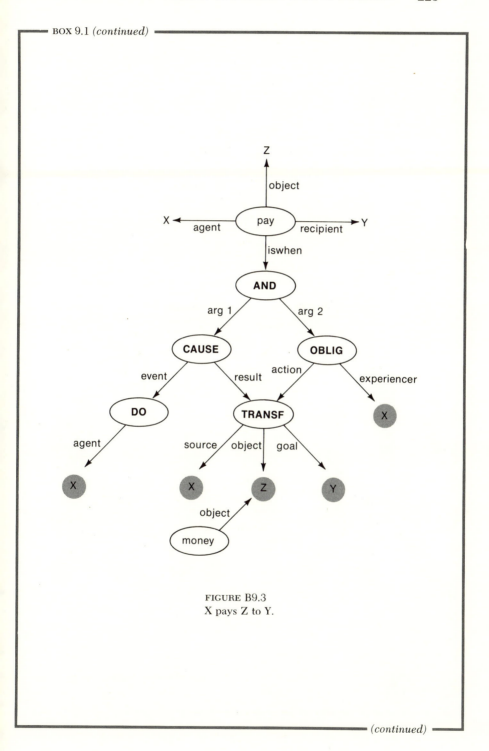

FIGURE B9.3
X pays Z to Y.

BOX 9.1 *(continued)*

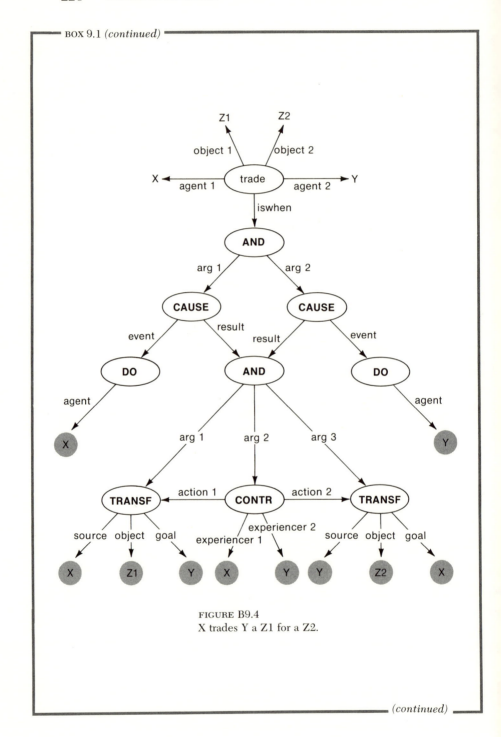

FIGURE B9.4
X trades Y a Z1 for a Z2.

(continued)

BOX 9.1 *(continued)*

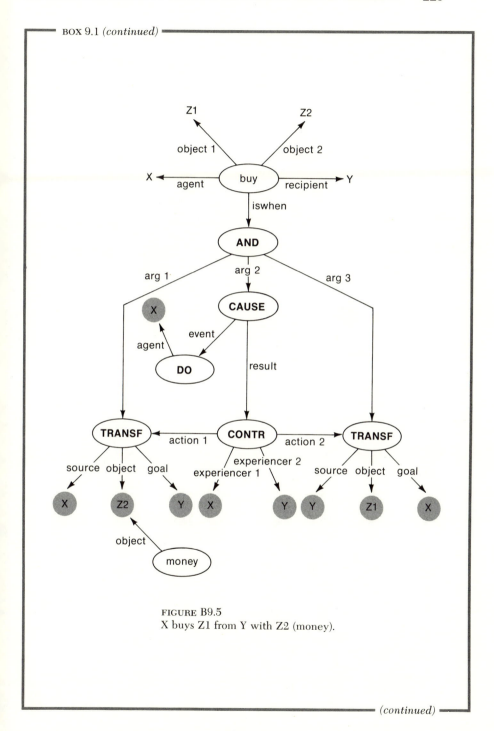

FIGURE B9.5
X buys Z1 from Y with Z2 (money).

BOX 9.1 (*continued*)

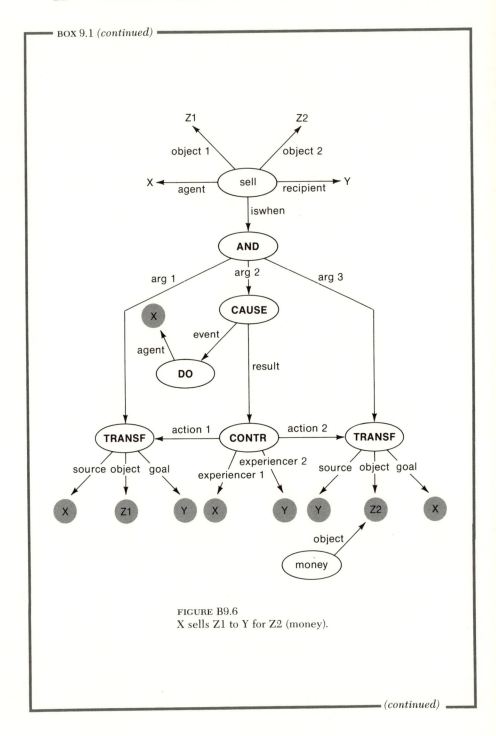

FIGURE B9.6
X sells Z1 to Y for Z2 (money).

(*continued*)

BOX 9.1 (continued)

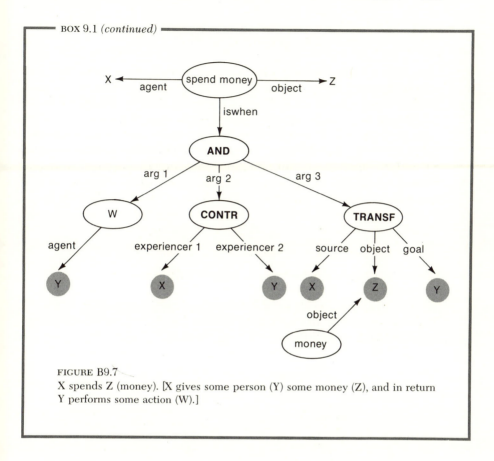

FIGURE B9.7
X spends Z (money). [X gives some person (Y) some money (Z), and in return Y performs some action (W).]

MEMORY FOR CHUNKS

To understand the meaning of a sentence, it is necessary to expand the lexical items to their semantic components and to link these components in the way specified by the sentence. To read out a sentence from memory requires the production of a set of words that correspond to the interrelated chunks. This process of going from the semantic components to the surface words is akin to the linguistic notions of predicate-raising (McCawley, 1968a) and "conflation" (Talmy, 1972). There are usually several ways to combine the chunks into words. A set of chunks may be read out as "went by foot" or as "walked," for example. Usually it is not possible to predict exactly what lexicalization should result from a given structure. However, we can make some general predictions.

Confusions among Semantically Similar Verbs

If verbs are stored as interrelated sets of chunks, then recall for verbs should depend on the recall for chunks. An immediate implication is that verbs whose underlying structures overlap should be more confusable than verbs whose structures are very different.

In an experiment designed to test for such confusions, I showed subjects triads of sentences. The verbs in two of the sentences (types S1 and S2) had chunks in common; the verb in the third sentence (type D) had little or no semantic overlap with the other two verbs. All three sentences had the same agent, as in the following triad:

(11A)   Ida received the backpack. (type *S1: similar*)

(11B)   Ida borrowed the tablecloth. (type *S2: similar*)

(11C)   Ida ruined the drafting set. (type *D: different*)

Figure 9.6 shows the structural networks for sentences 11A, B, and C. The sections of the networks for "receive" and "borrow" that overlap (the **CHANGE** of **POSS** sections) are shaded.

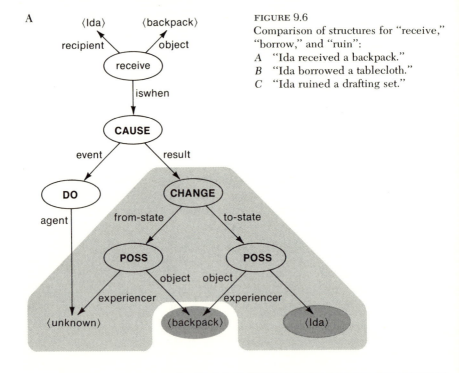

FIGURE 9.6
Comparison of structures for "receive," "borrow," and "ruin":
A   "Ida received a backpack."
B   "Ida borrowed a tablecloth."
C   "Ida ruined a drafting set."

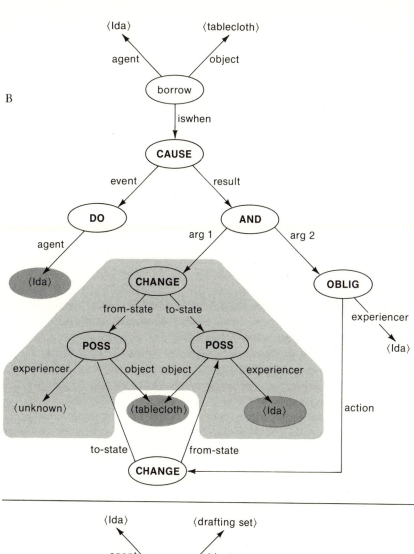

B

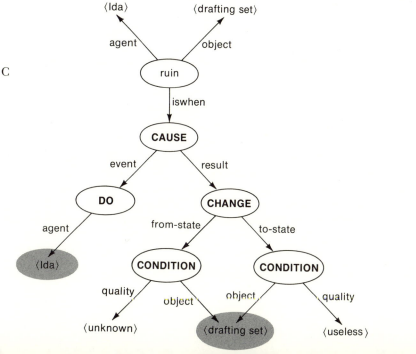

C

Consider a subject who has seen three sentences of the form shown in (11A, B, and C) and who has forgotten some of the underlying components. In particular, consider the subject who has retained some of the information shown in the shaded portions of Figures 9.6A and 9.6B, but who has lost the links with the rest of the network for the verbs. Suppose we now test him by presenting one of the following probes:

(12A)   Ida borrowed _____.

or

(12B)   Ida received _____.

Both probes contain substructures (the shaded areas in Figures 9.6A and 9.6B) that are consistent with either of his partial networks: the structure concerning possession of the backpack and the structure concerning possession of the tablecloth. The subject who has lost the connecting links for these substructures should be unable to tell which fragment belongs with which probe. Since sentences of type D have little or no overlap with the other sentences, a probe derived from a sentence of type D

(13)   Ida ruined _____.

should seldom lead to confusion. The theoretical prediction is that because of the overlap in the structures, there should be more object confusions between sentences of types S1 and S2 than between sentences of types S1 and D or S2 and D.

Since the predictions for the experiment concern only errors, subjects were deliberately overloaded in an effort to increase the number of errors. Each subject heard 40 sentences. The stimuli were 8 S1-S2-D triads (making 24 sentences) randomly interspersed with filler sentences. The subjects were instructed to remember the sentences for a recall task. In addition, they were told that they would have to write a brief impression of each of the 4 people who were the agents of the 40 sentences: Ida, Frederick, Sam, and Violet. (For each agent there were 2 triads and 4 filler sentences.) The subjects were asked to write the impressions in order to encourage them to comprehend the sentences, not simply to memorize them. Within each triad the pairing of verbs and objects was counterbalanced over 3 groups of subjects.

Under these conditions subjects made a large number of errors. Only 31 percent of the responses were correct; another 55 percent were omitted entirely. The errors of interest were the confusion errors, in which an object that was presented with one verb was mistakenly recalled with another verb. These constituted 8 percent of the responses. As predicted, confusions between objects of overlapping verbs greatly outnumbered confusions between objects of nonoverlapping verbs. Eighty-one percent of the confusion errors occurred between S1 and S2 sentences, although by chance alone these errors should have constituted only one-third of the total number of responses. Table 9.1 presents the proportions of confusion errors of each type. The overlap between verbs S1 and S2 existed wholly at the level of semantic representation. The high proportion of confusions between them is strong support for a componential treatment of meaning.

TABLE 9.1
Confusions in which the object presented with one verb is mistakenly recalled with another verb.

Confusion type	Sentence used for agent-verb cue	Sentence in which recalled object was actually presented	Proportion[a]
similar-similar	S1 S2	S2 S1	0.81
similar-different	S1 S2	D D	0.13
different-similar	D D	S1 S2	0.06

[a]$F(2,60) = 6.66$; $p < 0.01$.

Shifts between General and Specific Verbs

When parts of the structure for a verb are forgotten, the verb may be recalled as a more general verb, one that lacks some of the chunks of the verb actually heard. For example, the sentence

(14)   Ida bought a lawn mower.

might be recalled as

(15)   Ida got a lawn mower.

if the structural information necessary for the more specific verb "bought" has been lost. Palmer (personal communication) obtained this specific-to-general shift in noun recognition. In his experiment subjects were less likely to notice the substitution of a general noun (such as "flowers" in sentence 16B) for a specific noun (such as "tulips" in sentence 16A) than the substitution of a specific noun for a general noun.

(16A)   The boy noticed the tulips in the park.

(16B)   The boy noticed the flowers in the park.

It is also possible to produce general-to-specific errors. If chunks are added by context to the network for a general verb, the resulting structure may look identical to the one for a more specific verb. In this case the extra chunk will sometimes be recalled as part of the verb, producing a shift from a general verb to a specific verb.

For example, consider the pair of words "give" and "pay." The meaning of "pay" is almost the same as that of "give" with the addition of the specification of the object as money and of the element of owing (a state of **OBLIG** to **TRANSF** something). Suppose someone hears a statement that combines "give" with a prior condition of owing and with the notion that the object involved is money. He should construct a structural representation that looks like the structure for "pay." One would then expect him to use the word "pay" when he recalls the passage.

In a simple demonstration of this phenomenon, I presented subjects with one of two stories, each ending with the same final sentence:

(17)   Max finally gave Sam the ten dollars.

In one story, Max was described as owing money to Sam. In the other story, Sam simply asked Max for some money. The two groups of subjects were then asked to recall the story as accurately as possible. The results of their recall of the critical sentence, sentence 17, are presented in Table 9.2. When sentence 17 was presented in the story that involved owing, subjects used the phrases "paid" and "paid back" considerably more often than they used the correct word "gave" (47 percent compared with 30 percent). Subjects who had heard the story that involved asking for money recalled sentence 17 quite differently. No subjects used the words "paid" or "paid back." One-third of the subjects used the word "loaned": the same fraction that used the correct word "give."

Since no subjects heard the word "pay" in the experiment, the high incidence of false recalls of "pay" and "paid back" in the "owing" version is not the result of simple memory for lexical items. Further, the fact that no subjects made the "pay" substitution in the "asking"

TABLE 9.2
Substitutions for the verb "give" after a story about Sam and Max.

Verbs recalled in sentence 17	When sentence appeared:	
	In a story containing "owing" (percent)	In a story containing "asking" (percent)
gave (the correct response)	30	33
paid	31	0
paid back	17	0
loaned	0	34
other	22	33

version rules out the possibility that "pay" simply fitted better in the sentence. I conclude that subjects constructed a componential representation that encompassed not merely the immediate verb presented ("give") but also its context. When they were asked to recall the story, they had to partition their semantic structures into words, which often yielded words that were different from those that they had originally heard. These results, like the results of the semantic confusions experiment, support a model of memory in which verbal material is stored as sets of interrelated components.

SEMANTIC STRUCTURE AND THE ACQUISITION OF MEANING: AN EXPERIMENTAL ANALYSIS

If word meanings are embedded within structural networks composed of interrelated semantic components, then acquisition of word meaning should be largely explainable in terms of the acquisition of components and the relations among them. There is considerable evidence that the development of word meanings proceeds by gradual addition of chunks to existing representations. The work of E. Clark and of Donaldson, Balfour, and Wales provides several examples of the gradual accretion of the "semantic features"[3] associated with a given word (E. Clark, 1970, 1971, 1973; Donaldson and Balfour, 1968; Donaldson and Wales, 1970). In the stages before all the necessary features are added to the representation of a word, the child's use of the word indicates that its meaning for him lacks some features of the adult meaning.

---

[3]For present purposes, E. Clark's "semantic features" can be considered to be roughly equivalent to what I have called chunks.

A verb whose representation includes chunks that are acquired late should be learned later than one whose chunks are acquired early. Further, verbs with few chunks should be used correctly before verbs with many chunks. More specifically, there should be a nested-chunks effect. If the structure for one verb is entirely contained within the structure for another, the former verb should be acquired first. Because a child's representation of a verb depends upon just how many of the underlying components have been acquired, a child's mistakes in interpreting complex verbs should in general reflect omission of the chunks not yet acquired.[4] His interpretation of a complex verb may be identical to his (correct) interpretation of a simple verb, at least until he acquires the necessary additional verb components. The order of acquisition of the underlying components of possession verbs should determine both the relative ages at which children can acquire the meanings of these verbs and the types of errors children will make if they attempt to use a possession verb before they have acquired all of its meaning components.

A weak order of acquisition among the chunks can be derived directly from the nested relations among the chunks. **CONTR** contains **OBLIG** as part of its meaning, and the composites **CONTR-TO-TRANS** and **OBLIG-TO-TRANSF** cannot be understood until their components (**DO, CAUSE,** and **TRANSF**) are present.

Additional ordering predictions can be inferred from the developmental psychology literature. The work of Piaget suggests that young children tend to rely very heavily on the notion of animism — the tendency to attribute animate causes to events (Piaget, 1955, 1965). This attribution of cause requires (implicit) knowledge of **CAUSE** and **DO. TRANSF** should also be learned relatively early, because the notion of change of possession is both more concrete than the notions of **OBLIG** and **CONTR** and more common in the experience of children.

The expectation, then, is that **DO, CAUSE,** and **TRANSF** should be acquired early by children. The other components enter into the child's representational system later.

To use **OBLIG** correctly as part of a verb, the child must understand something about the notion of social obligation. **CONTR**, which involves mutual social obligation, requires prior understanding of **OBLIG**. Accordingly, it should be the last chunk to be acquired.

Thus, the predicted ordering of acquisition is roughly **DO, CAUSE, TRANSF, OBLIG,** and finally **CONTR**. In addition to these conceptual

---

[4]This naturally applies only to verbs that the child has heard and that he attempts to use prior to acquisition of all the necessary chunks. If a complex verb is only first encountered after all the necessary chunks have been acquired, the course of acquisition may be quite different.

chunks, the function of money as an argument constraint must also be learned in order for the child to use verbs such as "pay" or "buy."

In order to predict the order of acquisition of the verbs themselves, it is necessary to consider not only the individual chunks, but also the nested relations among the sets that comprise the verbs. There are two nesting orders among the sets of subconcepts that make up the verbs under consideration. Figure 9.7 shows these nesting orders and the derived predictions for the order of acquisition of the verbs.

First come "give" and "take." Both these verbs should be acquired early in the development of the child since they require only **DO**, **CAUSE**, and **TRANSF**. The next two words to be acquired should be "trade" and "pay." Both these words add **OBLIG** (as well as other components) to the previous **DO, CAUSE, TRANSF** structures. Which of these two words comes first depends upon whether the child first learns about social contracts (**CONTR**) or about the use of money. There is no *a priori* reason to suspect the primacy of one of these concepts over the other. One would suspect that the relative order of acquisition of **CONTR** and of the notion of money varies from child to child.

Finally, after both **CONTR** and money have been acquired, then the child is ready to use properly terms such as "buy," "sell," and "spend money." Of the words that are examined in this chapter, these three should be the last to be acquired.

Confusions among the Verbs

At the stage when only **DO, CAUSE**, and **TRANSF** are understood, only the verbs "give" and "take" can be represented correctly by the child. More complex verbs such as "buy" and "sell" should be represented incompletely as some combination of **DO, CAUSE**, and **TRANSF**. The child who has not yet acquired **OBLIG, CONTR**, or the notion of money sees in an act of "buying" only a series of transfer, of which only the object transfer makes sense. He has no way of organizing the transaction as a whole. The most we can expect this child to store as his representation of a complex verb is some sort of object transfer.

Experimental Procedure

The details of the experimental study are reported in Gentner (1974). Here an outline of the study is presented, along with reasonably complete results. Children between the ages of 3 and 8 were asked to

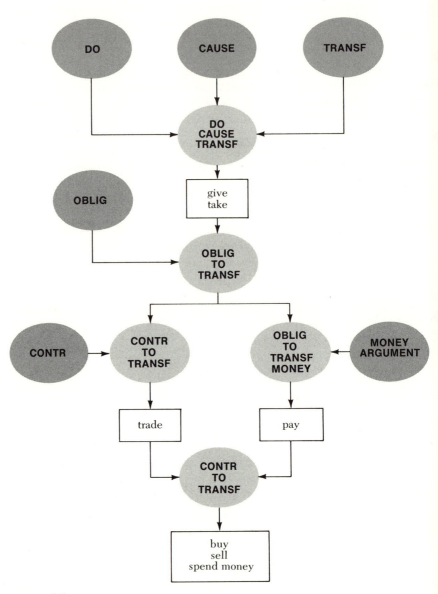

FIGURE 9.7
The nested relationships among the concepts underlying the verbs "give," "take,"
"trade," "pay," "buy," "sell," and "spend money." Semantic components (chunks)
are represented by darkly shaded ovals. The states that permit full understanding of
the verbs are represented by lightly shaded ovals. Age of acquisition of the verbs
proceeds vertically, youngest age at the top.

manipulate two dolls to act out sentences containing possession verbs. The experimenter observed and recorded the manipulation, taking particular note of the types of errors made. Special care was taken to ensure that the children fully understood the nature of the task, that the dolls (and their names) were well learned by the children, and that simple artifacts could not account for the results. In particular, care was taken that the number, type, and arrangement of the objects that were to be transferred could offer no clues as to the operations that should be performed, and a control experiment was performed to ensure that the children were in fact using their semantic understanding of the verbs that had been presented to them, and not simply responding to the surface ordering of the names of the dolls and objects used in the sentences.

The subjects were 70 children ranging in age from 3/6 to 8/6 years.[5] There were 14 children at each of 5 age levels, approximately evenly divided between males and females (see Table 9.3). Each child received one dollar and some candies for his participation.

TABLE 9.3
Distribution of subjects used in the experiment.

Age range (years/months)	Females	Males	Total per age
3/6–4/5	7	7	14
4/6–5/5	8	6	14
5/6–6/5	4	10	14
6/6–7/5	8	6	14
7/6–8/5	8	6	14
Totals	35	35	70

The experimental arrangement is shown in Figure 9.8. The experiment was performed with each child individually in the child's home. The child was seated on the floor and presented with two stuffed beanbag dolls. The dolls were known as "Ernie" and "Bert" and were the commercially available models of the dolls with those names used in the television show "Sesame Street." Usually the child was already familiar with the dolls and their names. If not, the experimenter talked to him about the dolls until he was able to name them easily.

---

[5] The age notation is that of years/months. Thus, age 3/6 means 3 years 6 months.

FIGURE 9.8

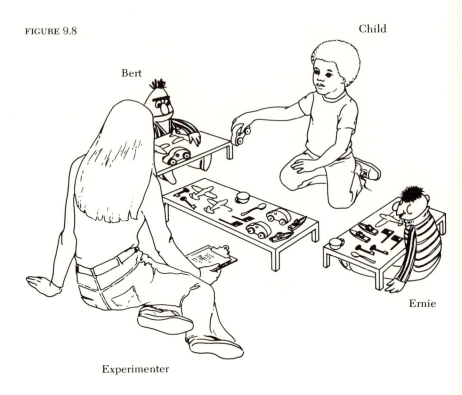

Child

Bert

Ernie

Experimenter

The experimenter spent considerable time with each child to ensure that he understood the names of the dolls, understood the seating arrangements, knew which table and which objects belonged to each doll, and was able to manipulate each doll to make it "pick up a toy," "move it over here," and "drop it down." The experiment began once the child had mastered all of these concepts and manipulations. Initially, each doll had the same set of toys: two each of cars, boats, flags, and keys; one each of a spoon and a cup. In addition, the experimenter placed some toys on the third "dining room table," saying, "Here are some things that Mother left on the dining room table." At least one of each type of toy was placed on the third table. This was done to allow confusions about the source and goal and the objects to be visible to the experimenter. However, children almost never used the objects on this third table.

The list of test sentences is shown in Table 9.4. At least two instances of "take" and two of "give" were administered. Then the experimenter said, "Now Mother comes in and says, 'You've been very good today, both of you, so you can both have some money.'" The child helped distribute play money to the dolls: two dimes and two

TABLE 9.4
Sentences used. Nonindented sentences are the ones normally used. Indented sentences are those used when checking for the effects of surface form. X and Y denote agent *and* recipient, *respectively. Z denotes* object.

Verb	Sentences	Verb	Sentences
give	Make X give Y a Z.	take	Make X take a Z from Y.
	Make X give a Z to Y.		Make X take from Y a Z.
sell	Make X sell Y a Z.	buy	Make X buy a Z from Y.
	Make X sell a Z to Y.		Make X buy from Y a Z.
	Make X sell a Z.		Make X buy a Z.

pennies to each doll. The experimenter continued with something like "Now they can do lots of things. Can you make Ernie buy a car from Bert?"

After this, the experimenter progressed semirandomly through a total of eight instances of each of the verbs "give," "take," "buy," "sell," and "spend money," and two each of "trade" and "pay." The objects and the dolls used as agents (or subjects of the sentences) were varied from sentence to sentence.

The experimenter avoided saying "good" and making other evaluative remarks. Instead, to encourage the child, the experimenter would often either comment on the action after the child had completed it (for example, "Now Ernie has lots of planes, huh?") or else speak for one of the dolls ("Gee, thanks Bert. The car was just what I wanted"). Remarks of this sort were made often, particularly whenever the child seemed to be flagging, and were independent of the correctness of his response.

Scoring of Responses

The responses were recorded by the experimenter. For each response the following information was recorded: *object* (which object was moved), *source* (from what place the object was moved), *goal* (to what place the object was moved), and *agent* (who moved the object). If there was more than one transfer, the information was recorded for each of them, along with the time order of the transfers. If, in any transfer, the experimenter failed to see the source, goal, or object used, that transaction was not recorded and another sentence of the same type was asked later. However, if only the agent was not seen, the transfer was recorded with the agent information missing. On some of the later transfers, children frequently failed to use an agent; that is, they moved the objects themselves instead of causing the dolls to move them.

Results and Discussion

Order of Acquisition.   The proportion of correct responses at each age level is shown in Figure 9.9. From this it can be seen that the order of acquisition of the verbs (where "acquisition" is arbitrarily defined as the point at which the child scores 75 percent correct) agrees quite well with the expected order. The verb group consisting of "give" and "take" is acquired first; then the group consisting of "pay" and "trade"; and finally the group consisting of "buy," "sell," and "spend."[6] The overall performance on a verb in any group is significantly different from the performance on verbs in the other two groups. Within the groupings the differences in performance are not significant, with one exception: "Sell" differs significantly from both "buy" and "spend." It is not clear whether the poorer performance on "sell" reflects some added conceptual complexity over "buy" and "spend" or whether "sell" is acquired later simply because the act of selling and the term "to sell" are relatively infrequent in a child's experience.

Another way to view the order of acquisition is shown in Table 9.5, which gives for each verb the conditional probability of achieving a high score on that verb, given a high score on each of the other verbs.[7] If a subject understands a verb belonging to one group, the probability that he will also understand the verbs from a simpler group is quite high, ranging from .91 to 1.0. The probability that he will understand a given verb from a more complex group is much lower, ranging from .33 to .76. For verbs in the same group, intermediate and approximately symmetric conditional probabilities appear.[8] The probability of understanding "trade" given "pay," for example, is about the same as that of understanding "pay" given "trade" (.77 and .83, respectively).

---

[6]For "Make X trade Y a Z1 for a Z2," either of two responses was counted as correct: either the transfer of Z1 from X to Y and of Z2 from Y to X, or the reverse transfer of Z2 from X to Y and Z1 from Y to X. Both these interpretations exist among adult speakers; 3 out of 14 adults tested on this sentence performed the reverse transfer.

[7]A "high score" on a verb or "understanding" a verb means that the subject scored 6 or more correct responses out of 8, or, in the case of "trade" and "pay," 2 correct responses out of 2.

[8]There are two exceptions to the several patterns observed in Table 9.5: "Give" and "take" have very high mutual probabilities, apparently because these verbs were well learned even by the younger children; in addition, "sell" does not appear to behave the same as "buy" and "spend." As noted before, "sell" appears to be acquired later than the other verbs in its group.

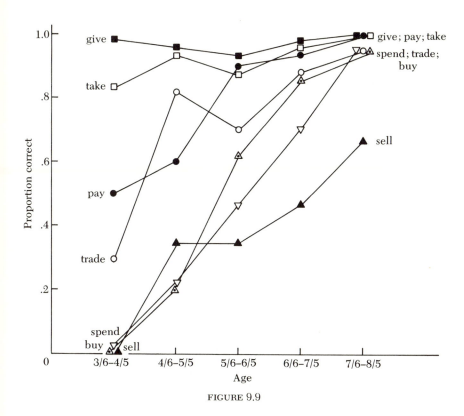

FIGURE 9.9

TABLE 9.5
*Probability of a high score on the column verb, given a high
score on the row verb.*

	give	take	pay	trade	buy	spend	sell
give	—	.96	.76	.70	.50	.48	.33
take	.99	—	.74	.69	.52	.48	.34
pay	.98	.92	—	.77	.67	.60	.39
trade	.98	.94	.83	—	.67	.63	.46
buy	.97	.97	1.0	.91	—	.77	.57
spend	1.0	.97	.97	.94	.84	—	.59
sell	1.0	1.0	.91	1.0	.91	.86	—

NOTES:

1. A "high score" is defined to be 6 correct responses out of 8 for "give," "take,"
   "buy," "spend," and "sell" and 2 correct responses out of 2 for "trade" and "pay."

2. The different shadings indicate the 3 different sets of probabilities: those below
   the diagonal (predicted to be high); those above the diagonal (predicted to be
   low); and those near the diagonal (predicted to be intermediate). All 3 differences
   were significant.

Children understand verbs that are conceptually simple before they understand verbs that are complex. It is rare for a subject to perform well on the verbs in a group unless he also performs well on the verbs in groups that are less complex. There are only 2 instances out of a possible 102 cases in which a subject achieves a high score on a verb in one group without also achieving a high score on at least one verb in every simpler group. More stringently, there are only 12 instances out of a possible 102 in which a subject scores high on a verb without also achieving a high score on *every* verb in every simpler group.

Errors.   Figure 9.10 shows the time course of acquisition both of correct responses and of the most common incorrect responses for the five complex verbs. For all of these verbs, the commonest incorrect response was some form of one-way transfer. This is in accord with the notion that **TRANSF** enters the semantic representations before the more abstract obligational notions (**OBLIG**) are acquired.

It is noteworthy that for all five complex verbs the erroneous one-way transfers are in the correct direction. Although the child's representations of the meanings of these verbs are incomplete, he nevertheless understands some components. For example, the young child acting out "buy" and "sell" completely disregards the money transfer that should be part of their meanings, yet performs the object transfer in the correct direction. He reacts to "buy" as if it were "take." He treats "sell" as if it were "give." The chunks that are present in the representations—notably **TRANSF**—can be used correctly, even though the complete representation is not present.

This pattern of correct one-way transfers shows up in the other complex verbs as well. For "spend money," the commonest error was simply to transfer money from the spender to the goal. As with "buy" and "sell," the object, source, and goal of the one-way transfer are all correct; only the other transfer is lacking. Notice that when money is explicitly mentioned in the sentence ("Make X spend some money"), even the young child performs a money transfer, though without performing the object transfer necessary to complete the **CONTR**. He can physically identify the objects called money, but he does not understand the abstract function of money. He interprets "spend money" as "give away money."

Another example of the young child's difficulty with the notion of money can be seen in the responses to the verb "pay." Here, the correct response is a simple one-way transfer of money. The commonest incorrect response is a transfer of the object to be paid for (a return) from the payer to the other doll. The child performs the one-

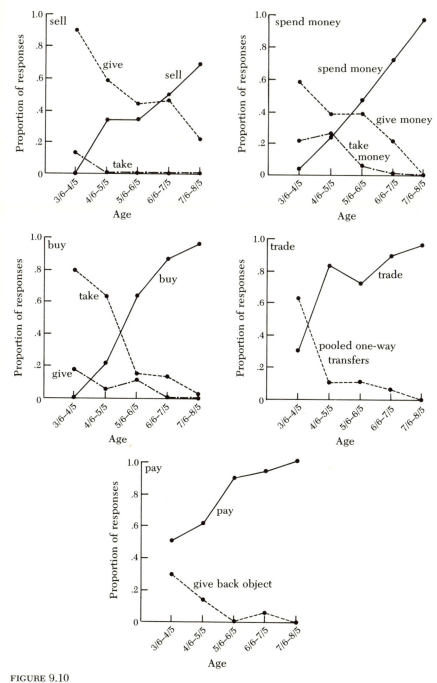

FIGURE 9.10

The proportion of correct responses and the proportion of the most frequent incorrect responses to the complex verbs. The correct responses are shown by solid lines; the incorrect responses are shown by dotted lines. (The verbs acted out for the incorrect responses are written on the graphs.) Responses that were denoted as "give" and "take" are transfers *to* or *from* the subject of the sentence, respectively.

way object transfer that is most appropriate and in the correct direction, again consistent with his lack of understanding of the money
argument involved in "pay."

The responses to "trade" show the lack of the **CONTR** chunk in the
younger children. One-way transfers outnumber the correct two-way
transfer at the outset. Notice that there are several likely one-way
transfers for the sentence form used in the experiment:

(19)   Make X trade Y the Z1 for the Z2.

Either Z1 or Z2 or both may be transferred, either in the direction
from X to Y or in the opposite direction.

A Check for the Use of Surface Cues.   I have argued for a semantic
interpretation of the fact that young children perform the correct
one-way object transfer before they understand the rest of the meaning of a complex verb. To justify this interpretation it is necessary to
rule out the possibility that the surface syntactic cues present in the
sentences determined the children's responses. The verbs "buy" and
"sell," in particular, occurred in sentence forms that could have been
matched, using surface cues, with the corresponding "take" and
"give" sentences. This would lead to the correct object transfer, but
for nonsemantic reasons. For the verbs "buy" and "sell," the sentences normally used were of these forms:

(20)   Make X buy a Z from Y.

(21)   Make X sell Y a Z.

Notice the similarity of these sentences to the forms most commonly
used for "take" and "give," namely:

(22)   Make X take a Z from Y.

(23)   Make X give Y a Z.

There are two possible surface strategies:

  1. The preposition ("from" or "to") could be used to deduce the
     direction of transfer of the object with respect to the agent.

  2. The order of the *object* and *recipient* (*goal*) in "buy" and "sell"
     sentences could be matched with the order in "take" and "give"
     sentences, respectively.

To check for the use of one of these strategies, 38 of the subjects were tested in a few examples of the verbs "buy" and "sell" presented in alternative sentence forms (shown in Table 9.4). In some of these forms, the words "from" or "to" and the nouns that followed them were omitted; in others the order of goal and object was reversed from the normal order in "take" and "give" sentences. Table 9.6 presents the results of these manipulations, averaged across all ages.

None of the surface variations produced any lessening of the tendency to perform the object transfer in the correct direction. This

TABLE 9.6
Effect of surface forms of sentences used.

	Buy		
	Order of object and recipient same as for normal "take"	Order of object and recipient reversed from normal "take"	Recipient omitted
	"Make X buy a Z from Y."	"Make X buy from Y a Z."	"Make X buy a Z."
Proportion correct	.57	.48	.76
Proportion of "take" responses	.25	.39	.11
Proportion of object transfers in correct direction (sum of rows 1 and 2)	.82	.87	.87
Number of responses	143	61	63

	Sell		
	Order of object and recipient same as for normal "give"	Order of object and recipient reversed from normal "give"	Recipient omitted
	"Make X sell (to) Y a Z."	"Make X sell a Z to Y."	"Make X sell a Z."
Proportion correct	.43	.38	.56
Proportion of "give" responses	.53	.59	.44
Proportion of object transfers in correct direction (sum of rows 1 and 2)	.95	.97	1.0
Number of responses	143	81	43

conclusion appears to hold when the data are analyzed by age. Unfortunately, since only four children from the youngest group—3/6 to 4/6—were tested with the altered sentence forms, there remains a possibility that very young children use nonsemantic strategies in their interpretation of "buy" and "sell" sentences. If this were true, the semantic interpretation proposed would still be valid overall: Children learn the complex possession verbs starting with the simple notions of **DO**, **CAUSE**, and **TRANSF**, and add more abstract chunks later.

SUMMARY

In this chapter I have presented an analysis of a set of possession verbs. Verbs of possession were hypothesized to contain an underlying set of more basic semantic components or "chunks." When these verbs are used in language, their differing underlying structures convey different meanings. A person who hears a particular verb may later make errors in recall of the verb, either because he had not recovered all of the verb components that were originally there or because, through confusions among the structures in his memory, he has added other components to the structure for that verb. Further, through loss of some of the chunks of a verb, a person may confuse the proposition centered around that verb with another proposition centered around a verb whose underlying structure shares some components with the original verb.

The proposed semantic structures allow predictions about the order in which children should acquire the meanings of the verbs. Accordingly, children ranging in age from 3 years to 8 years were asked to demonstrate their understanding of this set of possession verbs. They were found to understand verbs that contain relatively few and simple chunks first, and verbs with larger numbers of chunks later. The order of acquisition and the pattern of the errors were explainable in terms of sequential acquisition of the semantic chunks hypothesized in this chapter.

CHAPTER 10

Experimental Analysis of the Semantics of Movement

ADELE A. ABRAHAMSON[1]

Throughout this book we have argued that a model of cognitive and linguistic processing must go deeper than the surface level of language, that the mind has its own special "language." Both linguistic and nonlinguistic inputs are encoded into this common information format. The other chapters have argued that information at the underlying conceptual level involves units smaller than words. One word may communicate several conceptual units or *semantic elements*. Furthermore, a small number of semantic elements underlie a large number of words; they include basic concepts that recur in the encoding of our experiences. There is reason to believe that most semantic elements are universal, that all languages communicate the same elements in their various ways.

Examples readily come to mind: The concepts of change, of causation, of location, and of movement seem basic to much of human communication. These concepts have already been discussed in this

[1] I thank Carlton James for his suggestions. Completion of the analyses and the writing of this chapter were aided by grant 07-2128 from the Rutgers University Research Council.

book in the chapters on the structural representation (Chapter 2), the review of linguistics (Chapter 4), the language comprehension system (Chapter 8), and the analysis of semantic components in Chapter 9.

The studies reported in this chapter attempt to perform an experimental analysis of the semantic elements of movement by examining distortions produced by subjects asked to recall stories.

SEMANTIC ANALYSIS OF RECALL

The Recall Method

Consider what happens when a person attempts to recall an utterance heard earlier. Presumably, when the utterance is heard, the recipient forms some representation of its meaning. The representation of meaning includes some of the semantic elements asserted in the utterance, and it may also include inferences. People differ in how thoroughly they extract semantic elements from an utterance. Over time, a person forgets. At the time of recall, the stored meaning must be translated back to language. Occasionally, recall may be an accurate reproduction of what was heard, based on verbatim memory of the words. However, even when as few as one to five minutes elapse between presentation and reproduction, there is often little verbatim recall. Distortions may be introduced during the encoding of meaning, during the period of retention, and during the translation back into language. We can use these distortions as a tool to study the semantic elements that, in various combinations, make up the meanings of utterances.

Addition and Deletion of Semantic Units in Recall

Given the decision that recall of utterances can be a source of information about the meaning of utterances, still one must determine how to mine this source.[2] In the present approach the difference between the presented utterance and the recalled utterance is taken as the result of additions and deletions of one or more semantic elements.

---

[2]Bartlett (1932), Crothers (1972), Fredericksen (1972), and Kintsch and Keenan (1973) have analyzed recall with a semantic orientation. Their emphasis is on the relations among propositions, whereas my analysis emphasizes the semantic information within each proposition. The approaches are complementary.

The goal is to discover just what those elements are. In my system of analysis, if "seize" is recalled as "take," a semantic element of **INTENSITY** has been lost. The same reasoning applies to additions of elements.[3]

The Fisherman Story

To collect some utterances for analysis, I wrote a two-paragraph story, *The Fisherman Story*. I asked half of my 32 subjects to read Form 1 of the story and then to recall it in writing. The other half did the same with Form 2. The subjects were given thirty seconds to read the first paragraph. Then they immediately wrote it down as accurately as they could (from memory). This procedure was repeated with the second paragraph.

A comparison of the two forms of the story (see pp. 250–251) shows them to be essentially identical in content and to differ only by the use of related or synonymous words.[4] The paragraphs have a high information density to assure a high yield of errors, are of a length found to be appropriate for good recall of basic content, and have interesting variations in (the somewhat complex) syntax and semantics.

Written recall of the story was obtained from 32 undergraduates at the University of California, San Diego.[5] Some additional memory tasks followed, but are not discussed here. For analysis of these additional results, and of propositions other than movement propositions, see Abrahamson (1973).

---

[3]In keeping with the notation used throughout this book, semantic elements are indicated by upper-case English words in **THIS TYPE FACE: CHANGE, CAUSE, LOCATION** (or **LOC**), and **MOVE**. (In the other chapters, case relations are not treated as semantic elements and so are not capitalized; I do so because I treat them as basic semantic elements, whereas in the other chapters case relations are "ranges.") Elements differ from words in at least two ways: (1) Each semantic element represents one and only one concept, independent of context; (2) the rules of construction are different from those governing English syntax. A given word may have only one semantic element in its meaning (for example, "cause" has the meaning **CAUSE**), or it may have more than one semantic element in its meaning ("push" has several elements in its meaning in addition to **CAUSE**).

[4]The difference between the forms is unimportant for the present analysis. A detailed analysis of the differences between the forms is given in Abrahamson (1973).

[5]The University is located on and above the Pacific Ocean, and this had an effect on the recall responses. The shore in the vicinity of the University is mostly fairly steep, characterized by cliffs located near the water. There are large areas of kelp beds about 300 meters from shore, and the kelp (a form of seaweed) is visible from the shore. Fishing boats are often visible around the outer portions of the kelp beds. All these facts help constitute the body of world knowledge that the subjects used in interpreting the story.

BOX 10.1
The fisherman story.

FORM 1

The weathered old fisherman looked at the ocean as he made a knot in a line. It appeared incredibly blue and calm. Earlier, while talking with another fisherman, he had said that conditions seemed good for a large catch of tuna. He was confident that he would kill many fish that day. The knot completed, he ran to his boat, left shore, and sailed until he passed the kelp beds. His face reddened in the wind.

As he laid out his lines the lapping of the waves against his boat reminded him of his daughter playing in the waves by their home. He would give her the best fish and the villagers would buy the rest from him. Within a few hours, a number of fish had seized the bait and he began to return home. The air was cold, and he felt glad to finally enter the kitchen and sit by the stove. He warmed some porridge on the burner and devoured it.

ANALYSIS OF THE RECALL

A Preview Analysis: Some Basic Semantic Elements

There were sixteen attempts to recall each proposition of each form of the story. I compared each recalled proposition with its corresponding presented proposition and classified the differences between the two. This comparison and classification process resulted in the postulation of a relatively limited set of semantic elements. A detailed presentation of the analysis of all of the propositions in each story is too tedious to present here. In this chapter, I merely explain my analysis and the derived semantic elements by discussing in detail three propositions from each form of the story. The six propositions, three each from (1A) and (1B), concern the fisherman's sailing from shore, past the kelp beds:

(1A)   . . . (he) left shore, and sailed until he passed the kelp beds. (Form 1)

(1B)   . . . (he) pushed off, and kept sailing until he was past the kelp beds. (Form 2)

BOX 10.2
The fisherman story.

FORM 2

The weathered old fisherman scanned the ocean as he knotted a line. It was incredibly blue and calm. Earlier, while speaking with another fisherman, he had mentioned that conditions appeared good for a large catch of tuna. He felt confident that many fish would die that day. The knot finished, he raced for his boat, pushed off, and kept sailing until he was past the kelp beds. His face became red in the strong breeze.

As he put out his lines the lapping of the waves against his boat made him think of his daughter splashing in the waves by their home. He would let her have the best fish and the rest he would sell to the villagers. Within a few hours many fish had taken the bait and he began to return home. The air felt cold, and he was glad to finally hurry into the kitchen and squat by the stove. Some porridge warmed on the burner and he ate it hungrily.

The important information in (1A) and (1B) can be expressed more simply as a single clause with three propositions:

(1C)   The fisherman sailed his boat from shore past the kelp beds.

Most of the analysis in this chapter focuses on this simple sequence. I begin with a detailed look at the semantic representation of (1C), as shown in Figure 10.1, where I have superimposed a diagram of the situation on an outline of the structural network representation.

The structural network representation for a verb of *animate intransitive movement*, like "sail," seems to include at least three semantic predicates: **MOVE, IMPLEMENTATION,** and **CAUSE.** The two predicates, **MOVE** and **IMPLEMENTATION,** serve as the arguments of the third, **CAUSE.** The relations (event and result) indicate the role each predicate plays with respect to **CAUSE. MOVE** is a special case of the **CHANGE** predicate discussed in Chapter 2; namely, a change of location from one place to another. **IMPLEMENTATION** (related to the **DO** component of Chapters 2, 4, 8, and 9) represents the physical actions (for example, the motions of the fisherman's body) that implement the change of location. The **MOVE** and **IMPLEMENTATION** predicates also have their own arguments.

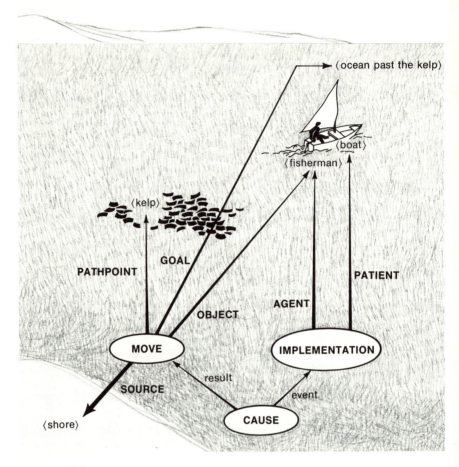

FIGURE 10.1
The sailing situation, with a diagrammatic representation of the semantic
analysis of the sentence "The fisherman sailed his boat from shore past the
kelp beds."

Some *movement verbs* equally emphasize the *abstract* change of
location (**MOVE**) and the more concrete, *physical* action (**IMPLEMEN-
TATION**). These are the verbs that give a specific **IMPLEMENTATION**
(for example, "sail," "row," and "run"). Other movement verbs
emphasize the *abstract* aspect, because the physical action is not
specified (for example, "come," "go," and "travel"). Finally, a third
group of verbs refer only to the physical action; there is no movement

along a path. These are therefore called *bodily action* verbs rather than movement verbs (for example, "*clap* hands," "*shrug* shoulders").[6] The emphasis of movement verbs can be modified by context:

An emphasis on the physical action:	He sailed so hard that he became exhausted.
	He traveled with great speed.
An emphasis on the abstract change of location:	He sailed out to sea.
	He traveled from shore to the fishing grounds.

To clarify the distinction, consider the difference between "run" and "run in place." "Run in place" is a bodily action verb; it communicates only a specific **IMPLEMENTATION** (running motions by the body). In contrast, "run" is used when there is movement along a path. The bodily action is not an end in itself, but is causing movement from one place to another. "Run" is a movement verb, one that equally emphasizes the abstract and physical aspects of meaning.

As illustrated in Figure 10.1, each of the predicates **MOVE** and **IMPLEMENTATION** takes arguments. **MOVE** and its arguments together represent the abstract notion of the fisherman's movement along a path; they make up an *abstract system* that is part of the meaning of sentences that use the verb "sail." **IMPLEMENTATION** and its arguments together represent the physical interaction of the fisherman and his boat. They make up a *physical system* that is also part of the meaning of sentences that include the verb "sail." Those predicates and their cases are defined in Box 10.3.

The particular **IMPLEMENTATION** used in the part of the fisherman story under analysis here is the act of sailing. I introduce a specific element **SAIL**, which refers very narrowly to the physical motions involved in the act of sailing. (In the sense used in this story, the existence of a sailboat is assumed, and the actions therefore include such things as adjusting the sails and controlling the boat.) When the English verb "sail" is used in the sense of "to sail a sailboat," then it implies both the abstract change-of-location predicate (**MOVE**) and the specific implementation element (**SAIL**). Thus, this sense of the verb "sail" is represented by the predicate **CAUSE**, with **MOVE** and **SAIL** as its arguments: **CAUSE (SAIL, MOVE)**.

---

[6]A similar distinction is made by Miller (1972).

BOX 10.3
The system of elements.

ABSTRACT SYSTEM OF ELEMENTS[a]

MOVE   The semantic element denoting change of loca-
                     tion. Any verb classified as a movement verb
                     includes this element.

Cases used by **MOVE**:

OBJECT   The person or thing that is moving. There may be
                     one or more **OBJECT**s, and they appear as sub-
                     ject or object of the verb.

> He sailed **the boat.**

---

[a]The definitions of the case relations are deceptively simple. The case relation between a noun and verb can be defined on syntactic, semantic, and pragmatic grounds. Typically, the syntactic devices of word order and prepositions mark the case relations, but sometimes these are deleted or are insufficient to determine the case relation. Also, a given sentence about a situation usually does not express all of the possible case relations; some are either left unknown or can be inferred. Figure 10.1 shows the case relations that are marked in sentence 1C (plus **GOAL**). Thus, the *instrumental* role of the boat (made clear by "He sailed with the boat") and the role of the wind ("The wind moved his boat") are ignored here.

Syntax alone determines neither whether the subject of a sentence is an **AGENT** or a **PATIENT**, nor whether the subject is also an **OBJECT**. Three examples show how these decisions are made:

(a) The boat sailed.   The boat is a **PATIENT** since some force or being (not stated) must be acting on it. It cannot be an **AGENT** because it is inanimate. It is an **OBJECT** because it is moving, though the points on the path are not given.

(b) The fisherman sailed the boat.   The boat has the same analysis as in (a) (**PATIENT** and **OBJECT**). The fisherman is an **AGENT** because he is an animate being performing an action. He is also an **OBJECT**, because of the pragmatic knowledge that he is moving along with the boat.

(c) The fisherman sailed hard.   The fisherman has the same analysis as in (b) (**AGENT** and **OBJECT**), except that pragmatic knowledge is not needed to determine the **OBJECT** relation. When there is only one noun phrase with a movement verb, it is always an **OBJECT**.

Notice that in movement propositions, both the subject and object of the verb must be assigned to a physical system case (**AGENT** or **PATIENT**), and at least one must also be assigned to an abstract system case (**OBJECT**). My definition of **AGENT** is similar to Fillmore's (1968), and my **PATIENT** is similar to Chafe's (1970). My case relation **OBJECT** has no direct analog in other case grammars, which do not make the distinction between abstract and physical systems.

(continued)

BOX 10.3 *(continued)*

SOURCE The initial point of movement. Usually marked by the preposition "from."

He sailed **from shore.**
He left **shore.**

GOAL The final point of movement. Usually marked by the prepositions "to," "toward," "for."

He sailed **for the ocean.**
He went **home.**

PATHPOINT Any intermediate point of movement. May be marked by such prepositions as "past" or "by," or by the verb.

He sailed **past the kelp.**
He sailed **through the kelp.**
He **passed the kelp.**

PHYSICAL SYSTEM OF ELEMENTS

IMPLEMENTATION The element that denotes the physical actions that implement the movement. Any verb classified as a movement verb includes this predicate, but not all movement verbs specify a particular **IMPLEMENTATION.**

He **went** past the kelp. (Unspecified)
He **sailed** past the kelp. (Specified: The fisherman is performing sailing actions.)

Cases used by **IMPLEMENTATION**:

AGENT The animate being acting to implement the movement. The **AGENT** is usually the subject of the verb.

The fisherman sailed the boat.

PATIENT The thing (occasionally, an animate being) passively involved in the implementation of the movement, being acted upon by the **AGENT**. The **PATIENT** is usually the direct object of the verb.

The fisherman sailed **the boat.**

There are, of course, many elements like **SAIL** that specify the details of the **IMPLEMENTATION** for various verbs. Thus, I distinguish between two kinds of semantic elements:

1. Those, such as **IMPLEMENTATION, CHANGE, MOVE, AGENT**, and **GOAL**, that ideally form a small, closed set representing the limited number of ways experience is organized.
2. Those, such as **SAIL, ROW, RUN**, that form a large, open set bounded only by how finely humans slice their experience.

I now turn to a detailed analysis of the recall protocols in order to show the way in which much of the data can be accounted for by these semantic elements.

The Recall Data

I now consider the subjects' recalls of these three propositions. In Form 1 (Box 10.1), the important components of the sailing were described as in (1A):

(1A)   . . . (he) left shore, and sailed until he passed the kelp beds.

There are three propositions of interest to us:

> he left shore
> he sailed
> he passed the kelp beds

Form 2 of the story (Box 10.2) described these same events slightly differently.

(1B)   . . . (he) pushed off, and kept sailing until he was past the kelp beds.

Here the three propositions of interest to us are:

> he pushed off
> he kept sailing
> he was past the kelp beds

Of the 32 subjects, 26 recalled something that was related to the propositions in (1A) or (1B). The individual recalls of these 26 subjects are shown in Figure 10.2.

The top part of the figure shows some of the fisherman's activities. Speakers would seldom wish to describe the movements so carefully or completely that they would describe each picture by a single, different proposition. Rather, they would use one or a few propositions to describe the event more generally. A subject who knows about sailing might use this knowledge to reconstitute the detail represented by the series of drawings. If so, memory for the particular segmentation of events used in the story could be lost.

The boxes just below the drawings show some of the ways the sailing event can be segmented. The event *left shore* is shown as being composed of the two subevents *pushed off* and *sailed away*. The segment *sailed out* overlaps *sailed away* (and therefore also *left shore*) and *kept sailing*. Thus, we see how it is possible to draw different psychological boundaries between continuous events.

The segmentations used by each story form are shown in the central portion of the figure. The forms differ in several ways:

- Form 2 gives a smaller, more specific segment at the beginning than does Form 1.
- Form 1 asserts the segments *left shore, sailed,* and *passed kelp. Passed kelp* refers to a process or movement; the outcome—he *was past kelp*—must be inferred. Hence, nothing in Form 1 corresponds to the last segment at the top of the figure.
- Form 2 asserts the segments *pushed off, kept sailing,* and *was past kelp.* Two intermediate segments must be inferred: *sailed away* (first dashed line) and *passed kelp* (second dashed line). Form 2 gives the outcome or final state, rather than the process.

The bottom portion of Figure 10.2 shows what the subjects recalled. Each recall is matched with the segments of the presented story.[7] For example, subject number 25 ("Set out to ocean") has one proposition that spans the whole situation. Within that proposition, the first two words match the beginning of the story segment and the last two words match the last story segment. The rest must be inferred (dashed line).

Even a quick glance at Figure 10.2 reveals that the recalls are organized differently from the presented sequences of three propositions. They look different because:

- Subjects deleted segments.
- Subjects made changes in the segmentation: by amalgamation into fewer propositions; by forming segments that overlapped the given segments.
- Subjects made changes as to which information was asserted and which information must be inferred.

---

[7]Whenever a preposition, rather than a verb, is used to express the "passing" information, the figure shows it as the last (final state) segment. This is arbitrary, but is an expedient way to classify the many sentences that combined a movement (process) verb and a preposition in one clause (for example, "sailed out past the kelp"). The question is whether the stative preposition, when preceded by a movement verb, is supplying information about the process (passing) or the final state (past).

LEFT SHORE	
PUSHED OFF	SAILED AWAY
	SAILED OUT

These events were described in Form 1 as:

   . . . (he) left shore, and sailed
until he passed the kelp beds.

The three clauses correspond to three of the segments
labeled above; the last segment is inferred (in parentheses):

Left shore	Sailed	Passed kelp	(Was past kelp)

The subjects' recalls can be laid out to match these segments:

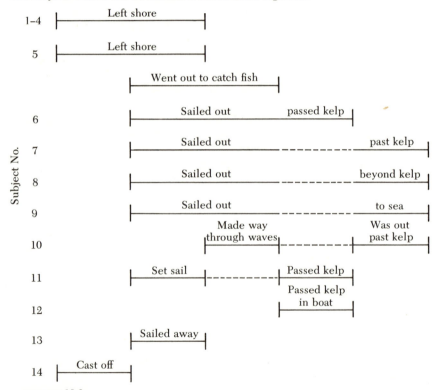

FIGURE 10.2
Segmentation of the sailing situation in the story and in subjects' recalls.
Across the top of the figure, successive parts of the movement are grouped into
segments. Each labeled box is a segment. Below the boxes, the segmentation
used in each story form is given. Each proposition, marked off by vertical bars,

258

(KEPT) SAILING	PASSED KELP (PROCESS)	WAS PAST KELP (STATE)
SAILED OUT		

These events were described in Form 2 as:

. . . (he) pushed off, and kept
sailing until he was past the kelp beds.

The three clauses correspond to three of the segments
labeled above; two segments are inferred (in parentheses):

| Pushed off | (Sailed away) | Kept sailing | (Passed kelp) | Was past kelp |

The subjects' recalls can be laid out to match these segments:

| Pushed off | | | | | 15–17 |

| Shoved off | | | | | 18 |

| Pushed off | | Kept going | Passed kelp | | 19 |

| Pushed out boat | | Kept going | Got out | past kelp | 20 |

| Shoved off in boat | | | | past kelp | 21 |
| | Moved | | | |

| Pushed off | Sailed boat out | | past kelp | | 22 |

| Rowed boat on out | | beyond kelp | 23 |

| Sailed far out | | to sea | 24 |

| Set out | | to ocean | 25 |

| Passed through kelp | 26 |

Subject No.

is a segment. Segments that must be inferred are labeled in parentheses (over
a dashed line). Each line in the bottom portion of the figure gives the recall by
one or more subjects. The parts of the recalls are lined up with the segments
in the presented form of the story. The propositions are given in abbreviated
form; for example, the subject (the fisherman) and the determiners are deleted.

259

Segmentation Changes. Only two subjects (subjects 19 and 20) used three propositions; all the rest used fewer propositions. Deletions could be attributed to forgetting, but the large number of amalgamations suggests additional factors. Apparently, three propositions were too many for this part of the story. The information could easily be communicated in two propositions, one of which was used to express "leaving shore" and the other for the remainder. At least, this is what most subjects did.

Assertion Changes. The recalls reflect the effects of comprehension. The distinction between asserted and inferred information is largely lost. In the production of a recall response, information that had been asserted in the original story is left to inference; information that had been left to inference in the original story is asserted. This is especially evident for the recalls of Form 2, where the asserted segments were not continuous in the presented story. (Notice, however, that there is also some evidence of verbatim recall.)

These characteristics of recall are characteristics of language itself. Discourse would probably be unbearably ponderous if speakers and writers did not leave many gaps to be filled in by the audience. When the discourse describes a physical event, the analogy of a series of snapshots or film clips suggesting the flow of the complete sequence seems apt. Though the shots contain less information about the events in one sense, they induce segmentation, focus, and innuendo.[8] Figure 10.2 illustrates this imposition of subjective organization on a continuous event.

Knowledge of the World. Inferring segments of action not asserted in the story is part of a general tendency to use knowledge of the world in order to construct meaning. For example, some subjects explicitly stated inferences about the boat that were not asserted in the story. Five subjects inferred that the fisherman got into the boat before leaving shore. Several others added a boat to the proposition about "sailing."

These inferences may seem unremarkable, but that is the point: It is a natural, essential aspect of language processing that one makes connections between current input, preceding context, and knowledge of the world.

---

[8] Edward Klima (personal communication).

SEMANTIC ELEMENTS FOR ANIMATE MOVEMENT

The Six Proposition Pairs

The recalls for the three proposition pairs about sailing, presented in Figure 10.2, represent only half of the data. The movement propositions occur in two sequences in the story: a running and sailing sequence, and a going-home sequence. There are a total of six pairs of propositions about movement. All refer to *animate* (self-propelled) *movement*.

(2A)   . . . he ran to his boat, left shore, and sailed until he passed the kelp beds. . . . he began to return home. [The air was cold, and he felt glad] to finally enter the kitchen. . . . (Form 1)

(2B)   . . . he raced for his boat, pushed off, and kept sailing until he was past the kelp beds. . . . he began to return home. [The air felt cold, and he was glad] to finally hurry into the kitchen. . . . (Form 2)

Because each of 32 subjects read 6 movement propositions, there were 192 opportunities for recall of a movement proposition. Of these, there were 77 deletions of a proposition and 4 cases that were not classifiable. This leaves 111 partial or full recalls of a presented proposition. (Amalgamated recall propositions count more than once in this total.) Five added propositions (on getting into the boat) make a total of 116 propositions to analyze.

Basic Semantic Elements in the Six Proposition Pairs

A particular subset of the basic semantic elements is asserted by each movement proposition in the fisherman story. Table 10.1 shows the occurrence of **MOVE** and **IMPLEMENTATION** and their respective cases in the recalls of the six proposition pairs. Those elements marked by parentheses occurred only in recall; the others were judged to be asserted by the propositions in the original story. (Because every **AGENT** and **PATIENT** is also an **OBJECT** in these propositions, the **OBJECT** relation is not listed separately.)[9]

The semantic elements in Table 10.1 are called basic because they include both of the two predicates (which by definition, are asserted

---

[9]**CAUSE** and its case relations event and result are not discussed in the following analyses. These three elements are a formal device for linking the two predicates, and are deleted precisely when **MOVE** and **IMPLEMENTATION** are deleted. It is therefore redundant to apply them to the analysis of recall.

TABLE 10.1
Basic semantic elements in recall for each of the six pairs of movement propositions. For cases, the argument (noun) is given. Parentheses indicate that the element was inferred in recall but not asserted in the story. All recalls include **MOVE** *and* **IMPLEMENTATION.**

The propositions of movement	Elements related to **MOVE**			Elements related to **IMPLEMENTATION**		
Form 1/Form 2	**SOURCE**	**PATHPOINT**	**GOAL**	**AGENT**	**PATIENT**	Specific **IMPLEMENTATION**
ran/raced			boat	fisherman		RUN
left/pushed off	shore	(kelp)		fisherman	(boat)	SAIL (ROW) PUSH
sailed/kept sailing		(kelp)	(ocean)	fisherman	(boat)	SAIL (ROW)
passed/was past		kelp	(ocean)	fisherman		(SAIL)
began to return/ began to return			home (shore) (village)	fisherman		(ROW) (SAIL)
enter/hurry into			kitchen (house) (home)	fisherman		

by any movement proposition) and also their case relations. Except for **SOURCE**, every semantic element is asserted in some recalls for at least two proposition pairs. **AGENT** and **MOVE** (and the general **IMPLEMENTATION**) occur in every recall.

These "basic" elements were originally discovered by careful examination of the 116 recalls. Every element was first noticed because it had been added or deleted from the story by at least one subject. Once the set of elements was established and each element was defined, intuitive judgments determined which elements were asserted by each presented and recalled proposition. An element could thus be assigned to the meaning of a story proposition even if no subject had exposed it by deleting it. For example, **RUN** was discovered by comparing the story verb "ran" with the recall verb "went." Once discovered, **RUN** was also assigned to the meaning of "raced," though it happened that no subject had deleted it from "raced." Thus, recall distortions were used to find the elements, and intuitive application of their definitions was used to decide which propositions asserted which elements.

Additional Semantic Elements in the Six Proposition Pairs

The question now arises: Are any additional semantic elements asserted in the story or in the recalls? Table 10.1 indicates that we have at least some of the elements needed for movement propositions, but there may be additional, more peripheral ones.

In fact, the procedure just described yielded a number of semantic elements in addition to the basic elements. If only the 3 proposition pairs about sailing are considered, 20 different elements are asserted in the 35 separate recall propositions, counting the elements at the most general level. (For example, the four specific **IMPLEMENTA-TION**s count as one element.) If the count is made according to the most specific level, there are 26 different elements. Of these, a majority (14) never appeared in the presented propositions, but were inferred in recall. Many recalls involve multiple changes (for example, two deletions and one addition). This fact, plus the large number of elements, contributes to the difficulty of analysis.

To account for the remaining 3 proposition pairs, only 7 additional elements are needed at the most general level (12 at the most specific level). This convergence suggests that additional propositions would add a limited number of additional general elements to those found here.

What are these elements? What kinds of information do subjects infer when they recall the movement propositions? Fortunately, the elements can be explained fairly systematically. In Box 10.4, the elements appear on the left and the explanations appear on the right. Indentation is used to indicate the hierarchical structure of the elements: leftmost elements are classes of elements (general elements); rightmost elements are members of those classes (specific elements). This is a relative, not absolute, distinction, and was used for the previous element count.

Recall that there are two ways of analyzing a movement. Each makes up a separate system, the abstract system and the physical system. Here these systems are extended, and a third group of elements ("other elements") is added. (**CAUSE** and its case relations are not shown.) Each system is subdivided into similar groups of elements by headings, which should not be mistaken for elements. All elements are set in **THIS TYPE FACE**.

BOX 10.4
The semantic elements.

ELEMENTS OF THE ABSTRACT SYSTEM

Predicate
===

MOVE   **MOVE** is the predicate used whenever an object moves from one place to another.

Path cases
===

SOURCE   An **OBJECT** moves along a path.
PATHPOINT   Important points along the path usually
GOAL   are associated with other objects, and
MEDIUM   depending on which point, we call them
OBJECT   **SOURCE**, **PATHPOINT**, or **GOAL**. The whole movement may take place within a **MEDIUM** such as air or water.

(continued)

BOX 10.4 *(continued)*

Adverbial relations

SOURCE-GOAL
  OUT
  DOWN
AGENT-SOURCE
  OFF

The objects have relationships to each other as well as relationships to the path. Some of these are adverbial; in a sentence, they may be expressed by prepositions functioning as adverbs. In the sailing sequence, the **SOURCE** (shore) and **GOAL** (ocean) are in a relationship **OUT**: "He sailed out to sea." It has something to do with distance, being outdoors, and (sometimes) enclosure. Another relationship is an **AGENT-SOURCE** relationship, **OFF**: "He pushed off" (from shore).

Locative relations

PATHREL
  PAST
  IN

These relations are expressed by locative prepositional phrases. When the preposition tells us more about the relation of the moving object to the stationary object along the path, we call it a **PATH RELATION** (**PATHREL**). It has a dynamic meaning, because the locative relation is changing as the object moves along the path. **PAST** is one of these: The moving object starts off on one side of the stationary object, and ends up past it. So, the whole event is **MOVE PAST**. Another **PATHREL** is **IN**, as in "enter" or "go in." In the story, **PAST** relates to a **PATHPOINT** (kelp), and **IN** relates to a **GOAL** (kitchen).

LOCATION
  IN$_L$

The other kind of relation expressed by locative prepositional phrases has nothing to do with movement, so it is simply called **LOCATION**. For example, some subjects infer that the fisherman is "in" his boat. [The word "in" therefore has at least two corresponding semantic elements, **IN$_M$** (the **PATHREL** for movement) and **IN$_L$** (the location). Usually the subscripts are dropped when context makes it clear which **IN** is intended.]

(continued)

BOX 10.4 *(continued)*

Specificity

SPECIFIC PATHREL **SPECIFIC SOURCE-GOAL**	Sometimes with these relations one has a choice of either a more or a less specific word. To describe the fisherman's **PATHREL** to the kelp, one could simply say he sailed "past" the kelp. But if one says he "passed through" the kelp, that statement is more specific about his path. If someone uses a more specific word, the difference is labeled **SPECIFIC** X; for example, **SPECIFIC PATHREL**. This happens with **SOURCE-GOAL** too, but with regard to distance: "He sailed *far* out to sea."

Attributes

ATTRIBUTE **WARM**	People and things are often described in terms of qualities or attributes. Usually, adjectives are used: "the *warm* kitchen."

ELEMENTS OF THE PHYSICAL SYSTEM

Action cases

AGENT **PATIENT**	The physical system has its own set of cases. They tell about the action roles of the different people and things in the situation. We need only two, though there are more: **AGENT** (the active participant) and **PATIENT** (the passive participant).

Action description

IMPLEMENTATION **RUN** **SAIL** **ROW** **PUSH** **JUMP** **MANNER** **INTENSE** **EFFORTFUL**	There are two ways to describe the action itself. **IMPLEMENTATION** tells what general kind of action it is: sailing, running, or whatever. **MANNER** tells more about how it is being done: intensely, casually, and so forth. One might think of **IMPLEMENTATION** as labeling the action, and **MANNER** as narrowing down the values of parameters, such as speed.

(continued)

BOX 10.4 *(continued)*

"He sailed" gives the **IMPLEMENTATION**; "He made his way through the waves," which one subject recalled, gives the **MANNER** instead (call it **EFFORTFUL**). "He ran" gives the **IMPLEMENTATION**; "He raced" adds the **MANNER** (paraphrase: "ran fast").

OTHER ELEMENTS

Modals-Temporals

Psychological

ATTAIN
REASON
MATRIX-VERB
  DECIDE
  GLAD
  READY
  PREPARE

There are a number of elements that are outside the physical/abstract systems. For example, sometimes subjects cannot resist saying how someone perceiving the motion would feel about it (for example, **ATTAIN**). Subjects often put ideas in the head of the human doing the moving; for example, "He decided to return" instead of simply "He returned," or "He sailed out to catch the fish," which gives his **REASON** for moving. The subjects added several matrix (higher) verbs to "return." Besides "decide," there were "glad to," "was ready to," and a few similar verbs. I have lumped them together as **MATRIX-VERB**.

Objective

TIME
  MP-TIME
  EVENT-TIME

These are the topics that the logicians and grammarians have always labored over: modal verbs, tense, and so forth. I have paid little attention to these, but do identify **MP-TIME** (expressed by a measure phrase, such as "he returned within a few hours") and **EVENT-TIME** (which gives the time by relating it to another event; for example, "after catching the fish").

(continued)

BOX 10.4 *(continued)*

Action Segments

Segments

LEAVE

Earlier, the point was made that although movements are continuous, we sometimes see them in segments. For example, sailing could be divided into leaving (shore), continuing on, and arriving (at the ocean past the kelp). In the recall analysis, if a subject said "he left shore" or "he set out," I put the element **LEAVE** in the analysis.

Deixus

COME/GO
  COME
  GO

Deictic terms also belong here. "Go" is like "leave" in that it focuses on the beginning; and "come," like "arrive," focuses on the end. The element **COME/ GO** represents this distinction separately, since additional factors are involved.

Aspect

INCEPTION
CONTINUE
NONCOMPLETION

Aspect is another way of segmenting movements. The elements **INCEPTION** ("began to return," "headed for shore"), **CONTINUE** ("kept sailing") and **NONCOMPLETION** ("raced for his boat") figure in the recalls here, though there are others. (**NONCOMPLETION** indicates only a possibility of not reaching the **GOAL**; from the context we know that he in fact reached the boat.)

Other

PREVLOC

Finally, **PREVLOC** (previous location) sees the movement as part of a larger sequence; recurrence is involved in a verb like "return."

The analysis described in Box 10.4 can be compared with Miller's (1972) semantic field analysis of the meaning components in a large group of related words: *movement verbs*. I found my meaning components by comparing presented clauses with recalled clauses, for a small subset of movement verbs. In general, Miller and I made similar distinctions in our analyses, despite differences in method and number of words studied. I included such elements as **REASON** and **MATRIX-VERB**, which are outside the semantic field of movement, but are associated with movement events by subjects when hearing a story. Miller did not include two elements prominent in recall— **IMPLEMENTATION** and **SOURCE-GOAL**. I did not analyze the structure of causation as carefully as he. There were also some differences in the definitions of elements.

On balance, there appears to be cause for optimism about the generality of my analysis. The minority of Miller's verbs that I cannot analyze assert some of my elements, but also assert some new elements. A cursory look at these verbs suggests that I need to add elements at least for direction (for example, "retreats," "ascends"), for shapes of complex paths ("zigzags"), and for multiple people and things ("accompanies"). (Miller combines these and other distinctions under his very general component, *directional*.) Miller limits his analysis to verbs (and, indirectly, to prepositions), so there must be further gaps in my analysis of whole propositions that are not uncovered by this comparison.

THE REPRESENTATION OF THE RECALLS

The Path Diagram

It is not sufficient to list and define the semantic elements; it also is important to know just how the elements combine into propositions. The graphic display in Figure 10.3 shows some of the combinations that subjects employed. The data used in this figure include all the recall propositions that most closely correspond to the phrases:

(3A)   . . . he passed the kelp beds. (Form 1)

and

(3B)   . . . he was past the kelp beds. (Form 2)

Fifteen subjects mentioned either "kelp" or "sea" or "ocean." These 15 subjects are indicated in Figure 10.3 by the 15 lines entering at the top. All 15 subjects recalled the elements of **IMPLEMENTATION**,

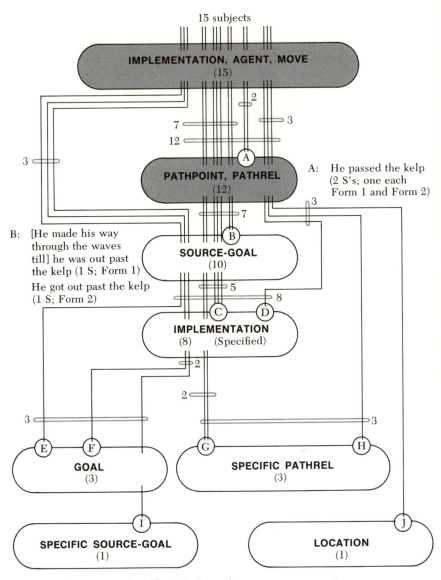

15 subjects

IMPLEMENTATION, AGENT, MOVE
(15)

PATHPOINT, PATHREL
(12)

A: He passed the kelp
(2 S's; one each
Form 1 and Form 2)

B: [He made his way
through the waves
till] he was out past
the kelp (1 S; Form 1)

He got out past the kelp
(1 S; Form 2)

SOURCE-GOAL
(10)

IMPLEMENTATION
(8)   (Specified)

GOAL
(3)

SPECIFIC PATHREL
(3)

SPECIFIC SOURCE-GOAL
(1)

LOCATION
(1)

C: He sailed out past the kelp (1 S; Form 1)
    He sailed out passed the kelp (1 S; Form 1)
    He sailed [his boat] out past the kelp (1 S; Form 2)
D: He shoved [off in his boat] past the kelp (1 S; Form 2)
E: He set out to the ocean (1 S; Form 2)
F: He sailed out to sea (1 S; Form 1)
G: He sailed out beyond the kelp (1 S; Form 1)
    He rowed [his boat on] out beyond the kelp (1 S; Form 2)
H: The line passed through the kelp (1 S; Form 2)
I: He sailed far out to sea (1 S; Form 2)
J: He passed the kelp in his boat (1 S; Form 1)

FIGURE 10.3
Path diagram of the 15 recalls to the presented propositions
. . . [till] he passed the kelp beds (Form 1) and . . . [till]
he was past the kelp beds (Form 2). Each subject's recall is
represented as one of the 15 downward paths through the
semantic elements. The number of recalls that include each
element is in parentheses. The bottom of each path (or each
set of identical paths) is labeled with a letter. The recall(s)
for that path are listed to the side. To make comparison
easier, irrelevant features of the recalls are standardized; for
example, the grammatical subject of the verb is always a
pronoun, "the" and "his" are the only determiners used, and
"kelp beds" is shortened to "kelp." The number of subjects
giving each recall, and the story form presented to those
subjects, follow each recall. Elements from the presented
propositions are shaded; all other elements appeared in the
recalls as additions only. (Note: strictly speaking, "the line"
in recall H is a **PATIENT**. Since the **AGENT** was replaced by
an inanimate object only once in all the recalls, as a
simplification "the line" was analyzed as **AGENT**.)

AGENT, and **MOVE**. Moreover, all 15 added more elements to the
recall. This is indicated in the path diagram by the fact that all 15 lines
that enter the **AGENT**, **MOVE** oval also leave. (Some of these additions
are due to amalgamation with another proposition.)

Of the 15 subjects, 12 retained the elements of **PATHPOINT** or
PATHREL from (3A) or (3B).[10] Two subjects stopped at this point (the
two subjects marked as point A who both said simply, ". . . he
passed the kelp"). Seven subjects added a **SOURCE-GOAL** specification to the **PATH** or **PATHREL** and **AGENT-MOVE** specification, and
so on. By following the lines, one can determine just what semantic
elements each subject added to his recall. By seeing where the lines
terminate and matching the label on that termination with the recalls
listed on the figure, one can tell what each subject said.[11]

Notice that the elements in the path diagram are ordered in terms
of relative frequency. Thus, the higher up in the diagram the element
appears, the larger the number of recalls in which that element has
appeared.

---

[10]The dynamic element **PATHREL** was assigned to both verbs ("passed") and prepositions ("sailed past"). In context, both forms refer to a process; the locative result of
that process is not analyzed here (cf. Figure 10.2).
[11]In my dialect, "beyond" entails a greater distance than does "past," and thus has in
it the element **SPECIFIC PATHREL**. Not all speakers of English share this interpretation.

Interpretation

What regularities does the diagram suggest? First, there is one path to the bottom that includes the paths of 9 of the 15 recalls; some of the 9 drop off sooner, some later, 2 not at all.

Three recalls (at the right of Figure 10.3) show idiosyncratic deviations, skipping elements from the main path or branching away from the path entirely. The remaining 3 recalls (shown at the left) skip **PATHPOINT** and **PATHREL** and include **SOURCE-GOAL**; they may or may not include **IMPLEMENTATION**; all 3 include **GOAL** (one goes on to **SPECIFIC SOURCE-GOAL**). Thus, **GOAL** ("to sea") would seem to be a minority alternative to **PATH**, each being a case associated with a major stage in a change of location. There is no syntactic reason that both cases could not be given (as in the sentence "He sailed past the kelp to the ocean"). This tendency to substitute rather than add a semantically similar element is seen with other propositions in the story, and should be taken seriously despite the small number of recalls in Figure 10.3.

SOURCE-GOAL and **IMPLEMENTATION**, it can be seen, can occur separately or in combination. They are not alternatives to any other element; they are additions only, and apparently are independent of one another.

SPECIFIC SOURCE-GOAL and **SPECIFIC PATHREL**, on *a priori* grounds, should occur only if **SOURCE-GOAL** and **PATHREL**, respectively, occur. This situation appears in Figure 10.3. They are thus less free to occur independently than **SOURCE-GOAL** and **IMPLE-MENTATION**, for example.

Finally, one subject recalled **LOCATION**. Of the 15 subjects who deleted ". . . to his boat" in the recall of the "running" proposition, 6 compensated by adding "boat" as a **LOCATION** or **PATIENT** in the sailing propositions. Thus, **LOCATION** and **PATIENT** were substitutions for the earlier **GOAL**.

SUMMARY

Information Limits

Semantic Elements. When an element is added in recall, some other element is usually deleted from the word or clause. Only the simplest verbs and clauses seem immune. Perhaps this is due to a constraint on the number of elements that may be comfortably asserted by one proposition.

To see if this is the case, we could simply gather the movement proposition recalls, count the number of elements in each proposition, and see what distribution emerges. For example, "The fisherman went out to sea" has 12 elements:

- 3 predicates: **CAUSE, IMPLEMENTATION, MOVE**

- 5 case relations: **EVENT, RESULT, AGENT, OBJECT, GOAL**

- 2 arguments: fisherman, sea

- 2 modifying elements: **COME/GO, SOURCE-GOAL**

It can be seen that certain types of words typically are associated with only one semantic element. In the whole clause, however, there are more elements than words.

Twelve elements in a six-word clause seem not unreasonable. Is the constraint somewhere in this ballpark? In a word, no. Far more complex verbs can be processed with ease. Consider the verbs of transfer analyzed by Dedre Gentner in Chapter 9. A clause with the verb "sell," at the most detailed level of her analysis, has more than 70 semantic elements. If there is a constraint on the number of semantic elements in one clause, it is clearly a large number.

What we are looking for is a measure of semantic complexity applicable to the difficulties subjects have in performing a memory task. The number of semantic elements is a measure of the perceived complexity of the situation referred to, but not of the processing complexity. One function of language is to make simple the communication of complex ideas. As long as the complex idea is important enough to have been named, speakers of the language can communicate the idea by the name, rather than by a long description.

Clearly, however, the word is not the unit of complexity. The number of words in a clause gives only a rough estimate of the memory load. Semantic elements are often lost without an entire word being deleted, suggesting that there is some psychological reality to a representation that is more abstract than words.[12] The fact that "seize" is often recalled as "take" suggests that **INTENSITY** is not always retained in the memory system, though the basic idea is retained.

Processing Units. Suppose one used the number of *separable* units of information in a semantic representation as the measure of processing complexity. In recall of a verb, certain sets of predicates

---

[12]See Kintsch (1972a) for a different approach to this issue.

are added or deleted in an all-or-none fashion. For example, if animate movement is recalled at all, the three predicates **CAUSE**, **IMPLEMEN-TATION**, and **MOVE** (with their relations event and result) are all included. For movement propositions, the basic predicate structure is treated as a unit: **CAUSE** (**IMPLEMENTATION, MOVE**). A specific **IMPLEMENTATION**, however, is separable: **SAIL** can be lost while **IMPLEMENTATION** is retained. To distinguish these units from semantic elements, I call them *processing units*. One processing unit may be one semantic element, or a whole group of semantic elements (for example, the predicates linked together in a subnetwork).

The suggestion is that, although complex representations are needed to model the meaning in a clause, the elements in the representation are combined into higher units, which are the determinants of processing complexity. The question, then, is, What level of units should be counted for each type of verb?

An Estimate of the Processing Unit Constraint. I am now in a position to count the number of processing units in each recalled proposition of movement or transfer.[13] The count is made according to the following guidelines:

- Each modifier supplies one processing unit. For example, "out" has the unit **OUT** (a member of the class **SOURCE-GOAL**).

- Each noun phrase supplies one processing unit.

- Each noun phrase has a relation to the action, sometimes marked by a preposition and sometimes by word order, which supplies one processing unit.

- Each verb supplies one or more processing units, the number determined by the criterion of separability in recall. For example, "go" has two units, **CAUSE** (**IMPLEMENTATION, MOVE**) and **COME/GO**.

By this analysis, two-thirds of the recalled verbs have 2 units. Half of the remaining verbs have only one unit (for example, "take": transfer of goods) and half have 3 units ("sell": transfer of goods, transfer of money, and the existence of a social contract).

Analysis of the entire clause shows that the average number of processing units is 7.3: 2.0 units from the verb, 4.6 units from the 2.3 noun phrases (including the noun and its case relation to the action),

---

[13]The transfer verbs in the story are "laid," "put," "give," "let have," "buy," "sell," "take," and "seize." They are included in this analysis to increase the range of propositions.

and 0.7 units from other words. It is hard to resist thinking of Miller's (1956) paper on "the magical number seven."

Miller's paper also supplies our rationale for counting noun phrases as one unit. The paper gives the first suggestion, now a truism in the memory literature, that "chunking" of information into hierarchical structures can expand the amount of information processed beyond the numerical capacity limit. Noun phrases and embedded propositions are obvious candidates for this treatment. The hierarchical structure permits clauses to be rich in structure, yet not exceed complexity limits.

The processing unit analysis provides the framework we wanted for discussing verb recall. The original question was: Are processing limitations responsible for the fact that additions of semantic elements are often accompanied by deletions of other elements? The data for answering that question are at hand. No verb in the 198 recalls analyzed had more than 3 processing units. Most had 1 or 2. Typically, a core unit for the movement verbs can be combined with one, and only one, modifying unit, a unit at the semantic element level. A choice must be made as to which modifying element will be asserted. Here are some examples:

Verb presented	Verb recalled	Element lost	Element gained
returned	sailed	**PREVLOC**	**SAIL**
ran	went	**RUN**	**COME/GO**
seize	bite	**INTENSITY**	**BITE**

As far as the verb is concerned, it seems impossible for the subject to give more than the core predicate structure and one extra piece of information in recall of animate movement. If an inference is made, some old information is "bumped." Of course, the lost information might possibly be reinstated in an adverb or adverbial phrase—but it is not. There is a linguistic constraint (the number of elements per verb), but there is also a linguistic device (modifying words) for circumventing the constraint. Why is it not used?

The Jumbled-Closet Model.   The data suggest to me that the linguistic behavior I observed can be described by the following scenario. The subject opens up a jumbled closet crammed with old knowledge of the world as well as with a new layer of information directly asserted in the story that was just heard. The core predicate structure comes tumbling out. The subject notices a modifying element at the top of a heap, quickly finds a handy verb, and shuts the door, ignoring everything else in the closet.

According to this view, subjects pick a very few salient elements and use whatever language is handy to express them, with little concern for what else is dragged in or excluded by the choice. In turn, people listening to this sentence would put the elements into closets of their own. Unimportant information supplied by the speaker passes right through the listener's system, without contributing to processing load, while important information not supplied by the speaker is inferred. Communication would be considerably more cumbersome if all information to be communicated had to be asserted or if the listener were not permitted to ignore unimportant distinctions. (It is interesting to consider the conversational postulates described in Chapter 3 as an implicitly agreed-upon structure for aiding communication by permitting speaker and listener to minimize processing loads.)

Evaluation of the Structural Network Representation

At the beginning of this chapter, the basic elements of the sailing situation were shown within the network representation developed in this book. I have been forced to incorporate additional elements in my analyses. What does this imply for the structural network representation?

Some of the elements present no problem: They simply involve additional predicates. However, adding the whole set of elements would be, at best, inelegant. Some (for example, **MANNER, COME/ GO, ATTAIN**) could be added to one or another of the predicates (**CAUSE, IMPLEMENTATION,** or **MOVE**); others might be separate predicates (taking existing nodes as arguments; for example, **SOURCE-GOAL**). There is something unsatisfying in this, however; most of the additions appear as *ad hoc* violations of the simple, basic structures.

When Brown (1973) studied children's early language acquisition, he found that basic action structures are uttered first, in Stage 1 speech. He calls them the *Basic Meanings*. In general, our network representation is at that stage. The second half of Brown's book is about Stage 2 speech. Brown calls it *Modulations of Meaning*. This is when children start forming plurals, tenses, locatives, and other modulations. Mostly, it is done by adding affixes to root words, or by using prepositions.

Perhaps the memory model, at its present stage of maturity, is best regarded as a Stage 1 model. There are five stages in Brown's analysis, so according to this view, the memory model has made a good start, but it has a long way to go.

PART VI

STUDIES OF VISUAL PERCEPTION AND PROBLEM SOLVING

Visual Perception and World Knowledge: Notes on a Model of Sensory-Cognitive Interaction

STEPHEN E. PALMER

Imagine that you are visiting a psychological laboratory —
probably around 1915. As you walk in, a psychologist comes over
and, without waiting for introductions, asks what you see on the
table.

"A book."

"Yes, of course, it is a book," he agrees, "but what do you
really see?"

"What do you mean, 'What do I *really* see'?" you ask,
puzzled. "I told you that I see a book. It is a small book with a red
cover."

The psychologist is persistent. "What is your perception
really?" he insists. "Describe it to me as precisely as you can."

"You mean it isn't a book? What is this, some kind of trick?"

There is a hint of impatience. "Yes, it is a book. There is no
trickery involved. I just want you to describe to me *exactly* what
you can see, no more and no less."

You are growing very suspicious now. "Well," you say, "from
this angle the cover of the book looks like a dark red
parallelogram."

"Yes," he says, pleased. "Yes, you see a patch of dark red in the
shape of a parallelogram. What else?"

"There is a grayish white edge below it and another thin line of the same dark red below that. Under it I see the table—" He winces. "Around it I see a somewhat mottled brown with wavering streaks of lighter brown running roughly parallel to one another."

"Fine, fine." He thanks you for your cooperation.[1]

This exchange between subject and experimenter was invented by Miller to make a point about perceptual experience: Normal perception is concerned with seeing real-world objects, not patches of color. The viewer finds it extremely difficult, even if pressed, to attend to an uninterpreted sensory image. Visual information may begin with patches of color on the retina, but the visual system rapidly interprets those patches as objects in the world. The end result is a mental model of the viewer's surroundings. He does not see colored shapes; he sees such things as books, tables, and people in various spatial relationships to each other and to himself.

The mysterious ways by which people manage to arrive at meaningful interpretations from retinal information have long fascinated and puzzled psychologists. Helmholtz (1925) proposed the notion of "unconscious inference," whereby the cues present in the retinal image form the basic data of a problem-solving process. In this process, prior knowledge of the world is used to infer the physical situation that gave rise to the retinal data. Similar ideas are found in Brunswik's (1956) "probabilistic cue-association," Bruner's (1957) "hypothesis testing," and Neisser's (1967) "analysis-by-synthesis" approaches to perceptual interpretation. All these proposals make a certain amount of sense in their attempts to deal with the complexities involved in the interaction of external sensory information with internal knowledge. None, however, is specific enough to be evaluated critically.

In this chapter I discuss certain aspects of an information-processing model of perception in which stored information about the world plays a central role in the interpretation of sensory data. Although the model is by no means complete, I outline the main proposals for:

- A representation for visual information capable of specifying this knowledge;

- A procedural system that generates expectations on the basis of stored knowledge.

---

[1]From George A. Miller, *Psychology: The science of mental life.* New York: Harper & Row, 1962, pp. 103–104. Copyright 1962 by George A. Miller. Reprinted with permission of author and publisher.

The discussion is largely concerned with visual processing of objects and scenes, but the basic theoretical framework is applicable to other visual tasks (for example, reading) and to tasks in other sensory modalities.

VISUAL REPRESENTATION

Representational Formats

The first issue in formalizing a model of visual perception and knowledge is that of specifying a representation for the information. Several candidates are available. One form is an "iconic" representation such as a template (see Neisser, 1967) or a "holographic" image (Pribram, 1971). Iconic representations are found at the initial stages of visual processing—for example, some of the line, edge, and angle detectors discovered by Hubel and Wiesel (1962) and the iconic or sensory memories proposed by Sperling (1960) and Neisser (1967). Iconic representations are particularly useful in early processing as a veridical form of representation for temporary storage of sensory input. However, their use in operations requiring conceptual abstraction (for example, categorization and other similarity-based operations) is severely limited. (For a critique of analog representations in this regard, see Pylyshyn, 1973, and the discussion in Chapter 1 of this book.) I return to the discussion of iconic representations shortly.

An alternative to iconic representation is a "feature" representation (Selfridge and Neisser, 1963). Features are elementary units—lines, curves, and angles, for example—of which the visual image is composed. The representation of a figure is a list of such features. Simple feature representations fail for the opposite reason that iconic representations do. They are inherently too flexible in that they do not specify the manner in which the elemental units are combined. More sophisticated feature representations can overcome this difficulty by specifying higher-order features that are (explicitly or implicitly) relational. Given relational definitions, feature representations become virtually indistinguishable from propositional representations, the format to which I now turn.

A format for representing visual information that has attracted interest recently is that of the proposition (for example, Baylor, 1971; Winston, 1970). A proposition is an assertion about the relation between informational entities. In a propositional representation for visual information, the relationships are primarily concerned with spatial location, shape, color, size, and texture, and the informational entities are structural units and values along relational dimensions. The structural units can be primitive (for example, **POINT**) or higher-order (for example, squares and cubes). In a propositional system, an angle might be represented by a proposition expressing the relation between the component lines and the vertex point of the angle. Similarly, a triangular pyramid might be represented by a set of propositions about the intersection between the four component triangles at the six edges and four vertices of the pyramid. Specific propositional representations are presented more formally in later sections.

Propositions are attractive because they are capable of encoding diverse types of information in a single, easily interpretable format. The relation **COLOR**, for example, holds between an object (or part of an object) and its color value specified, say, by hue, saturation, and brightness. Similarly, the primitive location relation, **LOC**, holds between an object and a reference point with a value specified, say, by a direction and a distance. In a memory system, this separability of information allows for the ability to account for partial forgetting of visual information. It is possible to forget (or fail to encode) the orientation of an object while remembering (or successfully encoding) the location of the same object relative to other objects (Frost and Wolf, 1973). A related advantage of propositions is that they are modality independent. They can be used to represent linguistic information (as shown in other chapters of this book) as well as visual information. This is important, as it allows for easy translation of equivalent information between modalities. Chase and Clark (1972) have argued persuasively for the necessity of this in their cross-modal verification experiments in which sentences must be matched against pictures.

There have been a number of debates over the relative merits of propositional versus analogical (or iconic) representations (for example, Pylyshyn, 1973; Sloman, 1971; also see the discussion in Chapter 1). The arguments in favor of analogical representations tend to emphasize the relative ease with which certain operations can be performed on them compared to the difficulty in performing the same operations on propositional representations. These arguments, however, generally overlook the fact that propositions can encode quantitative as well as qualitative information. In addition, it is not often recognized that propositions are capable of encoding an analog image. Higher-level propositions can be decomposed into lower-level propositions until they are reduced to primitive propositions about points. A triangle, for example, can be decomposed into propositions about its component angles; these angles can then be decomposed into propositions about their component lines; and the lines can be further decomposed into propositions about their component points. (A mechanism for decomposing propositions is discussed later in this chapter and by Rumelhart and Levin, in Chapter 8.) At its lowest level, a propositional encoding becomes essentially equivalent to an analog representation. Indeed, given a medium in which to construct an image, a fully decomposed propositional encoding can generate the corresponding analogical figure. This means, among other things, that so-called analog operations, such as mental rotation (Cooper and Shepard, 1973; Shepard and Metzler, 1971), can be performed with equal ease on analogical and propositional representations once the latter have been decomposed into primitives.

Consider how the rotation of a two-dimensional figure might occur in a propositional representation. Suppose the location of a point X in the figure is represented propositionally by polar coordinates: **DIST** (X, P, r) and **DIREC** (X, P, θ), where r is the distance of X from the reference point, P (the center of rotation), and θ is the direction of X from the reference point, P. According to this view, then, the process of rotating the figure is simply the process of updating θ for each point. In order for this theoretical point of view to be capable of accounting for the results of experiments on mental rotation (for example, Shepard and Metzler, 1971), θ must be changed successively in small increments. Note that the "analog" aspect is in the process of updating θ, not in the nature of the representation. Three-dimensional rotation could take place in the same way, except that a second direction parameter (ϕ) is required.

Structural Descriptions

In Two Dimensions. Assume that the equivalent of a lexicon of appropriate informational units exists, by which the retinal image can be described. The lexicon contains all possible relationships (for example, shape, color, location, size, orientation) and their possible values. These values may be numerical, categorical, or propositional.

The structural description of a two-dimensional shape can be specified by perceptual units and the relationships between them. I assume that points are primitive perceptual units. Primitive units can be combined into higher-order units (schemata) that summarize the information included in the collection of points. Figure 11.1A shows the format of some simple schemata. Each token of a **POINT**, line, angle, square, and so forth is denoted by angular brackets, representing a node specified by some set of parts and some set of parameters. **POINT** differs from the others because it is assumed to be

A

Schema	Token	Part schemata	Parameter relations
POINT	⟨A⟩	—	LOC
line	⟨AB⟩	⟨A⟩, . . . , ⟨B⟩	LOC, ORIENT, LENGTH
angle	⟨ABC⟩	⟨AB⟩, ⟨B⟩, ⟨BC⟩	LOC, ORIENT, DEGREES
square	⟨ABCD⟩	⟨AB⟩, ⟨BC⟩, ⟨CD⟩, ⟨DA⟩, ⟨ABC⟩, ⟨BCD⟩, ⟨CDA⟩, ⟨DAB⟩	LOC, ORIENT, LENGTH

B

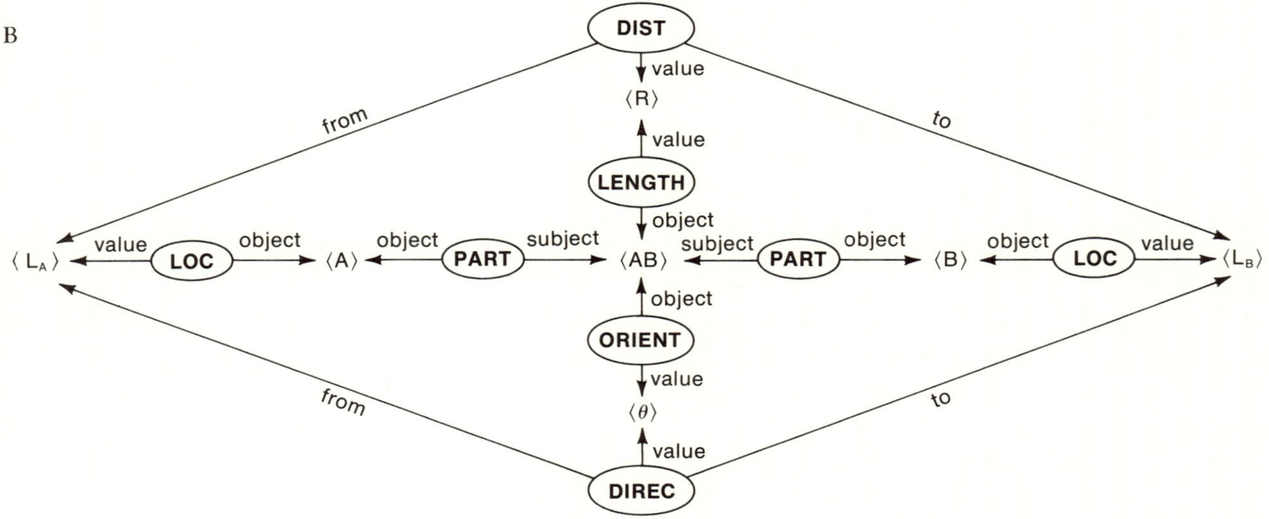

FIGURE 11.1

A shows a few simple structural schemata, their component parts (but not the spatial relationships between them), and the parameters used to define specific instances. B shows the length and orientation of a line in relation to the location of its end points.

primitive; it has no parts, and it has only a single parameter of location, **LOC**. Line has **POINTS** as parts (represented in Figure 11.1A by the end points) and parameters of location (**LOC**), orientation (**ORIENT**), and length (**LENGTH**). The location of a line is represented by the location of its midpoint, the orientation by the direction (**DIREC**) from one end point to the other, and the length by the distance (**DIST**) between the end points. Note that length and orientation are "emergent" properties of a line in that they do not appear as parameters of its component parts. The values of emergent properties, however, are derivable from the values of properties of subparts, as illustrated for **LENGTH** and **ORIENT** in Figure 11.1B. An angle has two lines and a **POINT** as parts. An angle's location is the location of its vertex, its orientation is the mean orientation of its component lines, and its angular size is the orientational discrepancy between its lines. Finally, a square has lines and angles as parts and parameters of location (of its center), orientation (of one of its sides), and length (of one of its sides). All parameters of a **POINT**, line, angle, or square must be specified to encode any particular instance of these perceptual concepts. The more concepts that remain unspecified, the more abstract and general is the representation.

Figure 11.2 illustrates the complete structural description of square ABCD. The figure shows the structural **PART** relationships between the square's component parts (lines and angles) and the parts of its component parts (**POINTS**). Notice that although the representation seems to have 28 parameters—a location for each vertex, a location, orientation and length for each line, and a location, orientation, and angular size for each angle—there are really only 3 independent parameters: the location of the square, its orientation, and its length. (All nodes that have the same value for the same parameter would ultimately point to one node representing that value. Parameters are not shown in Figure 11.2 because of space limitations.) Thus, the schema for a square represents the informational redundancy of its shape, as indeed it should (Attneave, 1954).

As more complex shapes are encountered, it becomes obvious that structural descriptions must make use of higher-order units. Giving completely expanded descriptions is too clumsy. If one could define a shape in terms of a more general class of shapes that have the same qualitative structure and then "decompose" (replace by definition) that higher-order definition into its component parts, the problem would be greatly reduced. For example, a square might be defined as a polygon with four lines of equal length and four angles of 90°. "Polygon" would then be defined in terms of n lines and n angles and the structural relationships between them (for example, the end point

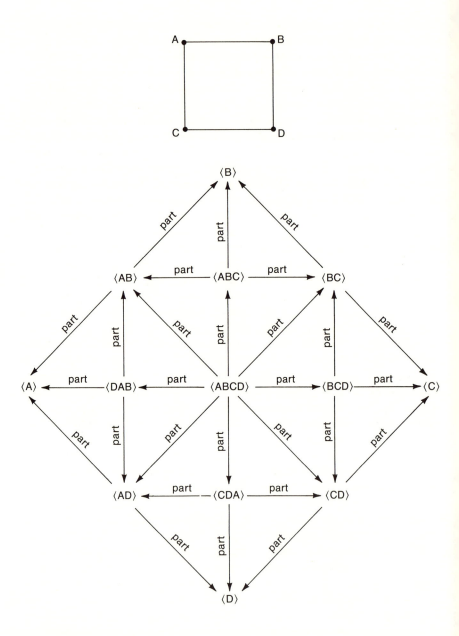

FIGURE 11.2
The structural description of square ABCD. Nodes represent the component
POINTs, lines, and angles of the square (see Figure 11.1A). Parameters of
the component parts are not shown.

of each line is the vertex of an angle). When the procedural definition of **square** is then executed by the interpreter (see Chapter 7), it passes the parameters of the particular square to **POLYGON**. **POLYGON** is then executed with these parameters by replacing **ANGLE**s and **LINE**s with their respective definitions. After all definitions have been executed, the result should be a complete structural schema for the square, as shown in Figure 11.2. The procedures being suggested are analogous to those used to decompose the representation of verbs into underlying structures (see Chapter 8). The important point is that higher-order encodings can be reconstructed in their complete form by such a system, ultimately generating an analog image with an interpreted superstructure of higher-order propositions.

In Three Dimensions. At the level of three-dimensional inference, the schemata for shape are more complex than those for two dimensions, but the same principles apply. Any given shape can be represented by three-dimensional relationships among its component parts. Now, however, location and orientation are specified in three-space rather than two-space, and the shapes generally require more parameters. Figure 11.3 shows the structural schema for a **cube**. Note that the first-order parts of a **cube** are **squares**, a higher-order unit whose internal part structure is given in Figure 11.2. It should be possible to write procedural definitions capable of generating the complete schema for a **cube** from its parts. Given such procedures, the reconstructive expansion down to particular points is always possible. It is necessary, however, only when detailed information about low-level constituents and their interrelationships is required, as in Baylor's (1971) block visualization task.

Complex shapes can be represented by putting together simple shapes with the proper relationships (Winston, 1973). To do this rigorously, representations must be developed for predicates that specify the structural relationships between parts that are not explicitly represented in the higher-order encoding. For example, if one cube is on top of another cube, the relationship between the top surface of the lower cube and the bottom surface of the upper cube is important and implicit in the predicate "on-top." The solution is to define the complex predicate in such a way that the implicit information is made explicit. Operators such as **bottom-of (X)** and **top-of (X)** can be defined that evaluate to the node representing those surfaces of their argument, object X. Thus, for the cube shown in Figure 11.3 (call it **cube-1**), the operator expression **bottom-of (cube-1)** would evaluate to the **square EFGH**, and **top-of (cube-1)** would evaluate to the **square ABCD**. Now, the relationship between

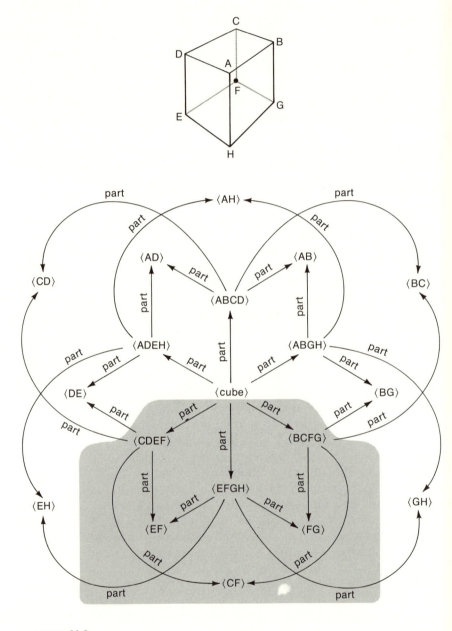

FIGURE 11.3
The structural description for cube ABCDEFGH expanded to the level of lines.
(Vertices are not shown.) Nodes representing parts of the cube not visible from the
perspective shown above are within the shaded area.

the upper and lower cubes in the expression **on-top (upper-cube, lower-cube)** can be specified by the proposition **AGAINST (bottom-of- (upper-cube), top-of (lower-cube))**, where **AGAINST** is a zero-degree planar angle between the two surfaces. This expansion is then the definition of the higher-order relation **on-top**.

Representing Objects. The schemata for real-world objects are specified by the structural descriptions of their shape as previously outlined, modified by such properties as color, scalar size, texture, location, and orientation within their superordinate schemata. For each concept certain properties are encoded (more or less) absolutely — for example, shape and color. There are also properties that are encoded relative to the corresponding properties of the superpart — for example, location, orientation, and scalar size. The notion is that higher-order concepts constitute a "frame of reference" for their sub-parts with respect to these relative dimensions.

Consider the representation for a human face. The location, orientation, and size of the eyes are specified relative to the location, orientation, and size of the head. These properties of the head, in turn, are specified relative to the same properties of the whole body. If the representation is to have any generality, these properties must be encoded with locations and orientations specified relative to one another, since the absolute parameters vary considerably across different views of a face. The relative encoding of location and orientation is especially important for those parts that are movable with respect to each other and to their superordinates. The position and orientation of a person's head, for example, is not fixed relative to his body, but can vary only within a small, specifiable range of values. Relative encoding with superordinate reference frames allows this information to be represented in a simple and natural way.

A possible representation of a person's face is given in Figure 11.4A, which illustrates the relative encoding of spatial relationships. The predicates are shown in shorthand notation for relative locational predicates (the vector symbols), relative orientational predicates (the degree values), and relative-size predicates (the ratio values). Predicates of the same type (location, orientation, or size) represent the same information except for the values along the encoded dimension. This is illustrated in Figure 11.4B, which gives the definition for a relative locational predicate (the vector symbol). This predicate encodes the distance (**DIST**) and direction (**DIREC**) between the locations (**LOC**) of the object (A) and the referent (B). It is the values of the distance parameter, R, and the direction parameter, θ, that determine the particular vector used in the shorthand predicate.

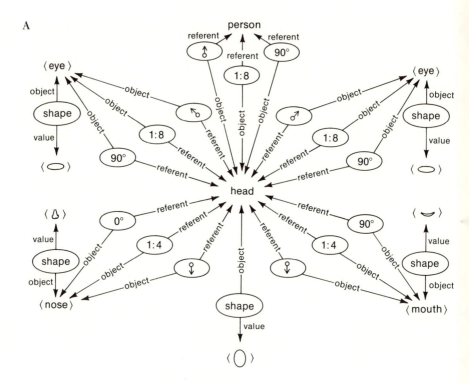

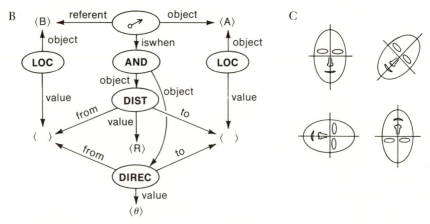

FIGURE 11.4

A shows a schema for a two-dimensional projection of a face such as drawn in C.
The definition for a relative locational predicate in B illustrates the potential
expansion of the representation in A. C illustrates the invariance of the relationship
between the reference frame of the eye relative to that of the head when the face is
translated and rotated in two-dimensional space.

The relationship of each part of the face to the face as a whole is specified relative to the reference frame established by the whole. I presume that each shape has an intrinsic frame of reference defined by its parameters. For example, the eye can be represented as a 3 by 5 oval, with a major axis (the longer dimension) and a minor axis (the shorter dimension). Similarly, the head has a major and minor axis. The location, orientation, and length of the major axis establish the intrinsic frame of reference for each shape. Specifying the contextual (or relative) location, orientation, and size of the eye, then, is simply a matter of specifying the relationships between the reference frame of the eye, and the frame of reference of the referent node (in this case, the head). These relationships state the translation, rotation, and scaling transformations required to bring the two shapes into the proper spatial configuration. The result is the relative encoding of the two intrinsic frames of reference, which remains invariant with rotations, translations, and size changes of the object represented (see Figure 11.4C). The two-dimensional encoding given here can easily be modified to represent three-dimensional relations. It can also be extended to include the encoding of a part with respect to another part (as opposed to the superordinate). These part-part relationships are implicit in the schema shown in Figure 11.4A.

Representing Scenes. A person's knowledge about the world goes far beyond knowing the intrinsic properties of objects and their parts. He also knows the types of environments in which objects are characteristically found—bread in kitchens, mailboxes in front yards, and television sets in living rooms. Clearly, if an observer knows what kind of scene he is looking at, he has important information about what types of objects are likely to be found there. In a recent experiment (Palmer, in press) I have demonstrated that people are more likely to identify a briefly presented picture of an object correctly when it is preceded by an appropriate contextual scene than when the same object is preceded by a blank slide. In addition, my subjects were less likely to identify an object correctly when it was preceded by an inappropriate context than when it was preceded by a blank slide. Thus, people not only *have* knowledge about scenes, they *use* this knowledge in interpreting sensory information.

The format I propose for the representation of the structure of scenes is the same as that used earlier to represent the structure of objects. Figure 11.5 shows part of a generalized schema for a kitchen. The schema focuses on objects that might be found near a loaf of bread on a kitchen counter. Although each object is shown as a single node, each node stands for a whole schema representing that object's

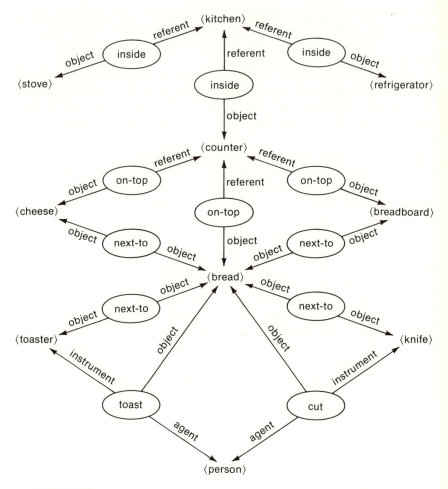

FIGURE 11.5
A partial schema for a kitchen scene that includes a counter with several objects
on it. Locational relationships are represented abstractly to illustrate the lack of
specificity in general schemata for types of scenes.

internal structure. Similarly, the locational relationships between
objects (on-top, next-to) are higher-level encodings that have defining schematic expansions, similar to those outlined earlier for
on-top. The abstract nature of these relationships illustrates the lack
of specificity inherent in general schemata for most scenes. The
spatial relationships between objects in a type of scene are seldom as
definite as those between parts within a "unitary" object. Naturally,

in a particular kitchen, many of the relationships are well specified, and in a particular kitchen at a particular time, all of the relationships are well defined, even though people seldom seem to encode all this information.

Many readers are no doubt troubled by the complexity of the representations proposed. If the kitchen representation were expanded to primitive units, for example, the resulting network would be truly mind-boggling. However, a number of considerations should be kept in mind. First, the amount of potentially perceivable information in the corresponding kitchen scene is equally mind-boggling when considered in detail. It would be naive to expect that the richness of such a complex visual stimulus could be captured in full by a simple representation. Second, the important aspects of a scene can be captured by the higher-level superstructure of the schema. This level of representation is relatively simple and comprehensible. Most importantly, people seldom (if ever) perceive or remember visual information in microscopic detail. In both perception and memory, a stack of books is simply a number of books piled on top of each other, not a collection of specific volumes in a particular order with definite orientations relative to each other. On some occasions an observer might notice how neatly the books are stacked or whether the pile is leaning precariously to one side. But a great deal of information is simply ignored in everyday life unless there is some good reason to attend to it. In other words, the ratio of perceived information to potentially perceivable information is low, probably astonishingly low. Any reader who doubts this is referred to the discussion of my informal experiment on people's memory of the Psychology-Linguistics Building at the University of California, San Diego (see Chapter 1). Many things people "see" every day for years are known only in terms of their most general visual properties.

Categories, Prototypes, and Specific Instances

In line with recent studies on categorization that emphasize the importance of prototypes (for example, Rosch, 1973, 1974; Reed, 1972; Rips, Shoben, and Smith, 1973; Smith, Shoben, and Rips, 1974), I propose that representations of categories include information about prototypical values. In some cases this information concerns a central tendency such as the typical dimensions of a face, but in other cases this information concerns ideals such as the purest, most saturated shade of blue. This prototypical information plays an important part in the process of categorization discussed later in this chapter.

Naturally, the rule for specifying prototypical values of properties depends on the nature of the property. Some properties vary continuously over a single range of values (for example, the length of a nose in Reed's (1972) family resemblance experiment). The prototypical value along such dimensions would be well suited to the mean of the distribution of observed values. Discrete properties, such as a person's sex, are clearly inappropriate subjects for an averaging rule. Either the modal value or the linguistically "unmarked" value (see H. Clark, 1973b) would be the most likely candidates. In still other cases, a property varies continuously over a number of discrete ranges. An apple, for instance, can be any one of a number of shades of red, green, or yellow. Its prototypical value might well be the mean value of the modal range.

I am assuming that there are such things as perceptual categories. These may or may not be the same as linguistic categories. The analysis developed to this point leads to the view that perceptual categories exist by virtue of similar structural descriptions. Thus, the set of four-legged mammals might well be a strong perceptual category, whereas the set of biological mammals (including whales, bats, and people) might not be. Whales seem to be closer to the perceptual category of fish than to that of mammals, bats seem to be closer to birds than to mammals, and perhaps people should comprise a perceptual category of their own. These are simply guesses, of course, since there is little evidence on this matter.

There are many linguistic categories that are mainly functional in nature. A vehicle is something for transporting other objects, and food is something that is consumed by eating. Often there are lower-level categories that are more strongly perceptual—for example, cars, planes, and boats within the category of vehicles. In such cases, the general category would be represented structurally as a set of unrelated or very distantly related perceptual categories whose unifying feature is their functional relatedness.

VISUAL PROCESSING

Now that a representation for visual information has been presented, the problem of how perceptual processes manage to interpret sensory data can be approached. The goal is to devise a perceptual system that not only will recognize visual stimuli, but will do so faster and more accurately when:

- the stimulus is well known rather than novel (Broadbent, 1967; Reicher, 1969);

- the stimulus appears in an appropriate context rather than out of context or in an inappropriate context (Biederman, 1972; Palmer, in press; Tulving and Gold, 1963);

- the stimulus is typical of its category rather than atypical (Rosch, 1973, 1974).

Since all these effects can only be explained by some facilitation due to prior experience with the stimuli, a workable model must specify how the interpretive process makes use of stored knowledge to facilitate processing.

The proposal presented here incorporates a constant interplay between external sensory information and internal conceptual information. This interaction is the heart of the perceptual system. Sensory features "look for" possible interpretations within the available conceptual schemata, and the possible interpretations "look for" confirming sensory information among the features being extracted. Generally speaking, the facilitating effect of this type of system is that once a member within a schema has been advanced as a candidate interpretation, the rest of the units within the schema provide "expectations" about what else should be found and where these things should be located. The specific mechanisms involved in such a system are discussed more fully later.

The Parsing Paradox: Bottom-Up or Top-Down

If perceptual interpretation is a matter of mapping sensations onto structural schemata, which happens first: interpreting the whole or interpreting the parts? How can someone recognize a face until he has first recognized the eyes, nose, mouth, and ears? Then again, how can someone recognize the eyes, nose, mouth, and ears until he knows that they are part of a face? This is often called the parsing paradox. It concerns the difficulties encountered with either a pure "bottom-up" (part-to-whole) or a pure "top-down" (whole-to-part) strategy in interpretive processing.

The solution I propose is that, under most circumstances, the interpretation of parts and wholes proceeds simultaneously in both bottom-up and top-down directions. The final interpretation is reinforced by consistency between a number of levels in the structural schema. For an example of the interactions of part-to-whole and whole-to-part strategies, consider without context the differences between how well a nose must be drawn to be recognizable when it is shown in the context of a face and when it is shown by itself. Most any

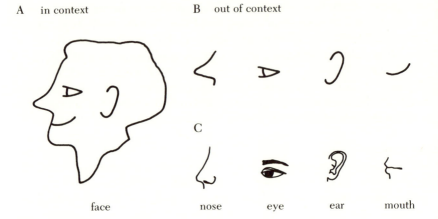

FIGURE 11.6

An illustration of part-whole context. Facial features recognizable in the context of a profile (A) are not recognizable out of context (B). When the internal part structure of the facial features is differentiated (C), however, the features become recognizable out of context.

sort of bump is adequate when it is part of a profile (see Figure 11.6A) —if it is in the appropriate position. But the same bump will not suffice when it is shown alone (see Figure 11.6B). It is obvious from Figure 11.5B that the same is true for other parts of the face. In context, all that is needed is a hint of the overall structure of the facial features and the proper spatial relationships between them. Alone, however, the internal part structure of the facial feature must be represented (see Figure 11.6C). A similar demonstration can be made for the head itself. In order to be recognized, it must be seen either as part of a person's body (that is, along with other body parts in the proper spatial relationships) or with its own part structure clearly represented. Now, if one can recognize a nose when it is part of a face, and a face when its part structure is represented, then one can recognize both nose and head without further information. This simple example illustrates the interdependence of part-whole structure in a particularly illuminating way, and emphasizes the sufficiency of just a few structural levels for interpretation.

I mentioned previously that facial features have "overall structure" as well as "part structure." For every node in a schema there is some information specifying its "global" properties: general size, location, dimensionality, orientation, and so forth. It is these global properties that allow perceptual analysis to begin at virtually any level in a schema and work its way upward and downward. A demonstration that appeals to one's intuition of what global properties might be is to defocus the image of an object until the specific parts become unrecognizable. What is left might be the global properties of the object as a whole. Naturally, the same analysis applies to parts of objects: A nose has global properties (Figure 11.6B) as well as part structure (Figure 11.6C). Regardless of exactly how global information is defined, it is essential to a workable perceptual system for reasons that will be discussed shortly.

The Process of Identification

The components of the visual system proposed thus far are:

- a lexicon of two-dimensional shapes from which higher-order structural descriptions can be generated to encode a retinal image;

- a lexicon of three-dimensional shapes from which higher-order structural descriptions can be generated to encode a three-dimensional representation of the retinal image; and

- a set of structural schemata for objects and scenes known from previous experience.

Although there could be a set of structural schemata for known objects at the two-dimensional level—corresponding to different views of the same object—this would proliferate stored representations beyond manageability. Rather, there could be procedures, called projection rules, which would map two-dimensional structures onto three-dimensional structures according to the laws of perspective.[2] For example, it must be known or derivable that an ellipse is a projection of a circle viewed from an oblique angle. Along these lines, Shepard (personal communication) has demonstrated that people are quite accurate at determining whether a particular three-line vertex could be the projection of a corner of a cube.

The question now is how the perceptual process interprets the retinal image in terms of meaningful objects and scenes. It is clear that sensory data must play a bottom-up role. The data are incorporated

---

[2]At short viewing distances, it may be that the three-dimensional structure of an object is "directly available," thus bypassing the two-dimensional level. Powerful depth information from the binocular disparity of the two retinal images and eye convergence may provide an immediate interpretation in three dimensions. In any case, perception in three-space probably operates differently at short distances than at long distances or when interpreting a two-dimensional picture. The present discussion concerns the last two situations.

into a structural description and eventually into a conceptual description of meaningful objects in a scene. Within each kind of description, possible data interpretations activate superparts within the schemata of which they are part. These two bottom-up processes—activating higher-level interpretations and activating higher-level structural units—move the perceptual process constantly toward a global interpretation of the visual stimulus at a meaningful level. Fragmented interpretations can occur, of course, if no global interpretation is available within existing schemata. A set of unrelated objects placed arbitrarily within the visual field is a case in point.

Expectations based on prior knowledge play a top-down role. They are generated within schemata on the basis of analyzed data and then influence processing at lower levels. The expectation of seeing a particular object, for example, produces expectations of seeing the parts of that object.

Tuning Functions. There are a number of particular methods by which the mapping of input information onto interpretations might be accomplished. Perhaps the most promising is a system in which scores are computed according to the "fit" (or similarity) of the sensory data to the informational unit making the computation. For instance, the face schema would be "tuned" to the typical shape of a face—say, an oval of particular length-to-width dimensions. This prototypical shape produces maximum activation of the face node. A thinner or fatter oval produces lower activation of that same node, the value being determined by the particular tuning function for the face schema (see Figure 11.7). The tuning of a concept, then, represents both its central tendency (or its ideal) and its variance.

Pursuing the tuning notion a bit further, we see that specific concepts will be very finely tuned relative to general concepts. While a fat face will activate the general face node less strongly than a typical face, the fat one will activate the nodes corresponding to particular fat-faced people more strongly than a typical face will (see Figure 11.7). Also, given that the tuning function represents the frequency distribution of the property for a particular category, it should be true that exemplars falling far from the typical value will be easier to discriminate from other exemplars than a typical exemplar is.

Processing an Object. To get a feel for the kind of bottom-up, top-down interaction proposed, consider how the retinal image of an object might be processed in the absence of higher-level expectation based on context. Suppose that a lower-level, two-dimensional description in terms of points, lines, and curves gets constructed from

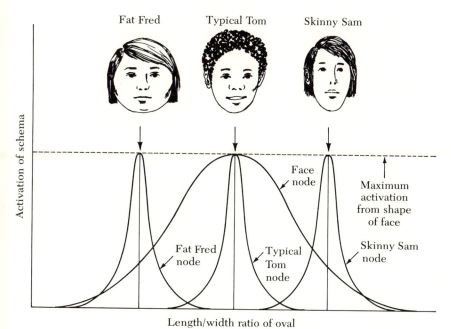

FIGURE 11.7

Hypothetical tuning functions for the general face schema and three specific face schemata regarding the length-to-width ratio of the face shape. The tuning function for the general face schema is broad, representing the frequency distribution of this property for the category. The specific tuning functions are more finely tuned to specific values.

the image. Each line activates a number of alternative interpretations at the three-dimensional level. A line might be interpreted as the edge between a surface and background, an edge between two surfaces of the same object, a border between two parts of the same surface, or simply a line. Because lines are parts of angles and vertices, the vertex schema gets activated. This schema "looks for" vertices within the description of points and lines within the scene and then computes the parameters of each vertex that has been found: number of sides, angular size, and so forth.[3] At the same time, the vertices found begin to activate their possible three-dimensional interpretations: a convex corner of a rectangular solid, a concave corner of a rectangular solid, and various other types of edge combinations.

---

[3]Alternatively, this process may be thought of as a large set of angle networks, each of which is computing its fit to angles present in the scene. This is compatible with the tuning hypothesis, but, in practice, may prove to be a more difficult process. The net effect, however, is similar.

Waltz (1972) has demonstrated that the constraints imposed by just this simple information are usually sufficient to separate a complex scene of blocks into objects. Waltz's analysis does this by discarding inconsistent interpretations of lines on the basis of the interpretations of vertices. As one would hope, the process converges until each line has a single interpretation that fits the interpretation of its vertex (see also Marc Eisenstadt and Yaakov Kareev's description of bottom-up and top-down processing of board configurations in the games of Go and Gomoku in Chapter 12).

In the present system, however, the process continues to more complex levels of interpretations. Since lines and angles are parts of polygons, the polygon schema gets activated and begins to look for closed areas within the network thus far constructed. If any polygons are found, they activate their possible three-dimensional interpretations according to the projection rules. These polygons are parts of shapes in the three-dimensional lexicon. Thus, the schemata for possible three-dimensional shapes provide expectations of what types of surfaces are likely to be found adjacent to what others. These predictions can also help fill in missing lines and vertices. Simultaneously, the three-dimensional interpretations begin to activate the object schemata of which they are part to a degree that reflects their fit to the encoded parameters of the concept. These candidate schemata also provide specific expectations about their components within the structural description being constructed at lower levels.

The whole process can be seen as a series of bottom-up "hypotheses," top-down "queries," and a set of quantitative answers to those queries. The end result should be a structural description of the two-dimensional image, a corresponding structural description at the three-dimensional level, and a set of scores for the goodness-of-fit of each conceptual interpretation advanced as a candidate. During the initial analysis, there are certainly multiple interpretations for any given structural unit. Under normal circumstances, one interpretation will stand out as the best fit at all levels within the schema.

The Role of Global Properties.   I omitted from the previous discussion an important component of the identification process: the use of global properties. It is a good bet that information can be extracted that does not require the discrimination of specific lines and angles at the level of analysis just implied. When a person views a face, for instance, it is probably the color, general ovalness, and dimensionality of the face that initiate the hypothesis of seeing a face, not the specific contours of the cheek or shape of the eye. Specific lines and angles are *not* required to discriminate a face from most other objects; a person can make the discrimination from a poorly focused image.

A closely related phenomenon is a person's ability to interpret "stick figures" and other reduced representations. As an illustration, consider Figure 11.8. In Figure 11.8A all objects are given moderately detailed three-dimensional representation. In Figure 11.8B, however, the objects and parts of objects are represented very abstractly. The

FIGURE 11.8
Global information and stick figure representations. *B* illustrates the amount of the information in *A* that can be captured by the drastically simplified representation. All objects are readily recognizable as members of classes of objects (person, chair, table), although they cannot be identified as specific examples of those classes.

back of the chair and top of the table are simply two-dimensional rectangles (in three-dimensional space), whereas the legs of the chair and table are one-dimensional lines. Still, however, the figures capture enough of the global properties of the objects they represent to be interpretable. Experience with such representations and contextual information no doubt help in interpreting these figures, but the phenomenon is more fundamental than that. A chair's back is *essentially* two-dimensional in both perceptual properties and in functional properties, but its legs are *essentially* one-dimensional in both perceptual and functional properties.

The importance of global information is that it can be used to generate higher-level hypotheses rapidly on the basis of low-resolution information. The expectations derived from the hypotheses could then be used to direct further processing at levels that require more finely resolved data. This would give the system a more efficient, top-down mode of analysis. It would also provide information from portions of the retina where resolution is poor. Global information from peripheral areas of the retina is especially important for the process of visual search.

Ambiguous Figures and Multiple Interpretations.   It was proposed earlier that one interpretation usually stands out as the best fit at all levels within the schema. In these cases there is a single schema whose components provide consistent interpretations for the bulk of the structural description—each component is the best fit for its corresponding structural part, and the highest concept in the schema is also the best fit for the entire structure. In unusual conditions, however, multiple interpretations are perceived. Multiple interpretations can result from ambiguous figures such as the "wife-hag" and the "rat-man" (see Neisser, 1967), even though the visual stimuli are the same, because there are two distinct sets of interpretations, each of which can succeed at all levels. Thus, the two interpretations are in competition for the same data. Significantly, when a person looks at the "chin-nose" of the "wife-hag" and forces one interpretation (say, the wife's chin), the rest of the wife interpretation follows rather automatically. This phenomenon would occur in the present system in the following way. Forcing the chin interpretation increases the activation of the superordinate **wife-face** interpretation. The increased activation of the **wife-face** schema produces specific expectations for seeing the other facial features of this interpretation, which then become more strongly activated. Thus, the **wife-schema** comes to dominate the **hag-schema** at all levels. The change in interpretation can be initiated at a single subpart because of the structure of the schemata and the bottom-up, top-down nature of the activation process.

Two other interesting cases of multiple interpretations are illustrated in Figure 11.9. The "fruit-face" shown in Figure 11.9A exemplifies interpretive rivalry between local and global interpretations. Part of the image is interpreted as a watermelon representing a head, another part as a pear representing a nose, and so forth. While the face interpretation succeeds at the global level, the fruit interpretations succeed at the local level. In other words, each part is best fit by the schema for a kind of fruit, while the structure as a whole is best fit by the schema for a face. This drawing provides some good evidence for the power of global properties. If the image is presented quite briefly, what is seen is a face (though a rather strange one), not the fruit of which it is composed.

A   A fruit-face   B   A hordograffe

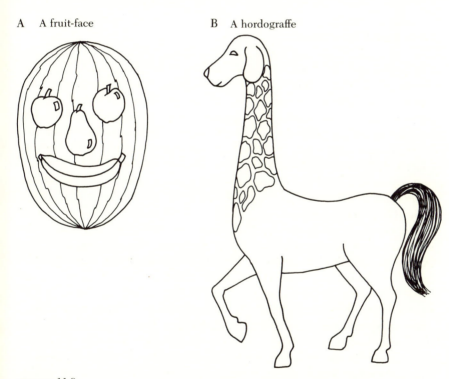

FIGURE 11.9
Illustrations of discrepant part-whole interpretations. *A* shows a "fruit-face," each part of which is best interpreted locally as a piece of fruit, while the whole configuration is best interpreted as a face. *B* shows an unfamiliar animal whose parts are identifiable as those of specific animals. Their combination, however, is inconsistent with the configuration of any single known animal.

Figure 11.9B illustrates another interesting perceptual interpretation. The strange animal depicted here is not any animal one might know about from past experience. Nevertheless, it is easily describable as having the head of a dog, the neck of a giraffe, and the body, legs, and tail of a horse. The fact that it can be identified as an animal indicates that the general category of four-legged animals has the best fit to the structure as a whole. But at the level of specific kinds of animals, no single known schema succeeds. The dog schema finds a good fit to the head area, the giraffe schema finds a good fit to the neck area, and the rest of the body parts fit well within the horse schema. This fragmented interpretation is a rather sophisticated one, but seems quite natural for people and plausible within the interpretive system outlined here.

Data and Expectations

Up to this point, the interaction between bottom-up data and top-down expectations has been formulated only very sketchily; analyzed data produce expectations that somehow facilitate further processing. In this section I discuss some proposals about how this facilitation might take place. The proposal is based on the notion of a limited-capacity system in which processing resources (or attention) can be differentially distributed. The ideas were inspired by Norman and Bobrow's (1975) analysis of data-limited and resource-limited processes.

Suppose that each node in a schema is a procedure that computes the concept represented by that node. "Computing" a node is the measurement of the goodness-of-fit between the sensory data and both the encoded properties and part structure of the concept. The nodes representing the part structure of the concept, however, compute themselves in the same manner. The face schema (Figure 11.4A), for example, computes a face by testing for the appropriate shape, color, location, size, and color (its global properties) and by integrating these results with results computed by its subschemata. The integrated results are transmitted to its superordinate schema, person. Similarly, the eye schema computes an eye by testing its global features, integrating these results with those computed by its subschemata, and transmitting its current measures to the face superordinate. Thus, three functions are performed by the procedures:

- computing the similarity of the eye's global features to those present in the uninterpreted structural description;

- integrating these results with results transmitted from subordinate procedures;

- transmitting the current goodness-of-fit to superordinate procedures.

Each schema will succeed to an extent determined by its goodness-of-fit score. For a particular sensory stimulus, then, there is some asymptotic level of success that can be achieved. This level will be reached when all pertinent data have been analyzed. Now, assume that the *rate* at which this asymptote is achieved depends on the amount of processing resource allotted to the given procedure (and, indirectly, its subprocedures). The more resources a procedure is allotted, the faster and more completely it will be able to compute its concept and make its results available to other procedures.

Consider the proposal that expectations affect the distribution of processing resources. Strongly expected schemata receive large resource allocations, whereas unexpected schemata receive small resource allocations. Within the active relational network developed to this point, an "expectation" is simply a request for data from an associated node (property or subpart). A "request for data" from another procedure produces an increment in the amount of resource allotted to that procedure. The more processing resource a procedure has, the more rapidly it can compute its fit to the available data. The facilitating effect of expectations, then, is to increase the rate at which predicted information is analyzed. Note that resource allocation is largely "data driven," since expectations are derived from the interpretation of prior data. In general, such a system exhibits "intelligence" by concentrating its effort on the computation of information known from experience to be likely, given what has already been identified within a context.

One intuitively appealing aspect of the distributed resource system is that it models an active information processor. If datum D_i is expected at location L_i, which is not within the visual field, the procedure requesting D_i will generate an eye movement to L_i only if it receives sufficient resource allocation. If D_i is not expected at L_i (or is less strongly expected), this eye movement might never be made. Clearly, the same type of analysis is applicable to situations in which no eye movement is required. Resource allocations will eventually filter down to procedures computing concepts at specific locations in the sensory image (see also Rumelhart, 1970). It is possible, then, that processing can be differentially directed to areas that are "conceptually defined," thereby concentrating on parts of the sensory image that contain information about objects "on the table" or "along the sidewalk."

It follows from this analysis that expectations can have varying amounts of specificity, in terms of both expected data and expected location. An observer could expect to find some specific data at a very specific location, within a small range of locations, or just somewhere in the scene. Similarly, at a very specific location an observer could expect a very specific set of data, a limited range of data, or just any data. The more specific the expectations, the more resource should be concentrated on a particular schema. Diffuse expectations will distribute resource over more alternatives, and, given that the alternatives require more than the limited pool of resource, will lower the efficiency of testing for the alternatives.

As an illustration, suppose a person is looking for a fire hydrant in a city street scene. Global information from the buildings and street have already activated the **street-scene** schema. From the knowledge of street scenes contained in the schema, the expectation is derived that the hydrant will be located somewhere along the street. The request for hydrant data is made from within the schema by allocating processing resources to the **hydrant** subschema, which makes further requests for relevant data in relevant locations. The resource allocations thus are passed down to particular data procedures at particular locations. These processing resources are then used either to scan actively along the street by means of eye movements or to facilitate the extraction of hydrant data from attended areas already present within the visual field. In either case, the hydrant would be found sooner if it were located (as expected) along the street than if it were located, say, on the side of a building. The hydrant on the side of the building, of course, would eventually be noticed, assuming that at least some processing capacity were allocated to analyzing this part of the scene for hydrant data. This type of analysis is consistent with Biederman's discussion of his results of scene-scanning experiments (Biederman, 1972; Biederman, Glass, and Stacy, 1973).

The effects of global properties and peripheral vision are particularly interesting and are important in the distributed resource system. Suppose that the fire hydrant is expected to appear somewhere over a range of locations at the periphery of the eye. Given the limited resolution in the expected region, it is plausible that only the global information of a fire hydrant would be available. If an object with the appropriate global properties is located within the expected region, these data will increase the activation of the **hydrant** schema. The additional activation can then request that more resource be allocated to the subschemata of hydrant parts.

In many cases, in order for a schema to achieve the necessary resolution for its tests, the eye must be moved to pick up information from the area of the potential hydrant. The eye movement is required because only the central, foveal region of the eye is capable of analyzing the visual scene with the necessary resolution. Only after the eye movement has been made can the "hydrant hypothesis" be confirmed or disproved by the local tests. This implies that eye movements will be made to locations containing objects that are similar to hydrants in terms of their global properties, but not to objects that can be discriminated from a hydrant at the global level of analysis. At least informally, this seems to be consistent with the way in which we search for objects in the real world. It is also consistent with Williams' (1966) finding that some properties can be used to direct visual search among many alternatives whereas others cannot.

SUMMARY

I have touched on a wide variety of issues related to the processing of visual information. Given our current piecemeal knowledge of perception, one can formulate either detailed models for specific problem areas or more diffuse models that address a wide range of problems. I have opted for the latter because I believe it is equally important and much more interesting. My intent has been to outline what I see as critical problems in visual perception, particularly those related to how people's knowledge of the world affects the way they perceive their environment. At the same time I have formulated a theoretical framework within which I believe this jigsaw puzzle of problems can be confronted with some hope of successful resolution. A great deal of work is required to finish the job. Certainly the problem of world knowledge is an important issue — perhaps *the* most important issue — and it will have to be solved before we can claim more than trivial knowledge of how people process visual information.

CHAPTER 12

Aspects of Human Problem Solving: The Use of Internal Representations

MARC EISENSTADT and YAAKOV KAREEV

In this chapter we explore some aspects of human problem solving by observing people playing board games. In particular, we focus on the internal representation of board positions and the representation of hypothetical states of knowledge. Evaluation and move generation, although important aspects of game playing, are examined only insofar as they relate to our model of internal representation. In the studies reported here we used two different board games, both of which are sufficiently difficult to play that the choice of a move at any particular point in the game is not a completely well-structured problem.

This chapter consists of two sections. First, we present a brief description of our experiments with and observations of the game-playing behavior of subjects playing two different board games. Second, we undertake a theoretical analysis of the structure of the problem-solving procedures used by our subjects. Here, we use the theoretical technique developed in the study of active structural networks to examine both the representation of the perceptual aspects of the board game and the representation of the strategies that people use to play these games. The strategies are described as a set of procedures in the SOL language. Thus, this chapter extends the analyses presented in this book to cover how people might apply procedural knowledge to the solution of problems.

SECTION 1   Experimental Analyses

THE GAMES

We used two board games, Go and Gomoku. The boards and pieces used in the two games are the same, but the rules are quite different. Both games are traditionally played on a board that contains a grid formed by the intersections of 19 vertical lines and 19 horizontal lines. The pieces are black and white stones, and they are placed on the intersections of the grid lines. To simplify the games we used a board with a grid that was 9 squares high and 9 squares wide (10 horizontal lines and 10 vertical lines). We used X's and O's instead of stones, and we placed the pieces in the squares instead of the intersections. The essential change in the games, of course, was the reduction from a 19 by 19 grid to a 9 by 9 grid of board positions.

In this chapter, it is essential that you be thoroughly familiar with the rules of both games as well as with some simple strategic concepts. We suggest that you read the rules and examples in Box 12.1. We also recommend that you play several games of Gomoku, and perhaps one game of Go. (Gomoku is considered an easy game, and it is often played by children. Go is considered very complex, perhaps even more complex and difficult than chess.)

BOX 12.1
The rules of Go and Gomoku.

The rules given here are the rules that were shown to the subjects. Both games are traditionally played with black and white stones on the intersections of the lines that make up the 19 by 19 board. We played with pieces placed on the squares rather than on the intersections, but the game played on the squares is isomorphic to the one played on the intersections. We also used a smaller board: 9 by 9 rather than 19 by 19. The reduced size of the board simplified the design of the computer programs that played against the subjects (especially for the game of Go), but the games on the 9 by 9 board were still challenging.

(continued)

BOX 12.1 (*continued*)

GO

Go is played with black and white stones (or X's and O's) on 81 squares, which comprise the 9 by 9 square board. At the beginning of the game the board is empty. The players alternately place one of their pieces at a time on any vacant square (except for "Ko," described in a subsequent paragraph). Once placed, pieces are never moved, unless captured, in which case they are immediately removed from the board.

Rule of Capture

A group of pieces is captured and removed from the board by the opponent when he has occupied every square that is adjacent to those pieces, either vertically or horizontally. In other words, a group is captured when it has no "breathing spaces" left (when it does not touch any empty squares in a vertical or horizontal direction or any friendly pieces that lead in a vertical or horizontal path to an empty square).

For example, if X plays at C4 (see Figure B12.1), the O at C5 is captured and removed from the board, since it has no adjoining breathing spaces. X does not have to play at B4, D4, B6, or D6 in order to capture the O at C5.

If O plays at A1, he captures the group of two X's at A2 and A3. They would have no breathing spaces, because the edge of the board forms a natural boundary.

Although the group of three O's in the upper right-hand corner of the board is "surrounded," it is not yet captured because it still has one internal breathing space at I9. *All* horizontally and vertically adjacent vacant intersections must be filled in by the opponent in order for a group to be captured. Thus, if X goes to I9, the three O's on H9, H8, and I8 would be captured. Although the X at I9 will itself be without breathing spaces the instant that it is placed there, X's turn is not truly over until any captives have been removed from the board, at which time the X at I9 would have breathing spaces.

Scoring

The score of each player is determined at the end of the game by adding the number of pieces of his opponent that he has captured to the number of vacant squares that remain under his "control" (that is, within his own walls).

Rule of Ko

A piece that has just captured an opponent's piece cannot be immediately recaptured if that recapture leads to a repetition of the original

(*continued*)

BOX 12.1 (*continued*)

board configuration. The recapturing move must be delayed at least one turn.

If O goes to G3 (see Figure B12.1), he captures the X at F3. X is not allowed to recapture the O at G3 immediately because of the rule of Ko. The rule forbids making a recapture that causes a prior board configuration to be repeated. X must instead move elsewhere, but on his following turn he may capture the O at G3 by moving to F3, if O has not meanwhile moved to F3 himself.

The End of the Game

The game ends when both players agree that there are no more profitable moves. (A player is allowed to "pass.") The player with the highest score wins.

FIGURE B12.1
Illustrative Go positions.

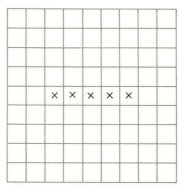

FIGURE B12.2
Winning Gomoku position for black.

GOMOKU

Gomoku is played with black and white stones (or X's and O's) on the 81 squares that comprise the 9 by 9 square board. The players alternately place one of their pieces on any empty square on the board. The first player to succeed in forming an unbroken straight line of five of his own pieces (either vertically, horizontally, or diagonally) wins the game, as illustrated in Figure B12.2.

(*continued*)

BOX 12.1 (continued)

Technical Configurations

The following terms all refer to pieces that belong to one player and are positioned along a straight line.

An Open-Four.   A line of four adjacent pieces with a vacant square next to each of the two extreme members is called an open-four (see Figure B12.3). An open-four assures a win to the player who owns it because no matter what the opponent does, the open-four can be extended to a five on the next move.

A Closed-Four.   A line of four adjacent pieces that is open on only one end (that is, has an opponent piece immediately next to one of its extreme members) is called a closed-four (see Figure B12.4). The creation of a closed-four by one player forces the other player to block it or else the player who owns the closed-four can win the game on the next move.

An Open-Three.   A line of three pieces that can become an open-four in one move is called an open-three. There are two types of open-threes. A *continuous open-three* consists of three pieces next to each other with two consecutive vacant squares next to (and in line with) at least one of the extreme members, and one vacant square (or more) next to the other extreme member. Obviously, placing a piece on one extremity of a continuous open-three transforms it into either an open- or a closed-four. A *noncontinuous open-three* consists of a line of two pieces, a vacant square, and then another piece. The two extreme pieces (the single one and the outermost of the two) have a vacant square next to them. A noncontinuous open-three becomes an open-four if a piece is placed in the middle vacant square. Figure B12.5 shows some cases of open-threes.
  Both types of open-threes have to be blocked immediately upon their creation, or else the open-three can be converted into an open-four. There are two possible ways of blocking a continuous open-three (by moving next to either of its ends), and three ways in which a noncontinuous open-three can be blocked (by moving next to either end or to the middle vacant square).

A Double-Threat.   Any configuration that has two lines demanding an immediate reaction is called a double-threat (that is, two closed-fours, a closed-four and an open-three, or two open-threes). Figure B12.6 includes some examples of double-threats. A double-threat assures a win, since only one of the two offenses can be responded to and then the other either becomes a win or assures a win in one move.

(continued)

BOX 12.1 (continued)

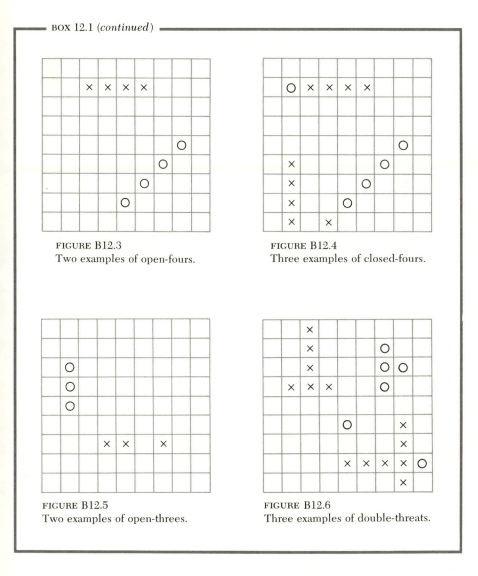

FIGURE B12.3
Two examples of open-fours.

FIGURE B12.4
Three examples of closed-fours.

FIGURE B12.5
Two examples of open-threes.

FIGURE B12.6
Three examples of double-threats.

THE APPARATUS

In the experiments that are reported in this chapter, we always had our subjects play Go and Gomoku with a computer program that played the part of the opponent. This gave us some control over the strategy and skill of the opponent, and assured us that all games were played under the same conditions. The Gomoku computer program was written by modifying a static evaluation function for the game suggested by Naddor (1969). The program played an excellent game: The program consistently wins (or draws) with beginning players, but skilled players can consistently beat it. The Go program was specially designed to play on a 9 by 9 board and it does not have general applicability. The Go program played a good game, better than that of our beginning subjects.[1]

The experiments were controlled by the laboratory's PDP-15 computer. The game-playing programs were incorporated as subroutines in the set of programs that ran the experiments. The computer generated images of the 9 by 9 board and pieces and transmitted them to a scan converter, which, in turn, relayed them as a television image to a 19-inch television monitor located in an acoustically isolated booth. A light pen located in the booth allowed the subject to make his moves by pointing at the desired square on the television monitor. The computer noted where and when the subject pointed (time was measured to the nearest millisecond) and then displayed the subject's move on the screen. Then the computer made its move. An overall view of the laboratory setup is depicted in Figure 12.1.

STUDIES OF THE INTERNAL REPRESENTATION

A "problem space" consists of all the problem solver knows relevant to the problem at hand (see Newell and Simon, 1972). For board games, this includes knowledge of the rules of the game, where the opponent has just moved, and what the current board position looks like. Although the configuration of pieces on the game board clearly exists in some objective sense, the player plays according to his subjective perception of the board.

Subjective Organization

The mapping between a configuration of pieces in the real world and the subjective perception of those pieces is not perfect. Figure 12.2A shows an arrangement of pieces that may be subjectively organized in different ways, depending on whether that board position is seen

---

[1]The Gomoku and Go computer programs were designed to serve two main functions: First, they served as standard opponents for our subjects. Second, they made very rapid moves, an important property for some of our experimental conditions. The programs are of little theoretical interest, except possibly to the extent that their static evaluation functions capture the elements of the games that are important to human players.

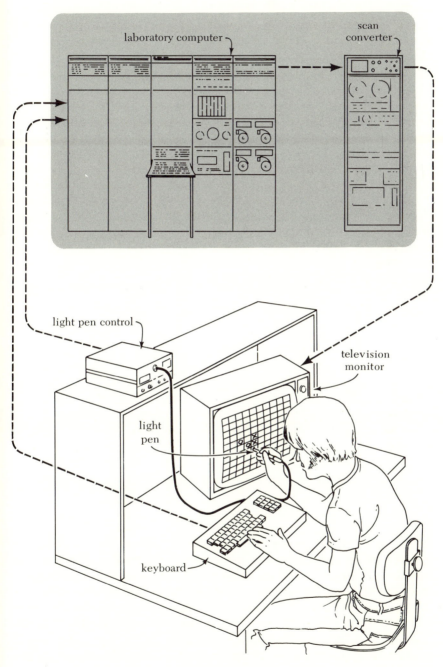

laboratory computer

scan converter

light pen control

television monitor

light pen

keyboard

FIGURE 12.1

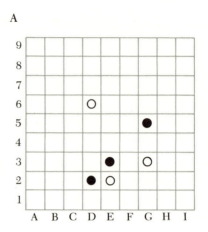

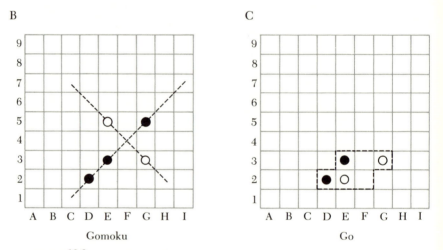

FIGURE 12.2
A board position (A) and different subjective organizations of that position for Gomoku (B) and Go (C).

as occurring in the course of a Go game or in the course of a Gomoku game. We can describe the subjective organization of the pieces in the following way. When Figure 12.2A represents a Gomoku position, the important pieces are described by the "X" (shown in Figure 12.2B) that consists of the three black pieces and the two white pieces at G3 and D6. When Figure 12.2A represents a Go position, the subjective organization is that shown in Figure 12.2C, centering around the white piece at E2, which is caught in a possible trap by its two neighboring black pieces, with the same white piece helping its cohort at G3 control the lower right-hand corner. Note that in the

Gomoku interpretation the white piece at E2 is left out of the organization, while in the Go interpretation, the pieces at D6 and G5 are
left out. Thus, when we talk about "what is seen," we are effectively
talking about "what is perceived," and perceptual organization refers
to internal representations, which can differ for different analyses of
the same scene.

To illustrate this point, we performed the following experiment.
Subjects were asked to analyze the board position shown in Figure
12.3A by trying to make the best move for black, after being told that
this position was taken from a Gomoku game. After making this
analysis, the subjects were asked to reconstruct the board position
from memory. The subjects then performed two more analyses of
the same form, except that they were not asked to reconstruct the
positions from memory. After they solved these two intervening
problems, the subjects were shown the board position depicted in
Figure 12.3B, told that it was taken from a Go game, asked to make
the best move for white, and then asked to reconstruct this board
position from memory. Since the board position shown in Figure
12.3B is a transformation of the one shown in Figure 12.3A (the
board is rotated counterclockwise 90° and reflected across the vertical axis, and the colors of the pieces are reversed), the reconstructions could be directly compared. We identified 6 pieces that were
crucial to the Gomoku analysis and 6 pieces that were crucial to the
Go analysis, and labeled these pieces "Gomoku template" and "Go
template," respectively. Accuracy of the reconstructions was scored

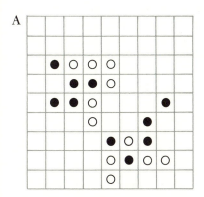

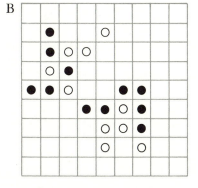

Gomoku game, Black's move   Go game, White's move

FIGURE 12.3
Board problems shown to our subjects. *B* is a transformation of *A*, arrived
at by rotating *A* counterclockwise 90°, reflecting it across the vertical axis,
and reversing the colors of the pieces.

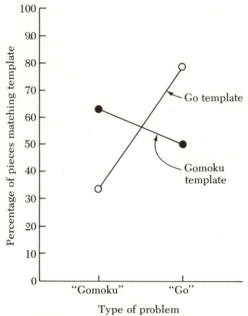

FIGURE 12.4
Percentage of crucial Go and Gomoku pieces
(labeled "Go template" and "Gomoku template,"
respectively) that were correctly remembered,
as a function of which game the subjects were
told the problem represented.

by noting how many of these crucial pieces the subject placed correctly. As Figure 12.4 shows, the nature of the board problem (that is,
whether it was presented as a Go game or a Gomoku game) determines the types of pieces remembered [$F(2,8) = 65.00, p < 0.01$]. This
result clearly demonstrates the effect of the nature of the game on
subjective organization.

Simple Perceptual Factors

It seemed plausible to us that the way in which the board is scanned
is affected by three of the Gestalt principles of perception: *proximity*,
continuity, and *similarity* (Koffka, 1935). Proximity should affect the
scanning of the board so that if one piece is being looked at, nearby
pieces are more likely to be noticed than distant pieces. Continuity
should dictate that straight lines (consisting of contiguous pieces) are
easy to detect. Similarity should operate by making groups of similar

pieces (typically pieces of the same color) easier to detect than groups consisting of different pieces.

The game of Gomoku is won as soon as one of the players gets 5 of his pieces in a row, regardless of the orientation of that row. Rows that lie along diagonals should be more difficult to notice than horizontal or vertical rows because the separation between individual pieces on a diagonal row is $\sqrt{2}$ times the distance between pieces on the other rows. This simple fact explains the following observation: 71 percent of the losses of subjects playing their first 6 games of Gomoku occur when the opponent completes a diagonal string of 5, even though the number of possible different winning diagonal strings is only 36 percent of the total number of possible winning strings.

To demonstrate that this is because the diagonal squares are farther apart than the horizontal and vertically contiguous squares and not because subjects are predisposed to examine only horizontal and vertical orientations, we tried altering the board. We rotated it 45° (to form a diamond) and replaced the square grid by dots to eliminate any possible effect on scanning caused by the presence of lines on the board (see Figure 12.5A). Subjects still lost 59 percent of their games on the former "diagonals" that were now running horizontally and vertically. Then when we distorted the normally square board

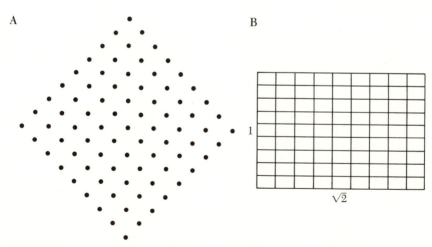

FIGURE 12.5
Altered boards used to test the effects of proximity during the game of Gomoku. A shows the rotated board with grid lines removed. Fifty-nine percent of the losses occur on the former "diagonals," which are now running horizontally and vertically. B shows the elongated board. The ratio of losses occurring on the horizontal axis to those occurring on the vertical axis is 4 to 1.

into a rectangular one with sides in the ratio of $\sqrt{2}:1$ (see Figure 12.5B), subjects lost 4 times as many games to strings of 5 on the long axis than to strings on the short axis. This occurred both when the long axis was vertical and when it was horizontal. In addition, of course, because strings on diagonals were still separated more than strings on the other axes, most of the games on the rectangular boards (69 percent) were still lost on diagonals.

Scanning Behavior

An understanding of the perceptual aspects of problem solving can be aided by data revealing what the subject is viewing at any given instant. We restricted each subject's view of the board by using a movable one-by-one window. This effect was achieved by displaying only the board, not the pieces, on the television monitor. The subjects pointed with the light pen to the single square they wished to examine. When they pointed to a square, its contents were displayed, and the contents of the previously examined square were erased.

This procedure (which we call Window Mode) allowed us to collect scanning data that were in many ways analogous to eye movements. Three of the virtues of Window Mode (as opposed to eye-movement studies) were:

- We could collect simultaneous verbal protocols.

- The subjects were involved in their own actual games.

- We had a good idea of what the subjects were attending to, since they had no peripheral vision.

The scanning behavior of a subject can be divided into episodes if we assume that a long pause between two window movements defines a boundary between episodes. Our definition of a "long pause" is two seconds, based upon the two-second boundary used by Chase and Simon (1973) to isolate chunks during the reconstruction of board positions.

Here we present an example of a subject's performance in Window Mode. For illustrative purposes, we selected a sequence that contained more than 10 but less than 50 window movements before the subject had decided upon his move. The example chosen here was taken from a game of Gomoku played by subject RE. The game was at the fifteenth move, and the computer had just moved. The board position at that move is shown in Figure 12.6A. (The computer's pieces are shown by O.)

Start with Figure 12.6A. Here, O (the computer) has just moved to square F4, giving him an open-three (see the discussion of these technical configurations in Box 12.1). X is obligated to block this by going to either C4 or G4. Figure 12.6B shows X's sequence of window movements, which comprise his first episode superimposed over the board position. This first episode starts with the subject examining D4. The subject confirms the fact that O's move has not only given him an open-three but a diagonal open-two as well (running from D2 through G5). The confirmatory nature of this episode is supported by the fact that the subject looked precisely at the crucial squares necessary to identify the two relevant strings of O's on the board.

Episode 2, shown in Figure 12.6C, appears to be more exploratory in nature than is Episode 1. Since the subject is obligated to move to either C4 or G4, he must determine which move is more profitable by finding out what other strings of pieces are present in the vicinity of

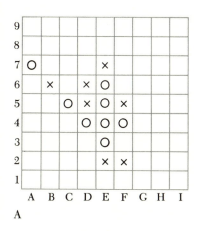

A

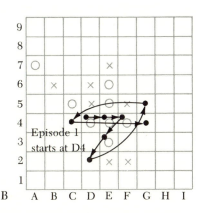

B

FIGURE 12.6

Board position from move 15 of Gomoku game played by subject RF in Window Mode. The computer (O) just moved to D4, and it is now the subject's (X's) move. Note that only the square being pointed to is visible to the subject at any moment. A: board position. B: window movements 1–8 of Episode 1 (*continued*).

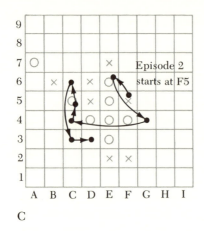

C

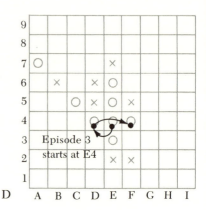

D

FIGURE 12.6 (continued)
C: window movements 9–16 of Episode 2. D: window movements 17–19 of Episode 3.

the 2 squares in question. If, for example, O had a vertical string of O's on C5, C6, and C7, then if X went to G4, O would win by going to C4, simultaneously creating a vertical and a horizontal string of 4.[2] We can assume some prior knowledge on the part of the subject (for example, we assume that he knows that column G is empty), but he must still explore the diagonal string extending from G4 through E6 to see either if a threat of an O group exists or if he can link up with another X to form a threat of his own (by going to G4). Discovering that neither X nor O can form a viable string on that diagonal, the subject then moves over to explore the relevant square around C4. He finds a potential string of O's in column C, and an empty diagonal through C4 and D3.

In Episode 3, depicted in Figure 12.6D, the subject points once again to the horizontal group of O's at D4, E4, and F4. Since this group of O's is the most important group on the board, and since the subject just looked at them 13 seconds earlier, it is fair to assume that the subject definitely knows they are there, but is looking at them in order to maintain his mental image of them (that is, to "rehearse" them). The subject did not point to the blank squares on either side of the three O's (that is, at C4 and G4), which we interpret as meaning that he did not have to confirm the presence of an open-three.

After three more episodes (yielding a total of 40 seconds in Window Mode), the subject moved to C4, which was his best possible move at

---

[2]X would lose by going to G4 anyway. The sequence is: X:G4, O:C4, X:B4, O:C3 (creating two open-threes, which guarantees a win for O), X:F6, O:B2.

that point. On the basis of this type of analysis, four types of episodes can be seen in the behavior of each of the subjects:

Confirmatory.   The subject looks at a particular location or group of locations in order to verify a hypothesis about what is actually there. "I think this gives O an open-three," is an example of a protocol that accompanies a confirmatory scan.

Exploratory.   The subject looks at a particular location or group of locations to find out what is actually there, but he has no specific hypothesis regarding the contents of the location(s) in question. For example, exploratory scans may be accompanied by statements like, "Let's see, what do we have here?" Also indicative of exploratory scans are "interrupts," occasions when the subject suddenly becomes aware of a configuration that he was not actively looking for. For example, subject RE says at one point during a Go game, "Oops, I just realized that O is about to capture this X. Why didn't I notice that before?" Note that interrupts may also occur during *confirmatory* scans if the scanner's hypothesis about the contents of a particular square is incorrect.

Revival.   The subject looks at a location whose contents he is "certain" of. Since it is possible for the subject to be incorrect, revival episodes can actually serve the same function as *confirmatory* episodes. The main distinction is the degree of confidence that the subject has in his hypothesis, and the fact that revival episodes involve squares that the subject has just looked at recently. A sample protocol from a revival episode is the following: "I must block this string of O's." Another aspect of revival episodes is repeated window movements to the same squares.

Imaginary.   The subject looks at a square where he is imagining a future move. For example, subject RE says at one point, "If I move here," while pointing with the light pen to the square in question.

A complete model of the subject's scanning behavior would have to include his precise knowledge of the contents of the board at any given instant, since it is otherwise extremely difficult to distinguish between *exploratory* and *confirmatory* scans. A model that took account of the subject's knowledge of the board position would also be able to explain why the subject did not look at certain squares during his scan of the board.

Although we do not attempt to construct a complete model of the subject's scanning behavior, we have found the type of analysis presented here to be useful in identifying the major characteristics of scanning behavior. The four varieties of episodes serve as constraints on our model of internal representation. In particular, our model must be capable of constructing internal representations as a result of both *confirmatory* and *exploratory* scans. The internal representation must be subject to decay, which can be forestalled by *revival* scanning episodes.

SEARCH THROUGH THE PROBLEM SPACE

Game playing offers a unique opportunity for studying search behavior. It differs from most other problems in that an opponent exists whose actions are not under the control of the player, and whose goals are opposed to those of the player. That fact, together with the fact that moves are irreversible, calls for careful planning before making a move. In many problem-solving situations, a "bad" move only results in wasted time; in game playing the choice of a bad move may be disastrous.

The assessment of possible moves is normally thought of in terms of "static" and "dynamic" evaluation. *Static evaluation* refers to the assessment of a particular position by examining the properties of the pieces involved in that position. In static evaluation, we assume that the player does not "lookahead," that is, he does not consider the effects of possible moves and countermoves in assessing the position. *Dynamic evaluation* refers to the assessment of a particular position by evaluating the positions that might result from looking ahead at additional moves. (These positions themselves, of course, may be evaluated either statically or dynamically.)

There are at least two other types of evaluation. The first we refer to as "extrapolative." *Extrapolative* situations involve the repetition of circumstances on the board, such as the "chase" of Go stones depicted in Figure 12.7. One or two moves must be visualized for the repetition to be noticed, so these visualizations are not really "static." However, once the repetitiveness is realized, the entire sequence may be extrapolated rather than visualized move by move, so the evaluation is not "dynamic" either.

The second case of evaluation we call semidynamic. In *semidynamic evaluation* it is possible to assess the outcome by imagining the moves of only *one* of the players. Neither extrapolation nor static evaluation will work, yet the situation does not require the player to look ahead at all possible moves and countermoves. This occurs, for example, when one player can apply a sequence of forcing moves, regardless of what his opponent does. Figure 12.8 shows such a situation, taken from a Gomoku game.

Skilled game players possess a repertoire of familiar patterns that are associated with move responses. This repertoire allows many

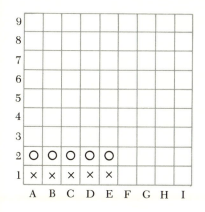

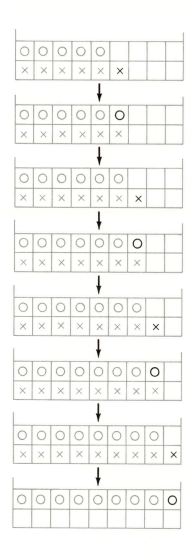

FIGURE 12.7
Example of extrapolative evaluation from the game of Go. It is X's move, and he is doomed because O can run him into the right-hand edge and capture all of his pieces. It is *not* necessary for X to visualize the entire sequence dynamically as it is depicted here.

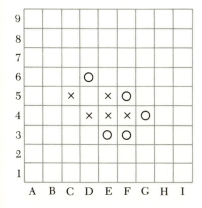

FIGURE 12.8
Example of semidynamic evaluation, taken from the game of Gomoku. X needs only to imagine his sequence of forcing moves; he does not have to imagine O's exact responses. The forcing sequence proceeds as follows:

X: C4;   O: somewhere to block.

X: C3;   O: somewhere to block one of the open-threes.

X: F6 or C6;   O: somewhere to block.

X: somewhere to make five in a row.

situations to be evaluated statically by an expert, even though the same situations might require a semidynamic evaluation by an average player and perhaps a dynamic evaluation by a beginner. (Evaluation strategies and their implication for the representation of search behavior are more fully discussed in Eisenstadt, 1974.)

Most planning is performed mentally, and is therefore not accessible to the experimental observer. To make the effects of the planning process more visible, we developed two experimental methods. One, called Preview Mode, provided the players with a computer facility to plan moves ahead on the board. This procedure was intended to simplify the mental activities necessary in planning (most especially, to lighten the memory requirements), thereby making it an attractive option to the players. The other method, a procedure we call Blitz Mode, was intended to enforce rapid playing. In rapid playing, we assume that much of the planning involves static evaluation. We were interested in seeing the differences between Blitz play and normal play.

Planning Ahead

Preview Mode provided the capability of looking ahead for any number of moves without increasing the load on memory. Following each of the computer's moves, subjects were allowed to plan ahead on the game board by pointing with the light pen to display "hypothetical" pieces for either player. (The hypothetical pieces were indicated by dotted lines.)

The use of Preview Mode was optional; some subjects used it frequently, others hardly used it at all. Players were most likely to plunge into extensive lookaheads in cases in which a move of high value (as determined by our Gomoku-playing program) was made by the opponent, but for which there was no obvious immediate response. Players were least likely to use extensive lookahead when the opponent's move created a situation demanding an immediate reply, presumably cases where straightforward static evaluation elicited a previously stored response to a similar situation.

When subjects did explore sequences in Preview Mode, they had a strong tendency to use a progressive deepening type of search—a search scheme characterized by successive extensions of a given hypothetical move sequence, but having almost no capability to retrace one's moves by mentally "backing up" the search process: Once one path has been explored, the next search starts back at the beginning, from the position originally existing on the board. This "backup" type of search has been found before in game-playing situations — see De Groot (1965) and Newell and Simon (1972). It was used here despite the fact that one of the features of Preview Mode enabled the subjects to mark possible branching points and to return to these points without having to go all the way back to the position existing on the board at the beginning of the search.

While looking ahead a player has to generate hypothetical moves for his opponent as well as for himself. To maximize the usefulness of the lookahead, the player should assume that the opponent would make the best move available to him. The identification of the best move at a given point, of course, depends upon what situation will ultimately result from each move, given that future moves are also selected in the same way. The only way to determine this formally is to continue this lookahead analysis all the way through to the end point of the game, and then proceed backward to find the path of moves that leads to the best final outcome (for oneself), given that the opponent will try to make his own best possible move at each opportunity. This is known as a "minimax" analysis (cf. Samuel, 1963). Although a lookahead analysis terminating at the end of the game is impractical for obvious reasons, it is possible to perform a minimax analysis that terminates at some particular configuration of pieces, which may then be assessed in some way in terms of its value for each player. Although people probably attempt to perform this type of lookahead, they fail on occasion to notice good moves that are available to the opponent. Almost any player can recall instances in which he has "totally overlooked" some good move for the opponent, or in which a seemingly defensive move by the opponent turned out to be offensive as well.

We hypothesize that a player's belief about whether he is on the offensive or the defensive at a given point plays a crucial role in determining when and which possible moves by the opponent will be overlooked. Such beliefs are typically very difficult to assess, but in the game of Gomoku that possibility does exist. When we compare the nature of the moves (that is, offensive versus defensive) hypothesized by the subject for his opponent (the computer) with the nature of the moves the computer would actually have made in that situation, we found that subjects were fairly accurate: About 65 percent of the predictions were correct. Many of the incorrect predictions reflected the effect of the subject's belief about his current offensive or defensive status. About 67 percent of their errors could be attributed to the following type of event: The subject hypothesizes that the computer will react to his offense with a defensive move, and thus he completely overlooks a better offensive move available to the computer (which it invariably makes).

Subjects spent less time generating hypothetical moves for their opponent than they did for themselves. This result shows up consistently, even when lookahead moves are equated on the basis of their nature (offensive or defensive) and their value.

Together these results indicate that players do not analyze their opponent's moves as thoroughly as they do their own. This asymmetry in analysis may account for the types of errors evident in human play.

The Time to Select a Move

When we analyzed the lengths of time required by 3 of our subjects to make their moves in normal Go and Gomoku games, we found that the median time to make a Gomoku move was 9 seconds, whereas the median time required for a Go move was 6 seconds: 93 percent of all the Gomoku moves and 85 percent of all the Go moves were made within one minute. It is hard to attribute this speed to mastery of the games on the part of the subjects, since the subjects lost 42 percent of the Gomoku games and 33 percent of the Go games from which these move-time statistics were taken. The games can realistically be considered somewhat of a challenge to all of the subjects, yet they make most of their moves very quickly. These quick moves exemplify what we refer to as "Blitz planning": planning that does not involve deep lookahead.

Blitz planning may be an underlying element of normal play, but how important is it? How well can subjects do if forced to rely on Blitz planning? By forcing subjects to make only rapid moves, we can characterize the quality of their play and the types of moves they make, and thus gain further insight into Blitz planning behavior.

Three subjects were told that they had 4 seconds in which to make their moves. If they did not move in the allotted time, the computer would make a random move for them.

Subjects lost 42 percent of their Blitz Gomoku games which is identical to their normal performance when they are given unlimited time. We suspect that this lack of deterioration in play is a result of the rather simple nature of defensive play, which can be used to obtain a draw against the computer. If subjects adopt an entirely defensive strategy in Blitz Mode, then they are less likely to lose than if they try to plan offensively and make a blunder in the course of their play.

The 3 subjects lost 67 percent of their Blitz Go games. This performance is easier to account for than the Gomoku result: There is no simple defensive strategy that allows the subject to make simple move responses throughout a game of Go. There are local conflicts that can be handled with elementary defensive responses, but a more global strategy is generally considered necessary to play a decent game of Go (see, for example, Ryder, 1971).

In order to assess the quality of these moves, we sought to use the subjects as their own standards of performance for Blitz play versus normal play. Subject HC observed the replay of a Gomoku game that we claimed had been played by another subject against the computer (though in reality the game was one that HC had played in Blitz Mode several days earlier). Before each of X's moves, the subject was asked to "kibitz" (that is, suggest moves for X), taking as much time as he wished.

Subject HC spent a total of 90 minutes performing deep analyses of the very same moves that had taken him a total of only 65 seconds to make when originally playing the same game in Blitz Mode. Although some increase in time spent on the game must be due to additional processing required to output a verbal protocol, an increase by a factor of 83 clearly indicates the existence of some deeper planning behavior during the kibitz analysis. Even with all of that deep analysis, both the Blitz player and the kibitz analyzer (that is, subject HC on two different occasions) made identical moves 69 percent of the time. Ninety-five percent of the time, the moves made by HC in Blitz Mode were among his top 6 move choices in kibitzing. These results indicate that even in Blitz Mode, the player is capable of making many of the same moves that otherwise would require a deeper analysis.

SECTION 2   Theoretical Analyses

This section presents a theoretical account of some aspects of the problem-solving activities described in the preceding section. The discussion of the theoretical aspects of internal representation deals with two questions: the way in which external information becomes available to the problem solver, and the way it is internally represented. We start with an analysis of the constraints imposed by the existing data on the form of a viable model of the scanning of the outside world; then we show how our model meets these constraints. The problems of scanning and of internal representation turn out to be intimately related. We then discuss planning behavior as manifested in search through a problem space. We describe how progressive deepening, a major characteristic of human search behavior, can be represented as a natural result of the properties of human short-term (working) memory.

THEORETICAL ASPECTS OF INTERNAL REPRESENTATION

The results of our experimental studies provide a set of guidelines for the construction of a model of internal representation:

- The board reconstruction study demonstrated that subjective organization is affected by the nature of the problem. This organization centers around configurations of pieces that are meaningful in the context of the game being played. Thus, internal representations must be able to represent the external world in terms of meaningful or highly familiar segments.

- The studies of perceptual factors demonstrated the importance of proximity and continuity for noticing crucial Gomoku patterns. Thus, internal representations must be composed of elements grouped on the basis of these Gestalt principles of perception.

- The Window Mode studies of scanning behavior indicated the existence of *confirmatory* episodes. This means that the construction of internal representations can occur through an *active* search for elements of a pattern thought to exist in some location.

- The Window Mode studies also indicated the existence of *exploratory* episodes. This means that the construction of internal representations can also occur through a passive "discovery" of elements of a pattern.

Using these guidelines, we outline a model of internal representation. We describe our model in the terms of the memory representation of this book, using **SOL** definitions of many components. The use of **SOL** definitions provides a level of specificity otherwise lacking in theoretical discussions.

TOP-DOWN ANALYSIS: SEARCHING FOR A PATTERN

We illustrate the basic principles of the model by examining the internal representation of board configurations, with special emphasis upon the procedures that recognize significant configurations of pieces. To begin, we follow the guideline that says that internal representations can be constructed as the result of an *active* scan of the board. This is a "top-down" analysis, for the aim is to devise procedures that examine the representation of the board to determine if a particular configuration is present. In a later discussion we show how simultaneous "bottom-up" procedures might operate, automatically informing the problem-solving routine whenever relevant data configurations show up.[3]

A pattern is defined as a member of the class of *operators* (see Chapter 7). The definition of a pattern consists of procedures that determine whether all of the necessary subparts of the pattern exist. Whenever a pattern is found, it is represented by a particular instantiation of its procedural definition. This instantiation is a token of the procedure, and its parameters are bound to particular values. We call the token instantiation of a procedure an activation of that procedure. Activations are stored in the data base with one of three truth values, each of which corresponds to one of three types of patterns:

- Patterns known to exist (truth = true)
- Patterns known not to exist (truth = false)
- Patterns that we are in the midst of looking for (truth = unknown)

Suppose we wish to know whether a particular pair of pieces (say, at coordinate locations C4 and D4) exists. We can say

(1)   If you find a pair at C4 and D4, print "Eureka!"

The procedure find is in charge of finding old activations of patterns. If an old one cannot be found, find creates a new activation and executes it. Thus, if a particular pattern is already known to exist, an activation (which is the internal representation of that pattern) will be present with the truth value true, so that future attempts to find that particular pattern need not bother to re-execute a procedure that has already succeeded. Similarly, there is no need to re-execute a procedure that has already failed.[4]

---

[3]The terms "top-down" and "bottom-up" are used extensively throughout this chapter. The terms come from computer science, and refer to the manner in which an internal representation of some structure (typically, a grammatical string of words) is arrived at. Top-down analyses start with hypotheses and then attempt to verify them by looking at the stimulus (for example, "Is there a noun phrase here?"). Bottom-up analyses start by analyzing the stimulus, trying to determine which structural description applies to a given input (for example, "What part of speech is this word?"). As used here, the term "top-down analysis" refers to goal-directed activity, whereas "bottom-up analysis" refers to stimulus-driven activity. These terms are more than simple metaphors, because they concisely characterize the actual computer programs used to analyze stimulus inputs.

[4]These constraints apply only during the scan of a given configuration of pieces. After some change occurs on the board (that is, after a move has been made), we may want to re-execute a procedure because its truth value may have changed.

Our top-down definition of pair is as follows:

(2)   Define as operator pair.
       The definition frame for pair is:
       Pair at L1 and L2.
       The definition is:
       If you find a piece at L1 and you find a piece at L2,
          then note success, return true,
             otherwise note failure, return false.
          ##

Note is a procedure that changes the truth value of the stored activation (of piece in this case). Future attempts to find this particular
instance of the pattern need not actually execute the pair procedure,
but can simply inspect the truth value of the prior activation.
    Piece is an operator that is defined in a way analogous to the defi-
nition of pair:

(3)   Define as operator piece.
       The definition frame for piece is:
       Piece at L1.
       The definition is:
       If L1 contains any FEATURE-1,
          then note success, return true,
             otherwise note failure, return false.
          ##

Contains looks for L1 on a node called world (which we use to
simulate the external world[5]) and sees if L1 is connected to an instance of FEATURE-1 (which is our symbolic representation of the
primitive features constituting a piece).
    Suppose now that the board has pieces at C4 and D4 (see Figure
12.9A). If we say

(4)   If you find a pair at C4 and D4, print "Eureka!"

and no activations are present in the data base, the procedures are
executed in the following way: Pair first looks for a piece at C4, which
in turn looks for some FEATURE-1 in the world at location C4 and
succeeds, causing piece at C4 to succeed. Then pair looks for a piece
at D4, which succeeds in a way similar to piece at C4, causing pair to
succeed. The word "Eureka!" is then printed out.
    Figure 12.9B depicts the structure of the data base after execution of
statement 4. Due to the construction of activations performed by find
and the assignment of truth values performed by note, the nodes

---

[5]The world node is conceptually distinct from our model, but is necessary because we
do not have a hardware "eye" to input features from the real world.

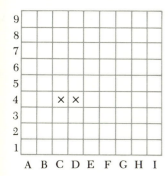

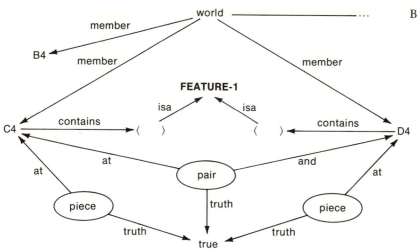

FIGURE 12.9
A board configuration (A) and its internal representation (B) after interpretation of the sentence If you find a pair at C4 and D4, print "Eureka!". The activation of pair and the two activations of piece, shown in ovals, are added to the data base by the procedure find.

depicted as ovals in Figure 12.9B have been added to the data base. The model would thus know of the existence of a **piece** at C4, a **piece** at D4, and a **pair** at C4 and D4. If some other procedure were looking for the existence of these items (say, as part of a larger pattern that included them), **find** would discover that they already existed, and would save the model the trouble of re-executing these procedures.

The definitions discussed so far have all been of a top-down nature; that is, familiar patterns have been defined only in terms of their subparts. If the existence of a pattern is hypothesized, then the discovery of the appropriate subparts will confirm the hypothesis. The procedural definitions specify where to look for the subparts, and thus constitute a framework for hypothesis testing, or a form of analysis-by-synthesis, which is characteristic of top-down mechanisms.

Top-down mechanisms satisfy one guideline for internal representations suggested by our Window Mode studies: They account for the *active* search for patterns that are suspected to exist. If we have a repertoire of patterns that are associated with a specific game (for example, Go or Gomoku), and if some higher process (such as **play Go** or play Gomoku) is responsible for the activation of the procedures associated with these patterns, then the top-down mechanisms can also satisfy a second guideline for internal representations: The model's representation of the external world will be sensitive to the particular task at hand (that is, which game is being played), just as were the subjects in our reconstruction experiment.

BOTTOM-UP ANALYSIS: SUGGESTIONS FROM THE STIMULUS

Top-down analysis is only part of the story. A good deal of pattern recognition is associated with "bottom-up" or "stimulus-driven" processing, processing that is not based on expectations. Bottom-up processing can be intuitively characterized in terms of messages of the form "Here I am!", which originate from low-level processes. Top-down processing is more appropriately characterized in terms of messages of the form "Are you there?", which originate from high-level processes.

The message "Here I am!" can be sent from an activation of a particular pattern to activations of larger patterns that might possibly contain it. Thus, if pair is known to be part of a three-element pattern called trio, we could extend the definition of pair this way:

(5)   Define as operator pair.
        The definition frame for pair is:
        pair at L1 and L2 orientation O1.
        The definition is:
        If you find a piece at L1 and you find a piece at L2,
           then note success,
           suggest trio at L1 and L2 and beyond L2 orientation O1,
           suggest trio at before L1 and L1 and L2 orientation O1,
           return true,
        otherwise note failure, return false.
        ##

The definition frame has been expanded to include the orientation, or axis, of the pattern. What this definition means is that whenever a pair is observed, the pair procedure automatically suggests that one of two possible trios may also exist along the same axis. If, for example, the orientation of the pair is "horizontal," then the third piece that comprises the trio may be either to the left or to the right of the pair. Suggest creates new activations if it cannot find old ones. Bottom-up processing of this kind enables us to meet another of our criteria for internal representations: Patterns may be recognized in a *passive* manner.

In our model, all familiar patterns are defined as a mixture of top-down and bottom-up procedures, thus producing a recognition scheme that we call convergence. Convergence is conceptually similar to the scheme proposed by Stephen Palmer (Chapter 11) for scene analysis, and it also incorporates many of the features discussed by Kaplan (1973) for the parsing of language.

With a convergence mechanism, we can simulate both a top-down, goal-driven approach to the scanning of a board position ("Does my opponent have five in a row? If not, does he have four in a row?", and so on) and a bottom-up, stimulus-driven approach ("Let's see, what does he have here?"). The bottom-up aspects of the convergence model **suggest** certain low-level patterns, which in turn will **suggest** higher-level patterns, and so on, until an internal representation of the world is obtained. Most importantly, convergence allows top-down and bottom-up processing to coexist, as we know to be the situation with our Window Mode subjects (who, for example, get interrupted by noticing one pattern while in the process of actively looking for another). As the model has been described so far, this coexistence occurs sequentially, with bottom-up suggestions being made after existence has been verified in a top-down fashion. Later on in this chapter we will show how both aspects of convergence can be smoothly integrated by an executive controlling the processing of activations within a working memory.

Gestalt Principles.   One of our guidelines for internal representations was that they must be sensitive to Gestalt principles of perception in the same way as our subjects were. In other words, pieces that are close together are easily noticed, as are pieces in a continuous line. The arguments L1 and L2 in the definition of **pair** represent two locations that are next to one another. Although this "next to" constraint does not appear in the definition of **pair**, in actual practice the procedure is suggested only when L1 and L2 are next to one another. This is done by expanding the definition of **piece** as follows:

(6)   Define as operator piece.
        Give the definition frame for piece:
        Piece at L1.
        The definition is:
        If L1 contains any **FEATURE-1**,
            note success,
            for each neighbor of L1
            suggest pair at L1 and that neighbor
            oriented in the direction from L1 to that neighbor,
            return true,
        otherwise note failure, return false.
        ##

Neighbor of X finds all squares adjacent to X. This guarantees that activations of pair will have arguments L1 and L2 in the proper relation to one another. This relation, in fact, is one of proximity. The neighbor procedure looks out from its target square in an expanding circle so that, for the coordinate notation we use to represent the external world, horizontal and vertical neighbors are found before diagonal neighbors. The suggest procedure in (6) is re-executed for each neighbor of L1, and thus diagonal pairs of pieces are the last to be suggested. Pairs that are suggested earlier may in fact lead to suggestions of trios, and thus horizontal and vertical groups will tend to get noticed before diagonal ones. If any of these horizontal or vertical groups lead to acceptable move suggestions in a Gomoku game, then diagonal threats may be completely overlooked, which is exactly what we find with our Gomoku-playing subjects.

The definition of pair takes advantage of the principle of "continuity," since a straight-line pattern suggests a continuation of that line (that is, trio). Another Gestalt primitive, "similarity," can be handled by specifying, say, "color" as a parameter, requiring that certain classes of patterns all have constituents of the same color. In principle, there is no restriction as to which attributes of a pattern may be specified as parameters, but in a simulation model, clearly one would use only those attributes found to determine perceptual units.[6]

Extensions

The convergence mechanism previously described constructs internal representations that meet four of the criteria dictated by our experimental observations:

- They can be sensitive to which game is being played.

- They can reflect Gestalt principles of perception.

- They can drive an active scan of the external world.

- They can result from passive "discovery."

---

[6]Rather than specifying the location of each constituent of a pattern as a separate parameter (for example, "at L1 at L2 at L3"), one may designate entire patterns themselves as constituents of larger patterns. This is particularly useful when defining large patterns such as "double-open-three", whose constituents cannot be specified in a precise, templatelike fashion. In addition, this mechanism provides the model with a natural "chunking" ability—the ability to incorporate subparts of a pattern into the larger pattern as a whole.

Despite these virtues, the convergence mechanism fails in these respects:

- Subjects do not have perfect memory for board positions; when subjects are not allowed to see the board, they exhibit degrees of uncertainty about the existence of a given item or configuration of items. The "revival" exposides exhibited by our subjects in Window Mode indicate that internal representations are subject to decay and rehearsal.

- Subjects cannot take in all of the features of the external world at once, but must instead make eye movements or window movements in order to gather such features.

Our model must exhibit the same characteristics as our subjects with respect to both of these observations. Some of these characteristics can be handled by extensions to the model — specifically, by considering the roles of eye movements and working memory.

Eye Movements.   The representation of the external world is built up by having the model "look" at the world. This is accomplished by the statement:

(7)   Notice each feature which is present in the world.

Notice causes the execution of all the primitive features that are attached to locations connected to the "world" node. The features (for example, **FEATURE-1**) are defined as procedures that suggest simple patterns (for example, piece) so that activations of familiar patterns get added to the data base.

However, people do not perceive the entire world at once. The only features of the world that are noticed are those that are within the scope of the model's imaginary fovea. To simulate this process, we let fovea be a node in the data base that contains the coordinates of the location of the fovea. Let subtend be a predicate that determines the locations in the world that are within the scope of the fovea. The examination of the external world can now be accomplished in a more realistic fashion by the statement:

(8)   Notice each feature which the fovea subtends.

Stimulus-driven activations thus proceed only from those features in the world that are actually "visible." Eye movements themselves can be driven by procedures that actually attempt to find features at specific locations. Suppose that some procedure that is checking for the presence of a particular pattern needs to check position L1 for the presence of a piece. The procedure first checks to see whether L1 is within the scope of the fovea. If not, it requests the action

(9)   Move the fovea to L1.

which brings about the necessary eye movement.

If we allow some features that are not within the scope of the fovea to be noticed peripherally, then the model can be made still more realistic. The model need only notice enough features peripherally to satisfy top-down expectations. If these peripheral features do not provide enough information, then the necessary eye movements can be explicitly requested.

Working Memory.   In addition to accounting for eye movements, a good model must also account for the failure of subjects to remember perfectly what they were looking at. To incorporate the process of decay of internal representations, the model stores activations in a working memory instead of in the permanent data base. Such activations are no longer executed directly by the find or suggest procedures that create them, but rather sit idly in working memory until an executive routine explicitly requests their execution. The structure of activations is altered to include a strength value in addition to a truth value. Find and suggest must now check for a strength greater than some threshold value. Truth values thus represent the existence of essential subparts of a pattern. (*All* subparts are essential for the simple types of patterns we define for board games.) Strength values represent the saliency of the internal representation of a pattern within working memory. Working memory is treated as a resource allocator that distributes a finite amount of processing capability among its elements. When this finite capacity is exceeded, the strength of each activation is decremented as that activation is processed. The strength of an activation is incremented each time it is accessed via the suggest or find procedures, and thus patterns that are frequently sought and/or recommended will remain in working memory longer than those that are ignored.

If the strength of an activation decays, then it may be incremented by once again searching for the crucial elements of the pattern. This renewed search corresponds to the "revival" episodes exhibited by our subjects in Window Mode.

The Control Structure.   At this point we are ready to define the control structure that activates the general game-playing routines.

Procedures may only be executed if they represent either primitive features in the external world or activations in **working memory**, corresponding to peripheral processes and central processes, respectively. The controlling executive routine for game playing looks like this:

(10)   Define as action play.
        The definition frame for play is: play.
        The definition is:
        While the game is in progress, notice each feature which
            the fovea subtends, process each node from working
            memory.
        ##

The **process** routine looks at activations within working memory and executes them only if they have a truth value of **unknown** or if they are close to threshold strength.

Procedures are all defined in terms of the activations that they place into **working memory** by means of the actions of **find** or **suggest**. For example, statement 9

(9)   Move the fovea to L1.

would create an activation of **move** in **working memory**. When its time came to be processed, the **fovea** node would be updated. This would alter the model's view of the world as soon as the next cycle through **play** (10) reached the statement:

(11)   notice each feature which the fovea subtends,

This control mechanism is conceptually similar to that used for production systems (Newell and Simon, 1972; Newell, 1973) that execute procedures as the result of a match between patterns in short-term store and long-term knowledge of the "meaning" of such patterns.

THEORETICAL ASPECTS OF SEARCH THROUGH THE PROBLEM SPACE

Progressive Deepening

Our experiments, along with the experiments reported by DeGroot (1965) and Newell and Simon (1972), all suggest that humans search through their problem space by means of a strategy best described as a "progressive deepening." This means that the game player or problem solver explores in some depth a sequence of hypothetical actions, but with little or no branching and only a limited backup capability.

It is possible, of course, to define algorithms that produce progressive deepening forms of search. One such algorithm is described by Newell and Simon (1972, p. 721). Our goal is to outline a realistic set of processes that captures our understanding of the human problem-solving and general information-processing mechanisms, which by themselves might automatically yield a progressive deepening search strategy.

Consider the procedures that a person has available to him. He can use either bottom-up or top-down invocation of problem-solving procedures, but however he performs his planning, he works within the limits imposed by his working memory. We suspect that he uses working memory deliberately, both to guide his search and also automatically to help constrain it.

Suppose the player's opponent has just made a move. When this happens, we presume that the movement of the opponent's piece attracts the player's attention to the appropriate location on the board, bringing that location within the domain of the fovea. This automatically activates the appropriate processes within working memory and the processing routines, in manners already discussed. (When the player is not observing the actual placement of the piece on the board, he can re-create the changes by systematically scanning the board, looking for discrepancies between his internal representation and that of the real world.) Thus, placing a new piece on a board automatically starts a bottom-up chain of processing.

A very similar pattern of events can occur when a player plans hypothetical moves. When he imagines the placing of a piece, the imagining process could lead to the same series of bottom-up processing as would be invoked by a real move. There are differences, of course. One major difference is that perceptual processes are not invoked, so there is no confusion of the internally imagined piece with a real, actually present piece.

A procedure called **imagine** allows such hypothetical moves to be made by creating an activation of **piece** (at the appropriate location) with a strength above threshold. This will cause the model to act as if the piece were present, activating any suggestions associated with its analysis, and forming a new internal representation of the world. Since the activation exists only in **working memory**, it is subject to decay, as described earlier. When it decays, the suggestions associated with it decay as well, leading to a deterioration of the model's lookahead. The activation can be revived only by re-executing the procedure **imagine**. Note how this contrasts with pieces that actually exist in the real world: Their activations are constantly revived by suggestions from the features that are present in the world (provided that they are within the scope of the **fovea**). We need only pick up enough primitive features of items that actually exist in the world to satisfy our top-down expectations for the existence of those items. However, we must reimagine imaginary items to keep them from disappearing from **working memory**. This is considerably harder than picking up the features in the world, which is done automatically whenever the **fovea** happens to be in the right area. Reimagining an item is by no means automatic, since we have no way to reinvoke that **imagine** procedure except by reliving the circumstances in which it was invoked in the first place. "Reliving" means returning to the real-world scene and performing once again the operations we have just performed; weak activations of imagined moves that are still in **working memory** now get strengthened, allowing a slightly deeper lookahead each time through (until there are so many activations that they are decaying faster than they can be revived). This strengthening by reimagining will yield the progressive deepening behavior characteristic of human game players. Since we do not allow any special bookkeeping to keep track of hypothetical actions and pieces, a return to the real-world board configuration automatically results in the disappearance of the internal representation that had been associated with the model's lookahead. This is true because as the imagined pieces decay, execution of the procedure (10) will do the sequence

(12)   Notice each feature which the fovea subtends.

reconstituting an internal representation of the real world.

Note one more important property of this method of invoking search: The depth of search is limited by the capacity of the working memory to keep nodes active. A player may plan ahead by imagining that a previously well-learned pattern is invoked at any given point, thereby effectively increasing the depth of his search. But a beginner will have an apparently smaller depth of plan-ahead, even though both expert and beginner are subject to the same laws of memory activation. The difference, of course, is that the expert can take advantage of previously acquired larger units of analysis. For example, a beginner requires four lookahead moves to realize that the pattern of "two open-threes" in Gomoku is a winning configuration, whereas an experienced Gomoku player realizes this without any lookahead.

Backup

Now consider what happens when the human planner has progressed in his planning, either to the limit of his memory capacity or simply as far as seems profitable with the particular sequence he is investigating. How does he try alternative plans? Because we have postulated that the search is guided through the invocation of nodes within working storage, true backup is not possible.

Suppose the player wishes to back up two moves: How can he accomplish this? The only procedure available to him is to invoke an imaginary removal of a piece:

(13)   Imagine removing a piece at L1.

Invoking (13), of course, *adds* another process to working memory rather than simply erasing one. Thus, the player is able to backup through his original planning sequence only if he has sufficient capacity left within his working storage to contain both the planning sequences and the backup instructions. Backing up one move is thus moderately difficult, but it can still be done. Backing up two moves is much more difficult. To back up several moves, it becomes easier simply to let the imaginary pieces decay, rescan the real-world board, and start again. These procedures yield a progressive deepening-type search.

There must be some memory for hypothetical configurations that were previously evaluated and that are not to be repeated in the next lookahead episode. People do, of course, go over parts of the same path more than once, for that is how progressive deepening is defined: continual reworking of a path, and extending it further. If this reworking is considered a rehearsal mechanism, then the hypothetical moves or configurations that are rehearsed will remain active and can be avoided in future searches.

IMPLEMENTATION

Most of the constructs described in the preceding sections have actually been implemented, including:

- The ability to define complex patterns.

- A working memory in which all activations reside.

- The generation of eye movements (movements of the **fovea**) in order to get information about squares that are not visible.

- The generation of hypothetical moves.

The constructs described in this chapter appear to be capable of accounting for the behavior of people who are playing board games. The actual simulation of the behavior of a given subject, however, requires much finer tuning of the model than we have been able to provide. For example, parameters must be fit (for example, those that specify decay rates, activation thresholds, magnitude of excitation associated with find and suggest, and the criterion for deciding when to reactivate a decaying activation). In addition, simulation of, say, a sequence of Window movements requires the making of many assumptions about what the subject knows immediately before embarking on that sequence.

To illustrate the actual operation of the computer model, we present a portion of the computer output as it looked when it was simulating the behavior of a subject in a Window Mode experiment. The game that is simulated is, in fact, the same one that was analyzed earlier in this chapter. The board position was originally shown as Figure 12.6: it is repeated here for your convenience as Figure 12.10.

We start the simulation with the fifteenth move of the game. The subject has just moved by placing an O at location F4. At this point, the computer is examining the new piece, so the fovea is pointing at F4. The text that follows is the actual output of the computer as it appeared on the typewriter terminal, with the exception of minor typographical changes. (The actual output was all in capital letters and the statements were not numbered.) The statements in parentheses refer to movements of the fovea. The other statements refer to internal processing of the patterns.

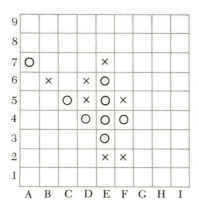

FIGURE 12.10
Position used for computer simulation
of Window Mode.

(14)   *OK, we have an O at F4.*

(15)   *Let's see what's happening around F4.*

(16)   *(Looking at F5) . . .*

(17)   *OK, we have an X at F5.*

(18)   *What else? . . .*

(19)   *(Looking at G4) . . .*

(20)   *(Looking at F3) . . .*

(21)   *(Looking at E4) . . .*

(22)   *OK, we have an O at E4.*

(23)   *Which gives us a horizontal pair of O's at F4 E4.*

(24)   *Hmmm, there might be a horizontal trio of O's at F4 E4 D4 . . .*

(25)   *(Looking at D4) . . .*

(26)   *Yup!*

(27)   *Hmmm, there might be a horizontal four of O's at F4 E4 D4 C4 . . .*

(28)   *(Looking at C4) . . .*

(29)   *Nope!*

(30)   *But we have a horizontal sub-open-three.*

Although the program's "verbal protocol" was added as a frill to enable us to follow what the program was doing, it was added in a way entirely consistent with the model. In other words, the act of "saying" something also resides in **working memory**, so the model can remember what it has just said. This enabled us to add some output production rules in a natural, consistent way. Thus, if the model discovers something based on an earlier discovery, and that earlier discovery has just been announced (for example, statement 22), the model says *Which gives us . . .* (statement 23). Whenever the model discovers something that was preceded by the disconfirmation of something else, it precedes its output with the phrase *But we have . . .* (for example statement 30).

The model begins at statement 14 by noting the presence of the latest piece. Unlike the actual subject, the model starts without knowing anything about the board configuration. As a result, its first strategy is simply to look around the square from which it has started. The model does this by placing the procedure **lookaround** within its **working memory**. Now the simulation begins. The model first looks at F5 (statement 16) and notices the X there. The existence of this X does not generate any hypotheses, so the model inspects **working memory** to see what it was doing at the time it noticed that X. The procedure **lookaround** is still active within **working memory**. Statement 18 is the result of a rule about the generation of output text that states that the resumption of a process need not be explicitly mentioned. (Without this rule, statement 18 would have been a repetition of 15: *Let's see what's happening around F4.*) The model looks at several more empty neighbors of F4 (statements 19, 20, and 21) before it discovers the O at E4 (statement 22). It remembers that there is an O at F4, so it realizes that a larger pattern is present (statement 23). This larger pattern is a "potent" one (that is, it is above threshold), so the model interrupts the scan around F4 by suggesting a possible larger pattern (statement 24). Statements 25 and 28 reflect an active search for a hypothesized pattern. Although the second active search fails (statement 29), the fact that C4 is blank is immediately used by the model: It discoveres a sub-open-three, which it was not actually looking for (statement 30).

These criteria for the model are fulfilled by the implementation:

- The scans are game-specific.

- The scans obey Gestalt principles of perception.

- The scans may be active or passive.

- The scans can generate eye movements.

- The internal representation of patterns is subject to decay.

The parameters remain to be specified, but the central mechanisms of the model appear to be confirmed.

SUMMARY

This chapter shows how experimental and theoretical studies of game playing and of internal memory representation can be combined to form a useful tool for the investigation and simulation of human problem-solving behavior.

Our experimental studies show that perceptual processes and problem-solving strategies work together. The internal representation of a board game seems to incorporate meaningful, interpreted structures. The internal representation for a particular configuration of pieces will depend both upon the game from which it has arisen and upon the skill of the player.

Our subjects played rapidly, even when not required to do so. Combining this finding with other evidence, we conclude that planning ahead by considering possible new board configurations is a difficult task. A player prefers to use previously acquired knowledge and strategies rather than to engage in new planning activities. As a result, game-playing performance often falls below the level that is possible for a given player.

We found that our players examined the board by means of active searches for specific patterns as well as by searches that seemed to be driven by the "accidental" discovery of new configurations of pieces. Because of this finding, we suggest that the search mechanism is one that allows for convergence between top-down, hypothesis driven searches, and bottom-up, stimulus-driven searches. Those features actually present in the world guide the processing in a bottom-up fashion, whereas the planning process of the subject guides the top-down processing.

To account for this behavior, we suggest that the internal representation of familiar patterns is most likely an active procedural representation, not just a static listing of the configuration of the pieces. This allows patterns to be activated from "below," when the external world gets analyzed in terms of features that suggest possible patterns. Alternatively, patterns can be activated from "above," when the planning or analysis process requests information about the patterns present (or possible) on the board.

When a subject plans ahead, the same kinds of search processes can be used. The placement of "imaginary" pieces within the internal representation of the problem space automatically invokes the planning processes in a bottom-up manner. Determining which pieces to consider in this fashion is, of course, a top-down, hypothesis-driven situation. This helps explain one of the standard observations about human problem-solving behavior: People follow a "progressive deepening" search strategy rather than a depth-first or breadth-first one. Evidently, this results from the fact that once imaginary moves have been considered within the working (short-term) memory, they cannot be erased. Thus, backup in the planning sequence can easily overload the capacity of this memory. As a result, subjects tend to start a search process over rather than to back up a few steps.

PART VII

EXTENSIONS

CHAPTER 13

Answering Questions about Processes

GREG W. SCRAGG

(1)   If you were to make a chocolate fudge upside-down angel food cake, what ingredients would you need? What utensils would get dirty?

To answer questions of the form illustrated by (1) — questions about the results and implications of performing a process — it must be possible to evaluate the effects of a set of known procedures. Although it might be feasible to maintain a list of all the ingredients used in preparing each type of food (including the ingredients that, themselves, have ingredients that must be prepared), it would not be feasible to maintain a list of all of the extraneous effects of the act of making each food item: which utensils get dirty, where each utensil is, or how much of an ingredient is used.

I call a question about the performance of an action a *process question*. Although there have been many studies of question-answering systems, they have been primarily concerned with questions that can be answered by consulting a table or by simple deduction. The problems of answering process questions have been little explored (but see Brown, Burton, and Zdybel, 1973).

This chapter examines what is necessary to develop answers to questions about processes, questions that ask "How?" "Why?" "What if?" or "Is it possible?"

LUIGI

Purpose

To explore the problems of answering questions that require a knowledge of processes, I have developed a system that knows about kitchens and cooking. The system, called **LUIGI**, was developed within the **MEMOD** computer system (described in Chapter 7). **LUIGI** has two parts: a data base, called **Kitchenworld**, which contains information about objects found in a kitchen and a set of procedures for manipulating those objects; and a set of procedures for answering questions using the data base. **LUIGI** can simulate simple actions within **Kitchenworld** such as cooking and preparing foods. More important, he can examine his own procedures for performing actions and calculate or predict the results of those actions.[1] Although **LUIGI** is designed to operate within the world of the kitchen, nothing in his question-answering abilities depends upon the environment. Thus, were **LUIGI** moved to some other context (say, American history or a sport such as baseball), once the data base, containing information about the facts and actions of the new domain, were constructed, then **LUIGI**'s procedures should also apply to the new domain.

Guiding Principles

Certain principles were established to guide the development of the system. I wanted a system that could answer questions about processes and that could also alter its data base and refer to it in a format reasonably like English. I used the following principles to guide this development:

- There are many questions that cannot be answered without knowledge of how actions are performed. The system should be able to check these actions, but the only information it should have about a process is the instruction for performing it.

- The system should not be limited to a few preselected facts. Its knowledge should be easily extendible by presenting the system

---

[1]**LUIGI** cannot actually make a sandwich but he can simulate the process. To answer certain questions, it will be necessary for **LUIGI** to "simulate his simulation." For convenience, I refer to **LUIGI** as if he could actually make a sandwich and I refer to his "simulations of simulations" simply as "simulations."

with definitions or descriptions of objects, actions, or events. The system should be able to change its own world.

- All high-level reasoning should be done in a manner similar to the way in which a person would reason.

A Sample Dialogue

The dialogue that follows was originally created to help guide the development of **LUIGI**: It is now possible to hold this conversation with **LUIGI**. Some of the stilted nature of the dialogue reflects the minor idiosyncracies of the system. The dialogue is useful to present at this point as a guide to the types of processes and representational structures that are discussed in the remainder of this chapter. In this dialogue the statements of the user are printed in this type face and preceded by the symbol >. **LUIGI**'s responses are shown in this type face.

(2)   > Where are the eggs?

Perhaps the eggs are in the refrigerator. Should I check?

> Yes.

Yes, the eggs are in the refrigerator.

> Where are the cookies?

Perhaps the cookies are on the shelf. Should I check?

> Yes.

No, the cookies are not on the shelf.

Maybe they are on the counter.

No, the cookies are not on the counter.

I can't find the cookies.

> I ate the cookies.

OK.

> Where are the cookies?

There are none.

> Make a baked Virginia ham and very sharp Cheddar cheese sandwich.

OK.

> What did you use to make the sandwich?

Baked Virginia ham, very sharp Cheddar cheese, lettuce, mustard, butter, knife, plate.

> What utensils would I need if I toasted bread?

I know one utensil. A knife.

> How do you toast bread?

If I want to toast bread, then I must do the following:

   I put the bread in the toaster.

   I wait until it is done.

   I pick up the toast.

   I put the toast on the plate.

   I spread the butter on the toast with the knife.

> Don toasted bread.

OK.

> Did Don toast rolls?

No, but Don toasted bread.

> Did Don spread the butter on the toast?

Yes.[2]

REPRESENTATIONAL STRUCTURES

To answer questions, a system must have a well-defined method of representing the actions, concepts, and objects in the data base. In this section I discuss the representational structures for actions and objects, and for descriptive phrases that are constructed from a concatenated sequence of modifiers.

---

[2]All of this dialogue actually took place, although never all in one sequence. This restriction occurs because although the answers look simple in the dialogue, in fact, many require enormous amounts of machine computation and memory space. For example, to answer the question that asks which utensils are needed to toast bread, **LUIGI** required approximately 16 seconds of processor time and 4 seconds of input-output time. About 1.5 minutes of elapsed time were required before the time-shared Burroughs 6700 computer actually produced the answer. To answer that question, **LUIGI** recursively examines all of the components of making toast to find out if any use utensils. Only one does: To spread butter on toast requires the use of a knife. (A toaster is classified as an appliance, not as a utensil.)

Actions

LUIGI must know about the actions that he can perform, including the components of that performance, what the preconditions are, and what the results will be. The active structural network representation and the Semantic Operating Language (**SOL**: see Chapter 7) provide the basic capabilities needed to accomplish this self-knowledge. In **MEMOD**, all actions are encoded as part of a semantic network and are accessible by any **SOL** procedure. But they are not necessarily in a form that other procedures may readily interpret. I have introduced special constraints to ensure a uniform structure for procedures. All actions are divided into three classes: *conscious*, *semiconscious*, and *unconscious*.

Conscious Actions. Conscious actions are actions that can be broken down into constituent parts, each of which the performer is aware of. For example, the conscious action **move** X may be defined to have these parts:

(3)   move X:
　　　　pick-up X
　　　　transport X
　　　　put-down X

The definition of each conscious procedure should contain meaningful names of subprocedures; that is, the simulation should be composed of simulated substeps, each named appropriately. It thus becomes possible for the system to describe one of its routines to a human in an easily understood form. In a similar fashion, a person can give English-like instructions to **LUIGI** that reflect his own procedure for performing the action.

Semiconscious Actions. Semiconscious actions correspond to the lowest levels of conscious actions, those that humans are barely aware of performing. **Pick-up** is probably a semiconscious act. Humans are conscious of the act of picking up an object. But they need not think of the process by which they grasp the object with fingers and thumb. The definitions of semiconscious actions do not need to be clear descriptions of the actions, but they must yield the proper results when executed.

Unconscious Actions. Unconscious actions are those that do not play a direct role in the simulation of human performance. These include routines for which there is no human analog, but that must be done by the program in order to perform the simulation (bookkeeping, printing, and so on).

Procedures. In the definitions of procedures, I require that descriptions of conscious actions include as few explicit unconscious actions as possible. These should be contained within the semiconscious actions if possible. Semiconscious actions may not entail conscious actions, and unconscious actions may entail neither conscious nor semiconscious actions. The intent is that a semiconscious action will be a sort of primitive action for people and that unconscious actions will be invisible to the processing routines. Following these criteria, the definition of a conscious action should be an ordered list of conscious and semiconscious actions that are needed to perform the action being defined, resembling a list of instructions a human might be asked to follow.

Each procedure is simultaneously a set of directions for performing a task, an outline of the effects of performing the action, a plan for performing the act in the future, and a guide for determining which other acts would be performed. Thus, if **LUIGI** is told to perform an action, he does so by executing the appropriate procedure. If he is told that an action has taken place, he notes that fact. If he needs to know about any subactions that might have occurred or about the results of the action, he must derive them from the procedure. He answers questions by examining the procedure in varying levels of detail, either looking only at the surface level actions, or going deeper, perhaps recursively examining each subaction. Thus, a question like

(4)   How do you make cookies?

is answered by examining the program **make** X, substituting "cookies" for the formal parameter X. Questions like

(5)   Can you make cookies?

can be answered by examining the preconditions for **make** X. To answer questions like

(6)   What utensils do you need to make cookies?

LUIGI must **trace** the operation of **make**, and all of **make**'s subprocedures, noting the use of any utensil.

Real and Mental Worlds

It is important that there be a distinction between **LUIGI**'s understanding of the state of the world (his "Mental World") and the actual state of the world (the "Real World"). **LUIGI** may believe that there is cheese in the refrigerator, whereas the cheese is actually on the table. Similarly, there may be ham in the refrigerator even though **LUIGI** is not aware of the fact. **LUIGI** may freely consult his mental world. However, if he wishes to consult the real world, he is constrained by limitations analogous to those faced by a human. That is, to find cheese, **LUIGI** can examine his mental world to see where he believes it to be, but he cannot determine the real-world location of the cheese without simulating the act of going to the appropriate location and looking.

The data base is actually two data bases stored together as one, the **Real World**, which represents the objects in the world (a kitchen), and the **Mental World**, which represents **LUIGI**'s mental image of the real world. The distinction is similar to that made by traditional dualist philosophers. The **real world** contains only descriptions of real physical objects. The **mental world** contains abstract concepts and mental images of the real-world objects.

The major hierarchical relation between *type nodes* in the **mental world** is the relation **superset**. *Tokens* are connected by the relation **isa**. The distinction between the relations **superset** and **isa** is exactly the same as between the set-theoretical relations "superset" and "element." **Real-world** objects may not be related to any other nodes by either **superset** or **isa**, but are linked to their **mental-world** correspondents by **mental-image** (the converse relation is **real-image**). Since there are no *type nodes* in the **real world**, each **real-world** token is linked to the appropriate *type node* in the **mental world** via the relation **mental-class**.

In Figure 13.1, node ✳3[3] is a **real-world** red block, correctly aligned with its **mental-image** and concept. Node ✳5 is a green block existing in the **real world** but unknown in the **mental world**. The concept of "green block" must exist in the **mental world** in order for a **real-world** green block to exist, even though there are no known examples. Node ✳9 is a mental blue block, but no real blue block exists. Node ✳7 is a yellow block incorrectly believed to be blue. In Figure 13.2 the cheese is correctly believed to be in the refrigerator, but the ham, which is also in the refrigerator, is believed to be on the table.

---

[3]The nodes in the figures in this chapter are numbered consecutively for convenience of reference. The numbers have no further significance.

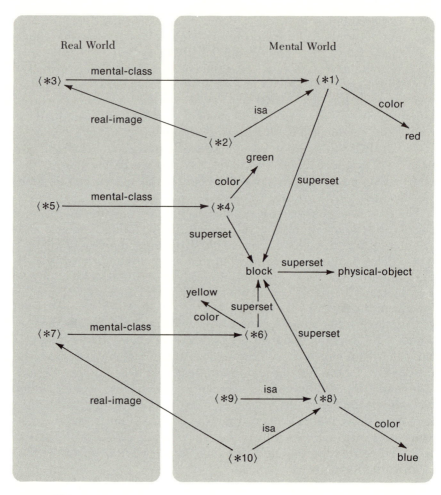

FIGURE 13.1
Real- and mental-images of several objects. Node *3 is a red block, correctly aligned with its mental-image and correct concept. Node *5 is unknown in the mental world. No real-image for node *9 exists and the mental-image of node *7 is incorrect.

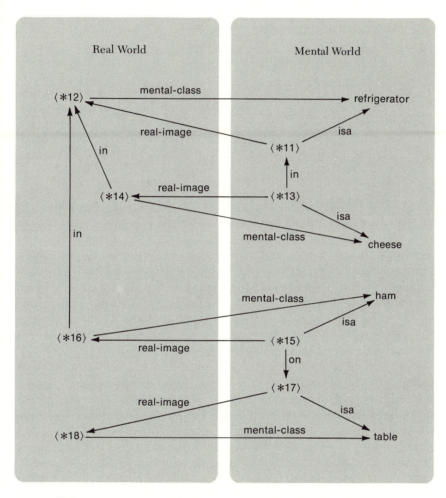

FIGURE 13.2
A confusion regarding the actual location of an object. The cheese (node *14) is correctly believed to be in the refrigerator, but the ham (node *16) is incorrectly thought to be on the table.

Modifiers

Consider the noun phrase

(7)   a very sharp Cheddar cheese sandwich

To understand (7) one must understand several underlying concepts, including "sandwich," "cheese sandwich," "Cheddar cheese," "sharp Cheddar," and "very sharp Cheddar." It must be recognized that the words "very sharp" modify the type of Cheddar, not the sandwich. That the nature of the modification is not obviously governed by syntactic considerations can be seen by such phrases as

(8)   an open-faced Cheddar cheese sandwich

(9)   a hot melted Cheddar cheese sandwich

Phrases 7, 8, and 9 show that the first two modifying words (not counting the determiners "a" and "an") can sometimes modify the type of Cheddar (as in 7), sometimes the variety of the cheese (as in 9), and sometimes the form of the sandwich (as in 8). The representational structure for such modifying phrases turns out to be a central issue in the entire process of question answering. Therefore, I examine this representational issue in considerable detail.

One particular problem in the understanding of modifying relations is that the type of modification required depends upon both the modifier and the object being modified. The modifier "cheese" means quite a different thing when it is used to modify "sandwich" (cheese sandwich: a sandwich that contains cheese) from when it is used to modify knife (cheese knife: a special kind of knife used for cutting cheese). In **LUIGI** it is important that these different forms of modification be mapped into different representational structures. The structures in Figure 13.3 can be generated after the relation (called the modification-word) between the object and the modifier is determined by consulting a list of allowable classes of objects that the adjective can modify.

FIGURE 13.3
Two structures created to represent modification by "cheese":
"a cheese sandwich" (*left*) and "a cheese knife" (*right*).

Concatenated Modifiers

When two or more modifiers are concatenated with one noun, there are a number of syntactically valid interpretations of how they modify and interrelate with one another. In a phrase of the form *"modifier1 modifier2 noun,"* *modifier2* clearly modifies the *noun*, but *modifier1* may modify the *noun*, *modifier2*, or the concept represented by the pair *"modifier2 noun."* It is a nontrivial problem to determine which of these is correct for a given noun phrase. Indeed, a sentence may be ambiguous even in context. In general, any number of modifiers may appear in one noun phrase. In this discussion, I treat only the two-modifier case, but there is a natural extension to the many-modifier case.

Orthogonal Modification. Two modifiers (*mod1* and *mod2*) are said to be orthogonal with respect to a noun (*N*) if insertion of *mod2* between *mod1* and *N* in a sentence does not affect the relation holding between *mod1* and *N*. Orthogonality is the simplest relation that can hold between two modifiers and an object. In the model there are two tests for orthogonality:

- Both modifiers must be legal modifiers for the noun.

- No special conditions (described later in this chapter) may apply.

Examples of modifier-noun pairs that fail the first condition include "green ideas" and "very blocks."
Structurally, the concept referenced by two orthogonal modifiers and their noun is the intersection of the two subsets denoted by *mod1 N* and *mod2 N*. The representation for "large red block" is shown in Figure 13.4. In the figure, it is apparent that the concepts

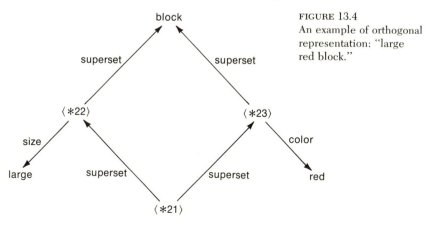

FIGURE 13.4
An example of orthogonal representation: "large red block."

for "large block" and "red block" both appear just as if the other modifier had not been used (that is, they are orthogonal) and that node *21 represents the intersection of the two subsets.

An Experiment.   To determine if the orthogonal representation is always sufficient to represent meaningful noun phrases, I conducted a small survey to determine the appropriate representations for sandwiches and omelets. I asked fifty people (who were both familiar and unfamiliar with semantic networks) to answer the following four questions:

(10A)   Is a ham and cheese sandwich a special type of ham sandwich?

(10B)   Is a ham and cheese sandwich a special type of cheese sandwich?

(10C)   Is a ham and cheese omelet a special type of ham omelet?

(10D)   Is a ham and cheese omelet a special type of cheese omelet?

If the orthogonal representation were correct, then the answer to each question should be "Yes." (Everyone was required to answer either "Yes" or "No" to each of the four questions in example 10.) The following results were obtained:

	Answer (percent)	
Question	Yes	No
Is a ham and cheese sandwich		
a ham sandwich?	52	48
a cheese sandwich?	14	86
Is a ham and cheese omelet		
a ham omelet?	20	80
a cheese omelet?	46	54

The results show that many people believe that a ham and cheese sandwich is not a cheese sandwich and that a ham and cheese omelet is not a ham omelet. Most people feel that some feature is possessed by ham and cheese omelet that it does not gain by virtue of a position in the intersection of "ham omelet" and "cheese omelet."

The sample questions contain two clues to their structure. First, the word "and" connects the two modifiers. This suggests that the two modifiers are working in a parallel fashion. The other clue is that "ham" and "cheese" have the same modifying effects when their object is a food product. (They both indicate an ingredient.) Again these modifiers would appear to be operating in parallel.

Parallel Modification.   Two modifiers will be said to be "parallel" with respect to an object *N* if they are conjoined by "and" and they each have the same modification word with respect to the object.

The structure for representing such concepts is a single subset of the noun, modified by each of the modifiers via the appropriate modification word. The structure for "ham and cheese sandwich" is shown in Figure 13.5. Note that whereas **node *24** is a subset of omelet, it is not a subset of either "ham omelet" or "cheese omelet."

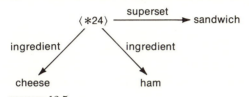

FIGURE 13.5
An example of parallel modification: "a ham and cheese sandwich."

Modifier Affinity.   So far, it has been assumed that both modifiers modify the terminal noun of the noun phrase. But this is not always true. In "blue cheese dressing," "blue" clearly modifies "cheese" not "dressing." This is a dressing made with blue cheese. A "large green grape" is not necessarily a large grape, but only large for a "green grape." The tendency of a modifier to refer to an object is referred to as its *affinity* for the object. Affinity is a measure of the node-space distance between the modifier and its possible objects.

A *named subset* is a subset of a class that has special properties not derivable from the name. "Green grape" is a named subset of grape that, besides being green, has the additional properties of being small and being seedless. An *idiom* is a construct that represents a concept not related to its apparent syntactic superset. A "white elephant" is neither elephant nor white. The structure for "large green grape" is shown in Figure 13.6. Note that the concept of the named subset

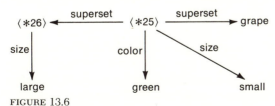

FIGURE 13.6
An example of a named subset, modified by a second adjective: "a large green grape."

"green grape" (represented by **node** ✳25) is treated exactly as if it were a single noun. **Node** ✳25 may have additional properties since it is a named subset rather than just a subset. Note that the relation "large" is always relative to the normal size of the prototypical member of the superset. Thus, **node** ✳26 is "large" relative to "green grape." **Node** ✳25 indicates that "green grapes" are "small" relative to the normal size of a grape.

Adverbial Modification. If *mod1* has a strong affinity for *mod2*, then *mod1* may behave as an adverb modifying *mod2*. It is not necessary that the modifier be known to be an adverb. In the phrase "Swiss cheese sandwich," "cheese" behaves syntactically as an adjective, "Swiss" as an adverb. Swiss modifies cheese, indicating that the sandwich is made with Swiss cheese but it is still a cheese sandwich. The structure is shown in Figure 13.7. The concepts for Swiss cheese, cheese sandwich, and Swiss cheese sandwich all appear in the structure as **nodes** ✳29, ✳27, and ✳28, respectively. The relation **ro** (restriction-operator) indicates that the **node** ✳28 is the subset of **node** ✳27 formed by restricting it to only those cheese sandwiches that are made of Swiss cheese (**node** ✳29). The relation **replaces** indicates that **node** ✳29 is used in place of cheese.

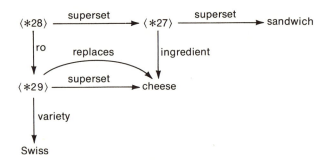

FIGURE 13.7
An example of the structure used when an adjective has high affinity for another adjective: "a Swiss cheese sandwich."

Selecting the Modification. The determination of which of these modifying structures to generate in a given case is fairly complex. In noun phrases with more than two modifiers, the representational structure is built recursively. The **SOL** parser causes the last modifier to be evaluated first because in English, an adjective modifies only the portion of the phrase to its right. Each succeeding adjective (working from right to left) is evaluated in succession operating on the structure built by the previous adjectives. A set of precedence rules is used to help select the appropriate structures when two or more seem appropriate. For example, the noun phrase

(11)   large baked ham and sharp Cheddar cheese sandwich

is represented by the structure shown in Figure 13.8. Note the position of each relevant concept necessary in the structure. For instance, node *34 is "sharp Cheddar cheese," node *37 is "baked ham and cheese sandwich," and node *39 is a "large" subset of the intersection of "baked ham and cheese sandwich" and "ham and sharp Cheddar cheese sandwich."

ANSWERING QUESTIONS

Sentence Understanding and Simple Fact Retrieval

The understanding of English and the answering of simple questions are two closely related tasks. Often it is necessary to answer a question in the process of comprehending an input sentence. ("Is the referent of this noun phrase really capable of performing the action described by the verb?") If a question simply requires a *yes or no* answer or an identification, frequently almost all of the work necessary to answer the question will have been performed by the time parsing is complete. To take advantage of this situation in answering a question, the system need only look at the memory structures that correspond to the object and retrieve the answer directly from that location. To answer the question

(12)   "What color is the cheese?"

the system converts it to the declarative form,

(13)   "The cheese is what color."

The referent of "the cheese" can be examined to see if color connects it to any other node. If it does, then that node can be returned as the answer. Note, however, that in **LUIGI** the referent is actually the mental-image of the cheese, so that he can really only answer what color he *thinks* the cheese is. To verify this answer, **LUIGI** must go to

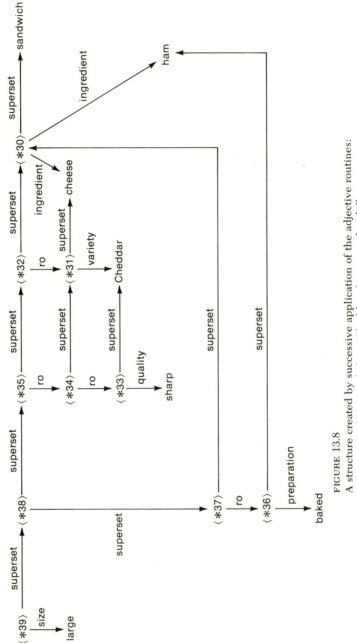

FIGURE 13.8
A structure created by successive application of the adjective routines:
"a large baked ham and sharp Cheddar cheese sandwich."

the cheese and look at it (which would force him to ask himself, "Where is the cheese?"). Similarly, a *yes-no* question can be answered by checking to see if the desired construct is present. To answer

(14)   Did John hit Mary?

LUIGI can examine each known event pointed to from the node history. If any event is an **act** of "hit" with subject "John" and object "Mary," then a "Yes" answer can be returned.

   An extension of direct retrieval is simple deduction. The semantic network provides a natural tool for simple deductions such as syllogisms. Suppose that we know that Fido **isa** dog and dog **has-as-part** fur. If the question

(15)   Does Fido have fur?

is asked, examination of the node **Fido** provides no answer. However, whatever is true of **dog** must also be true of **Fido**, since **Fido** is an element of **dog**. So the node **dog** is examined and the answer found. If there is conflicting information on the **superset** of a node, the principle of local information should be used. If birds can fly but ostriches cannot (even though they are birds), the more local information "Ostriches cannot fly" should be returned as the answer to the question "Can ostriches fly?"

Inferential Reasoning and Procedural Questions

It is not always possible to find an answer by looking it up or by simple deduction. Yet it may still be possible to infer an answer from data in the data base. Questions about processes are often of this sort. For instance, the extraneous effects of making a sandwich are not stored anywhere, but they can be inferred by careful examination of the recipe. I now show how each of several classes of questions may be answered. Note that each of these classes is answered by very similar reasoning processes.

   "How Do You" Questions.   To see how **LUIGI** answers questions like

(16)   How do you make a ham and cheese sandwich?

let us examine the format of the recipe for sandwich. A general form of the recipe, applicable to a wide variety of ingredients, is entered into the system in this format:

(17)   Define sandwich as recipe.
        The definition frame for sandwich is:
        (subject) sandwich X.
        The definition is:
            Place a slice of bread on the counter.
            Spread preferred spread of X on the bread.
            Place each ingredient of X on the bread.
            Place a second piece of bread on the bread.
        ##

Now, when **LUIGI** is asked question 16, he must first determine the form of the sandwich ("ham and cheese" in this case), and then trace through the steps of (17), substituting the appropriate form of the sandwich for the variable **X**, and reconstructing each conscious or semiconscious action. In this case the output would be:

(18)   *If I were to make a sandwich, then I would do the following things:*
        I place slice of bread on the counter.
        I spread mustard on the bread.
        I place ham on the bread.
        I place cheese on the bread.
        I place lettuce on the bread.
        I place second piece of bread on the bread.

To produce this output, a procedure called **trace** finds each conscious or semiconscious subact in the proper sequence. **Trace** is capable of recursively examining the procedure and each of its subparts. The procedure **how** runs along with **trace**, evaluating each **act** node that **trace** finds. **How** must find a suitable English name for each argument to each substep and translate the node into English. To obtain the results that ham, cheese, and lettuce are needed, the argument **X** of **ingredient** must first be converted to the node representing the concept "ham and cheese sandwich." The operator **ingredient** is then executed, returning with the list **ham**, **cheese**, and **lettuce**. Each of these names must be substituted, one at a time, in the appropriate spot on the node that is the token of the action **place**. Then the resulting node structure is used to guide the English output.

"Did (or Will) an Action Occur" Questions.   Sometimes it is desirable to predict the results of future or hypothetical actions or to calculate the results of a past process. To answer the question

(19)   Did Bill use a knife?

LUIGI can examine each known event involving Bill to determine if it was an act of using a knife. If there are no such events, **LUIGI** must recursively trace each recent event to see if any of its substeps might involve the use of a knife. To search for a semiconscious event (such as **use**), all conscious and semiconscious steps must be checked. But to find a conscious event, only the conscious substeps need to be checked. For hypothetical questions ("will"), only the process definition needs to be checked. The past events are not relevant.

"What," "Where," "Who," and "When" Questions. Questions such as

(20A)   What did John do?

(20B)   Where did John make omelets?

(20C)   Who made omelets?

(20D)   When did John make omelets?

can all be answered with a simple modification of the "did" question-answering routines. To answer each of the preceding forms, **LUIGI** asks the *true-false* ("did") question obtained from the given question by replacing the *Wh-question* word with the corresponding indefinite pronoun or adverb (anything, anywhere, anyone, ever). If a "Yes" answer is returned, the description of the event is examined for the appropriate argument (action, location, subject, or time), and the content of that argument is returned as the answer.

Next-Step Questions.   This form of question asks for the next step of a process or for an explanation for a particular step.

(21A)   What do you do after you put toast in the toaster?

(21B)   What happened after Bill made the sandwich?

The method used to answer such questions is simply an extension of the "How do you" question-answering method. To answer (21A), **LUIGI** traces the procedure **toast**, exactly as was done for "how" questions, except that no output is made until the desired step is reached (an act of putting toast in the toaster, in this case). The next step is evaluated and printed out as for a "how" question. If more detail is needed to find the desired step, **trace** must follow through each of the substeps of the action, recursively. In (21B), which asks about a real rather than a hypothetical event, **LUIGI** must check each of the known events rather than just the procedure for the event under consideration.

"What If" Questions.   To answer questions of the form

(22)   What utensils would I get dirty if I made a cake?

it is necessary to think through the entire process of making a cake and to determine at each step if a utensil were being dirtied. The mechanism for doing this is to ask "Does making a cake get any utensil dirty?" However, the entire process must be examined: It is not possible to stop when one utensil is found, as in the *true-false* questions. If a process changes the state of the world (as many of them do), the prediction results might be difficult. If the output of one step of a process depends on a previous step, and if the question inquires about the state of the world at some particular time, it may be necessary to simulate the simulation in a hypothetical world. In such a space, **LUIGI** can manipulate hypothetical objects while remembering the actual locations of their real-world counterparts. Thus, to answer

(23)   What utensils would be left on the counter after I made cookies?

it would be necessary to simulate the entire process and then examine the counter for utensils. The step-by-step method used to answer (22) would not work because a utensil might be placed on the counter and later removed, and the question only asks about the end state.

"Why" Questions.   A "why" question could have any of several meanings. The method of answering a "why" question should depend on the intent of the question. An expected answer to the question

(24)   Why did John take a frying pan out of the cupboard?

might be the use to which he put the frying pan. To provide such an answer, **LUIGI** can examine the sequence of events in which the frying pan was removed, just as if it were a "next-step" question, and return the step immediately following the removal. Such a reply might be *"He fried some eggs."* In the question

(25)   Why did Oliver put peanut butter on bread?

an answer that gave the event in which Oliver used the peanut butter would be sufficient. To obtain such an answer, trace can be run just as in a "did" question. When the event of putting the peanut butter on the bread is discovered, the name of the procedure that is being traced can be returned as the answer:

(26)   Oliver made a peanut butter and jelly sandwich.

To answer the question

(27)   Why does water boil?

a cook might say that water boils because (when) it is put into a pan and heated. To derive such an answer, **LUIGI** behaves as if he were asked a "how" question.

The determination of which form of "why" question to answer is actually harder than the actual answering of the question. Unfortunately, **LUIGI** does not do a very good job of this selection and much more work is needed.

Generated Questions. If **LUIGI** believes that the bread is in the pantry but it is actually on the counter, he cannot find it by simple means. But he can generate the question

(28)   Did anyone move the bread?

In other words, he can look for changes in the desired property (location). Even if **LUIGI** finds an answer to (28), this need not lead to the solution. He will still have to verify that the bread is at the new location because it may have been moved twice or it may have been used up.

The Processing Routines

Overall control of the processing of input sentences and questions is performed by a group of routines collectively called the *real-world compiler*. The compiler has three components: the *parser*, the *adjective compiler*, and the *comprehender*. The parser is not actually a part of **LUIGI**, but is the augmented transition network parser of the MEMOD system discussed in Chapters 5 and 7. The adjective compiler is a part of **LUIGI** designed to aid the parsing process by semantically disambiguating input, generating modifier structures, and searching for referenced objects. The comprehender, also a part of **LUIGI**, is not invoked until a complete parse has been made. In general, the comprehender controls the response to the input.

The Adjective Compiler. Normally, the **SOL** parser locates a possible noun phrase and then executes (from right to left) the programs representing each adjective, determiner, or operator. I have replaced this mechanism with the adjective compiler. Now, whenever the parser finds a noun phrase, it calls the adjective compiler, which can consider semantic and contextual information before selecting the routine to build the structure to represent the input noun phrase. Most of the rules governing the selection of structures were given in the section on representation. The compiler can reject a noun phrase if it decides that it is not semantically valid. An example of a phrase to which it can object is an adjective-noun pair for which the noun is not within the known scope of the adjective. (The phrases "yellow ideas" or "cheese wrench" would be rejected as nonsensical.)

In addition to the syntactic and semantic rules, the compiler can derive some information from knowledge of the world. Suppose the nodes shown in Figure 13.9 are included in the data base. If the adjective compiler were examining the phrase "baked ham sandwich," it could discover that ham is something that can be baked, although sandwich is not. As a result, it selects "ham" as the argument of the adjective, and does not attempt to bake a ham sandwich. If the compiler analyzes "baked macaroni casserole," then it finds no help from its bake list: Neither macaroni nor casserole is listed as bakeable. But there are recipes for casseroles, and if any recipe involves baking, the compiler can conclude that "casserole" (or "macaroni casserole") is the appropriate object.

The Comprehender. Once the parser believes that it has successfully parsed the sentence, the comprehender becomes responsible for the remaining processing of the sentence. It is the job of the comprehender to call the question-answering routines. Sometimes the comprehender can modify the structure created by the parser. For example, when processing the question

(29)   How do you make a tuna sandwich?

the comprehender notes that **make** belongs to a special class of actions that refer to other actions. **Make X** is defined as

(30)   Follow the recipe for X.

The comprehender must find the recipe for sandwich and replace the object of **make** by the recipe. Now, execution of **how** will provide a

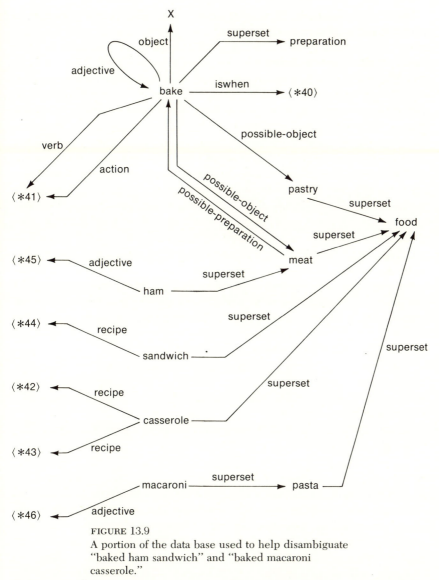

FIGURE 13.9
A portion of the data base used to help disambiguate
"baked ham sandwich" and "baked macaroni
casserole."

list of the recipe rather than a list of the **make** routine. The comprehender can also refuse to run the program generated by the parser. It
sometimes does this when the input is a declarative sentence. There
is sometimes more than one procedure for finding the answer to a
given question (such as a "why" question). It is the comprehender's
duty to select an answering procedure and then to attempt an alternative procedure if the first one fails.

Here is an example of how the comprehender might proceed in attempting to answer the question

(31)   "Where is the cheese?"

The cheese is recognized as a particular entity in the mental world. The comprehender decides that since cheese has a preferred location in the refrigerator, the actual search should begin there. The heuristic for physical searching is called to look in the refrigerator for the cheese: Suppose it fails to find any? The comprehender then checks recent events, but suppose the event-checking routine finds no references to cheese? The event-analyzing routine is then called. Suppose it discovers that Bill made Welsh rarebit? In analyzing the procedure for rarebit, it discovers that cheese is used. The routine then concludes that since the cheese cannot be found, Bill probably used it up. This may be the wrong answer, but if so, it is an error that is typically human.

Because the comprehender always has a reason for selecting the question-answering procedures that it invokes, when it fails it can say why it failed. Thus, if asked (31), it can respond

(32)   Bill used it up in making Welsh rarebit.

SUMMARY

Progress Report

At the time this chapter is being written, all of the procedures discussed here are in a state of continuing development and change. Although several of the features described herein are complete, many others are not. The noun-modifying procedures all work and mechanisms for automatically adding new adjectives to the data base of Kitchenworld are available. All of the special features required of verbs are automatically appended. Routines for adding new items to the world are provided. All of the simple forms of inferential question-answering described are implemented ("how," "why," "who," "how many," "which," "did," and "what if").

A large number of common objects found in kitchens are present in Kitchenworld and several basic actions can be performed (pick-up, move, put, clean, clean-up, use, eat, follow, tell-about, go, spread, and so on). In addition, several other actions are known (mix, pour, bake, place), but their definitions are naive. **LUIGI** contains simple recipes for *toast, s'mores, sandwiches, omelets* and *spaghetti*. **LUIGI** does not yet understand the concept of a piece of the whole. Consequently, sandwiches are made with whole loaves of bread and entire jars of peanut butter.

There are one or more procedures for answering each of the question forms: "how," "where," "why," "who," "when," "how many," "what," and "true-false." The comprehender is working, but it is now governed by limited rules. It performs no analysis of recent conversation and it cannot estimate the complexity of the answering routine very well. The generation of the imaginary world needed for certain "what if" questions is incomplete.

On the Size of a Data Base

It is interesting to note how large the data base for **Kitchenworld** must be to solve even very simple problems. At this time there are more than 5000 nodes in the data base, and it is still very elementary.[4] To see why this size is required, consider what is required to represent a "knife." Corresponding to the primary node for "knife" there is a node to represent the **mental-image**, one for the **physical-image**, and one for the concept. The knife is a utensil and the utensil is an object, and so this requires more nodes. The knife is in a drawer, which also contains forks, spoons, and other utensils. The knife is sharp and made of metal. All of these facts must be represented by nodes. Then there is cheese for the knife to cut and a board for the cutting to be performed on. The board is on the counter (above the drawer), which is between the stove (which gets hot and has a pan on it) and the refrigerator (which is cold and has food in it). All of these are located in the kitchen of a house. In order for the knife to cut the cheese, there must be a person who can perform the action, and a procedure for cutting. It is obvious that the descriptions are growing rapidly, yet we are still concentrating on "knife." There still are food items, the

---

[4]The 5000-plus nodes in the data base have an average of 4.1 links to other nodes. It is interesting to note that the number of links to other nodes has remained fairly constant as the data base has grown. Thus, the actual storage required for the data base has increased linearly with the number of nodes. The present size is 27,000 (48-bit) words. However, temporary use of nodes by the **MEMOD** system during processing can rapidly increase the storage requirement to more than 50,000 words (plus 10,000 words used for the **MEMOD** system itself). **LUIGI**, the system, is specified by about 4000 lines of **SOL** statements.

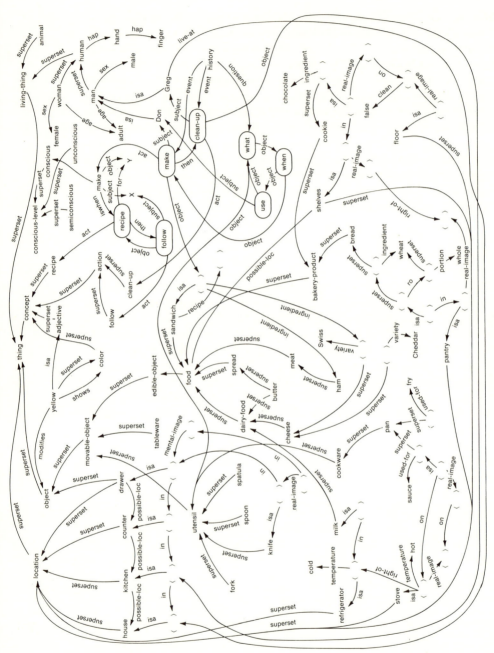

FIGURE 13.10

other utensils, the descriptive words of the vocabulary, and the many actions that can be performed and recipes that can be used. Everything requires more nodes. It should also be noted that these descriptions are rudimentary. The stove simply "gets hot." We do not bother to describe the level of flames from each of the burners. Still the data base is enormous. A rough schematic of only a small part of the data base is provided in Figure 13.10. I estimate that over one-half of this data base is filled with procedures for simulation and for question answering, and the rest contains the representational structure for the objects, concepts, and lexical entries for the world of a kitchen.

CHAPTER 14

Memory for Real-World Events

MARIGOLD LINTON

(1)   Which came first, the death of Charles De Gaulle or the landing of the first man on the moon?

Most people today have heard of both these events. Many remember their occurrence. But very few people can recall which of the two events occured first. Such a decision is often made with great difficulty and after a good deal of inferential problem solving.

It is clear that a person maintains the knowledge of a great number of events and personal experiences within his memory. Many occurrences are remembered without difficulty even after long periods have elapsed. Often memories that are quite old can be remembered in detail, and the act of recalling one often allows other, related events to be recalled. For example, if someone thinks back to the time when President John Kennedy was assassinated (in November 1963), events that took place at about this time seem sharp and clear within his memory. It is as if the dark areas of memory have been illuminated by a searchlight, with those things that occurred near the illuminated areas readily visible, often in considerable detail.

If some events can be recalled with reasonable accuracy, even after a long period, why do people have difficulty with the type of problem posed to them in statement 1? The events seem to be clear, but their temporal relationship is not. The organizational structure of memory seems to allow for recognition of events, but not necessarily for the determination of the ways by which two differing events are related to one another.

In this chapter, I describe the steps of a systematic investigation of the changes that occur in an individual's remembrance of daily events in the real world. The study is a long-term one, and detailed results will not be available for several more years. But at this point, it is useful to examine some of the theoretical and practical problems faced by one who wishes to study the memory for real-world events.

When one starts to examine the memory for occasions long past, several fundamental issues about memory and event structures arise. First, before we can readily study the memory for an event or for the interrelationships among events, we must specify what an event is. Second, assuming that a satisfactory determination of an event exists, then what is the means by which the memory structure is organized? Just how are different events related? Finally, we must know the mechanism by which the data base of human memory is searched in order to determine the information that is crucial to the questions asked.

TEMPORAL JUDGMENTS OF EVENTS

The Specification of an Event

Simple events have been described throughout this book. Here is an event that is typical of the ones illustrated in other chapters:

(2)   Helen played a game of tennis with Lew. She beat him.

To encode this event, the propositions that underlie the two sentences would be formed (in this case, in a relatively straightforward way), and the result would be entered into the memory system. When the structure for sentences such as in (2) is studied, the fact that it is examined in isolation from all the other existing structures in memory simplifies many of the problems that are associated with memory structures. In actuality, the memory must contain thousands, perhaps millions, of propositions similar to those in (2), and because many of them share common structures, it is not at all clear how one isolates the unique set of structures that characterizes a particular event. Part of the problem is that so many different areas of the memory share common features. Another aspect of the problem is that all non-primitive actions can be expanded into a large set of structures, and each of those structures can be expanded until finally the underlying primitives are reached. What, then, is an event? How many different events must there be in the playing of a tennis match? The answer depends upon the specification of event: There could be one event, or there could be as many events as there are swings of the rackets, or movements of the bodies. Alternatively, the tennis matches might simply be a subpart of a larger event within which they are embedded, perhaps a tournament. Thus we see that the richness of the overall memory structure makes it difficult to divide that structure neatly into separate, isolatable events. Further, temporal information may not be equally available for all specifications of events. It seems reasonable that subset events will often be less datable than superset events. For present purposes I bypass the problems of explicitly defining events and assume that the intuitive characterizations will suffice.

Still, one more problem remains in specifying an event: the problem of reference, akin to the issues discussed in Chapter 3. When a person is asked about an event in memory, it is necessary, among other things, to search for the appropriate structure that represents the event in question. Suppose the event is a tennis match, perhaps the one referred to in (2). If there were only one tennis match, then it would not be too difficult (perhaps) to recover the event. But suppose Lew and Helen played regularly. Then the description in (2) does not suffice.

When one person asks another about an event, it must be specified in sufficient detail that it can be located in memory; clearly, however, specification will not be so precise that the question itself contains the answer. Suppose we wish to question Helen about the match mentioned in (2). How would we do that? The problem is related to the problem faced by Olson's subjects (Olson, 1970: described in this book, Chapter 3), who were asked to describe under which block on a table a gold star had been placed. The description depended on the set of alternatives that were to be discriminated. Suppose Helen had played only one tennis game with Lew. We could say to her:

(3)   Do you remember your tennis game with Lew?

But suppose Helen had played Lew numerous times, and they were well-matched players, each winning about half the games. Then we would have to increase the number of details in order to specify the event unambiguously. Including a date often permits us to locate a recalcitrant event. However, it would not make sense to say to Helen:

(4)   Do you remember the first Sunday in December last year when you beat Lew at tennis? Well, was that before or after the game you played last week with Judy (and lost)?

The Organization of Events

The difficulty that subjects have in ordering two events in time, even though they do remember both events, indicates that simple time tags are not invariably associated with events. Logically, however, temporal information could be encoded in a number of different ways.[1]

Perhaps the simplest assumption is that an event has an explicit temporal tag that is encoded with the item at the time the memory is established. If the information in the tags is relatively permanent, it is a trivial matter to determine when an event in such a system occurred: find the event, search for the temporal tag, and read off the information. To determine the order of two events, the system finds the events, searches for the respective temporal tags, compares them, and assigns "earlier" to the event with the older date. Temporal tags may be hypothesized to include widely varying amounts of information. Although everyday observations immediately reject such a suggestion, it is possible to conceive absolutely explicit tags for day, date, and hour. Such tags might be consistently or probabilistically available when the item is recalled.

A more plausible suggestion, given the known difficulty subjects have, is that temporal information is only probabilistically associated with any item. Under this assumption, some items may have one specific tag and other items may have other tags, even perhaps no tags. For example, one might know that the event occurred on a Tuesday, or last week, or in the afternoon. Temporal encoding might occur at the time the particular event is originally stored, or be added at a later time (perhaps with increased probability that the information is incorrect). Specific temporal tagging need not, however, be assumed to explain availability of comparative temporal judgments. Temporal order is often derivable from the memory structure itself because

---

[1]This discussion does not necessarily apply to determining order for very brief periods, or for materials other than events.

explicit temporal overlap exists between target items. Consider how a subject (Helen) might answer the question:

(5)   Which came first, your tennis match with Judy or your tennis match with Lew?

Assuming for the moment that both matches are unique so that each can be identified, and assuming that neither match has a specific date associated with it, then to answer the question requires the study of the interrelationships of the memory structures for the two. Suppose that Helen knows that Judy has been out of the country for two years and that Lew has only been here since last summer. It can be readily inferred that the game with Judy came first.

A single subject may have available a variety of strategies for producing temporal orderings: Explicit temporal tags may be available for some item pairs, whereas overlapping events or sequences may be useful in generating order and explicit dates for other items. When an event is to be dated, the subject may begin working through a sequence of strategies. For example, the subject might first search for an explicit temporal tag. If a date is found, the problem is solved. If no explicit temporal tags are found, then there might be a search for temporally overlapping or coinciding events. If the first overlapping event bears a date tag, then the problem is solved (except for details). If the first overlapping event is not dated, then a person might look for additional details of the target item to help to relate it to the overlapping event; or he might find a second overlapping event that is related either to the target item or to the first overlapping event. A temporally tagged new event solves the problem. If the event has no temporal tag, the search continues for additional details on the target event or for other potentially tagged overlapping events.

The strategies used to determine the relative time of occurrence of two events depends on their mutual relationship. If two events are quite dissimilar, then the strategies used to date them may differ considerably from those used when both events are members of the same general class of events. Consider:

(6)   Which came first, the death of Robert Kennedy or the death of John Kennedy?

Judging the relative times of deaths of these two political figures is quite different from judging the relative times of events that are much less closely related, such as the death of John Kennedy and the awarding of the Academy Award to the motion picture *The Sound of Music*.

EMPIRICAL STUDIES

The task of these studies was to collect evidence about memory for real events in ways that would provide evidence about the representation of events in memory and about the strategies subjects use in answering queries about the events. The problem is not an easy one, and many difficulties occurred with each of the several techniques that I used.

One decision seemed clear: to use a naturalistic data base. The challenge was to find a data base of sufficient richness that I could study memories varying in age over an extremely wide range, without the danger that my subjects would use the artificial types of structures and memory strategies that are common to studies of memory conducted in laboratory settings. Because the hope was to collect data about memories encompassing periods measured in years, the initial attempts were aimed at the study of a person's already-existing knowledge of world events. Accordingly, two different studies were performed. In the first, subjects were asked to judge the relative temporal order of two events, both of which they could remember. This study is entitled *The Which-Came-First? Study*. The second study explored the interrelations between a person's personal experiences and his memory for a well-known event. The subject's task was to recall what he was doing at a specific time. This study is entitled *The What-Were-You-Doing? Study*. Both of these studies were unsuccessful, for reasons that I now describe.

The Which-Came-First? Study

Subjects were asked to think aloud as they ordered pairs of events or provided a specific date corresponding to the time that an event occurred. The events were a list of items selected from an original list of 1000 national headline items from the years 1957–1967. Because the tests were performed in 1972, only the most memorable of the items were retained, providing a pool of the 352 best-remembered items from that 10-year period.

Subjects of different ages, educational backgrounds, and so on differed markedly in the detail with which they remembered items and the extent to which they could date items. The strategies they employed varied from vague feelings to extremely precise strategies for defining exact periods. The variety of these strategies is represented by the four protocols shown in Box 14.1, which come from my interactions with the individual subjects.

BOX 14.1
Protocols from the temporal dating experiment.

Subjects were presented with a newspaper headline and asked to determine when the event described took place. They were asked to think out loud, and their comments were recorded. (Comments that are not part of the protocol are enclosed in square brackets [−] and are *printed in italics*. The experimenter is denoted by E; the subject by S.)

Subject P1
[*This is a 63-year-old subject who insisted she could not date most of the items presented to her and who had to be coaxed into making replies. The headline read:* **Savage killer methodically massacres eight young nurses in their Chicago residence.** *The incident took place on July 14, 1966.*]

S: Yes. I read just the other day where he has been delivered from life sentence . . . uh, they have commuted the life sentence.

E: *How reassuring.*

S: I don't remember the year on that; I remember reading about it all in the paper and what a terrible thing it was. The one nurse was saved, I think she pretended to be dead.

E: *Do you have any guess on what the date is?*

S: No, I haven't.

E: *Can you make a guess, like how. . . .*

S: Well, it's been in the 1960's, I know that.

E: *Could it have been last year [1971]?*

S: Oh, no. It was much further back than that. Maybe 1965.

(continued)

BOX 14.1 (*continued*)

Subject P2
[*This is a highly verbal, very accurate 27-year-old graduate student. The headline read:* **Actress Elizabeth Taylor and Eddie Fisher, singer, marry in Las Vegas, Nevada.** *The incident took place on May 12, 1959.*]

S: Let's see. That was after she . . . that Mike Todd died, which happened while Elizabeth Taylor was making, uh, either *Suddenly Last Summer* or *Butterfield 8*, one of those movies. Let's see, when would she be doing that? That would be after *Around the World in 80 Days* was produced, because Mike Todd produced it and he was alive when he produced it which must mean it was before she married Eddie Fisher. However, she didn't stay . . . , I mean, she practically married Eddie Fisher during her period of mourning or something like that, so it wasn't long after Mike Todd died. When was it . . . when in fact did Mike Todd die? Let's see. She's been married to Richard Burton for a good — ten years, and uh, the whole thing happened when *Cleopatra* was being made, and I remember seeing half of *Cleopatra* at a drive-in in 196-ummm-4, so, I'd say 1961.

E: *1961.*

S: I have no idea what time of year.

Subject P3
[*This subject is a 40-year-old professional (psychologist). The headline read:* **The United States Surgeon General's report scores cigarettes as a major factor in lung disease.** *The report was published on January 11, 1964.*]

S: [*long pause*] I'd say 1960. The reason for that being — as soon as that news came out, Professor A., being a heavy smoker, found it necessary to tell his class why there were certain statistical faults in that report. And I happened to be in his class at that time, and I believe that was 1960.

(*continued*)

BOX 14.1 (continued)

Subject P4
[*This last protocol shows the logical structure of a search by a subject who was willing to describe each step quite explicitly. The headline read:* **Vice President Nixon and Senator Kennedy face each other in first of series of television debates.** *The debate was held on September 26, 1960.*]

S: [*long pause*] Well, I really can't say that I remember—except that I can remember watching them on television. I can remember some of the content of the debates, I can remember reasonably vividly seeing each man, that it was a set debate, and that there was quite a bit of controversy over the format of the debate; ah, I was probably watching the debate with someone else. I don't remember who. I don't even remember the year. Let me try. Uh. I remember going to hear Kennedy at the Coliseum when he was running for the Democratic nomination prior to his being nominated. I remember going with the S's. I think it might have been [*long pause*] somewhere between '56 and '59. I think I could get the year by figuring backwards, but that seems like a ridiculous way to go about doing it [*pause*] Am I sure that I could?

E: *What seems ridiculous about it?*

S: It doesn't seem fair.

E: *That's fine.*

S: Well, since you told me earlier this afternoon that Kennedy was assassinated in November 1963, and that was sometime in his second term, or was it in his first term? [*long pause*] How strange. Who would have run against him? [*long pause*] Well, it seems to me that Eisenhower was elected President somewhere in '52. [*long pause*] How long did he serve? At least two terms. Did he die in office? No. I don't think so. It must have been about '58. [*long pause*] It couldn't have been '58 because elections are in even-numbered years. [*Hence the debates would have preceded that.*] Let's try '57. '57 or '59. Let's suppose that he was elected in '58. Then if he was assassinated in '63 it would have been the beginning of his second term. I think it was. I will say that he was elected in '58. Therefore, these debates could have been in '57. Uh. Now elections are usually in November. Ahh. Now the plot thickens. Let's see. Wait a minute. Now elections occur in November, presidential elections being in even numbered years. Now what is the next presidential election going to be? I should be able to figure backwards from that. This is currently '72 [*February 2, 1972.*] There's certainly not going to be an election in '72. We haven't even had a nominating convention. Could it be in '74? [*incredulous*] '74, that means there must have been one in '70, one in '66, one in '62, and his election must have been in '58; November of '58. But that's toward the end of the year. I would say that these debates probably occurred in 1958 rather than in 1957. Will that do?

The four protocols in the box illustrate the dating of individual items. When the task is to determine the temporal ordering of two events, usually the ordering can be produced much more quickly than is indicated by these protocols, and it is seldom accompanied by much explanation. If an explanation for the ordering of two events is requested, it usually is generated by individual searches for the dates of the two events.

The protocol for subject P4 illustrates an interesting and fairly common observation: The ability of subjects to date items is cyclic. Six months after this protocol was recorded, this subject would have produced a more accurate date because the impending elections would have fixed the election year in a sequence extending back from 1972 rather than 1974. As it was, the assumption that elections occurred in even years (rather than in years divisible by 4) yielded a misleading date. Similar errors are produced by a failure to recall whether it is elections or inaugurations that occur in years divisible by 4.

Three major problems are encountered with these data. First, memory is generally relatively poor (see P1). Even when recall is good, it often seems to be tacked on, as an extraneous afterthought and not intrinsic to the memory base of the individual. Frequently recall followed the form shown in P3. Individuals, however, were generally successful at two tasks. One of these was ordering pairs of events, and the other, an extension of the former task, was the serial ordering of 10 to 15 events.

Second, the rich matrix of associations that the descriptions were to yield, and from which it was hoped we would eventually detect the fabric of long-term recall, did not materialize. For most subjects, and especially for their memory of older items, the network is extremely impoverished. A marked exception to this is shown in P2. There is little overlap among the items (sometimes several hundred familiar ones) about which the subject was tested. Perhaps newspaper headlines are simply too broad a domain, both in scope and duration, for such a network to be possible.

Third, the course of change in recall cannot be mapped. There are potentially many differences between a 5-year-old item, a 10-year-old item and a 15-year-old item. It is impossible to tell whether differences in recall of two items are due to an item's age, its importance, or encoding differences. A final problem is that the experiment could not be run on subjects younger than 25 or 30 years of age. Unless they had learned about the incidents at some later time, younger persons had virtually no information about news items from the earliest periods — that is, about events that had occurred before they were 13 to 15 years of age.

The What-Were-You-Doing? Study

The second preliminary study attempted to guarantee a rich memory network by ensuring that at least one of the events being tested was richly encoded. The prototypic question was:

(7)   What were you doing when John Kennedy was assassinated?

The subjects were told that, for most people, a period preceding or following the assassination would stand out in memory from the background of dimly remembered events. The subjects were instructed to examine the highlighted sequence and to describe the events from it. They were to date the event and to describe it in as much detail as possible.

The early results were reassuring. The protocols were rich and complex:

(8)   It was the twenty-second of November, 1963. And at the time I was in Dallas, Texas. Before it happened, the preface to it, I was marching in a band up and down the playing field when this person came and shouted to the person who was overseeing this operation that Kennedy had in fact been killed. Now just after that happened there were all sorts of wild things, wild rumors flying around. . . . The time of day would have been about 1:25. As a matter of fact somewhere between 1:15 and 1:45. Well, that's when I remember hearing about it so I would suppose I might have been delayed as much as an hour or two in hearing it. It could have happened, I would say, as early as 11:00, although I don't remember exactly. . . .

Obviously, the event was well encoded. The test could be used on fairly young adults because persons as young as 10 or 12 years of age at the time of the assassination could recall related events clearly.

The first disadvantage of this method is the reliance on very few target events and the absence of equivalent events to be studied. With very few exceptions, the well-remembered event is idiosyncratic to the individual. The second disadvantage is that the study of particular events leaves unanswered the question of what happens to recall for less thoroughly encoded and rehearsed events.

This effort ended in dismal failure, however, when I performed the experiment on someone whom I had known well at the time of the assassination.

(9)   When I'm reminded of that date, particularly by you, I remember that you were the one who told me about the assassination, or at least that's

the way I remember it. . . . I believe that you, I *know* that you came down and told me about what you . . . had heard on the news. I don't know what time it was. Because down in the hole in F———— Hall one tended to lose track of time. . . . I had been working for some extended period of time and I was very much concentrating on what I was doing when I was interrupted by you having heard something about it. You said, I'm sure it was you who said, "The President has been assassinated, or shot—shot." And I probably looked up and said, "What?" and you said, "Kennedy, he's been shot." And I said, "What do you mean? Where?" and you said you didn't know. . . .

The problem with this method is revealed in a dramatic fashion. Because I am one of the participants described in the recall, I can provide a check on its veracity. The protocol is not correct: I was not present. Of course, one does not immediately know whether it is not simply my recollection that is wrong. However, examination of a variety of documentable external events demonstrates that the two of us could not then have been at the same place. In short, the events described in great detail, and with great emotion and conviction, *could not have happened*, at least not in the form described, or at least not with the putative cast of characters.

This exploration illustrates again the lesson that has been learned repeatedly since the last century: The researcher must know (or perhaps control) the details of events being remembered. It is the only way to judge the accuracy of the recall.

THE TAKE-TWO-ITEMS-A-DAY-FOR-FIVE-YEARS STUDY

To study very long-term natural memory it would seem necessary to collect items from an individual over a period of five years or so, and provide systematic tests. The individual must be someone with whom the experimenter has relatively constant access. It must be someone who will still be there in five years. Finally, it must be someone willing to make a fairly substantial investment of time over this extended period. Most people are eliminated by one or the other of these requirements. Only one natural choice for a subject remains: the experimenter. The decision to perform the study on oneself meets all of the demands but creates additional problems. One aspect of the difficulty is expressed in Crovitz' (1970) comment on Pearson's lament: "While Galton had broken new ground . . . , nobody among English psychologists had carried the work forward. Pearson supposed the reason might be that *it is easier to experiment with another person's mind than with one's own*" [p. 23, *emphasis added*]. A different aspect is perhaps best summed up by a comment by a colleague who remarked, upon hearing the details of the study: "Had you persuaded someone to serve as the subject in the experiment I would have described it as ingenious. Your plan to serve as the subject yourself leaves me speechless."

A Description of the Study

A Brief Summary.   Three major classes of tasks are involved. First, events must be recorded. Second, events must be scheduled for test. Third, events must be tested. I begin by describing the procedures, and then discuss the difficulties with them in a later section.

Each evening I write down a short description (up to 3 typed lines) of 2 or 3 events that have occurred during the day. The events are typed onto separate 4 in by 6 in (10 cm by 15 cm) white filing cards. On the reverse of each card the date of the event is listed, and the event is rated on a number of different scales (to be described). At the end of each month, I collect cards from that month, shuffle them thoroughly, and code each with a quasi-randomly selected number. The cards are nonsystematically sorted into 14 groups for testing during the next 3 years.

On the first day of each month, the accumulated cards from previous months are tested. After a recall exercise, designed to minimize warm-up effects, the descriptions on two randomly paired cards are turned up simultaneously, and I attempt to determine which of the two exposed events occurred first. Then, in turn, I attempt to determine the absolute date of occurrence of each of the two events. The dates and the times taken to reach a decision are recorded. Finally, the cards are rated on scales similar to those on which they were originally rated, and the types of strategies used for the dating tasks are recorded by categorizing them into one of several possibilities. Two typical cards are shown in Figure 14.1. (These are actual event cards. Card 2941 was discarded because of failure to recall the item. Card 2227 was discarded because of failure to discriminate the item from others.)

Recording the Events.   An event is defined by my (*American Heritage*) dictionary as "an occurrence, incident, or experience, especially one of some significance." A good deal of intuition is used to guide the selection. Additional constraints are added: Because an event is often not recorded until 24 or more hours after it has occurred,

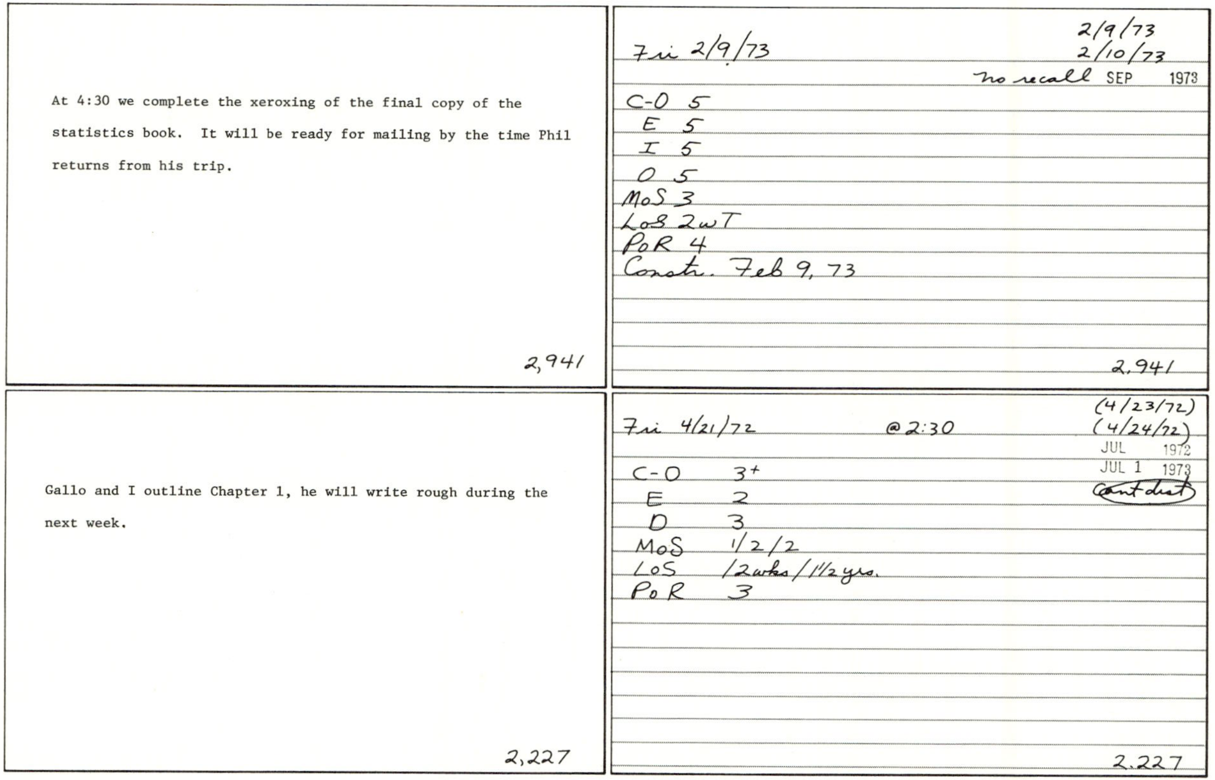

At 4:30 we complete the xeroxing of the final copy of the

statistics book. It will be ready for mailing by the time Phil

returns from his trip.

2,941

Gallo and I outline Chapter 1, he will write rough during the

next week.

2,227

Fri 2/9/73

C-O 5
E 5
I 5
O 5
MoS 3
LoB 2wT
PoR 4
Constr. Feb 9, 73

2/9/73
2/10/73
No recall SEP 1973

2,941

Fri 4/21/72   @2:30

C-O 3+
E 2
D 3
MoS 1/2/2
LoS 12wks/1½yrs
PoR 3

(4/23/72)
(4/24/72)
JUL 1972
JUL 1 1973
Conduct

2,227

FIGURE 14.1

Two different event cards. The event is described and a randomly assigned event number is written on the front of each card (the left half of the figure). The date of the event and the initial ratings are written on the back of each card (the right half of the figure). The dates of testing are shown in the upper right corner of the back of the cards. Once the card is written, an event and its number are never viewed together. The randomly assigned event numbers permit the date and the ratings to be retrieved blindly in order to be coordinated with the event. (These are real event cards that were discarded because of failure to recall or to discriminate the items: see text.)

some natural selection has already taken place in my memory for the day's occurrences. An event must not be confusable with other events or items I remember at the time I write it. However, if some items become confused as subsequent similar events occur, these later confusions are legitimate. In addition, the description of an item cannot exceed three 82-character lines. The style in which events are recorded varies greatly: Some are expressed in complete and literary sentences, others are presented in telegraphic form. Such unconstrained (natural) variation has existed from the beginning of the study.

At the end of every day (or as soon thereafter as possible), I record a set of items or events that have occurred during the last 24-hour period. During the first 4 or 5 months of the study, at least 5 items were recorded each day. (The number often ran to 10.) Because it was not feasible to test so many items, only 2 or 3 items were recorded each day during the subsequent months of the experiment.

Rating the Events.   After the event described has been typed on a card, the card is turned over. The day, date, and hour of the event are recorded, as well as the date on which the card was prepared. Then, the event is rated according to each of 7 different categories: confusability-distinguishability, emotionality, importance, datability, member of sequence, length of sequence, and probability of rehearsal. (The same ratings are also obtained each time an item is tested.) Examples of how ratings are recorded can be seen on the back view of the cards as shown in Figure 14.1. All ratings (except the sequence ratings) are on a 5-point scale.

- *Confusability-Distinguishability (C-D)* This scale rates how clearly I believe the item can be distinguished from others presently remembered. The most distinctive events receive a rating of 5. Events that would be completely confused with others would receive a scale value of one, except that such nondistinguishable items do not get encoded in the first place. Hence, for this category, initial ratings run from 2 through 5.

- *Emotionality (E)* Considerable emotionality (delight, shame, pleasure, fear, happiness, agony) earns a rating of 5. Essentially no emotionality is indicated by one. Items for which there is little felt emotionality but at which one's psychiatrist would raise an eyebrow ("Come now, you felt *nothing* when this happened?") are tagged separately.

- *Importance (I)* Importance is rated most often in terms of perceived steps toward life goals, both personal and professional. In general, final outcomes tend to be rated as more important than intermediate steps.

- *Datability (D)* This scale signifies my estimation of how well I will later be able to determine the date of the item.

- *Member of a Sequence (MOS)* This indicates whether the event is thought to be at the beginning (1), at the end (3), or in the middle (2) of some identifiable sequence. An item that is not a member of a sequence receives no rating.

- *Length of the Sequence (LOS)* If the item is seen as a member of a sequence, the length of the sequence is indicated.

- *Probability of Rehearsal (POR)*   How probable is it that I will rehearse or be reminded of the event? If it is virtually certain that the event will be thought of (often), the item is rated 5; if it is certain that I will not think about the event, or have not thought about the event, the item is rated 1.

When Events Are Tested.   At the end of each month, all events written that month are assembled and each card is assigned a number selected by means of a quasi-random procedure. The content of the card is hidden from view as I write the identification number in the bottom right corner of both sides of the card. All numbers are 4 or 5 digits between 0,001 and 19,999. Cards are shuffled thoroughly before assignment of numbers. Following their code assignment the cards are thoroughly reshuffled and haphazardly sorted into 14 sets, with approximately equal numbers of cards in each pile. Twelve sets are randomly assigned to each of the following 12 months for testing; the remaining 2 sets are held for testing 2 and 3 years later.

Each month, after items have been tested, the backs of the cards are stamped with the test date, and the cards are thoroughly shuffled and sorted into 17 sets. The sets are again nonsystematically assigned for their next testing to each of the following 13 months and to the second, third, fourth, and fifth years.

All events are tested on the first day of the assigned month, or on the closest preceding or subsequent day in the case of schedule conflicts. Occasionally, when it is impossible to complete the testing on a single day, it extends into a second day.

Test of the Items.   The test includes the following steps. Before the ordering task begins, events for the preceding year are recorded in a free recall procedure. There are no more specific instructions. My impression is that the strategies for recall and the particular events recalled fluctuate from month to month. (These data have never been examined.) Although this preliminary recall may yield some interesting results in its own right, the procedure was designed primarily to provide a reasonably substantial warm-up period for the task that follows. This should reduce the differential accessibility of the memory network that would otherwise be expected as increased numbers of events are recalled during the test.[2] The free recall warm-up procedure may take as long as 30 minutes, but it usually requires less time.

The items for the test month are thoroughly shuffled, separated into two numerically equal stacks, thoroughly shuffled again, and then placed face up (but covered) on the desk. I have a calendar that shows the days and dates from the beginning of the study to the present, but contains no additional information. (Holidays and other events are not shown.) Stop watches are used for timing recall.

The code numbers of the items (visible at the bottom of the cards) are recorded on the data sheet, the items themselves are then exposed, and timing begins. A stop watch runs until the order of the two events is determined; then a second stop watch is immediately started and I attempt to determine the exact date of the left-hand item. Immediately after that, I date the right-hand item. Times for the ordering and dating are recorded.[3]

For each pair of items, I determine whether the two events are from the same domain, and whether they are sequentially related. (The two events illustrated in Figure 14.1, "outline Chapter 1" and "xeroxing of the final copy of the . . . book," are sequentially related.) Then, I try to determine just what strategy has been used to do the dating. The possible categories are that

- The date was known.

- An approximate period was known.

- I counted time:
  backward from the present ("three weeks ago").
  backward from some known date ("three weeks before Easter").
  forward from some known date ("three weeks after Easter").

- I guessed.

---

[2]Since I process items for many hours on a test day, a reasonable concern was that some systematic error might occur over any particular test period. It was to help ensure relatively stable performance throughout the test procedure that free recall preceding the test was deliberately instituted. An examination of the average error over the course of the testing shows it to be stable. There are apparently no major effects that consistently occur during the course of the test.

[3]Initially I was concerned that I would be processing and dating the second item while I was dating the first. Although the argument may be made that ordering the items involves a search that overlaps with the dating, the introspective impression is that the search for the first date is sufficiently active that all thoughts of the second item disappear. A common experience is that when a date has been found for the first item, the second item is no longer remembered and it must be reread.

Which of these 6 categories was used is recorded, but specific details of the search are not.

Finally, each item is rated according to the same 7 dimensions that were used in the original construction of the item: confusability-distinguishability, emotionality, importance, datability, member of a sequence, length of the sequence, and probability of rehearsal. In addition, a set of dates is recorded that marks the earliest and most recent dates that the item could possibly have occurred.

It takes approximately 3 minutes to record the information for each item, or about 6 minutes for each pair. (The time varies markedly with time of day and is substantially greater for morning than for afternoon or evening.) The number of items tested in any month has ranged over the course of the experiment from 92 (the first month) to 215 (the third month). This rapid and unmanageable increase to more than 200 items demanded a modification in the method of allocating items to test, and in the number of items to be written each day. Items were distributed over longer and longer periods so that the mean time between viewing items increased from 2½ months to about 6½ months. With the present method of allocating events (described in a preceding section), the number of items stabilized at slightly more than 100 items at 10 months, and has gradually increased to about 175 at 20 months.

If an item cannot be recalled, or if it cannot be distinguished from another (that is, it might refer to two or more events in memory), the item is tagged "no recall" or "can't distinguish," and it is removed from the file. (The cards shown in Figure 14.1 were removed in this way.) Initially, it was intended that items must fail to be recalled twice before being permanently retired from the file. Because of the demands of the experiment, this desirable feature has not been consistently implemented. It is difficult to distinguish whether an event is remembered or whether I know only that the event must have occurred (for example, because it is a logical step in a series of events). An item in this category is specially coded. Because of the expected low reliability of this rating, however, these items, duly coded, remain in the file.

Difficulties with the Procedure

Problems Relating to the Definition of an Event.   One of the most difficult problems encountered in the study is the number and kind of details permitted to specify any single event. If too much detail is included, at test the event may be completely localizable temporally for irrelevant reasons. If too little detail is included in the description of the event, it is not possible to distinguish it from a variety of similar events in the domain. To take a specific example,

(10)   I had coffee with Jeff.

is an inadequate item because there are a number of occasions on which I have had coffee with Jeff. The item

(11)   I had coffee with Jeff and we talked about his research.

may or may not specify the event more closely, depending on the number of times drinking coffee with Jeff is accompanied by discussing his research. However, consider the item

(12)   I had coffee with Jeff before his colloquium presentation and we talked about his research.

With this last item I may well be searching, not for the memory of the event of drinking coffee, but for the temporal location of Jeff's colloquium. In one sense, this is not a significant problem, and for my definition of event, either item is perfectly legitimate. Moreover, it is possible that the end of statement 11 contains this same information: Jeff and I may very well have discussed his research only before his colloquium.

Problems Relating to the Choice of Events.   A frequent criticism is that the exclusion of "nonevents" from the study precludes the possibility of estimating the probability of a real event being correctly identified as real. Were this a standard recognition task, the exclusion of nonevents would make it a very strange task. (All items are "old.") For this study, the "nonevent" criticism is not critical: I am measuring accuracy in the dating and ordering of items; I am not studying recognition memory.

The present procedure is, in fact, an extremely conservative one. It assures that all items that I think I remember are dated and ordered. Only items not remembered at all, or ones that are not distinct from other items, are removed from the pool. Frequently "recalled" items include elements I do not remember: I find myself asking, "Is that with whom I saw the movie?" "Is that who drove me to the airport?" Such items might well be eliminated by the imposition of a stricter criterion requiring me to be certain of all the features of an item. The effect of a stricter cut-off point would be to improve the apparent accuracy of my performance. In other words, if a decision had to be made as to whether an item was genuine, and all confused items were removed, many of the items with which I had greatest difficulty would be removed, leading to greater mean accuracy and lower variability.

There are enormous difficulties in introducing nonevents into the data pool. Who should write the nonevents? It has been argued that when I devise a nonevent, it enters my memory in a way similar to entry by a "real event." Although this position may be extreme, a legitimate question may be asked about what constitutes a reasonable nonevent. Let us suppose that

(13)   I took the Volvo in for the 50,000-mile checkup.

is an event.

(14)   I took the Porsche in for the 50,000-mile checkup.

certainly does not comprise a reasonable nonevent because I know I do not have a Porsche: I can always distinguish the nonevent from a real event.

(15)   I took the Volvo in for the 100,000-mile checkup.

is a nonevent today, but may become an event during the course of the study. Other permutations could be generated by the person tested. For example,

(16)   John drove me to pick up the Volvo after its 50,000-mile checkup.

might be a nonevent that becomes confusable with real events with the passage of time. Perhaps a separate procedure for testing probability of recognition or recall for detail should be established. Events that vary in the critical details may be generated and tested without involving the elaborate mechanisms of this already cumbersome study.

Results

General Comments. During the first 20 months of the study, 2003 items were written and a total of 3006 items were tested (1538 new items and 1468 retests). Originally, it had been assumed that events (items) would be eliminated from the study rather rapidly because of recall failure. On the basis of that assumption, tests were arranged so that most items were first tested soon after their occurrence (half of all items were tested in the first month), with the probability that any given item would be tested diminishing over time. This assumption was wrong. Because events need only be recognized, and because the dating is a kind of cued recall task, forgetting of the events was much less rapid than had been expected. During the first 10 months of the study, a total of 8 items failed to be recognized and were dropped from the pool. During the second 10 months an additional 90 items were lost. The temporal distribution of these items from the 20-month period is unsurprising: 80 percent of them are from the earliest 6 months of the study, 20 percent from the second 6 months, and none from the 8 most recent months.

An examination of the items removed from the pool because they were not recalled shows a few surprises, but it is clear that most of the forgotten events should have been forgotten, either because they were insignificant events, or because in those first few months of the study I had a tendency to include events of too repetitive a nature. Here is a typical example of an item that was discarded for this reason:

> **Item 8,455**   After two sets in which J. L. and I beat J. B. and
> E. A., E. A. and I team against J. L. and J. B. and
> beat them 7–5. Very surprising. We led all the way.

This is a prototype of the kind of item that should be forgotten. It is highly confusable with other similar items. It was not remembered on its first test 2 months later. Since year after year finds me playing tennis several times a week, most often with the same people, forgetting this particular sequence, even after such a short period, creates no surprise.

Another aspect of forgotten events is illustrated by the first item from Figure 14.1:

> **Item 2,941**   At 4:30 we complete the xeroxing of the final copy
> of the statistics book. It will be ready for mailing by
> the time Phil returns from his trip.

This item refers to completion of the copying of the manuscript for my book *The Practical Statistician*. It was given high discriminability and emotionality ratings; yet 7 months later, on the first test date, it was not remembered. This seems surprising. I can reconstruct what must have happened from the date and the description. The manuscript was 750 pages long, so it must have taken 5 or 6 hours to copy. It is rated as being a big event: I can almost recapture the feeling of exhilaration: finally finishing the manuscript! But manuscripts are unexpectedly returned for revision, and judging from the date, this "final" completion was the second of four such events of finishing, copying, and sending off the manuscript during the course of a 12-month period. At the time it was recorded, this item was rated as the end of a sequence (MOS = 3). Presumably, I meant the end of the sequence of "preparing the manuscript." One's intuition is that important terminal events in sequences should be well remembered, but in this case, what was thought to be an important *terminal* event did not remain one.

Error Probabilities and Response Times.   In this section I present the quantitative analysis of the results obtained during the first 20 months of the study. Since most items are retested, data associated with a single event may contribute to a number of different points in a figure or may even contribute more than once to the same point. At the moment, these results are inconclusive, but they do suggest trends. It will take several more years before sufficient data are available to produce stable results from these analyses.

Figure 14.2 shows the percentage of errors made in judging the temporal order of two critical events as joint functions of the number

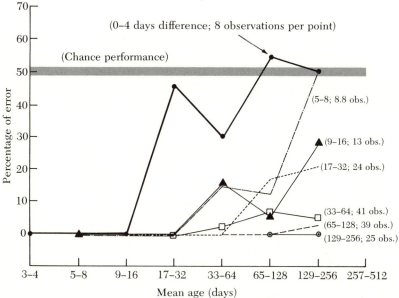

FIGURE 14.2
Percentage of sequencing error (the probability that two events are incorrectly ordered) increases from zero when the item is very young to 50 at some later time. Event pairs that are separated by only a few days become temporally confused more quickly than do event pairs that are separated by longer periods.

of days that had elapsed between the two events and the mean age of the two items. The expected outcome was that there would be a graceful series of curves, rising from zero errors when the items were young to chance performance (50 percent errors) when they were old. Curves for event pairs separated by only a few days should become temporally confused at a younger age than event pairs separated by months or years. Although some of these curves are based on relatively few items, this general shape seems consistent with the expectations. The figure shows that if the 2 events that are being compared occur fewer than 4 days apart, chance performance is reached around a mean age of 65 to 128 days. Items separated by 5 to 8 days can be ordered at better than chance level until the mean age of the items reaches 129 to 256 days, or about 4 to 9 months. All of the curves are based on relatively little data and are highly irregular.

Figure 14.3 indicates the time it took to determine which of two test items came first as a joint function of the age of the paired items and the age differences for paired members. These curves include both correctly and incorrectly ordered pairs. The curves generally suggest an increase and then a decrease in sequencing time as age increases for each family of pairs. For items differing in age by 5 to 32 days (consider the three curves together), there is a suggestion that the time required to determine their sequence is greater when the mean item ages are between 33 and 64 days. (The ages of the younger items range between 17 and 62 days, although most of them are between 30 and 48 days.) The apparent decrease in sequencing time for older items may simply reflect the fact that the search ends quickly if it is clear that ordering is not possible. For recent items it is quite reasonable that ordering should be rapid. For older items it may be possible to determine quite rapidly that information for making a reasonable decision is not available. Only for intermediate items would more time be necessary, either to finally determine an order, or to decide that sufficient data for such a decision are not available.

Figure 14.4 shows the average error made in estimating the dates of the items. The curve for absolute error ignores the direction of the error and indicates only size of error. Examination of this curve indicates that estimates are excellent for items less than 16 days of age. (Errors average less than one day.) Poorest estimates occur when the items are 4 to 8 months old. (Average error is about 12 days.) Although the absolute error increases with the age of the item, the percentage error in dating is relatively constant.[4]

---

[4]The drop in the curve at the end should not be taken seriously since it is probably the result of constraints imposed by the temporal limits of the study, possibly in combination with the overlearning associated with the early events in the study. (This last factor will be discussed later in this chapter.)

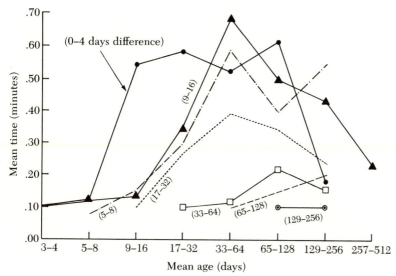

FIGURE 14.3

The mean time to sequence events (in minutes) is short when item pairs are young. The time increases and then decreases again as items become older. These curves suggest that, when age of the pairs to be sequenced is constant, less time is required to order event pairs separated by long intervals than to order those separated by short intervals.

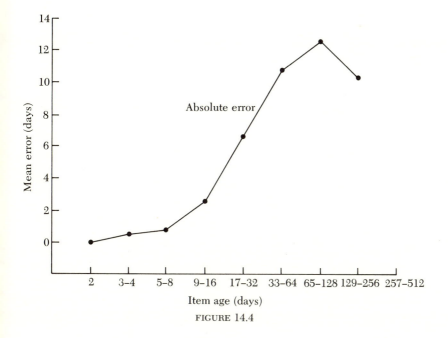

FIGURE 14.4

Figure 14.5 shows that as the number of tests of an item increases, the amount of time required to date the item decreases. Since each new test of the same item must necessarily test an older item, and since the previous figures have indicated that age of items is not monotonically related to dating time, this finding cannot result simply from the age of the item but must be due to some other factor. A number of possibilities come readily to mind. First, there is the *selective item hypothesis*: Only a few well-remembered items remain in the pool sufficiently long to survive six tests, and dating of these select items is easier. Second, there is the *rehearsal hypothesis*: The earlier tests are also "learning" trials. This hypothesis suggests that I simply remember the information by which I determined a date previously; either I receive practice on particular strategies for retrieving the appropriate information on these items, or I remember the particular outcome (the date) from these earlier retrievals. It is likely that these often-tested items came from the earliest months of the study, and as I shall indicate later in the chapter, these first few months may be subject to some unique problems. An analysis that examines both age and number of tests may clarify the factors involved, but it must await the collection of more data.

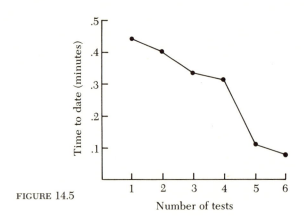

FIGURE 14.5

Protocols

Perhaps the most interesting aspects of the study are the strategies and techniques performed in reconstructing the events. To illustrate these, I collected a few protocols as I tried to recollect some of the events. This procedure has its dangers, for the attempt to probe my own strategies too deeply might bias future collection of data, especially for the particular items for which I happened to collect protocols. Therefore, protocol collection has been extremely limited, and the major reason for collecting this set was to provide some data on strategies and other aspects of the recall process for inclusion in this chapter.

The protocols were obtained by typing my thoughts as I tried to date the individual items. This task is ordinarily performed after I have attempted to order the two items that were selected for test. Here is one of those protocols.

Item 6,096   Dedre Gentner gives her presentation in Norman's research seminar on the semantic treatment of verbs.

[This event actually occurred on May 1, 1972. The protocol was recorded on February 3, 1974.]

> Fairly late in spring semester, 1972. Everyone was to have their papers ready for presentation sometime much earlier—perhaps April 3. I kept referring to it as the April 1 deadline although I knew it was somewhat after that. Dedre was perhaps the first person who did give her paper, or was it Steve Palmer? Could have been as late as June 1 because things were pretty well over for the summer by then. (Absolutely no recall for the event itself. I can, of course, remember that a number of people gave talks, and I can remember Dedre giving a talk. Perhaps can even recall her talking about verbs.) What might she have said? Do remember the session in which we heard the folk story and then tried to recall it. That was probably Kris's or Adele's. Of course, it might have been Dedre. But what would that have had to do with verbs? I know she was working with Steve on the project, but I don't think that they gave the presentation together. This was after the verbs of motion lecture by Fillmore. The meetings were held on Wednesday? Let's pick April 26, 1972. [*There were nine possible Wednesdays to choose among.*]

The time required to complete this protocol was 7 minutes, 52 seconds. A number of major markers can be identified. First, there was the putative April 1, 1972 deadline for the paper. That deadline was violated so radically that it became a standing joke to ask people, in April, or even May, if they had finished their April 1 paper yet. So the talk could not have been before the deadline. But the quarter ended on June 1, so it could not have been after that. Frank Restle had visited for a series of colloquia and seminars between April 10 and April 12, so it could not have been then. It could not have been May 3, since I was not there that week.

These factors illustrate the problem-solving nature of the recall. In this case, it was to no avail. Although the item was dated with reasonable accuracy, it was marked as NO RECALL. In most cases, recall is dependent on finding a set of reliable markers in memory and on drawing inferences from these. The nature of these markers is difficult to specify. The simplest case involves identifying an important dated event, and then providing a date for the target event by reasoning from the marker. But I suspect that I am equally likely to reason from other kinds of quite different "markers," such as affective tone, and from a global sense of the age of the event. Such qualities as the "good feeling" I had and the recency of the event seem more akin to independently retrievable attributes of the memory itself than to the "independent event" markers suggested by the simple case.

The amount of time required to produce a date and the accuracy of the date itself are not always an adequate measure of the quality of the mental activity that has gone on. A rigorous set, combined with a high internal demand for accuracy, produces fairly long times, and occasionally improved dating. This set requires that every possible lead be followed before the date is finally determined. A less rigorous set produces a date more rapidly. In one protocol, a date is produced in 80 seconds; the next 4 minutes produce a variety of information, but no improvement in the date.

REFLECTIONS ON THE STUDY OF MEMORY

"It *is* easier to experiment with another person's mind than with one's own." I must confess that after research first on rats and later on introductory psychology students, I looked forward to working with a completely tractable subject, one who would come on time, and who would be motivated and consistent. This impression simply is not true. I am frequently intractable, resentful, and distractable, especially as a long test day drags on. To be sure, I have never forgotten to arrive for a major test, but on some days I forget to enter my "two items a day." The experimenter/subject, just like all other subjects, would prefer fewer items, shorter tests, or both.

Probably the question I am asked most often concerns the effect of the study on my way of encoding materials. "Don't you spend considerable time thinking about encoding strategies and rehearsing materials?" "Isn't the data overload from all of this material going to create problems in your memory?" My impression is that, except when I am discussing the experiment scientifically, I spend little time thinking about the items in the pool. In fact, I frequently have to check whether I have written yesterday's items. (This involves a glance at the date of the last entry, not at the item itself.)

Are peculiar items selected for the pool? Although there are probably characteristic types of items that I prefer, in general a fairly broad range of items is included. As I indicated earlier, a serious attempt is being made to include items of different types, with a special effort to include items that lack distinct temporal cues.

Am I being trained to date items? There are several answers to that question. First, people probably differ in the amount of ordering and dating that they do spontaneously. I would guess that my spontaneous (prestudy) rate was fairly high. I feel comfortable asking and answering questions about when things happened. Other people may do this less, or even not at all. Imposing such a study on someone whose style it did not complement would probably produce changes in their method of processing. I suspect it has affected my basic approach very little. However, serving in the study has probably changed some features of my recall. Finding dated, important, and stable items makes it easy to date other items. Once these tagged items are found, they do receive considerable practice during the course of the study. For a teacher, the beginning of school is always a significant marker. I have probably always known approximately when the school year began. My recall is probably much more precise now because, in any test during the year, I am likely to use this information in dating other items.

Has performance improved over time? In studies on learning, one expects either improvement in performance (learning the task) or impaired performance (interference, motivational decrements). It is not clear whether either of these has occurred. I suspect, however, that a peculiarity of the study has produced permanently elevated recall of the first months of the study relative to the intermediate months. At first this appeared to be simply another example of the serial position effect. The first items entered into the pool were simply more salient and, of course, later recall of them was better. At least one additional factor is probably involved. At the end of the first month I tested 92 items, all of them from a single month. The month was fresh in my mind, and my estimates were extremely accurate. Significantly, however, I had repeated opportunities to look at the month. I was able to organize the month in my mind and to rehearse the sequential relationship of the events. For most other months I tested a maximum of 10 items. Performance on these recent items was good, but the smaller number involved does not encourage organizing and integrating any of these months in the same way that I did the first one. The first month is also peculiar because it has an anchor point: It is impossible for any items to be dated earlier.

As the experiment continues, the item pool should increasingly represent the total range of my memory contents. Some few events should stand out as vivid markers by which other events are located. Other less salient events, if they are similar, should be assimilated and become indistinguishable. I should be able to explore, within the context of this study, the phenomenon described by William James in 1890:

> the foreshortening of the years as we grow older is due to the monotony of memory's content, and the consequent simplification of the backward-glancing view. In youth we may have an absolutely new experience, subjective or objective, every hour of the day. Apprehension is vivid, retentiveness strong, and our recollections . . . are of something intricate, multitudinous, and long-drawn-out. But as each passing year converts some of this experience into automatic routine which we hardly note at all, the days and the weeks smooth themselves out in recollection to contentless units, and the years grow hollow and collapse [p. 625].

Epilogue

In this book we have presented the results of our explorations into the problems of cognition. Starting with a single basic philosophy about the nature of human memory and the representation of the information contained within it, we have explored the implications of our views for a reasonably wide variety of areas. The work reported here is but the beginning; there is still much to be done. Our main accomplishment has been to create an analytical tool with which to approach the study of the problems of cognition. Many of the chapters in this book point to the significant areas in which we will be working in the future. Many chapters point out the obvious advantages and strengths of our approach as well as the obvious problems and weaknesses.[1]

One of the more important aspects of our research effort has been an emphasis on broad generality. It has been of critical importance that we be able to understand a wide variety of cognitive phenomena within a single theoretical framework. This demand for consistency in our approach has imposed a severe test upon our developing theory, for it has required that the procedures developed for one problem be the same as or compatible with the procedures developed for another. The construction of a computer simulation model acted as a further check on our ideas, forcing us to be honest in the claims that we made for each new development. The computer was used for a variety of

---

[1] For example, despite the fact that there are two chapters in this book that deal with different aspects of question answering, none even addresses the problems raised by Norman (1973), let alone suggests how they might be solved. To be able to answer questions in an intelligent fashion, it is important to consider both the intent and the knowledge of the questioner. To do this properly is not easy. It requires understanding of the mechanisms that underlie the conversational postulates discussed in Chapter 3. It also requires that the answerer of the questions have a model of the knowledge structure of the asker. This problem has not yet been dealt with here for obvious reasons: It is still beyond our understanding. Clearly, then, here is one area that seems ripe for future research.

purposes (compare the analysis of verbs of Chapter 8 with the game-playing routines of Chapter 12 and the analysis of question-answering processes in Chapter 13). This forced us to make good our claim that we were indeed studying general cognitive processes, processes that applied to a wide variety of cognitive skills and that were not limited to, say, linguistic analysis.

The work goes on. At the time of the completion of this book, several new developments were under way, all directly resulting from the work described here, but all too new to be included. These developments have resulted from the study of two different aspects of cognition: first, the organization of higher-level conceptual units; second, the processing structure that underlies human cognitive processes.

HIGHER-ORDER CONCEPTUAL UNITS: SCHEMATA

One recent active effort on the part of the LNR research group has been to develop our understanding of higher-order conceptual units, units of knowledge that are larger than the structures for verbs we have been studying. We are interested in ways to characterize the structure of stories, the structure of the knowledge of large, complex topic matters, and, in general, the structure of knowledge and experiences that encompass a wider range than the relatively simple sentences, visual scenes, and problem-solving episodes that we have examined in this book.

Schemata

We have examined the manner by which one might organize material into *functional schemata*. We define a *schema* to be a framework that interrelates the different aspects of a body of knowledge. It is indexed by the features and functions of the knowledge that it includes. It can be examined, modified, and applied to new situations.

In this book, we have presented several different examples of the organization of material into schemalike structures. The entire conceptual framework for our analysis of language is one form of schema. Thus, the way in which a *causal* verb is represented, in terms of the underlying structures of its primitive components of **DO**, **CAUSE**, and **CHANGE**, provides a basic framework (schema) to organize the structure of the information that is acquired about the event under consideration. In Chapter 8, David Rumelhart and James Levin show

how such structures are constructed and then used in the acquisition and retrieval of knowledge. In Chapter 9, Dedre Gentner shows how a child acquires these structures, and she illustrates that their acquisition requires the learning of linguistic concepts as well as general social skills and concepts. Gentner shows that a child may require up to five years to build up the appropriate schemata for the acquisition of the linguistic and social aspects of "buying," and "selling."

In Chapter 11, Stephen Palmer shows that "world knowledge" plays an important role in the analysis of visual scenes, and he presents several examples for the representation of the schemata that might underlie the visual perception of objects in the world. Finally, Marc Eisenstadt and Yaakov Kareev (in Chapter 12) discuss the learning of and application of schemata for perception and decision making.

These studies take place simultaneously with a reasonably large number of similar studies that are being conducted by other research groups. In psychology, much of classical learning theory has been concerned with problems related to these issues. Piaget and Bartlett have long been concerned with the organization of a person's knowledge into schemata, and in fact, we have borrowed that term from them (see, for example, Bartlett, 1932; and Piaget, 1955). More recently, workers in the fields of both artificial intelligence and psychology have shown a growing interest in the problems of representing higher-level conceptual information. Abelson (1973) talks about the structures for representing interpersonal relations. Minsky (in press) discusses the concept of *frames* as an organizing principle. A number of different papers concerned with these issues are included in the book edited by Bobrow and Collins (in press). Rumelhart's chapter in that book provides the outline for the representation of stories by means of schemata (Rumelhart, in press).

Learning and Teaching

Many of the issues that have been discussed in this book are intimately related to problems that arise in the study of learning and teaching; indeed, one current activity of our group is the study of these problems. For example, there are the problems of memory structure and of maintaining communication between teacher and student. In a paper presented at the Tenth Carnegie-Mellon Symposium on Cognition, Norman, Gentner, and Stevens (in press) discuss the beginning of an experimental and theoretical program to determine how the concepts that have been developed in the course of the research reported here might bear upon issues in education. In particular, they are interested in two problems: first, the communication of an appropriate representational structure to the student, a problem that is related to the issue of reference and the discussion of conversational postulates in Chapter 3; second, the development of organizing schemata by students who are attempting to learn a complex new topic. (The student's use of a schema can both aid and hinder the acquisition of the new material.) It is our belief that the ideas that have been developed in this book will be of fundamental importance to the development of a cognitive theory of learning.

PROCESSING STRUCTURES

In this book we have emphasized the representation of knowledge, and not the processing. There are exceptions to this statement. Our discussions of the memory model (especially in Chapter 7) are intimately concerned with processing structures, as is Ronald Kaplan's discussion (Chapter 5). Stephen Palmer (in Chapter 11) and Marc Eisenstadt and Yaakov Kareev (in Chapter 12) explicitly discuss the role of the underlying processes in determining the end results of the analyses they were studying. Despite these discussions, the processing structure has not been of primary interest to our group during the progress of the work reported here.

The study of processing structure cannot really be separated from the study of representational structure. Thus, the schemata and frames that are currently under active discussion in many different research centers are all intimately tied to the underlying processes and their control structures (see Winograd, in press, for a discussion of this issue). Norman and Bobrow (1975) have explored some of the implications of processing structures for cognitive systems. One of their ideas is that it is fruitful to distinguish between processes whose quality of output is limited by the quality of the input (*data-limited* processes) and those whose quality is limited primarily by the amount of processing that can be allocated to them (*resource-limited* processes). Norman and Bobrow demonstrated that these ideas are useful for understanding the current literature on attention and perception and, in Chapter 11, Palmer discusses how they might apply to problems in visual perception.

Combination of the ideas of conceptual organization (memory schemata) with issues of cognitive processing has led to further new developments and suggestions for new areas of research. Thus, Bobrow and Norman (in press) attempt to expand upon these to see whether any new insights about cognitive processes in general might emerge. We leave it to each reader to judge the outcome for himself, but clearly we believe that this area of study appears to be a promising and exciting one.

COGNITIVE SCIENCE

The concerted efforts of a number of people from the related disciplines of linguistics, artificial intelligence, and psychology may be creating a new field: *cognitive science*. This field would include those people interested in the understanding of cognitive phenomena, regardless of their orientation and background, as long as they share a common concern for the scientific analysis of the underlying structures and processes. Their aim would be to understand cognitive processes in order to understand what is involved in intelligent behavior. Many of the important aspects of the study of intelligence cannot be classified as belonging to any existing discipline at the moment, for all the current related fields emphasize different parts of the problem, and each field has its own particular philosophical approach. But these disciplines share a common ground. The field of cognitive science would appear to combine the efforts of the linguist who is primarily interested in the study of natural language, the researcher in the field of artificial intelligence who is interested in the development of artificial systems, and the psychologist who wishes to understand how the human cognitive system operates. All these disciplines study similar problems from different points of view. Given the current level of our understanding of these issues, much can be gained by this cooperative research into the problems of cognition.

The end of this book marks the beginning of our studies. We hope that the research reported in this volume will stimulate others to investigate these problems. If they do, their work will probably lead to revisions in the framework that we have presented. The end result will be a better understanding of human cognition. Our efforts will have been successful if they inspire others to perform their own explorations in cognition.

Donald A. Norman

David E. Rumelhart

Bibliography

THE STUDY OF COGNITIVE PROCESSES

Many of the workers who have exerted the greatest influence on our thinking do not receive sufficient credit within the body of the book, primarily because our interactions were so frequent and so involved that it was not always easy to determine where in the book to attribute specific credit. The people with whom we have most frequently interacted are named and thanked in the Preface. At this point, however, we wish to cite three works that have been seminal in the development of our own ideas. These books contain the ideas and papers that have been important to us:

Anderson, J. R., and Bower, G. H. *Human associative memory* (1973), for the work of Anderson and Bower.

Schank, R. C., and Colby, K. M. *Computer models of thought and language* (1973), for the work of Abelson, Becker, Colby, Schank, Simmons, and Winograd (and others).

Tulving, E., and Donaldson, W. *Organization of memory* (1972), for the work of Collins and Quillian, Bower, and Kintsch (and others).

While this manuscript was being completed, Bobrow and Collins organized a symposium on language processing and understanding. The symposium was held in commemoration of the late Jaime Carbonell, one of the early researchers in the use of semantic networks, especially as a means of developing a tutorial system for education. Many of the papers in this symposium report on issues directly related to the research described in this book, both our own and that of others. We recommend the report of that symposium to you:

Bobrow, D. G., and Collins, A. M. (Eds.), *Representation and understanding: Studies in cognitive science.* New York: Academic Press, in press.

The most recent work by Kintsch and his co-workers on semantic structures and propositional representation is contained in:

Kintsch, W. *The representation of meaning in memory.* Hillsdale, N. J.: Lawrence Erlbaum Associates, 1974.

REFERENCES

Abelson, R. P. The structure of belief systems. In R. C. Schank and K. Colby (Eds.), *Computer models of thought and language*. San Francisco: Freeman, 1973.

Abrahamson, A. A. *Meaning and form: A semantic analysis of verb changes in discourse memory*. Unpublished doctoral dissertation, University of California, San Diego, 1973.

Anderson, J. R., and Bower, G. H. *Human associative memory*. Washington, D. C.: Winston, 1973.

Anderson, R. C., and Ortony, A. On putting apples into bottles—a problem of polysemy. *Cognitive Psychology*, in press.

Attneave, F. Some informational aspects of visual perception. *Psychological Review*, 1954, **61**, 183–193.

Bach, E. Nouns and noun phrases. In E. Bach and R. T. Harms (Eds.), *Universals in linguistics theory*. New York: Holt, Rinehart and Winston,'1968.

Bartlett, F. C. *Remembering*. Cambridge, England: Cambridge University Press, 1932.

Baylor, G. W. *A treatise on the mind's eye: An empirical investigation of visual mental imagery*. Unpublished doctoral dissertation, Carnegie-Mellon University, 1971.

Bendix, E. H. *Componential analysis of general vocabulary: The semantic structure of a set of verbs in English, Hindi, and Japanese*. The Hague: Mouton, 1966.

Bever, T. G. The cognitive basis for linguistic structures. In J. Hayes (Ed.), *Cognition and the development of language*. New York: Wiley, 1970.

Bever, T. G., and Langendoen, D. T. A dynamic model of the evolution of language. *Linguistic Inquiry*, 1971, **2**, 433–464.

Biederman, I. Perceiving real-world scenes. *Science*, 1972, **177**, 77–80.

Biederman, I., Glass, A. L., and Stacy, E. W. Searching for objects in real-world scenes. *Journal of Experimental Psychology*, 1973, **97**, 22–27.

Bobrow, D. G. Dimensions of representation. In D. G. Bobrow and A. M. Collins (Eds.), *Representation and understanding: Studies in cognitive science*. New York: Academic Press, in press.

Bobrow, D. G., and Collins, A. M. (Eds.), *Representation and understanding: Studies in cognitive science*. New York: Academic Press, in press.

Bobrow, D. G., and Fraser, B. An augmented state transition network analysis procedure. In D. Walker and L. Norton (Eds.). *Proceedings of the International Joint Conference on Artificial Intelligence*. Washington, D. C., 1969.

Bobrow, D. G., and Norman, D. A. Some principles of memory schemata. In D. G. Bobrow and A. M. Collins (Eds.), *Representation and understanding: Studies in cognitive science*. New York: Academic Press, in press.

Bower, G. H. Mental imagery and associative learning. In L. W. Gregg (Ed.), *Cognition in learning and memory*. New York: Wiley, 1972.

Broadbent, D. E. Word-frequency effects and response bias. *Psychological Review*, 1967, **74**, 1–15.

Brown, J. S., Burton, R. R., and Zdybel, F. A model driven question-answering system for mixed-initiative computer assisted instruction. *IEEE Transactions on Systems, Man, and Cybernetics*, SMC-3, 1973 (May).

Brown, R. *A first language: The early stages*. Cambridge, Mass.: Harvard University Press, 1973.

Bruner, J. S. On perceptual readiness. *Psychological Review*, 1957, **64**, 123–152.

Brunswik, E. *Perception and the representative design of psychological experiments*. Berkeley: University of California Press, 1956.

Chafe, W. L. *Meaning and the structure of language*. Chicago: University of Chicago Press, 1970.

Chafe, W. L. Discourse structure and human knowledge. In R. O. Freedle and J. B. Carroll (Eds.), *Language comprehension and the acquisition of knowledge*. Washington, D. C.: Winston, 1972.

Charniak, E. *Toward a model of children's story comprehension*. Unpublished doctoral dissertation, Massachusetts Institute of Technology, 1972. Also, *MIT Artificial Intelligence Laboratory Technical Report AI-TR 266*, 1972.

Chase, W. G., and Clark, H. H. Mental operations in the comparison of sentences and pictures. In L. W. Gregg (Ed.), *Cognition in learning and memory*. New York: Wiley, 1972.

Chase, W. G., and Simon, H. A. Perception in chess. *Cognitive Psychology*, 1973, **4**, 55–81.

Chomsky, N. *Syntactic structures*. The Hague: Mouton, 1957.

Chomsky, N. *Aspects of the theory of syntax*. Cambridge, Mass.: The M.I.T. Press, 1965.

Clark, E. V. Locationals: A study of relations between "existential," "locative," and "possessive" constructions. *Working Papers in Linguistic Universals, Number 3*. Stanford, Calif.: Stanford University, 1970.

Clark, E. V. On the acquisition of the meaning of *before* and *after. Journal of Verbal Learning and Verbal Behavior*, 1971, **10**, 266–275.

Clark, E. V. What's in a word: On the child's acquisition of semantics in his first language. In T. E. Moore (Ed.), *Cognitive development and the acquisition of language*. New York: Academic Press, 1973.

Clark, H. H. The chronometric study of meaning components. Paper presented at the CNRS Colloque International sur les Problèmes Actuels de Psycholinguistique, Paris, 1971.

Clark, H. H. *Comprehension and the given-new contract*. Paper presented at the Conference on the role of grammar in interdisciplinary linguistic research. The University of Bielefeld, Bielefeld, Germany, 1973 (a).

Clark, H. H. Space, time, semantics, and the child. In T. E. Moore (Ed.), *Cognitive development and the acquisition of language*. New York: Academic Press, 1973 (b).

Clark, H. H., and Haviland, S. E. Psychological processes as linguistic explanation. In D. Cohen (Ed.), *Explaining linguistic phenomena*. Washington, D.C.: Hemisphere Publishing Corp., 1974.

Collins, A. M., and Quillian, M. R. Retrieval time from semantic memory. *Journal of Verbal Learning and Verbal Behavior*, 1969, **8**, 240–247.

Collins, A. M., and Quillian, M. R. How to make a language user. In E. Tulving and W. Donaldson (Eds.), *Organization of memory*. New York: Academic Press, 1972.

Cooper, L. A., and Shepard, R. N. Chronometric studies of the rotation of mental images. In W. G. Chase (Ed.), *Visual information processing*. New York: Academic Press, 1973.

Crothers, E. J. Discourse structure and the recall of discourse. In R. O. Freedle and J. B. Carroll (Eds.), *Language comprehension and the acquisition of knowledge*. Washington, D. C.: Winston, 1972.

Crovitz, H. F. *Galton's walk: Methods for the analysis of thinking, intelligence and creativity*. New York: Harper & Row, 1970.

Davidson, D., and Harman, G. *Semantics of natural language*. Dordrecht, The Netherlands: Reidel, 1972.

DeGroot, A. D. *Thought and choice in chess*. The Hague: Mouton, 1965.

Donaldson, M., and Balfour, G. Less is more: A study of language comprehension in children. *British Journal of Psychology*, 1968, **59**, 461–472.

Donaldson, M., and Wales, R. J. On the acquistion of some relational terms. In R. Hayes (Ed.), *Cognition and the development of language*. New York: Wiley, 1970.

Dowty, D. R. On the syntax and semantics of the atomic predicate CAUSE. In P. M. Peranteau, J. N. Levi, and G. C. Phares (Eds.), *Papers from the Eighth Regional Meeting of the Chicago Linguistic Society*. Chicago: Chicago Linguistic Society, 1972.

Fillmore, C. J. Review of Bendix's "Componential analysis of general vocabulary: The semantic structure of a set of verbs in English, Hindi, and Japanese." *International Journal of American Linguistics*, 1966, **32**, Part II, No. 2. Publication 41.

Fillmore, C. J. The case for case. In E. Bach and R. T. Harms (Eds.), *Universals in linguistic theory*. New York: Holt, Rinehart, and Winston, 1968.

Fodor, J., and Garrett, M. Some reflections on competence and performance. In J. Lyons and R. Wales (Eds.), *Psycholinguistics papers*. Edinburgh: Edinburgh University Press, 1966, 135–183.

Fodor, J., Bever, T., and Garrett, M. *The psychology of language*. New York: McGraw-Hill, 1974.

Frederiksen, C. H. Effects of task induced cognitive operations on comprehension and memory processes. In R. Freedle and J. Carroll (Eds.), *Language comprehension and the acquisition of knowledge*. Washington, D.C.: Winston, 1972.

Frege, G. *Conceptual notation and related articles*. (T. W. Bynum, Ed. and trans.) Oxford, England: Oxford University Press, 1972. (Originally published as articles, 1879–1882.)

Frost, N., and Wolf, J. How "visual" is visual memory? Paper presented at the 14th Annual Meeting of the Psychonomic Society, St. Louis, Mo., November 1973.

Gentner, D. *Towards a psychological theory of the meaning of the possession verbs*. Unpublished doctoral dissertation, University of California, San Diego, 1974.

Goodman, K. A linguistic study of the cues and miscues in reading. *Elementary English*, 1965, **42**, 639–643.

Gordon, D., and Lakoff, G. Conversational postulates. *Papers from the Seventh Regional Meeting, Chicago Linguistic Society, April 16–18, 1971.* Chicago: Chicago Linguistic Society, 1971.

Grice, H. P. *Logic and conversation.* The William James Lectures, Harvard University, 1967.

Haviland, S. E., and Clark, H. H. Acquiring new information as a process in comprehension. *Journal of verbal learning and verbal behavior*, 1974, **13**, 512–521.

Helmholtz, H. V. *Handbook of physiological optics.* (J. P. C. Southall, Trans.), New York: Optical Society of America, 1925.

Hill, L. A. *Prepositions and adverbial particles.* Oxford, England: Oxford University Press, 1968.

Hubel, D. H., and Wiesel, T. N. Receptive fields, binocular interaction, and functional architecture in the cat's visual cortex. *Journal of Physiology*, 1962, **160**, 106–154.

James, W. *The principles of psychology.* Vol. 1. New York: Henry Holt & Co., 1890. (Also reprinted by Dover Publications, Inc., New York, 1950.)

Johnson-Laird, P. N. Experimental psycholinguistics. *Annual Review of Psychology*, 1974, **25**, 135–160.

Kanouse, D. E. Verbs as implicit quantifiers. *Journal of Verbal Learning and Verbal Behavior*, 1972, **11**, 141–147.

Kaplan, R. M. Augmented transition networks as psychological models of sentence comprehension. *Artificial Intelligence*, 1972, 3, 77–100.

Kaplan, R. M. A general syntactic processor. In R. Rustin (Ed.), *Natural language processing.* New York: Algorithmics Press, 1973 (a).

Kaplan, R. M. A multi-processing approach to natural language. *Proceedings of the 1973 National Computer Conference.* Montvale, N.J.: AFIPS Press, 1973, pp. 435–440 (b).

Kaplan, R. M. *Transient processing load in relative clauses.* Unpublished doctoral dissertation, Harvard University, 1974.

Kareev, Y. *A model of human game playing.* Unpublished doctoral dissertation, University of California, San Diego, 1973.

Karttunen, L. *Discourse referents.* (Indiana University Linguistics Club Reprint.) Bloomington: Indiana University Linguistics Club, 1971 (a).

Karttunen, L. Implicative verbs. *Language*, 1971, **47**, 340–358 (b).

Karttunen, L. Possible and must. In J. P. Kimball (Ed.), *Syntax and Semantics*, Vol. 1. New York: Seminar Press, 1972.

Karttunen, L. Presupposition of compound sentences. *Linguistic Inquiry*, 1973, 4, 169–193 (a).

Karttunen, L. *Presupposition and linguistic context.* Paper presented at the winter meeting of the Linguistic Society of America, San Diego, California, December 1973 (b).

Katz, J. J. On defining "presupposition." *Linguistic Inquiry*, 1973, 4, 256–260.

Kay, M. The MIND system. In R. Rustin (Ed.), *Natural language processing.* New York: Algorithmics Press, 1973.

Keenan, E. L. Two kinds of presupposition in natural language. In C. J. Fillmore and D. T. Langendoen (Eds.), *Studies in linguistic semantics*. New York: Holt, Rinehart and Winston, 1971.

Kimball, J. P. The grammar of existence. In C. Corum, T. C. Smith-Stark, and A. Weiser (Eds.), *Papers from the Ninth Regional Meeting of the Chicago Linguistic Society*. Chicago: Chicago Linguistic Society, 1973.

Kintsch, W. Abstract nouns: Imagery versus lexical complexity. *Journal of Verbal Learning and Verbal Behavior*, 1972, **11**, 59–65 (a).

Kintsch, W. Notes on the structure of semantic memory. In E. Tulving and W. Donaldson (Eds.), *Organization of Memory*. New York: Academic Press, 1972 (b).

Kintsch, W., and Keenan, J. Reading rate and retention as a function of the number of propositions in the base structure of sentences. *Cognitive Psychology*, 1973, **5**, 257–274.

Kiparsky, P., and Kiparsky, C. Fact. In M. Bierwisch and K. E. Heidolph (Eds.), *Recent developments in linguistics*. The Hague: Mouton, 1971.

Koffka, K. *The principles of Gestalt psychology*. New York: Harcourt, Brace, and World, 1935.

Kolers, P. A. Three stages of reading. In H. Levin and J. Williams (Eds.), *Basic studies in reading*. New York: Harper & Row, 1969.

Lakoff, G. *Stative adjectives and verbs in English*. Unpublished manuscript, 1966.

Lakoff, G. Instrumental adverbs and the concept of deep structure. *Foundations of Language*, 1968, **4**, 4–29.

Lakoff, G. *Adverbs and modal operators*. (Indiana University Linguistics Club Reprint.) Bloomington: Indiana University Linguistics Club, 1970 (a).

Lakoff, G. *Adverbs and opacity: A reply to Stalnaker*. (Indiana University Linguistics Club Reprint.) Bloomington: Indiana University Linguistics Club, 1970 (b).

Lakoff, G. *Irregularity and syntax*. New York: Holt, Rinehart and Winston, 1970 (c).

Lakoff, G. Hedges: A study in meaning criteria and the logic of fuzzy concepts. In P. M. Peranteau, J. N. Levi, and G. C. Phares (Eds.), *Papers from the Eighth Regional Meeting of the Chicago Linguistic Society*. Chicago: Chicago Linguistic Society, 1972.

Langacker, R. W. Movement rules in functional perspective. *Language*, 1974, **50**, 630–664.

Lawler, J. Generic to a fault. In P. M. Peranteau, J. N. Levi, and G. C. Phares (Eds.), *Papers from the Eighth Regional Meeting of the Chicago Linguistic Society*. Chicago: Chicago Linguistic Society, 1972.

Lawler, J. Tracking the generic toad. In C. Corum, T. C. Smith-Stark, and A. Weiser (Eds.), *Papers from the Ninth Regional Meeting of the Chicago Linguistic Society*. Chicago: Chicago Linguistic Society, 1973.

Lees, R. B., and Klima, E. Rules for English pronominalization. *Language*, 1963, **39**, 17–28.

Lindsay, P. H., and Norman, D. A. *Human information processing*. New York: Academic Press, 1972.

Loftus, E. F., and Zanni, G. *Eyewitness identification: Linguistically caused misperceptions*. Paper presented at the meeting of the Psychonomic Society, St. Louis, Mo., 1973.

McCawley, J. D. Meaning and the description of languages. *Kotoba no Uchu*, 1967, 2, 10–18, 38–48, and 51–57.

McCawley, J. D. Lexical insertion in a transformational grammar without deep structure. *Papers from the Fourth Regional Meeting of the Chicago Linguistic Society*. Chicago: Chicago Linguistic Society, 1968 (a).

McCawley, J. D. The role of semantics in a grammar. In E. Bach and R. T. Harms (Eds.), *Universals in linguistic theory*. New York: Holt, Rinehart and Winston, 1968 (b).

McCawley, J. D. English as a VSO language. *Language*, 1970, 46, 286–299.

McCawley, J. D. Where do noun phrases come from? In D. D. Steinberg and L. A. Jakobovits (Eds.), *Semantics: An interdisciplinary reader in philosophy, linguistics and psychology*. Cambridge, England: Cambridge University Press, 1971 (a).

McCawley, J. D. Tense and time reference in English. In C. J. Fillmore and D. T. Langendoen (Eds.), *Studies in linguistic semantics*. New York: Holt, Rinehart and Winston, 1971 (b).

McCawley, J. D. Kac and Shibatani on the grammar of killing. In J. P. Kimball (Ed.), *Syntax and semantics*. Vol. 1. New York: Seminar Press, 1972.

Miller, G. A. The magical number seven, plus or minus two: Some limits on our capacity for processing information. *Psychological Review*, 1956, 63, 81–97.

Miller, G. A. *Psychology: The study of mental life*. New York: Harper & Row, 1962.

Miller, G. A. English verbs of motion: A case study in semantic and lexical memory. In A. W. Melton and E. Martin (Eds.), *Coding processes in human memory*. Washington, D. C.: Winston, 1972.

Miller, G. A. and McKean, K. A chronometric study of some relations between sentences. *Quarterly Journal of Experimental Psychology*, 1964, 16, 297–308.

Minsky, M. *Semantic information processing*. Cambridge, Mass.: The M.I.T. Press, 1968.

Minsky, M. A framework for representing knowledge. In P. Winston (Ed.), *The psychology of computer vision*. New York: McGraw-Hill, in press.

Morton, J. A functional model for memory. In D. A. Norman (Ed.), *Models of human memory*. New York: Academic Press, 1970.

Munro, P. *Mojave syntax*. New York: Garland, in press.

Naddor, E. Gomoku played by computers. *Behavioral Science*, 1969, 14, 71–73.

Neisser, U. *Cognitive psychology*. New York: Appleton-Century-Crofts, 1967.

Newell, A. Production systems: Models of control structures. In W. G. Chase (Ed.), *Visual information processing*. New York: Academic Press, 1973.

Newell, A., and Simon, H. A. *Human problem solving*. Englewood Cliffs, N.J.: Prentice-Hall, 1972.

Norman, D. A. Memory, knowledge, and the answering of questions. In R. L. Solso (Ed.), *Contemporary issues in cognitive psychology: The Loyola symposium.* Washington, D.C.: Winston, 1973. (Distributed by Halsted Press, Wiley.)

Norman, D. A., and Bobrow, D. G. On data-limited and resource-limited processes. *Cognitive Psychology,* 1975, **7**, 44–64.

Norman, D. A., Gentner, D. R., and Stevens, A. L. Comments on learning: Schemata and memory representation. In D. Klahr (Ed.), *Cognitive approaches to education: Proceedings of the 10th Carnegie-Mellon University symposium on cognition.* Potomac, Md.: Lawrence Erlbaum Associates, in press.

Olson, D. R. Language and thought: Aspects of a cognitive theory of semantics. *Psychological Review,* 1970, **77**, 257–273.

Ortony, A. *On the impropriety of marrying one's mother—a problem of reference.* Unpublished manuscript. Department of Educational Psychology, University of Illinois at Urbana-Champaign, 1973.

Osgood, C. E. Where do sentences come from? In D. D. Steinberg and L. A. Jakobovits (Eds.), *Semantics: An interdisciplinary reader in philosophy, linguistics and psychology.* Cambridge, England: Cambridge University Press, 1971.

Palmer, S. E. The effects of contextual scenes on the identification of objects. *Memory and Cognition,* in press.

Perlmutter, D. M. On the article in English. In M. Bierwisch and K. E. Heidolph (Eds.), *Recent developments in linguistics.* The Hague: Mouton, 1971.

Piaget, J. *The language and thought of the child.* New York: The World Publishing Co., 1955.

Piaget, J. *The moral judgment of the child.* New York: The Free Press, 1965.

Postal, P. M. On so-called pronouns in English. In R. A. Jacobs and P. S. Rosenbaum (Eds.), *Readings in English transformational grammar.* Waltham, Mass.: Ginn, 1970.

Pribram, K. H. *Languages of the brain.* Englewood Cliffs, N.J.: Prentice-Hall, 1971.

Pylyshyn, Z. W. What the mind's eye tells the mind's brain: A critique of mental imagery. *Psychological Bulletin,* 1973, **80**, 1–24.

Quillian, M. R. Semantic memory. In M. Minsky (Ed.), *Semantic information processing.* Cambridge, Mass.: The MIT Press, 1968.

Quillian, M. R. The teachable language comprehender. *Communications of the Association for Computing Machinery,* 1969, **12**, 459–475.

Reed, S. K. Pattern recognition and categorization. *Cognitive Psychology,* 1972, **3**, 382–407.

Reicher, G. M. Perceptual recognition as a function of meaningfulness of stimulus material. *Journal of Experimental Psychology,* 1969, **81**, 275–280.

Reitman, W. R. *Cognition and thought.* New York: Wiley, 1965.

Reitman, W. R. What does it take to remember? In D. A. Norman (Ed.), *Models of human memory.* New York: Academic Press, 1970.

Rips, L. J., Shoben, E. J., and Smith, E. E. Semantic distance and the verification of semantic relations. *Journal of Verbal Learning and Verbal Behavior*, 1973, **12**, 1–20.

Rosch, E. On the internal structure of perceptual and semantic categories. In T. E. Moore (Ed.), *Cognitive development and acquisition of language*. New York: Academic Press, 1973.

Rosch, E. Universals and cultural specifics in human categorization. In R. Breslin, W. Loner, and S. Bochner (Eds.), *Cross-cultural perspectives*. London: Sage Press, 1974.

Ross, J. R. Auxiliaries as main verbs. In W. Todd (Ed.), *Studies in Philosophical Linguistics, Series One*. Carbondale, Ill.: Great Expectations Press, 1969.

Ross, J. R. Act. In D. Davidson and G. Harman (Eds.), *Semantics of natural language*. Dordrecht, The Netherlands: D. Reidel, 1972 (a).

Ross, J. R. The category squish: Endstation Hauptwort. In P. M. Peranteau, J. N. Levi, and G. C. Phares (Eds.), *Papers from the Eighth Regional Meeting of the Chicago Linguistic Society*. Chicago: Chicago Linguistic Society, 1972 (b).

Ross, J. R. A fake NP squish. In C-J. N. Bailey and R. Shuy (Eds.), *New ways of analyzing variation in English*. Washington, D.C.: Georgetown University Press, 1973.

Rumelhart, D. E. A multicomponent theory of the perception of briefly exposed visual displays. *Journal of Mathematical Psychology*, 1970, **7**, 191–218.

Rumelhart, D. E. The structure of stories. In D. G. Bobrow and A. M. Collins (Eds.), *Representation and understanding: Studies in cognitive science*. New York: Academic Press, in press.

Rumelhart, D. E., Lindsay, P. H., and Norman, D. A. A process model for long-term memory. In E. Tulving and W. Donaldson (Eds.), *Organization of memory*. New York: Academic Press, 1972.

Rumelhart, D. E., and Siple, P. The process of tachistoscopically recognizing words. *Psychological Review*, 1974, **81**, 91–118.

Ryder, J. L. Heuristic analysis of large trees as generated in the game of Go. *Report No. CS-245*. Stanford, Calif.: Stanford University, Computer Science Department, 1971.

Samuel, A. L. Some studies in machine learning using the game of checkers. In E. Feigenbaum and J. Feldman (Eds.), *Computers and thought*. New York: McGraw-Hill, 1963.

Schank, R. C. Adverbs and belief. *Stanford Artificial Intelligence Project Memo AIM-171*. Stanford, Calif.: Stanford University, Computer Science Department, 1972 (a).

Schank, R. C. Conceptual dependency: A theory of natural language understanding. *Cognitive Psychology*, 1972, 3, 552–631 (b).

Schank, R. C. *Causality and reasoning*. (Tech. Rep. 1) Castagnola, Switzerland: Istituto per gli Studi Semantici e Cognitivi, 1973 (a).

Schank, R. C. Identification of conceptualizations underlying natural language. In R. C. Schank and K. M. Colby (Eds.), *Computer models of thought and language*. San Francisco: Freeman, 1973 (b).

Schank, R. C. The fourteen primitive actions and their inferences. *Stanford Artificial Intelligence Project Memo AIM-183.* Stanford, Calif.: Stanford University, Computer Science Department, 1973 (c).

Schank, R. C., and Colby, K. M. (Eds.), *Computer models of thought and language.* San Francisco: Freeman, 1973.

Schank, R. C., Goldman, N., Rieger, C., and Riesbeck, C. Primitive concepts underlying verbs of thought. *Stanford Artificial Intelligence Project Memo AIM-162.* Stanford, Calif.: Stanford University, Computer Science Department, 1972.

Searle, J. R. *Speech Acts: An essay in the philosophy of language.* Cambridge, England: Cambridge University Press, 1969.

Selfridge, O. G., and Neisser, U. Pattern recognition by machine. In E. A. Feigenbaum and J. Feldman (Eds.), *Computers and thought.* New York: McGraw-Hill, 1963.

Shepard, R. N., and Metzler, J. Mental rotation of three-dimensional objects. *Science,* 1971, **171**, 701–703.

Simmons, R. F. Semantic networks: Their computation and use for understanding English sentences. In R. C. Schank and K. M. Colby (Eds.), *Computer models of thought and language.* San Francisco: Freeman, 1973.

Simmons, R. F., and Bruce, B. C. Some relations between predicate calculus and the semantic net representations of discourse. *Proceedings of the 2nd International Joint Conference on Artificial Intelligence.* London: British Computer Society, 1971.

Simon, H. A. *The sciences of the artificial.* Cambridge, Mass.: The M.I.T. Press, 1969.

Simon, H. A. The heuristic compiler. In H. A. Simon and L. Siklossy (Eds.), *Representation and meaning.* Englewood-Cliffs, N.J.: Prentice-Hall, 1972.

Slobin, D. Recall of full and truncated passive sentences in connected discourse. *Journal of Verbal Learning and Verbal Behavior,* 1968, **7**, 876–881.

Sloman, A. Interactions between philosophy and artificial intelligence: The role of intuition and non-logical reasoning in intelligence. *Artificial Intelligence,* 1971, **2**, 209–225.

Smith, E. E., and Spoehr, K. T. The perception of printed English: A theoretical perspective. In B. H. Kantowitz (Ed.), *Human information processing: Tutorials in performance and cognition.* Potomac, Md.: Lawrence Erlbaum Associates, 1974.

Smith, E. E., Shoben, E. J., and Rips, L. J. Structure and process in semantic memory: A featural model for semantic decisions. *Psychological Review,* 1974, **81**, 214–241.

Sperling, G. The information available in brief visual presentations. *Psychological Monographs,* 1960, **11**, Whole No. 498.

Steinberg, D. D., and Jakobovits, L. A. (Eds.), *Semantics: An interdisciplinary reader in philosophy, linguistics, and psychology.* Cambridge, England: Cambridge University Press, 1971.

Strawson, P. On referring. *Mind,* 1950, **59**, 320–344.

Sudnow, D. (Ed.), *Studies in social interaction.* New York: The Free Press, 1972.

Talmy, L. *Semantic structures in English and Atsugewi.* Unpublished doctoral dissertation, University of California, Berkeley, 1972.

Thorne, J., Bratley, P., and Dewar, H. The syntactic analysis of English by machine. In D. Michie (Ed.), *Machine intelligence 3.* New York: American Elsevier, 1968.

Tulving, E., and Donaldson, W. *Organization of memory.* New York: Academic Press, 1972.

Tulving, E., and Gold, C. Stimulus information and contextual information as determinants of tachistoscopic recognition of words. *Journal of Experimental Psychology,* 1963, **66**, 319–327.

Turner, D. R. *The complete study guide for scoring high on the Graduate Record Examination aptitude test. 3rd ed.* New York: Arco, 1972.

van Dijk, T. A. *Some aspects of text grammars: A study in theoretical linguistics and poetics.* The Hague: Mouton, 1972.

van Dijk, T. A. A note on linguistic macro-structures. In A. P. ten Cate and P. Jordens (Eds.), *Linguistische perspectiven.* Tübingen, Germany: Max Niemeyer Verlag, 1973.

van Dijk, T. A. A note on the partial equivalence of text grammars and context grammars. In M. Loflin and J. Silverberg (Eds.), *Discourse and inference in cognitive anthropology.* The Hague: Mouton, 1974.

Vernon, M. D. The functions of schemata in perceptual activity. *Psychological Review,* 1955, **62**, 180–192.

Waltz, D. L. Generating semantic descriptions from drawings of scenes with shadows. *Memo AI-TR-271.* Cambridge, Mass.: *M.I.T.* Artificial Intelligence Laboratory, 1972. (See also Waltz, D. L., in P. Winston (Ed.), *The psychology of computer vision.* New York: McGraw-Hill, in press.)

Wanner, E., Kaplan, R., and Shiner, S. *Garden paths in relative clauses.* Unpublished manuscript, Harvard University, 1974.

Wanner, E., and Maratsos, M. M. *On understanding relative clauses.* Unpublished manuscript, Harvard University, 1974.

Wason, P. C., and Johnson-Laird, P. N. *Psychology of reasoning: Structure and content.* Cambridge, Mass.: Harvard University Press, 1972.

Williams, L. G. The effect of target specification on objects fixated during visual search. *Perception and Psychophysics,* 1966, **1**, 315–318.

Winograd, T. *Understanding natural language.* New York: Academic Press, 1972. (Essentially the same study is also available as Winograd, T. A program for understanding natural language. *Cognitive Psychology,* 1972, **3**, 1–191.)

Winograd, T. A procedural model of language understanding. In R. C. Schank and K. W. Colby (Eds.), *Computer models of thought and language.* San Francisco: Freeman, 1973.

Winograd, T. Frames and the procedural-declarative controversy. In D. G. Bobrow and A. M. Collins (Eds.), *Representation and understanding: Studies in cognitive science.* New York: Academic Press, in press.

Winston, P. H. Learning to identify toy block structures. In R. L. Solso (Ed.), *Contemporary issues in cognitive psychology: The Loyola symposium.* Washington, D.C.: Winston, 1973.

Woods, W. Transition network grammars for natural language analysis. *Communications of the ACM,* 1970, **13**, 591–606.

Woods, W. An experimental parsing system for transition network grammars. In R. Rustin (Ed.), *Natural language processing.* New York: Algorithmics Press, 1973.

Woods, W., and Kaplan, R. *The lunar sciences natural language information system.* Cambridge, Mass.: Bolt, Beranek, and Newman, Report No. 2265, 1971.

Yamanashi, M. A. Lexical decomposition and implied proposition. In P. M. Peranteau, J. N. Levi, and G. C. Phares (Eds.), *Papers from the Eighth Regional Meeting of the Chicago Linguistic Society.* Chicago: Chicago Linguistic Society, 1972.

INDEX

Abelson, R. P., 407

ABLE. *See* Semantic primitives

Abrahamson, A. A., 249

Acquisition of meaning. *See* Verbs, acquisition of

Actional component of verb definitions, 47, 53, 55, 180, 184, 199. *See also* Verbs, representation of

Active structural network, 8, 16, 30, 35, 160

Adjective compiler, 370

Adjectives, 56, 97, 358–363

Adverbs, 98, 99, 100, 109, 265, 362

Agenda. *See* Augmented transition network

AGENT. *See* Case relations

Ambiguous figures, 302–304

Ambiguous sentences, 206

Analogical representation. *See* Representation, analogical

Analysis-by-synthesis, 280. *See also* Processing strategies

Anderson, J. R., 59

Anderson, N. H., 82

Anderson, R. C., 83

Answering questions. *See* Question answering

Arguments, 41, 163, 221. *See also* Predicates

ATN. *See* Augmented transition networks

ATRANS. *See* Semantic primitives

Attneave, F., 285

Augmented transition networks, 121–135
   agenda of, 132–133
   computational effort, 135
   conditions, 129
   jumping, 134
   as a psychological model, 136–155
   scheduling in, 124, 132
   seek arcs, 125–128
   send arcs, 125, 127

Bach, E., 98

Backup. *See* Game playing, backup

Balfour, G., 233

Bartlett, F. C., 7, 248, 407

Baylor, G. W., 281, 287

BECOME. *See* Semantic primitives

Bendix, E. H., 211, 213

Bert, 237, 239. *See also* Ernie

Bever, T. G., 113, 120–122

Biederman, I., 295, 306

Binding of variables. *See* Computer implementation
Bobrow, D. G., 17, 122, 159, 304, 407–408
"Borrow." *See* Verbs, representation of
Bottom-up processing. *See* Processing strategies
Bower, G. H., 18, 59
Bratley, P., 122
Breadth-first processing. *See* Processing strategies
Broadbent, D. E., 294
Brown, J. S., 349
Brown, R., 276
Bruner, J. S., 280
Brunswik, E., 280
Built-in operations, 163. *See also* Interpreter
Burton, R. R., 349
"Buy." *See* Verbs, representation of

Case frame, 160
Case grammar, 171
Case relations
    AGENT, 221, 254, 263, 265, 266
    EXPERIENCER, 221
    GOAL, 221, 254, 255, 264
    IMPLEMENTATION, 53, 251–256, 261, 263, 266, 269
    INSTRUMENT, 254
    OBJECT, 48, 221, 254, 264
    PATHPOINT, 255, 264
    PATHREL, 265, 266
    PATIENT, 254, 266
    REASON, 267, 269
    RECIPIENT, 221
    SOURCE, 221, 255, 263, 264
Causality, 13, 51–53, 180, 184, 214, 247. *See also* Semantic primitives
    agentitive, 184
    instrumental, 185
CAUSE. *See* Semantic primitives
"Cause." *See* Verbs, representation of
Certainty, 106, 107. *See also* Truth
Chafe, W. L., 76, 113, 254
CHANGE. *See* Semantic primitives
Change-of-state component of verbs, 13, 47, 50–51, 180, 247. *See also* Semantic primitives

Charniak, E., 76, 85, 86, 87
Chase, W. G., 282, 320
Chomsky, N., 101, 103, 119
Cicourel, A., 77
Clark, E. V., 212, 233
Clark, H. H., 84, 85, 282, 294
Cognitive science, 409
Cohen, D., 85
Collins, A. M., 59–60, 407
Competence grammar, 119
Componential analysis, 211, 231. *See also* Semantic primitives
Comprehender, 177, 369, 370, 372. *See also* Interpreter; Computer implementation
Comprehension, components of, 117–121
Comprehension, partial versus complete, 203–206. *See also* Verbworld
Computer implementation, 159–178. *See also* Interpreter; **LUIGI**; MEMOD; Parser; SOL; Verbworld
    binding of variables, 164
    representation of information, 161
Concepts, 43–44. *See also* Nouns, representation of
Conceptual dependency analysis, 96
Context, 112, 137, 296
CONTR. *See* Semantic primitives
Control structure. *See* Processing strategies
Convergence mechanism. *See* Processing strategies
Conversational postulates, 68, 75, 77–87, 112, 405
Cooper, L. A., 283
Crothers, E. J., 248
Crovitz, H. F., 387

Data driven. *See* Processing strategies, bottom-up
Data-limited, 408
Davidson, D., 67
Definite description. *See* Reference, definite
Definition frame. *See* SOL, definitions in
DeGroot, A. D., 327, 339
Depth-first. *See* Processing strategies

Depth of processing, 203–206
Derivational theory of complexity, 120
Dewar, H., 122
Dictionary. *See* Vocabulary
DO. *See* Semantic primitives
Donaldson, M., 233
Dowty, D. R., 91–93, 95

Eisenstadt, M., 326
Elements, semantic, 254. *See also* Semantic primitives
Ernie, 237, 239. *See also* Bert
Evaluation of a node, 164, 168. *See also* Computer implementation; Interpreter
Event, 377, 393
    configurations of, 53–55
    organization of, 379, 380
    segmentation of, 258–260, 268
    temporal judgments of. *See* Time, judgments of
Expectations, 298, 304–306. *See also* Context; Reading, predictions in
EXPERIENCER. *See* Case relations

Fact retrieval. *See* Question answering, information retrieval
Fillmore, C. J., 171, 211, 213, 217, 254
Fisherman Story, The, 249–260
Floor plan problem, 21
Fodor, J., 120
Foregrounding. *See* Reference, definite
Frame of reference, 289
Frames, 407. *See also* Schemata
Fraser, B., 122
Fredericksen, C. H., 248
Frege, G., 98
Frost, N., 282
Fruit-face, 303
Functional definitions, 59, 406. *See also* Structural definitions; Schemata
Functionalism, 113

Game playing, 26, 345. *See also* Go; Gomoku
    backup, 326, 342
    perceptual factors in, 318–320

    planning in, 326, 328, 340, 341
    representation in, 314–345
    scanning, 320, 323, 324, 330
Garrett, M., 120
Generative semantics, 5, 63–64, 88–89, 113
Generic quantification. *See* Quantification, generic
Generic statements, 71, 103
Gentner, D., 235
Gentner, D. R., 407
Gestalt principles of perception, 318, 335–336, 345
"Give." *See* Verbs, representation of
Given-new distinction, 84
Glass, A. L., 306
Global information, 296–297, 300–301, 304, 306–307. *See also* Processing strategy, whole-to-part; Processing strategy, part-to-whole
Go, 26–28, 309–310, 313–314, 316–318, 323, 328–329, 333. *See also* Game playing
    Ko, rule of, 310
GOAL. *See* Case relations
Goal-driven processing. *See* Processing strategies, top-down
Gold, C., 137, 295
Goldman, N., 211
Gomoku, 26–28, 309, 311, 313–314, 316–320, 324, 326–328, 333–334, 336, 341. *See also* Game playing
    closed-four, 312
    double-threat, 312
    open-four, 312
    open-three, 312
    open-two, 321
Goodman, K., 137
Gordon, D., 77, 80, 113
"Grab." *See* Verbs, representation of
Graesser II, A., 202
Grice, H. P., 77, 80, 82

Harman, G., 67
"Have." *See* Verbs, representation of
Haviland, S. E., 84–85
Helmholtz, H. V., 280
Hordograffe, 303
Hubel, D. H., 281

Iconic, representation. *See* Representation, analogical
Identification of objects, process of, 297–304
Idiom, 361
Image. *See* Representation, analogical
IMPLEMENTATION. *See* Case relations
Implementation, computer. *See* Computer implementation
Implicatures, 80. *See also* Conversational postulates
Indefinite reference. *See* Reference, indefinite
Inferential reasoning, 365
Information retrieval. *See* Question answering, information retrieval
Instrument case. *See* Case relations
Intension. *See* Reference, intensional
Interpreter, 160, 162–165, 168–170. *See also* Computer implementation
Isa, 10
Iswhen, 49

Jakobovits, L. A., 67
James, C., 247
James, W., 404
Jennings, K., 77
Johnson-Laird, P. N., 48, 106

Kanouse, D. E., 105
Kaplan, R. M., 120, 122, 128, 134–135, 335, 408
Karttunen, L., 103, 107, 109, 112
Katz, J. J., 107
Kay, M., 122
Keenan, E. L., 107–108, 248
Kimball, J. P., 212
Kintsch, W., 59, 248, 273
Kiparsky, C., 108
Kiparsky, P., 108
Kitchenworld. *See* **LUIGI**
Klima, E., 103
"Know." *See* Verbs, representation of
Knowledge of processes. *See* **LUIGI**
Knowledge of the world, 5–6, 85, 113, 260, 291
Koffka, K., 318
Kolers, P. A., 137

Lakoff, G., 77, 80, 89, 91, 93–94, 97, 99–100, 106, 113
Langacker, R. W., 113
Langendoen, D. T., 113
Language comprehension system. *See* **Verbworld**
Lawler, J., 105
Lees, R. B., 103
Lexical decomposition, 89, 96, 285. *See also* Semantic primitives; **Verbworld**
Lindsay, P. H., 59
LNR, x–xi, xv–xvi
"Loan." *See* Verbs, representation of
LOC. *See* Semantic primitives
"Locate." *See* Verbs, representation of
Loftus, E. F., 79
Lookahead. *See* Game playing, planning in
LUIGI, 350–375

McCawley, J. D., 91–92, 101, 103, 113, 227
McKean, K., 120
"Make." *See* Verbs, representation of
Maratsos, M. M., 135
MEMOD, 160, 163, 165, 170–171, 173, 177–180, 187, 350, 353, 369. *See also* Computer implementation; Interpreter; Parser; **SOL**
Mental rotation, 283. *See also* Representation, analogical
Metzler, J., 17, 283
Miller, G. A., 48, 120, 253, 269, 275, 280
Minimax, 327. *See also* Game playing
Minsky, M., 6–7, 407
Mojave, 94
Morton, J., 137
MOVE. *See* Semantic primitives
"Move." *See* Verbs, representation of
Munro, P., 88, 94

Naddor, E., 314
Navon, D., 198
Negation, 217. *See also* Truth
Neisser, U., 280–281, 302

Newell, A., 314, 327, 339–340
Node space, 35, 39, 60, 160–161.
    See also Type node; Token node
    operations on. *See* Interpreter
Nonlinguistic information. *See*
    Representation, nonlinguistic
Norman, D. A., 59, 208, 304, 405,
    407–408
Nouns, representation of, 56–60, 98

OBJECT. *See* Case relations
OBLIG. *See* Semantic primitives
Olson, D. R., 65, 69
Operators, 172, 331. *See also* **SOL**
Organization, subjective, 314
Ortony, A., 83
"Owe." *See* Verbs, representation of

Palmer, S. E., 231, 291, 295
Paraphrase, 4
    invariance under, 45
Parser, 160, 171, 362, 369
Partial comprehension. *See* Compre-
    hension, partial versus complete
Passive sentences, parsing of,
    128–133
PATHPOINT. *See* Case relations
PATHREL. *See* Case relations
PATIENT. *See* Case relations
"Pay." *See* Verbs, representation of
Perception, 16–26, 279–307. *See also*
    Representation, analogical;
    Representation, nonlinguistic
    in game playing. *See* Game
    playing
Perceptual strategies, in language
    comprehension, 120–121
Perlmutter, D. M., 103
Piaget, J., 7, 234, 407
Planning ahead. *See* Game playing
Plans, representation of, 29–31. *See
    also* **LUIGI**; Game playing,
    planning in
POSS. *See* Semantic primitives
Postal, P. M., 103
Pragmatics, 113
Predicate-raising, 227
Predicates, 36, 97–102, 264
    definition of, 41–43
    as procedures, 63–64
    in **SOL**, 172, 180
Presupposition, 107–112, 217

Pribram, K. H., 281
Primitives, semantic. *See* Semantic
    primitives
Problem solving, 340, 345, 402. *See
    also* Game playing
Procedures. *See* Predicates, as pro-
    cedures. *See also* **LUIGI**;
    Verbworld
Processing strategies, 338–339
    bottom-up, 136, 295, 297–298,
        300, 303, 305, 331, 334–335,
        337, 340, 346
    breadth-first, 133, 246
    convergence mechanism, 335–
        337, 346
    depth-first, 133, 346
    part-to-whole, 295
    progressive-deepening, 329, 339–
        341, 346
    top-down, 136, 295, 298, 300,
        303, 330–335, 340, 346
    whole-to-part, 295
Production systems, 339
Progressive deepening. *See* Process-
    ing strategies
Pronouns, 69–70, 202–203
Propositions, 43–44. *See also*
    Predicates
Prototypes, 59–60, 293–294
"Put." *See* Verbs, representation of
Pylyshyn, Z. W., 18–20, 281–282

Quantification, 61–63
    generic, 62–63, 103–105
Question answering, 189, 192, 206,
    208, 349–350, 363, 367, 375
    information retrieval, 206, 363
Question types
    "Did (or will) an action
        occur?", 366
    "How do you . . . ?", 365, 367
    next-step, 367
    procedural, 365
    process, 349
    "What were you doing?",
        386–387
    "Which came first?", 381–385
    wh-questions, 192, 197–198, 367
    "why?", 368, 371
    yes-no questions, 192, 195–
        197, 368
Quillian, M. R., 59–60

Range, of arguments, 41
Reading, 136–155
    predictions in, 146–150
REASON. *See* Case relations
Recalls
    error in, 232, 397
    problem solving in, 402
    response times in, 397
    semantic analysis of, 232, 248,
        250–260, 269, 277
"Receive." *See* Verbs, representa-
    tion of
RECIPIENT. *See* Case relations
Reed, S. K., 293–294
Reference, 65–87, 378
    definite, 69, 72, 74, 76, 83, 110,
        201–202
    indefinite, 72, 201
    intensional, 70–72
    problem of specification, 69
    specific, 68
    in **Verbworld**, 201
Referents, 102
Reicher, G. M., 294
Relations, 35, 80
    inverse, 35
    isa, 10
    iswhen, 49
"Remember." *See* Verbs, represen-
    tation of
Representation, 314, 330, 345. *See
    also* Game playing, represen-
    tation in
    analogical, 16–20, 281–283
    of categories, 293–294
    nonlinguistic, 21–29, 69, 78
    of nouns. *See* Nouns, represen-
        tation of
    propositional, 16–20, 281–293
    of verbs. *See* Verbs, representa-
        tion of
    visual, 280–294
Representational constraints,
    44–47
Restle, F., 401
Rewrite rule, 54
Rieger, C., 211
Riesbeck, C., 211
Rips, L. J., 60, 293
Rosch, E., 60, 293, 295
Ross, J. R., 94–95, 101, 113
"Ruin." *See* Verbs, representation of

Rumelhart, D. E., 59, 96, 113, 137,
    305, 407
Ryder, J. L., 329

Samuel, A. L., 327
Scanning. *See* Game playing,
    scanning
Schank, R. C., 5, 48, 59, 96, 99,
    113, 211, 214
Scheduling. *See* Augmented
    transition networks
Schemata, 7, 283, 289, 292, 295,
    297, 303–306, 406
Search mechanisms, 324, 346. *See
    also* Processing strategies
Searle, J. R., 77
Secondary concept, 42. *See also*
    Token node
Seek. *See* Augmented transition
    networks
Segmentation of an event. *See*
    Event, segmentation of
"Seize." *See* Verbs, representation of
Selfridge, O. G., 281
"Sell." *See* Verbs, representation of
Semantic features, 233
Semantic networks, 9, 59. *See also*
    Active structural network
Semantic primitives, 12–13, 47–56,
    64, 89, 96, 188–189, 211, 227,
    234, 236, 246–248, 250, 254,
    255, 264, 272–273, 406. *See also*
    Recall, semantic analysis of
    ABLE, 101
    ATRANS, 214
    BECOME, 89
    CAUSE, 10, 53, 89, 96, 185, 188,
        221, 234, 246, 251–256, 406
    CHANGE, 10, 12, 50, 89, 96, 100,
        183, 188, 221, 251, 406
    configurations of, 54–56
    CONTR, 219–221, 234, 242
    DO, 10, 14, 51, 93–96, 98, 100,
        185, 214, 215, 221, 234, 246,
        251, 406
    INFORMATION, 191
    in motion verbs, 264–268
    LOC, 10, 12, 48, 181–183, 265,
        282, 285
    MOVE, 251–256, 261, 263–264
    OBLIG, 218, 221, 234, 242
    POSS, 48, 188, 189, 212, 221

spatial, 283–287
TRANS, 96
TRANSF, 214, 217, 221, 234, 242, 246
Send. *See* Augmented transition networks
"Sesame Street," 237
Shepard, R. N., 17, 283, 297
Shiner, S., 135
Shoben, E. J., 60, 293
Short-term (working) memory, 329. *See also* Working memory
Simon, H. A., 118, 314, 320, 327, 339–340
Simmons, R. F., 59
Siple, P. A., 137
Slobin, D., 120
Sloman, A., 282
Smith, E. E., 60, 137, 293
SOL, 165, 170–172, 177–180, 183, 308, 330, 353, 362, 370. *See also* **MEMOD**
definitions in, 165–167
SOURCE. *See* Case relations
"Spend." *See* Verbs, representation of
Sperling, G., 281
Spoehr, K. T., 137
Stacy, E. W., 306
Stative components of verbs, 181–182
Steinberg, D. D., 67
Stevens, A. L., 407
Strawson, D., 108
Structural definitions, 283–287, 298. *See also* Functional definitions
Structural networks. *See* Active structural networks
Sudnow, D., 77
Syntactic analysis, 6, 117–120, 208
in reading, 137–143

"Take." *See* Verbs, representation of
Talmy, L., 227
The. *See* Reference, definite

The Fisherman Story, 249–260
Thorne, J., 122
Time
judgments of, 377–379
representation in **Verbworld**, 198

Token node, 37–39, 163–164, 355. *See also* Type node
Top-down processing. *See* Processing strategies
"Trade." *See* Verbs, representation of
TRANS. *See* Semantic primitives
TRANSF. *See* Semantic primitives
Transformational grammar, 112, 120
Transition network. *See* Augmented transition networks
Truth, 105, 107. *See also* Negation; Certainty
Tulving, E., 137, 295
Tuning functions, 298–299
Type node, 37–39, 164, 355. *See also* Token node

Van Dijk, T. A., 113
Verbal protocols, 320, 344
Verbs. *See also* Actional components of verbs; Case relations; Change-of-state component of verbs; Semantic primitives; Stative components of verbs; **Verbworld**
acquisition of, 233–246
active, 93
auxiliary, 101
confusions among, 228–233
factive, 108
general versus specific, 231
implicative, 109–110
inchoative, 89
modal, 101, 106
motion, 184–187, 247–276
possession, 13, 48, 211–227, 180–181, 188–192
representation of
  "borrow," 219
  "buy," 218–220, 225, 236, 240, 242, 244, 246
  "cause," 187
  "give," 179–180, 190, 215, 218, 220, 222, 235, 236, 240, 242
  "grab," 215
  "have," 189
  "know," 196
  "loan," 219
  "locate," 182
  "make," 191

Verbs (*continued*)
   "move," 184, 187
   "owe," 218
   "pay," 220, 223, 236, 240,
      242, 244
   "put," 187
   "receive," 228
   "remember," 191
   "ruin," 228
   "seize," 215, 249
   "sell," 219, 220, 226, 236, 240,
      242, 244, 246
   "spend," 220, 227, 236, 240
   "take," 215, 218, 220, 235, 236,
      242, 249
   "trade," 218–220, 224, 236, 244
  stative, 93–96
Verbworld, 179–208. *See also* Computer implementation; MEMOD; SOL
Verification in Verbworld, 189–192

Vocabulary, 39–40, 161, 162, 375

Wales, R. J., 233
Waltz, D. L., 300
Wanner, E., 135
Wason, P. C., 106
Wiesel, T. N., 281
Williams, L. G., 307
Winograd, T., 7, 60, 76, 87, 408
Winston, P. H., 281, 287
Wittgenstein, L., 59
Wolf, J., 282
Woods, W., 122, 134
Word Index. *See* Vocabulary
Working memory, 338–339, 341, 344
World knowledge. *See* Knowledge of the world

Yamanashi, M. A., 108

Zanni, G., 79
Zdybel, F., 349